My Conscience

My Conscience

Spensir T. Blake

Copyright © 2011 by Spensir T. Blake.

Library of Congress Control Number: 2011910992
ISBN: Hardcover   978-1-4628-9740-7
               Softcover   978-1-4628-9739-1
               Ebook   978-1-4628-9741-4

All rights reserved. No part of this book may be reproduced or transmitted in any form or by any means, electronic or mechanical, including photocopying, recording, or by any information storage and retrieval system, without permission in writing from the copyright owner.

This is a work of fiction. Names, characters, places and incidents either are the product of the author's imagination or are used fictitiously, and any resemblance to any actual persons, living or dead, events, or locales is entirely coincidental.

This book was printed in the United States of America.

To order additional copies of this book, contact:
Xlibris Corporation
1-888-795-4274
www.Xlibris.com
Orders@Xlibris.com
100543

Prologue

Where are we going today? Nowhere! After the day we had yesterday, we deserve a break today. *What do you think this is: McDonald's or your life?* Oh! There we go, that sounds very nice, McDonalds . . . a Big Mac with cheese, some McNuggets, some McFries, and oh yeah, a big McDrink. Good stuff! *Then get off your McButt and let's go!* You know, you are very pushy for a conscience. *Get use to it buddy, your life is just beginning. Since you have finally learned to listen to me your life is about to get a lot better, and definitely more interesting . . . so let's go.*

Have you ever heard that little voice in your head that tells you to do things, and not to do other things? Well my little voice talked to me one too many times, I answered him and now we talk all the time. At first, I thought I was going crazy, and then realize if life was an interstate highway, I was already on that off-ramp headed to crazy town. With the results I get; I know I am crazy, but figured I'd make it work to my advantage.

I've got no god complex nor does my voice claim to be God, the Son of God, angel, or any other deity. He talks to God all the time, but refuses to let me. My voice in my head does claim to know God and he said God likes me, which is a very good thing. Through this voice, God and I converse quite a bit, but hey I'm not bragging. My conscience is the Santa Clause we all dream of, except that stupid chimney thing. I still can't believe kids believe that crap. Anyway, my voice gives me things to help me in my small part of the planet. My conscience decided it was time to help me through life since he discovered I was going to mess it up pretty bad on my own. But that is a different story all together.

Now it's my job to change the world and make it a better place for me, and the people around me. The only obligations to right and wrong for me come from the consequences I create. Whatever money I need is always in my pocket or accessible. The key is, knowing how to have money without being noticed by everyone.

So what do I do? That's up to me, a kid in tenth grade . . . weird huh? And believe me when you are put in that situation your world tends to get a lot smaller than you could ever imagine. It's like jumping from the ocean into a pond. I'm no longer a small fish either. I always heard that analogy about the fish but I always thought I would stay a guppy. Now, I just hope I don't end up in a frying pan.

We can all go through life hoping for the best and praying to God for all the answers, but most of us know that if we don't do something, life will just pass us by. Not even waving as it passes, it just passes us by. I'm not going to let that happen to me. We all know there are three types of people in the world; those that make things happen, those that watch things happen, and those that wonder what happened. I don't want to wonder what happened, I want to make things happen.

Chapter 1

Tenth grade sucks! And this is just the first day of school. Ah, I hate this school, I hate being poor, I hate having no girlfriend, I hate being stupid, I hate my miserable life, I just want out! If things in my life don't change I will have to just get out. *And go where?* Looking around the room I say to myself. What was that voice? I'll . . . I'll kill myself. *No you won't Wimp!* "What was that? Who said that?" I come back to reality and see my teacher staring intently at me, "Yes Mr. Dunn, that would be me." I'm surprised and look all around the room . . . the voice matches no one sitting near me. She barks at me again, "Can you answer the question or not?"

Trying to stall and buy some time I ask, "Could you repeat the question, please?"

"No Sir, it is on the board!"

Now I can hear the irritation in her voice growing. I glance over to the board. I hate Algebra; looking at the board I see letters and numbers all jumbled together. Who was the genius that came up with this math anyway? The 'new' math as my mother would call it. Poor simple country girl far from a genius, but sweet as the day is long. Most of us feel that way about our dear 'ole mom I guess.

Can you hear me? "Yes" There is a low chuckle from the classroom as the teacher looks at the board and then back at me, "Yes is your answer to this problem?"

No, the answer is y=24. There is that voice again. *Just say, y=24!*

"The answer is y=24"

The teacher smiles and says, "Thank you. Now you may go back to sleep."

She walks back to the front of the classroom and says, "Just kidding, please continue paying attention."

I smile back at her, "Yes Ma'am you got it." As she walks away I say much softer, "Back to sleep it is."

9

She goes back to teaching her precious algebra and I go back inside my head. Wow how did I do that? *You did that because you finally started listening to me.* Who is 'me'? *Your conscience moron!* Hey, you want to play with me you need to be a little nicer. *OK, you got it. I'll tone it down a bit.* Thank you! *Please continue paying attention. Who does she think she's kidding? You're not here anymore than I am.* Hey buddy, without talking out loud. Can you hear me and understand the voice you hear is in your head? Yes. *Good, excellent, now she is gonna come back in a moment and really try to shake you up but don't freak out again, just listen to me and you'll be fine.*

So what . . . is this a dream, some kinda joke. What? *No, you have finally opened a door most people ignore their entire life. That little voice in your head, well I'm here to make your life better. Hey watch out, here she comes again and the answer is x=32.*

I look up to the scary teacher staring down at me again, "Hope you are still paying attention?"

I look her dead in the eyes and answer, "Yes Ma'am, you are a great teacher why would I not pay attention, x= 32." *Kiss ass, brownnoser!*

Smiling she says, "Well thank you, your answer is correct. Could you please show me how you came up with the answer so fast," and she hands me the chalk. In horror I take the chalk and stand up "Yes Ma'am, be happy to." Walking to the chalkboard in my head I hear. *You know the difference between a brownnoser and a shit-head? Depth perception! HA-ha!* Please don't let me down this time or I will never trust you again because this seems real familiar. *You need to forget fourth grade and let me take over.*

At that moment I felt like a marionette watching my hand solve this math problem on the chalkboard. I was trying to pretend I knew what I was doing then all of a sudden I started to explain the problem and tell common misconceptions that people have about the problem. I look around the room and notice the jaw drop expressions on everyone's face. Holy cow . . . was I that stupid before. *Yeah!*

Now feeling like I was in charge of my senses I walk toward my teacher and hand her the chalk. Returning to my seat she stops me, "Seems my sources about you were incorrect."

"No Ma'am, I'm just finally going to quit fighting the system and just shut up and color, like a good boy." She gives a half smile, "Well then, welcome to my class."

She goes back to teaching as I return to my seat. My friend Kaye taps me on the leg and says, "Nice job!"

I smile and shrug, "Thanks I guess."

I pretend to listen as I return to my head and my new friend. You the same voice from when I was younger? *Yes.* Then no thanks, you got me in a lot of trouble back then. So why should I listen to you now? *Hey sorry, we were kids and it was fun at the time. Now I've seen the error of my ways, plus I see what our life could be or not be, and I choose . . . could be. The other life doesn't turn out well for us. Also I don't want you talking stupid like you were earlier. You have a lot to live for and now I'm going to make it enjoyable. Unless you lose your head and think you're God or something stupid like that. Then you'll be on your own, I'll shut up for good, and it will get really lonely in here. Who knows you may go to a nice institution like so many others that have opened their conscience doors.* So I am crazy! *Not yet but we can have a good or bad relationship, your choice.* Are you the only one in there? *Yes, what, you think this is a freak show or something?*

I think for a moment. It all sounds good to me so far. What are the rules, what are my limits, and are you going to interfere with my life forever? *Good judgment will guide you and I will help push you in the right direction, but you will still be in control. Consider me your not-so-silent partner.* So what do you mean a better life and how silent will you be? *Let's test the better life. Think of a monetary figure not too large for a kid your age then put your hand in your pocket and see what happens.* Why? There's nothing in there. I reach in my pocket and pull out a twenty-dollar bill. Wow, that was cool. *Now here is the trick, don't draw attention to yourself and you will be fine.* I look over and Kaye is staring at my newfound money and me. She smiles and holds out her hand as if to say give it to me. Curious I hand it to her to see what happens. She takes it and puts it in her bra and just smiles. *Don't get crazy and overdo it and you can have a great life or you can create a lot of trouble for yourself. As far as silent, I'm here when you need me and I am part of you, so I know when to be quiet and when to speak up.*

I think of an amount in British pounds and put my hand in my pocket and pull out a five-pound note. This is cool . . . but I have to show restraint or I'll get myself in trouble, the money has to be coming from somewhere. Kaye looks over again and sees the money, "What is that, foreign money? How much you got in there?"

"Why? How much you gonna take from me you bully?"

She chuckles and goes back to listening to the teacher. "Everything alright back there?"

"Yes Ma'am, everything's great."

The ringing of the bell startles me and concludes the class. Everyone starts gathering their things and begin to leave the room. "So Mr. Dunn, you are going to be a good student this year?"

I look at the teacher sitting at her desk, "Yes Ma'am, I am going to give you my best effort."

"I hope so, I'm counting on that."

"Have a nice day!" I smile and leave the room.

When I walk outside the classroom Kaye is waiting for me and says, "What's going on with you?"

"Nothing is going on. Why? Do I seem different?"

"Yes and no. That was not your personality at the chalkboard earlier."

"I know, but I'm starting to think seriously about college, I want to try harder and do better than I did in the past."

We start walking toward the lunchroom, "Cool! Which college do you want to go to?"

"Carolina! Why? Is there anywhere else?"

"Duh, you could go to State."

"No way!"

Looking at me in disbelief she says, "Why!"

"Too many reasons, and you don't want them."

She looks at me disgusted, "Give me one good reason!"

We stop walking, "One! I'll give you several; I don't want to be a veterinarian or a cowboy, I hate the color red, the girls are ugly there, I grew up to close to the campus, and I bleed Carolina blue."

She looks even more disgusted now, "I said give me one. State is where I plan to go to school."

I smile and chuckle, "Nope, you're too cute to go to school there, even though you are crazy enough."

We both laugh and she reaches into her bra and gives me my money back.

Pushing away the money, "Thanks but no thanks, now it has booby germs on it . . . you keep it."

"That didn't seem to bother you at Christy's party."

I look at the ceiling as if deep in thought and then say, "Yeah, you're right."

I grab the money and start walking towards the lunchroom and say, "I'm buying lunch though, so I can get rid of this tainted money."

We join our gang of outlaws we call friends to eat lunch, joke, and have fun. This was our normal time to unwind and relax, that's what we were good at. We're a group of clowns waiting for the circus to come back and take us with them.

Between meaningless conversations I would go back inside my head, still curious as to what happened earlier. Can you tell me how that is happening with the money? *Yes.* There is a long pause. Ok, how is it happening? Do I have to ask the question a certain way or something? *No, just wanted to mess with you. Some questions you want to ask can't be answered for a while because you just won't understand and it would be a waste of time trying to explain it. Like what is the meaning of life? That is easy to answer but hard to understand. The answer is different for everyone, and the easiest way to explain it is: some are food and others eat the food. So you eat or are eaten. People are just like the animals; just look around man proves that every day. God wants to see how we will respond to different situations and to see if we still put him first or if we forget him like so many have.*

What does all that mean? *See I told you, easy to answer hard to understand. Ask me again in ten years and it will make more sense.* I will as long as you promise to answer me when I can understand it. *Kid, by then you will be smart enough you won't have to ask the question.* That sounds good, you gonna make me much more smarter. *By hearing that I don't think we have much of a choice. I'm pretty sure we are going to have to try, and we can only go up from here.* Well then, just in case I forget to say it in ten years . . . thanks! *That makes it all worth it Buddy. Now let's have some fun.*

Chapter 2

I wake up to a smack on my butt and mom yelling, "Get your lazy butt out of that bed!"

"Good morning Ma, love you too."

Straightening my room as if she is looking for something she says, "I loved you the first time I called you, now you are just getting on my last good nerve."

"Ma, it's too early to be on your last good nerve or do you just have the one."

She stops and smiles, "Good morning Son, get up please."

"Ok, I'm up. What's for breakfast? Some eggs, bacon, pancakes, hash browns, donuts?"

She chuckles, "Yeah, but I put all that in the cereal box on the table for you."

Sitting up in bed I say, "You better be glad I love you or I'd trade you in for a real mother."

She laughs, "Good luck with that, I ordered a new son last week and he should be here any day now."

At least she gets what she asks for.

I get out of bed and give dear 'ole mom a hug, "Ha-ha, can't you just wake me up like a normal mother?"

"What's the fun in that?"

I head to the bathroom but the door is locked. "How much longer you gonna be?"

My sister responds, "Five minutes!"

There should be a rule or a law, two kids . . . two bathrooms. No, we only have one for the whole family. As I head back to my room I wonder if there would be any money in my pocket. I look for the jeans I had on the day before and they are nowhere to be found.

"Ma, where are my jeans from yesterday?"

"On the laundry room floor! Why?"
"I thought I left some money in the pocket."
"If it gets in the wash the person washing it gets to keep it."
"Oh, now you are laundering money?"
She chuckles "Sure, but don't tell the IRS!"

Finding the pants as promised on the huge pile of clothes on the laundry room floor. I look at the pile of clothes and wonder if I have clothes still in style in there? I check the pocket and there is the left over money from the twenty and the five-pound note.

Mom walks in, "Where did you get the British money?"
"Found it yesterday. What do you think I should do with it?"
She looks at it then at me, "Where did you find it?"
Looking at the money I tell her, "School."
"Then it must belong to someone. Turn it in or at least ask the office if anyone has mentioned they lost any foreign money. That way no one can lie and just say, yes it's mine."
"Yes Ma'am, good idea."

I walk back to my room and passing the bathroom I say in my best whiny voice, "Roxanne, how much longer?"

My darling sister replies, "All done! Leaving now."

I continue to my room and grab my bathroom stuff. I hear her leave the bathroom and she rushes back in and yells, "Just one more minute."

I walk to the door and watch as she continues putting on her 'war paint' like the Indians did as my dad and I like to refer to it, "You get out now and I'll buy McDonald's on the way to school."

Dabbing powder on her face she says, "Really?"
"Yes, but you have to get out right now."
She smiles, "Ok"

I jump into the shower and in less than ten minutes we are out the door and headed to school via McDonald's. Reaching into my pocket and hoping it had not been a joke or a dream the day before. I pull out another twenty.

She looks at me in surprise, "Where you getting all this money?"

Not sure yet if she could handle the answer, I reply. "You forget I have two jobs? My paper route and from busing tables at the restaurant!"

"Yeah, but I thought you were like dad, Mr. Save-every-dime."

Handing her the money I say, "Tell you what, since you are such a good sister, you keep the change from that."

She takes the money and rubs me on the head, "Thanks! So you will not be eating then. Right?"

I smile and chuckle, "Hey, what are little brothers for?"

"You know I have always wondered the same thing. That's good for us though, I forgot to ask mom and dad for gas money."

My sister is a senior and that keeps her pretty busy, plus president of the Beta Club, senior class secretary, volleyball, basketball, chorus, and band. She is a very busy girl and her boyfriend just moved away for college. So she has not been real happy lately, but she hides it well.

I reach into my pocket again, "Tell you what Sis . . . buy yourself something pretty."

I give her another twenty. She smiles big and gives me a hug, "Thanks! You are allowed to talk to one of my friends today."

I smile devilishly and say, "Which one? Any of them think I'm cute?"

"They all think you're cute, but you are only a sophomore. You are not going to be sitting at my lunch table for two more years."

"Hey, just knowing I have a shot with a good looking senior is enough for me."

Looking at me and smiling she says, "You look like dad and mom mixed, you are nice, sweet, and a good listener. You got a shot with almost any girl, so stay away from my friends."

"You never said anything nice like that to me before. What's wrong with you?"

"Shut up, I'm trying to order!" She starts yelling the order into the drive thru sign. Ok, she is all right. The money has finally worn off. It lasted longer than I had expected.

She never allows me to talk to her friends and half of them don't even know we are related. So this ought to be very interesting. As we get to school she jumps out of her red Mustang and hurries away, as not to be seen with me. I yell to her, "Remember you have to acknowledge my existence in public today. And who can I speak to?"

She stops in a huff, "Leigh, and I'll see ya."

"Thanks have a great day!" She turns and rushes off.

Walking the halls I wonder where my little voice is. *I'm right here. Good morning!* So you have your own little world you go to? *Nope, I sit here watching you, I'm just amazed that you can walk upright.* Ha-ha, anyway, I can kick your ass? *Sorry, no way . . . even if it were possible I know you couldn't because I'm the bad ass you want to be. Guess you could beat your own ass and that might teach me a lesson.* Thought we were gonna be friends. *Yeah you're right, sorry. Hey, there's a cute girl let's talk to her.* You still trying to get my butt kicked? That's Billy's girl, plus he is a friend, so no! "Good morning Christy," I continue walking slowly.

"Oh hey! How are you?"

"Good, see ya later." *She seemed to like you!* She is way out of my league. *Not for long my friend.*

I head to first period Biology. That is a tough subject to stomach this early in the morning. The fact that I dislike the teacher and the subject does not help. *Don't worry kid I'll get you through this and all subjects, I promise.* So now I can be on the football team and can keep my grades up? *Yes, we are going to have the good life from now on.* Can I tell people about this between you and I. *Sure you can, but are you sure you want to.* What do you mean? *Most of the smart people tell someone and they go under the microscope. How many geniuses you know that have a normal life.* Good point! Why is that? *Nature has a way of balancing it's self out.* You mean like people who balance blindness with smell and sound? *Exactly like that! Or why a guy weighing 350 lbs. and 7 feet tall does not rule the world or beautiful blonds can't think for themselves half the time.*

So what would you give to have a better life? That would be a tough one. Do I get choices? *No, you just lose them.* So I have to choose now or lose this gift? *No you just lose something but look at it like this, you use this gift a little and you only lose a little.* That's the best you can do? There's a long silence as I sit down in Biology.

The teacher starts the lesson about cell replication already boring me to tears when I hear, *Yeah, that's the deal.* What about with studying and tests? It has always been frustrating because I study and when I take a test I bomb. What's that about? I forget right after I read something. I just feel stupid. *That is my fault; from now on whatever you read I'll remember it for you and you will be able to just say it.* "Wow, you promise?"

The class stops and stares at me, "Yes Mr. Dunn that is what happens when the cell splits. Did you have a question?"

"No Ma'am, I just thought that was interesting." *Good recovery!*

The teacher continues teaching, but keeps a closer watch on me. I grab the biology book like it was a brand new toy on Christmas morning. Ok here we go, cover for me. I'm going to read this entire book to see if you are bluffing. *You go ahead I'll watch the teacher for you.* Before I start . . . what would be a downside to this. *None, this is a win-win situation. You can't lose on this.* With that I began to read like I have never read before. My body was in the classroom but my mind was in the Biology book. The book was like a pool of knowledge and I had just learned to swim. I read the entire book just as the class was ending.

The teacher approaches me as the bell rings, "Did you get all that?"

"Yes Ma'am just finished."

"Just finished?"

I realized this was not what she was expecting to hear, "Yes Ma'am, good lecture, thank you."

I get up to leave and she blocks me, "So what was the last thing I was talking about? Because it looked like you were more interested in the book than my lecture."

Knowing I was busted I answered, "No Ma'am, I just got so interested in what you were talking about that I wanted to read it for myself."

"So what was I talking about before the bell rang?"

"Homework . . . read chapter 2 and do the questions at the end of the chapter. Just do the even numbered questions."

Smiling she says, "What is mitosis?"

"Well on page 125 the book defines it as the process during cell division in which the nucleus of a cell is divided into two nuclei. Over on page 506 it talks about spores growing into multicellular gametophytes that were haploid and produced gametes by mitosis. I like how you were tying it all together though much better."

She looks at me in shock, "Ok, but I'm watching you."

I look back at her shyly, "Really, how do I look?"

"Very funny, now get out of here."

I leave the room and I can feel her stare at me as I leave. Wow, now this feels good to be smart, or at least being able to regurgitate information. *So how does that make you smart?* Yeah, good point.

I get to my locker and there is Kaye shuffling through her stuff in her locker and getting very aggravated. "Something I can help you with," I ask.

She looks up and answers, "Yes, thank God you are here! Here, hold this."

She begins loading my arms with books and searching frantically. "What is wrong girl?"

"I can't find my biology book and it is only the second day of school!"

"Here, take mine I just finished that class."

"Oh thanks!"

She begins throwing books back in her locker. Her girlfriends approach as she finishes her fit and they all calmly walk to class in perfect stride. I watch her cute butt walk away from me. *Now what do you think about spending the rest of your life with that one?* Kaye? That would be like marrying my sister. She is my friend, a crazy girl, too loud and poor like me. *You don't like her because she is poor?* No, I do like her, but I need a girl that can afford me. Plus I want a lot of women not just one. *Good luck with that Mr. Playboy. You could be with all the women and you still won't be happy without love. The women are all the same in bed anyway.* You sound like my dad, 'how do you think that girl got good in bed and is still a virgin?' Ha-ha! Don't get me wrong, she is cute but not drop-dead gorgeous like

I want. *Hope you are ready to fight and have lots of trust issues.* What do you mean by that? *Look pal, all women are all the same, some just take more work on your part. The pretty ones are never happy and a lot of work.* I think it will be worth it. *Again, good luck with that. Tell you right now though, that girl will be your best choice.*

Well I'm off to Bible class. *Good luck with that also.* What does that mean? *Just tell me you will consider Kaye, I promise you a good life with her.* No promise, but I will consider her. Right now, she's just a friend. In Bible class I think about the fact my P.E. coach, Varsity football coach and is also a pastor and my bible teacher. This should be fun this guy hates me. *He disliked the old you not the new you, he's going to love you now.* This guy is what I think of when the Bible said God created man. Strong, tough, wholesome and a good Christian, but his fatal flaw is his ego. The kind of man women wanted and men wanted to be. I still don't like him because he just looks at me with disgust because I am only half the man he is. He kind of reminds me of that actor Burt Reynolds.

As I sit there loathing him he says something that catches my attention. He is talking about relationships and he asks, "Does anybody know what marriage is?" The answers hit all sides of the spectrum from a chance to have sex to wanting someone to grow old with. None of the answers were the one he wanted to hear.

He looks at me, "What do you say?"

I look amazed by the question and say, "Funny thing is, before class I was asking myself the very same question. My answer has already been used twice with the sex thing. I'm thinking that it is not correct and I would like to hear your answer, Sir."

He looks stunned by my response but does not miss a beat, "A marriage children, is nothing more than a friendship that got out of hand!"

Wow he is good!

"That person you decide to marry should be your best friend. Someone you can confide in without retribution. If you want to avoid sexual diseases, then have sex with only your wife or husband and no one else. How many married couples do you see or hear about with sexual diseases? If you have heard of such, in most cases one or both of them are cheating on the other."

Wow he is really good. Listen to this guy he is right!

I listen to him and flip pages in the Bible still building my knowledge base. By the end of class I have a new respect for my teacher but still remember my past experiences, and my pain.

Next class is P.E. and I have the coach again; two classes back-to-back hope we are friends this year. On the way to the gym I see my sister and her cronies making their way to the next class. I see her and smile, "Hello ladies!" They all look shocked by an underclassman with the nerve to speak to them. They keep walking except for Leigh; she stops and says, "Hey Cutie, your sister says you have something for me."

Looking dumbfounded and thinking of all the things I would like to give her, "Yeah but, I left it in her car."

"Ok, see you after school."

"Sure, see ya then," Under my breath where she can't hear me I say, "Yeah, see ya then you good looking thing you."

Leigh walks away and tries to catch up to her group. I watch her trot away and notice my sis looking back at me smiling. What am I supposed to have for her? I know what I'd like to give her. *Yeah big-boy, easy now!*

Kaye approaches me now as she is entering the gym and says, "Add another one to your stable?"

Chuckling at her comment, "You must think I'm some kinda slut or something, Ms. Lewis?"

Looking me up and down, "I see a lot of potential there."

I start walking with her, "I'm no slut, Pal!"

"How many girls you been with?"

"None, I'm still a virgin!"

Stopping at the girls locker room, "Then why so defensive? How many times you get close?"

Smiling at her I say, "I think you remember one encounter."

She says nothing and continues staring at me and I say, "A couple of times I could see the promise land, but I did not enter the forbidden forest."

Laughing she says, "Cute analogy!"

"Thanks! Thought you would appreciate that one. How many times you . . . you know?"

"You'd better get to class. By the way you don't ask ladies such questions!"

Embarrassed by her reply I say, "Hey, if you were a real lady you would not be inquiring about such topics with me as well! I'll go to class, but we're not done here."

She walks in the girl's locker room and I move toward the boys locker room. Wish I could read her mind. *I can!* So what does she think about me? *Oh I thought you were not interested.* Hey you were the one that wanted me to consider her? *She is very interested but scared of you at the same time. You need to keep her faith in you strong always be honest with her no matter what. I'm telling you she is the one. When you reach your new fame many women are going to be after you. She is the one who will stand by you through thick and thin she will be there for you. You both start out poor and get rich together and appreciate each other more. Trust me, but I know you want to look around a bit . . . it's human.*

After P.E., I walk into my Spanish class and my teacher asks me in Spanish why I was late. I answer her in Spanish and she says, "Mochas gracias!" I take my seat and she continues with the class, "en ese mismo memento?" No one would answer her question or pretend to know what she was saying. I raise my hand and she points to me, "at that very moment"

"Exactamente! Gracias Señor!" She continues the class and smiles at me. This is not a good thing as I already have a crush on her. Just a push in the wrong direction would be all I need for her. She is a beautiful senorita! I spent the rest of the class fantasizing about her and some beach in Acapulco. At the end of class she thanked me for my attention and help in the class. I think and then in Spanish reply, "bienvenido!" She smiles and walks away.

The rest of my day I read during every class as much as possible. I can now, since I have been promised I can retain it. I'm like a sponge and the books in my hand are a puddle of water. I just keep soaking it up.

While walking to my locker I see my sister and she is alone so I stop her, "Hey what am I supposed to have for Leigh after school?"

She smiles and continues walking, "That my brother is up to you."

I chase her down and walk with her, "What is something she likes?"

"Sorry babe, that would be too much help. You have football practice, right?"

"Yes I do. But you did not say anything I supposedly had for her?"

"No, she just expects something, no idea what. See you after my volleyball practice, later trouble."

I stop and say, "Thanks I'll see ya. Hey, can I drive your car to the football field?"

"Soon as you get a license, love ya!" She gives me her best beauty pageant wave as she glides down the hallway.

You need a little help? Yes please! *She likes to read romance novels.* Ok, this is a Christian school where am I supposed to get one of those dirty books. *Wow you are really brain washed!* At least it is clean. *You are getting really good at being a smart ass.* Yeah I like it better than a dumb one. *Either way you are still an ass!* And what does that make you. *Front row center at the freak of the week show.* We done? *Yeah I got nothing.* So what do I need to do for her? *There is a book in the car for you to give her.* Really, thanks? *But let's make this fun; here is what you do . . .*

After school I walk out to the car and practice the conversation that has been prepared by my conscience. I waited for just the time to exit the building and start to accidentally have an unexpected meeting with

Leigh. I am just about to speak to her when my friend Chris walks up, "Hey aren't you going to football?"

I look at Leigh and then at him, "Yeah I just have to go to the car for something."

"What, your jock strap?" He gives a little chuckle and says, "I'll go with you."

I look at him in disgust and nod towards Leigh, but just my luck he was not looking when I made the gesture. He continues to walk with me, as I get closer to Leigh he starts talking about stupid things that girls don't like to hear. Just as I am about to tell him to get away from me she stops right in front of us and turns around and says, "Hey Tommy, do you have something for me in your sister's car?"

"Yes, I sure do."

We all just stand there in the parking lot and wonder if poor Chris will get a clue. We start walking and he stays right in stride with us. Guess he just really wants to be with me right now or is trying to avoid being embarrassed, either way he is being a pain. As we walk across the parking lot no one speaks. Then Kaye sees us walking and she decides to join. Now this is just getting out of hand. We get to the car and everyone stands there looking at me. I try to buy some time but they all just stand there staring at me.

"Kaye, Chris, would you guys excuse us for a moment I need to give Leigh something from my sister."

They say, "Oh sorry, we'll leave."

As they leave I hand Leigh a note. She begins to open it, I proceed to the inside of the car, and sure enough, there on the backseat is a typical dime store love storybook. I grab it and turn back to Leigh and say, "The note was a joke to break the ice, but here is what my sister had promised you. It is a story of a boy who falls in love with an older woman." *Oh no, bad choice of words!* I notice the expression on her face and say, "Or to put it better, a more mature woman that is out of his league." *Good recovery.*

She looks at me sympathetically, "That's sweet, but I have a boyfriend, sorry."

"Why are you sorry? Is he a bad guy or mean to you?"

"No, he is great!"

"Then don't be sorry."

She looks at the note that says do you like me check yes or no and then the book, "Thanks but I can't accept this."

She tries to hand them back. "No they are yours. Like I said," pointing at the note, "that was a joke. But you can feel free to check 'No' since you have a boyfriend. I was just having fun and I thought you would enjoy the book. I overheard my sis say you like those kind of books. So please enjoy."

She smiles, looks around and then gives me a kiss on the cheek. I blush as she walks away, then I just stand there in awe watching her. She turns back to look at me and gives a quick wave and a smile.

All I can do is smile as Chris walks back over to me, "You ok Romeo?"

I come back to reality and realize he is standing there and I look at him in disbelief, "Yeah you condom!"

"What?"

I push his chest and say, "The onetime I go out on a limb and try to put the moves on an older chick you step in to cock-block, thanks!"

"Hey sorry, didn't know! Not use to you hitting on seniors."

"Why did you bring your contraceptive butt over anyway?"

Leigh drives by and waves as she leaves the parking lot and I say to my friend, "She's why I gave you the nod!"

"Sorry, totally missed it. Let's go play football, you can get me back."

I smile, "You got it! What did you think of all that homework they gave us today?"

We start walking towards the locker room and he says, "Yeah what a load of crap!"

You can tell who your real friends are. They are the ones you can say whatever you want in frustration and they will still be your friends.

Chapter 3

Football, this is a great time to inflict pain and get away with it. I just wish I was as big as my attitude. *You have a high metabolism and are going to need to eat a lot.* Umm hello, remember me? I'm a kid with no money. Amazingly enough my parents can afford to send me to a private school but not feed my little butt. *I thought I fixed your money problems? Your parents just want the best for you and are scared public school would be trouble for you.* What are they scared of? I can handle myself. *They are afraid you will get into sex, drugs and rock and roll.* Now that sounds like a fun mix! All except for the drugs, I can get that stuff here if I want. Why and how is that fun? *The drugs are what they're the most concerned about and then the women.* Wish I could make them understand that is not an issue for me . . . well maybe the women. I would just like to get a chance to get a scholarship to a real college.

So you are stuck on going to Carolina. Yes, that is my only choice. *Then you are going to have to work hard.*

"Ok Ladies! Let's get this practice started. I would like to congratulate all of you for making the team." We all look around at each other stunned and giving each other high fives and cheering. "The amount that is trying out for the team is the max I can dress, so you have all made the team. You will have to earn playing time though." We go through our stretching exercises and calisthenics. Then at the top of his lungs the coach yells, "Now give me ten laps." No rest for the weary. We all take off running. A few of the linemen struggle, as is the norm for big guys, plus running in these bulky pads make it harder. You can almost tell the positions of the guys as they run. The coach is watching to determine just that. I sprint as long as I can and then trot a bit. I need to impress this coach, he already thinks I'm weak and I most likely won't get to play any or at most very little. *We'll just use this year to build his trust then.*

While we are running I notice the quarterback. If I can keep up with the quarterback and his three friends, collectively known as the four horsemen, I should impress the coach. The four horsemen are a tight group of seniors. Two of them are running backs, the quarterback and the other is the quarterback's preferred wide receiver. So we should be a good team this year since the guys have played together since grade school. They notice me and try to pick up the pace. I speed up but not enough to invade their space.

As an underclassman you have to know your place or they will put you in it real quick. It is tough going from hero to zero in one year. Here a sophomore on the varsity team is a guppy in the lake, unlike when I was a freshman on junior varsity I was a shark in a pond. They glance at me again and start to slow the pace. Now it is a chess game and it was my move. I slow down as well like a frightened dog, no need to get eaten by the sharks on the first day.

On the last lap they pick up the pace to a full sprint. I grunt and strain to keep up and I hear a roar of thunder behind me as the whole team started stampeding to the finish. I close my eyes for a moment, hoping to muster some strength and alleviate some pain from the sprint. As I look up there is the back of a running-back in my face. He had crossed the finish and rapidly slowed down. I try to slowdown and go left but there is someone there, so I try to dart to the right and that space is occupied as well. Now I have no choice but to bump the guy in front of me and use him as a brake with my chest on his back. "Sorry Scott!" He looks at me as we walk off the run, "That's ok punk," and he gives me a wink and a shove in the chest.

Nice guy, but I bet I pay for that little encounter later. *Oh yeah! But pain only last a little while and glory lives forever.* Hey mister silent partner how have you been? *Good. I'm going to help you with this.* Cool! What do you mean help, with what? *When you are playing football or any sport, the world will appear to slow down, but it will be regular speed. This will give you a chance to see it better and give you a small advantage. Plus, I will guide you on where to be to optimize the play.* Optimize the play? *Make you look good!* Nice!

We go through a variety of drills; passing, defensive and so on. With no real chance to shine as a performer just to see what we are best suited for. "Ok ladies, let's set up for some plays!"

The group gaggle around not really knowing where to go or what position to fill until the coaches start pointing and smacking guys on the head. The coach and assistant coaches start pushing and pulling saying, "You go here, you go over there!" Soon we had twenty-two guys in position to play and ten on the sideline. I'll give you two guesses where I ended up, and the first guess does not count. As I watch the coach yell out his scheme of play I listened diligently so if my time came I could jump in without a hitch.

I watch play after play after play, repeatedly. This is boring. Can't these boneheads get it right? I start running laps and watching the plays. After my second lap the assistant coach stops me, "You ever play safety position?"

"Yes Sir, seventh and eighth grade."

"Get in there and send out Thomas."

"Yes Sir!"

I step on the field, but this is a running play they are running so I am just a last resort or last chance for defense on this play. They run the play and I get to hit a wide receiver that is trying to block me. The runner gets hit by a lineman and goes down. Next play the defensive coach calls a safety blitz. This is my chance to shine. At the hike I sprint around the end of the line to get to the play just as the quarterback releases the ball. I was just about to dive for him when I notice I am too late, so I run past him, as there is nothing I can do to help stop the play. Luckily the receiver drops the ball so they at least could not have scored with me way out of position.

Next play the defensive coach calls a standard zone defense. Trying to see how we handle different situations. *This time they are passing over here. When the play starts back up ten feet and either knock the ball down or intercept it.* "Hike," the quarterback yells and everyone darts in different directions. I back up ten steps and wait. Sure enough the ball is flying straight towards me. I jump up to catch the ball and just when I think I have it there is a huge crash. The wide receiver runs into me at full speed. The ball goes bouncing out of bounds and the wide receiver and I bounce off each other in different directions.

The coach comes running over as I crawl to my feet, "Are you ok?"

"Yes Sir, did it look that bad?"

He looks troubled, "Yes!"

"I'm fine and not that fragile! Hey can we run that safety blitz again?"

He smiles at me, "You got it kid!"

Now is my time to really show off. I have the quarterback's timing down now. I tell the tackle I'm going to be flying over his head on the next play so watch out for me and to stay low.

I stare at the quarterback as he lines up with his troops. He surveys the defense and yells, "Down, set," this was my cue. I sprint toward him and go airborne just as he yells, "hike." Now I see what my conscience was talking about, the world appears to be in slow motion as I fly over the line of men on the field. I see the fear in the quarterback's eyes as I approach. Like a deer standing in the road in front of an oncoming car he stops dead in his tracks just as he has taken possession of the ball. I collide with great force into the quarterback. We both go down in a big bear hug like mass. I hear him grunt and groan as we hit the ground. Then I hear a whistle telling us the play is over.

When I get to my feet, I look around and everyone is amazed my little 120-pound butt just laid out their star 180-pound quarterback. One of the running backs nudges me out of the way as he helps his quarterback up. I return to my side of the field to a host of, good job, and nice work tough guy! At that moment when my glory was at its peak, my facemask is grabbed by the head coach, "What do you think you are doing?"

I reply in a stunned state of mind, "Playing football Sir! I am trying to make you proud of me and your defense!"

"Don't hurt your own team in the process!"

"Yes Sir!" He releases me and goes to the offense's huddle to change the game plan I presume.

The defensive coach slaps me on the helmet, "Nice job kid! Keep up the good work!"

You know the next play is running straight at you don't you? I figured that. Any suggestions? *Yeah, don't get dead!* Thanks! Good advice. *Try to stay centered on the running back, he will be all yours. His blockers will be taken out so it will be just you and him. Hit him and try to hang on for dear life.* I got it, deer light. *Ha-ha very funny, that's dear life!*

Now seeing the eyes of the offensive team I can tell they are gunning for me. I can do this, hit or be hit, kill or be killed. I hear the yell of hike and the whole team moves toward me, and my side of the field that I am protecting. The defense picks up blockers just as my conscience had predicted, and here I am face to face with the senior fullback running full steam straight at me. Oh, this is going to hurt; I lower my head, close my eyes, and yell in pre-pain anguish. I feel the collision and realize we are still moving. I open my eyes to notice he is dragging me down the field and trying to discard me with no luck as I hang from his waist. I slide my grip from his waist to his thighs in an attempt to stop him. It slows him but does not stop him. He's too strong my only hope is to trip him so I slide the rest of the way to his ankles and we stop as he crashes to the ground.

The running back gets up and runs back to the offensive side. I lie there and get up slowly. The coach comes over and says, "Sit this next one out."

I do against my will because I do not want them to think they got the best of me. The next play is a passing play and they connect for a touchdown. The momentum has definitely shifted in their favor. The next play I run out on the field. The coach yells, "Where do you think you are going?"

As I look at the coach, I point to the field. He shakes his head no and points to the sideline. I walk back to the sideline and say, "Thought you said sit the next one out not all of them."

He looks at me in disbelief, "So now you are ready to get your head knocked in?"

I look at him and the guys on the field, "Oh, I've been ready for that my whole life! That is what I came here for."

"Ok then, get out there, but I'm not going to clean you off my field again."

I run into position and see the offense pointing and laughing. They obviously thought my sack earlier was a fluke. Time to make some noise boys! I can feel the anger growing in my head. I feel like a bull snorting for the charge. On the hike I rush to the play but everyone is running the opposite direction. I give chase but to no avail. The play is over and I am no factor.

We huddle up for the next play and decide to stay in a zone defense. We take our positions and ready for the snap of the ball. I notice the eyes again and get excited; they are coming toward this side again. I am already prepared for the impact this time. I am face to face with Scott again, only this time on impact I keep my eyes open and my head up. On impact I see stars as we crash to the ground immediately. We both jump up and he slaps me on the butt, "Nice job rookie!"

Scott runs back to the offense, and I am ecstatic from my performance and the defensive coach runs over and says, "Nice job!"

I look at him and I say, "I saw stars on that tackle."

He chuckles, "You must have kept your eyes open that time!"

"What do you mean? How would you know that?"

He points toward the legs of the running back, "You should have seen stars!"

I look over at Scott and notice he has yellow stars on the calf part of his socks.

"He tried to hurdle you with no luck! Good job!"

With that we hear a whistle and the head coach yells, "Bring it in ladies!"

We crowd around the coach as he gives his pep talk and says hit the showers. On our departure from the field I overhear a young lineman ask, "What's with this ladies stuff? I have cherries hanging from my tree!"

An older player replies, "And a lil twig also." We chuckle as the guy continues, "We are ladies until we prove otherwise with the coach. One of my favorite expressions of his, 'Boy do you stand or squat to pee!' He does that one when you make what he calls a sissy play like missing a tackle or a pass."

We all get a laugh out of that one as we walk to the locker room. I get changed and leave the locker room with my friend Chris.

Chris says to me, "Sure wish we were still on JV so we could play more."

"Yeah, I know what you mean."

We walk past the coach and he says to me, "Mr. Dunn, could you step into my office please." I wave bye to Chris and head to the coach standing in his doorway.

He walks into his office and I follow, "Have a seat."

He walks to his desk as I walk over to sit down, "That was quite a display out there today Son."

I take a seat and in amazement I wonder, is this really coming out of his mouth, "Thank you Sir?"

"Why the doubt? You did well!"

I look at him in awe, "I thought we had a history, you and me? Remember last year all the paddling and detentions?"

"You were different then. You seem to have matured over the summer and if we can get some size on you . . . I think you have the potential to be the future terror of the league."

I look stunned at the coach, "Thank you Sir, but I never really thought of myself as a terrorist."

"On the field you will be, with some training!"

He hands me an aspirin type bottle, "Here, take these tablets. Read the label, research it to make sure it won't hurt you. They are vitamin supplements that should help you get bigger. Take them with your meals and try to eat more and healthier."

I look down at the bottle that he had given me, "Thank you Sir!"

"So what are your plans for the future?"

I look up at him as he sits on the corner of his desk, "Not real sure yet, but I know some things I want to do." He just looks at me as if to say, yes go ahead. I tell him how I want to fly planes and helicopters, I want to play professional football, I want to be a NASCAR driver and I want to write books about the path I took when I'm done.

He looks at me in shock, "Then I guess the buzz about you is correct. The teachers have mentioned a change in you this year and it seems they are right. So what are your immediate goals in school?"

"I want to be a good football player, good student and hopefully get a scholarship because I know my parents can't afford to send me to college."

The coach smiles boldly, "Well I've gotten boys scholarships to great schools like Liberty, Western Carolina, and even ECU."

I look at him excitedly, "So you think you can get me into Carolina?"

The coach comes back from his high horse, "Carolina? You don't want to go there. There is nothing there but a bunch of sinners and I hear you could be a great preacher or something good!"

I look sad but manage to say, "Jesus hung out with the lowest people and saved a bunch of them."

"Good point, but you are not comparing yourself to him are you?"

I continue, "NO! Not even close, but how do the lost know they are lost unless we go and find them. Good people are in good environments and don't need help, just encouragement once in a while."

Looking at the ceiling tiles the coach says, "Good point. So you think you can handle the lion's den Daniel?"

I study him for a moment, "Not today but with three more years of your tutelage, I think I will have a better shot at it. I'm not Christ or do I claim to be. He spent how many days in church as a child? I'm in church every Sunday and here every day. After twelve years of that I think I should be good to go religiously and should be able to fight all kinds of demons. Don't you?"

He gives a half smile, "Carolina huh? I'll get to work on it; you are only a sophomore so we should have plenty of time. If I pull that off you will owe me big time."

"I'll pay you back up front by getting you a state championship. So you will actually be paying me back with a scholarship."

Smiling at the thought, "Don't make promises you can't keep Son."

I point at him, "I'll promise if you will."

We both stand and head for the door; he starts to open it and stops, "So what position do you want to play for me?"

I smile, "I'd like to play safety and wide receiver this year and next year the same but also backup quarterback. My senior year I want to be quarterback and safety backup."

Looking bewildered he says, "You already have it figured out don't you? Why not quarterback this year, you scared of the four horsemen?"

"No Sir! I respect them and what they stand for. They worked hard for what they have and I would never take that away from them. Plus I feel they are going to do a great job for you this year."

He smiles boldly, "Me too! Think I've got Stanley a scholarship to State."

I look at the floor, and he says, "What? State is a good school!"

I look up, "Yeah for a cow farmer!"

He laughs and pats me on the back as he opens the door, "See you tomorrow."

I leave the office, "Yes Sir!"

Chapter 4

On the way home, I ask Roxanne what she thinks life is about and what we should expect. She has no idea, and not even a care. Her life revolves around her. If it is not about her she couldn't care less.

I say to her, "What do you think is for dinner tonight?"

"Mama's dried up steak, potatoes, and some kind of vegetable, but at least her biscuits are good."

"Think we can grab a pizza instead before she starts cooking?"

We are about to drive past the Pizza Shop when she hits the brakes and swerves into the parking lot. "Ok where are you getting all this money?"

She comes to a stop and puts the car in park and she says, "Well, I'm waiting?"

"I told you this morning."

She smirks at me, "That crap is not going to float this time; you're tight with money. So, what has changed?"

I look at her sadly, "You would not believe me and I'm not sure I do; so you just enjoy it while it last and I promise it is nothing stupid or illegal."

She stares at me in the eyes, "Ok, you are telling the truth or at least you believe you are. I was just trying to be a good older sister."

This is a gift our family thinks they have. We all think we are human lie detectors.

Thinking about earlier in the day, "Why did you pick Leigh, because you knew she had a boyfriend?"

Roxanne gets out of the car, "Oh yeah, how did that go?"

Looking at her angrily I say, "Very funny!"

As we walk in the restaurant she says, "She is the one that always mentions you to me so I thought you might have a shot with her."

Roxanne smiles at me as we walk into the Pizza shop.

Roxanne walks straight to the payphone and grabs the receiver. She dials and says in her sweetest southern voice, "Hey Daddy!"

I knew it was dad soon as I heard the, "Hey."

She continues, "Has mom started dinner yet? No! Good Tommy and I stopped by to get pizza. You want the usual? What about mom? Ok, love ya! Bye, see y'all in about 30 minutes." She hangs up the phone and places the order while I stand there in utter amazement. She says, "What?"

"You are really amazing sometimes! You have to teach me that!"

She smiles, "We just go with what works."

We played some Ms. Pac Man and have small talk about practice while waiting for our pizzas. The waitress approaches, "Your pizzas are done."

I walk over to the cash register and reach in my pocket and feel nothing. The lady says, "That will be $23.95." I look in shock and my sister notices my expression. I think $25 and reach in the other pocket and there it is.

Roxanne approaches, "You lose the money?"

I smile, "Nope, just wrong pocket."

I hand the lady the money and grab the pizzas and begin walking out. The waitress yells, "Your change!" I turn and say, "Keep it!"

Knowing it wasn't much, but then again she didn't do much while we were waiting. She yells again, "Thanks!"

I nod my head; as my hands are full, "See ya later."

We get home and the feast begins. Mom says, "Where did you get the money for this?"

Roxanne and I look at each other and then she says, "We robbed a liquor store on the way home."

Mom chuckles, "I thought the liquor store was after the pizza place on the way home. What did you do, go the other way to throw them off your trail?"

"See Sis, I told you we got our smarts honest."

"Very funny young man!"

There is an awkward silence then mom says, "No really, where?"

Roxanne looks at me, "He said he didn't mind spending some of his money."

I wait for the questions that parents seem to have but all I get is, "Thank you."

Roxanne looks at me again with that, I told you so look, and bites her pizza.

"Yes Ma'am, no problem."

Then dad speaks up in his normal abnormal humor, "Yummy pizza good!"

I look over at him, "Yes Sir, and I love you too!"

He starts off with, "Hey how was football? Make the team? How was volleyball? Make the team?"

The chaos went on from there. I look around our family table and think that my life is not that bad. *Yeah it could be a lot worse. Don't worry about your sister or your mom; I have a plan to get them both fixed. You just keep being your sweet lovable self and things will turn around, you will see.*

I watch my family eat and listen to their conversation and wonder if they have a clue what I have in store for them.

Chapter 5

"I have this player that someone there really needs to see!"

"Thanks Coach. Give me the stats on him."

Coach Bolton grabs his clipboard, "Grades 4.0, no SAT yet he is only a sophomore, position defensive safety and wide receiver now, and senior year starting quarterback/safety. One of the best I've seen. It is like he can see the play before it happens, a natural."

The athletic director waits for his opportunity to speak, "Ok Coach, send us a video at the end of the year so we can see him."

Coach says, "I'll do that and just so you know, your school is his first choice, but he will be looking at other schools for a full ride."

With that statement the athletic director was curious, coaches only use the term full ride when they have a blue chip player. "Tell me coach what other schools are interested?"

"None yet, he said he wanted you guys to have first dibs then open him up his senior year if you have not yet showed any interest."

"Coach I'll be honest with you. We don't normally look at small private schools, but if you are sure you have something there we will keep an eye and an ear out for him. What's the name?"

Coach seems pleased with his success, "Tommy Dunn, so do I need to contact you anymore or can we expect to hear from you?"

"We will contact you, but please feel free to contact us anytime if things change."

"What exactly does that mean?"

The athletic director sighs, "Well Coach, unfortunately these young hot shots have targets on their back. They seem to get hurt, or are in trouble with the law, a girlfriend problem, and so on. Unfortunately it seems to be the nature of the beast. Last year we had two prospects lost due to these types of circumstances. We gave up three good kids to get them and ended up with nothing."

The coach pauses before he speaks, "I understand your situation, I just wanted to make you aware of this up and coming kid. He has a strong interest in your school; I feel he is going to do great wherever he ends up."

The director chooses his words carefully, "Thanks Coach, and again please keep us informed of his progress and we will keep in touch." With that the conversation ended. Coach Bolton runs the conversation through his mind. They are not interested. I've got to make them interested without getting him hurt. This is doable!

Chris and I walk in the gym and I see the coach leaving his office, the coach sees his hot prospect he wants to make rich, and a better name for himself. "Hey Dunn, get over here!"

I run across the gym to see what could be the problem, "Yes Sir?"

"Remember what I was talking about in class this morning?"

I look to the high ceiling of the gym for affect, "No clue."

He looks at me very disgruntled just before he speaks I say, "Just kidding, you were talking about the time Christ raised Lazarus from the dead."

He smiles, "Think you could do me a favor and give a speech on it?"

Wanting to impress the man and stay on his good side, "Sure I could! When would you like me to do that? Tomorrow, next week?"

He looks at me firmly, "Now, in the Chapel! I was supposed to speak today but my stomach is not a hundred percent. Could you do it for me Son? I have some notes here to help you."

Realizing my fear of crowd's, I see an opportunity for a bargaining chip. I say, "Can you do me a favor and let me play in the game Friday night?"

"You've already earned a spot on the team Son."

"Yeah on the team that is great, but how much time do I get on the field?"

"What is your request?"

Not wanting to be too greedy, "At least one play per quarter at wide receiver and as much defense as you will allow."

He looks me up and down, "You've got a lot of nerve . . . and a deal. Now get to the Chapel . . . relax and have fun with it."

I grab his notes and take off toward the Chapel. *Girls you have fun with! Public appearances at our age . . . you just try to survive. What is he trying to prove here?* Reading the notes I say to myself, you are going to help me with this aren't you? I hear no answer. Hey you! *You are on your own on this one.* What? *Just kidding, your words will flow like a waterfall.* Ok, that doesn't sound good. *What would you like then a gentle stream?* That sounds much better. I just don't want to look like an idiot. *Don't worry we will be fine. Nice maneuver with the coach by the way. You pull this off and you will be golden with him.* That is good since my collective fate is in his hands.

I enter the Chapel and see my friend Chris. "What did Coach want?"

"He said I get to play Friday night."

He laughs, "Hey now that's good. What position, guard and tackle? You know . . . sit the bench and guard the water cooler and tackle anyone that comes close to it . . . ha-ha!"

I smile because he is my closest competition for my positions, "Safety and some wide receiver and backup quarterback."

He looks at me amazed, "What did you have to do for that, lick his balls?"

I look around the Chapel scared to death, "Hey a little respect for where we are please. But you are really going to love this; all I have to do is give his sermon right now for that opportunity."

Looking at me in disbelief he says, "You should have licked his balls . . . You are no public speaker . . . remember last year? Good luck!"

"Thanks! I'm going to need it."

He has known me since first grade and knows public speaking is not something I do well.

He chuckles and says, "Don't . . ." he grabs his own neck and makes the chocking sound and gesture and having a laugh as I walk away from him and towards the front of the auditorium.

I pass the seniors on the front row of the auditorium and see my sister sitting there with her friends. I wave and she looks angry and signals for me to come over. I approach her and she starts berating me, "What are you doing up here?"

I smile at her as I crouch down in front of her and her friends, "I made a deal with the devil and now it is time to pay for my sins."

Her and her friends smile at my comment, "You will see! It is time to make you proud of your little brother."

She looks around, "I'm already proud of you, now get to the back of the auditorium where you belong."

"Sorry Sis, not today. You can't keep a brotha down, no more back of the bus for me . . . I've got battered fish to fry!"

Trying to build up my confidence, I smile at her, stand up, turn and then stroll in front of the seniors and up to the stage. I take a seat and look out at the audience of my peers. As I sweat I think, what have I got myself into?

The principle moves to the podium and gives the announcements of the day. Then he says, "Coach Bolton was supposed to speak today but is unable to at this time. Speaking on his behalf is our own Mr.

Tommy Dunn." The crowd applauds because they have to, not because they want to. I approach the podium, "Thank you!" I look around the Chapel as the applause dies down. I notice Coach Bolton sitting in the back of the room smiling joyously at me. He is not sick, he just wanted to see if I would sink or swim. *Well, here is your chance to shine. Shall I take over?* Yes please! My Conscience took over and gave the most eloquent speech I have ever heard. I watched the faces as I spoke and I could see hearts being moved and lives changing right before me. No one looked bored or sleepy; it was as if they were hanging onto my every word. Hey maybe I should become a preacher and make the world a better place. My voice stops and in my head I hear. *Get me a larger pulpit then.* Then I start speaking to the crowd again. I look to the back of the Chapel and Coach Bolton stands up and motions to his watch and gives me the kill it signal across his neck. Guess when you get talking it can be hard to stop sometimes. "So in closing I would just like to say. God loves you and so does this school. Be kind to one another and have a great day. I would now like to turn the assembly back over to our Principal."

I turn to leave the podium area and there is a loud roar from the audience. The applause is almost deafening this time. I turn towards the audience and wave as I walk off the stage. The Principal gets them to quiet down and does the closing prayer. After the prayer I open my eyes and the seniors attack me with hugs and pats on the back. All were congratulating me and saying they enjoyed the sermon. My sister grabs me and hugs me, "That was awesome! I especially like the dramatic pause right before you did your summation."

I look at her in shock, "Who are you and what did you do with my sister?"

She and her friends laugh then she says, "I was going to ask you the same thing. What happened to my lazy twerp brother?"

I look at her with my head cocked, "Ha . . . never knew you felt that way." *That explains a lot doesn't it?* She leans in and whispers, "I liked the old you, but I love the new you."

She gives me a peck on the cheek and wipes away the lipstick residue and walks away, "See ya bro!"

As my sister walks away from me I notice Leigh standing in front of me, "Loved your speech! It sounded familiar though."

I smile as she takes my hand in hers and I say, "Thank you!"

I notice from my peripheral vision that the coach was approaching, "It was really the coach's speech I just read it."

I hear my voice, *Depth perception!* She smiles and shakes my hand, "I know! He is my father remember? You did a very nice job with it, almost as well as the old man."

She winks at her dad and releases my hand and walks away.

He says, "You two need to remember your place and watch the PDA!"

She turns and says as she walks away as we say, "Yes Sir."

He smiles at our submission and says, "Nice work up there Son. You've made me proud; keep up the good work."

He starts walking away and I say, "Good to see you are feeling better Coach."

He turns to me, smiles and gives a wave and continues to walk with another teacher out of the auditorium. What the heck is PDA? *Public Display of Affection, glad I am here to pay attention for you.*

Heading to the lunchroom I run into Kaye and she says, "How are you Sweetie?"

I smile at her, "Be careful Honey, I'm going to make your life hell!"

She laughs and says, "You proposing to me again?"

"No, you are going to love it when I do though!"

She looks stunned, "Don't make promises you can't keep!"

"Trust me; I'll make you an honest woman someday."

"There you go again making promises you can't and won't keep! What's for lunch today?"

"I have no idea but I am starving!"

We stand in the lunch line and I look at her and notice she is very pretty and I never really noticed before. Wonder why I never noticed before? She turns and says very loudly, "Nice speech up there today!"

I smile and think, ah ha there it is, "Thank you. Kaye Honey, think you could tone it down a bit?"

Looking around she says, "Why do I embarrass you? You embarrassed to be seen with me?"

"No! But I don't think everyone in the room deserves to hear our conversation."

"Sorry! I was just proud of you!"

I look at her sternly, "Again! That is way too loud, Girl!"

She grabs her food and storms off without paying. I look at the lady at the counter as she hands me my food, "I'll be paying for both of these."

Smiling at me she simply says, "Ok."

I walk into the cafeteria and see my friend Chris and some other football players sitting together. I go over and they make room for me to sit with them. I sit across from Chris and he says, "What did you say to Kaye?"

"You know me and Kaye . . . always one argument after another. You would think we are dating."

Chris shrugs, "She is too obnoxious and loud!"

"That was what I was trying to explain to her."

I pray over the food and then look up and Chris looks mischievous. "What?"

He looks behind me, and then points to me as if asking someone. This guy? He looks at me and says, "That girl back there wants you."

I turn around to see which girl is trying to get my attention. I see no one; everyone is busy with their lunch and little conversations. I turn back to the table and say, "Who? What girl?"

I look at Chris and he has a mouth full of food and so do the other guys sitting there. I look at my plate and there is nothing there. My food is gone! They all start chuckling at the joke they had just pulled off without a hitch. "Hope you guys enjoyed it as much as I had hoped to!"

They all start laughing. Chris pulls my plate of food off his lap from under the table, "Gotcha!"

I look in relief at my food, "Good one!" They continue laughing as I begin to eat.

Kaye approaches in a huff, "Mrs. Coats said you paid for my food. So here!"

She attempts to hand me the money. I take a bite of food, "That's fine. I don't want your money."

Chris reaches across the table and attempts to take the money, "I do!"

Kaye pulls it out of his grasp, "No Chris!"

She looks at me, "Are you sure?"

And she dangles the money at me. "I am sure, I was not trying to hurt your feelings just give you some friendly advice."

Without a word she turns and walks away. Chris looks at me, and then her walking away, "At least she looks good leaving. What was that all about?"

I look upset at him, "That obnoxious trait of hers and how she should fix it."

"Why do you care so much?"

I look at him as I take a bite of food, "Not sure yet, but I think we will see."

That afternoon at football practice I notice Kaye and her sister and two other friends sitting in the bleachers. I go on with practice in a normal manner and try to ignore her. I have a few good defensive plays and then the coach puts me in at quarterback. The four horsemen do not approve of this action. "He is going to be our backup quarterback and I want to see if he can run some plays." They look as if relieved but still not happy. I go to the huddle and call the running play the coach called. We line up and I take the ball from the center, the defense is rushing in like a pack of dogs released from a cage. I turn to hand off the ball to the back and he is not there. I tuck the ball under my arm and take off running. Why are these guys always testing me? Little help please! *Gotcha covered!* The defensive end is directly in front of me as I make the turn. I stick my arm out and place it on top of his helmet as he dives for me. I push off as hard as I can, and become airborne in the opposite direction. I land on my feet as my opponent falls to the earth face first. I continue to run as the rest of the defense tries to corner me in for a tackle. I notice my offensive guys seem to be standing around watching and are no help to me at all. So it is going to be like that, huh? I charge toward the sidelines and still making forward progress up the field. Now my field of vision slows dramatically. I see holes and gaps in the coverage like never before. I spin to avoid a tackle and when I see another hole in the group of men, I dart in that direction and avoid yet another attempt to grab me. Trying not to let the anger take over I see my buddy Chris, time for some payback. I head directly toward him and he is running toward me. Right before impact I stick my arm out again. As I push him down he grabs my arm in attempt to keep me from progressing. Pulling me down as he falls, I free myself just as he hits the ground. This was not much help for me though, now the defense had caught up to me and six guys pounce on me knocking me to the ground.

As the mass of bodies untangle I look around to see how far I managed to get on my escapade. I notice it was about ten to twelve yards, not bad. I head to the huddle, "Thanks for the help guys! Quarterback keeper left this time! Ready, break!"

As we walk to the line of scrimmage I say, "Glad most of you guys are graduating this year, maybe next year I can get some guys that will play and protect me!"

One of the linemen says, "Good luck with that, I'll be at Liberty."

I say, "Not if you continue to play like that you won't!"

I bark the commands, "Down, set, coming at you . . ." One of the defensive linemen jumps but manages to get back across the line in time. "Hike!" I get the ball and spin as if going left, just as I planned the team goes right and so do I. They block instinctively because if they don't they will be running laps until Christ makes his second coming. I see a hole in the group of guys and shoot through it at top speed. I glance to see if there is anyone near me and I see no one, so I slow to a trot. I cross the line for a touchdown and toss the ball to the coach. He starts barking at the team like a hungry dog. The defensive coach yells and no one seems happy. Not even me; it would nice if I could get some help.

As I head to the sideline I see the senior quarterback standing there, "Hey Chappy, could you go back in, I think I strained a hammy!"

"Sure! Nice run."

As he trots back onto the field I say, "Thanks!"

I grab a cup of water and sit down on the bench.

The coach comes over to me, "You ok?"

I look up, "Yes and no. What is with these guys?"

"They are testing you. It is your job to take charge of the situation like you did. They don't want some kid running the show. How would you have felt last year, if they brought in some hotshot seventh grader for quarterback?"

I stand up and look at him, "This is just me, but I'd be happy if he could make us win games."

He smiles, "Yeah it's just you then, because that kid just caused someone to lose a job and it is the nature of the beast to be angry about it."

I look at the ground, "Yeah, I guess you are right. Prospective is a funny thing sometimes; everybody wants to win and they also want to be the reason a team won."

He shrugs and says, "You ok?"

I look him in the eye, "Yes Sir!"

He grabs me by the shoulder pads and says, "Don't fake an injury on my field again."

"Can't promise you that Sir, I won't fake one to you . . . but I may have to fake one for you."

He looks to heaven, "Why me Lord?"

As he releases me I say, "Because he likes you! Hey, I got an interesting analogy for you coach. Instead of you asking why me Lord? Ask why not me Lord? Get it? From God's prospective what did you do not to deserve troubles in your life? Get it?"

He looks at me again, "Yes I get it! You sure you don't want to go to a Bible college? Go in at wide receiver!"

As I trot on the field, "Why? They will never throw me the ball!"

He trots onto the field with me, "Oh yes they will, Chappy likes you and trusts you."

Coach jumps in the huddle, "Ok Chappy, let's see some passes and hit the open man. Work it in to everyone but try to get the open man."

He exits the huddle and Chappy calls the play. We line up to the line of scrimmage. "Hike!"

We all run our individual routes. I see one of the four horsemen catch the ball and he is running my direction. I bump my defender and he falls to the ground. The runner gets closer to me and as he passes me I step in the way of the guy about to tackle him, giving the runner a wide-open field to run for a touchdown.

We run a couple more plays with minimal gains. From the huddle Chappy tells me to burn the right side line. I smile and say, "You got it Sir!" On the hike I give a stutter step to draw my defender in close. When I see him commit I take off running with all my might. I run past him and I am wide open. The ball is launched beautifully down the sideline by Chappy. I see the ball floating in slow motion and out of the corner of my eye I see Chris bearing down on me like I owe him money. I notice we are all three headed to the same point. If my physics class taught me anything I remember that is not a good thing. I watch the ball and ignore Chris. The ball is now my fish on a fishing line and I am just reeling it in. I speed up and slow down to place myself directly under the ball and where I expect it to land accounting for wind and temperature. I glance at Chris and he is still bearing down on me. As I reach out for the ball I notice Chris going into a diving motion to knock me down. I grab the ball with one hand and place my other hand on Chris' shoulder pad to help cushion the blow. I pull the ball in close to my chest in an attempt to hang onto the ball, my other hand instinctively pushes away from Chris as hard as I can. I look and see the end zone and think I must break free. I feel no force trying to drag me to the ground, instead I feel like I am floating toward the end zone. I snap quickly to look behind me to figure out what was happening. Chris is lying on the ground and the other defender that was originally covering me was tripping over him and I was free to trot to the end zone for a touchdown.

I hear the coach yell, "Nice work people!"

The defensive coach yells, "Defense, you need to stay with your tackle and don't let them break away from you!" He grabs my friend Chris by his facemask and talks softly and boldly to him. He releases him and smacks him on the butt as he runs back to the defensive huddle.

As I jog past the coach, he gives me a thumbs up gesture and says, "Good work Son, keep it up!" I continue to the offensive huddle and look to the sidelines to Kaye pointing at me and cheering. I smile and keep running to the huddle.

As I enter the group I hear, "On two, break!" Chappy comes up to me, "I know you were a long ways away but get back faster. Run a down and in on two!" I look at him, "Same position?" He nods yes and screams, "Down . . ." I run to my position and wait for the second hike. We run the play and then another which is why we practice to make the plays run smooth during a game. The older guys on the team are slowly accepting me. That will make life much easier.

At the end of practice I see Kaye and she comes toward me, "Good practice!"

I shrug, "I guess so, the coach seems happy. Why are you here?"

She looks at the ground and says, "I wanted to apologize for earlier today in the lunchroom, for my big mouth and my even bigger attitude."

I look at her and say, "Thank you, that means a lot to me. I don't want to tell you how to run your life because I am just your friend, but if you could tone it down a bit we could possibly have a future together."

She looks at me in shock, "Yeah right, me and Mr. Football hero!"

We walk to the gymnasium, "I am telling you the truth. I don't want a girl who is thought of as loud and obnoxious. Honestly I love your spirit, but not so loud."

Again shocked at my statement, "What are you saying?"

"Just think about it, we'll talk more if I can see a change."

I walk into the boy's locker room and I can still hear her saying, "Think about what?"

I put my gear down and go back out and say, "See that is what I'm talking about! Too loud!"

I walk back in the locker room take a shower and change. When I come out she is standing right where I had left her. She smiles and says, "I can be calm and softer, but why? What am I supposed to think about?"

"I see patience is also something I should have mentioned."

She shrugs, "I can't win with you. What do you want?"

I look around to make sure the coast is clear and then take her by the hand and start walking to the parking lot, "I want it all!"

I start to explain what kind of woman I want. Just as we are walking out of the gym I hear, "I'll see you two in detention tomorrow!" We turn around and notice the coach behind us. I quickly let go of Kaye's hand, "Yes Sir, sorry!"

I look to Kaye, "Sorry for grabbing your hand like that in public."

He gives his smirk, "Nice try! Both of you have detention tomorrow!"

Kaye and I walk out of the gym and I say, "Ok, why were you here anyway?"

She looks at the ground, "Obviously, so you can get me detention."

We laugh and then she says, "I wanted to apologize and watch your practice. When you fake an injury you need to limp more or at least act hurt."

I look down in shame, "You saw that did you?"

"Yeah! Work on that won't you?"

"Yes Ma'am I'll try."

She chuckles and says, "So that senior girl? You like her or what?"

"Kaye I'm a fifteen year old guy stuck in a Christian school. I like all women at this point not just one." We get near her sister's car where her sister is waiting for her and Kaye says, "Think you are capable of having just one or are you going to play the field?"

I look at her sister sitting in the car and give a little wave. "Kaye I have never really thought about it, but you are my friend. If I settle down you will be the first to know and you know that."

Kaye smiles and jumps in her sister's car and says, "See you tomorrow!" I wave bye as they pull away.

My sister drives towards me and pulls up next to me, "What was that all about?"

I look at her and say, "I have no idea. Pop the trunk."

I throw my stuff in the trunk and get in the car. As we drive out of the school parking lot I say, "I can't wait for our first game!"

She pats me on my chest since my ego is right there as well, "Me too! But good luck with yours. Are you getting bigger?"

I smile and say, "Yes finally! The coach gave me some vitamins and I have gained three pounds and can lift about ten pounds heavier than before. Plus now I can afford to eat. Speaking of which, let's pick up some burgers on the way home."

"What about your dinner?"

I smile and say, "No worries, I need both!"

Chapter 6

Game day! We are playing one of our toughest opponents on opening day. Not the best move but unfortunately a necessary one, according to the coach. As we walk the halls the atmosphere of the school is different. People that would normally say nothing to me are wishing me good luck in tonight's game. We are allowed to wear our football jerseys on game day so this makes the players stand out from our normal collared shirt-wearing peers. Some people seem intimidated by the number 13 on my jersey, but hey . . . fear can be a useful tool. Coach did not want me wearing number 13, but after I explained it's meaning for me to him, he allowed it. I never understood people's fear of a number. *You need me to explain it again?* No, I'm good.

I sit in Biology for my first test of the year. I receive my test paper and the teacher smiles at me and says, "Good luck." I look at the smirk on her face and in my mind I hear, Good luck loser. I look at her face and smile back at her. Question number one . . . to my surprise, I draw a blank. Mitosis? I have no idea what that is? *Calm down! What did I tell you? I am here for you, the answer is C.* I look at the test and reread the question. Oh yeah, I see it now. Thank you. The test is a breeze now that my voice tells me the correct answers. I look at the teacher and she watches me like I am doing something wrong. I continue and finish the test and take it to the teacher at the same moment the girl that use to be the smartest in the class does. I return to my seat and breathe in relief, thank you my friend. *No problem.*

We have our afternoon pep rally last period to get us ready for our games. They do cheers and chants and then announce the teams and players. The girls' volleyball team is announced first, due to them leaving for their away game across town. When my sisters name is called I get my buddies to scream for her, but we are still not as loud as the others. *Wow she has a lot of support!* She runs this place, drama, band, sports, teacher's aide, and beta club. They exit the gym floor and our coach grabs the microphone. As the girls exit and trot past us we all give each other high fives and good luck chants.

The coach gives a quick speech and then calls Chappy. The crowd goes wild, cheering and stomping of the bleachers. He calls the rest of the four horsemen and there is still cheering but nothing like that call for Chappy or Mr. Mike Chapman. They call us by grade; seniors first and then down the line. By the time they get to us sophomores the cheering had turned to a courtesy clap. When my name was called, it sounds like the cheers went up a bit louder but not that much. Just wait until my senior year; they will go nuts for me too I promise, just like Chappy.

At the end of the rally Kaye comes up to me, "Ready for detention?"

I look at her, "No, but ready as I am going to be. You have got to quit getting me in trouble all the time Ms. Lewis."

She hits me on the shoulder as hard as she can, which actually hurt. "You are the one always getting me in trouble!"

I point at her and say, "Ouch! You know a wise man once told me. You should never hit a Lady, but a lady will never hit you."

She looks at me oddly, "What does that mean?"

I smirk, "Since you hit me you are no longer a lady, just some girl. And I can smack you around like a three dollar hooker."

I pretend I am going to hit her and she takes off running. I give chase and catch her at the gym exit. I give her a devilish laugh, "You can't escape my grasp oh dear one!"

We laugh and start walking towards our library where our detention is held. When we enter the library we walk in and I grab a couple of books. Kaye pulls out some books to do homework. We check in with the monitor and take some seats. I read like it is the most interesting thing I have ever done. Kaye watches me curiously and then continues her homework. I finish one book and then start on the next. I turn page after page, absorbing information that I never knew existed. I finish the book and notice we still have thirty minutes left in this place.

I raise my hand and the monitor asks, "Yes what do you need?"

"I need to ask Ms. Lewis a question about our history homework."

"Go ahead."

"Thank you."

I whisper to her, "Hey Kaye! How you doing? How are your wife and kids?"

She smiles at me, "You are nuts!"

I smile and say, "Yeah I know. Please give me a piece of paper, a pen, and book, so I can do my homework also. Gracias Senorita!"

Kaye and I do our assignments. I finish it and hand it to her and whisper to her, "Next."

Kaye looks amazed and hands me algebra. I do the assignment for that and hand it back to her. She then hands me her home economics book. I take it and realize what it is, "I'm not in this class."

"Just do it!"

I look at the time and we have seven minutes left. She hands me what needs to be done and I turn to that chapter of the book. I read it and then do the questions at the end for her.

I close the book and look at the time. One minute to go and then I notice Ms. Leach the monitor standing next to me. She looks at the book I just closed and then at me and says, "Didn't know you were taking home economics?"

"I'm not! I just got bored there towards the end and was seeing what I could learn about running a home." I use effeminate voice, "A very informative book."

"You wouldn't be doing someone else's homework would you?"

"No, did you need me too. I'd be happy to help out."

She opens the book and says, "Then explain this?"

I look at the page she opened the book to and then I look up at her and say, "Well you see a stove is a complex heating device used for cooking food."

Kaye and another girl in the room start chuckling.

Getting angry with me she says, "So this is not your hand writing here?"

I look at the paper, "No Ma'am!"

Kaye looks at it, "That is mine."

We both write a few words on different papers and then show her. Reviewing the two papers and the one in question, she seems satisfied with the result and starts to walk away.

She turns and says, "I'm watching you two!" We gather our stuff and leave the library.

When we get in the hallway Kaye grabs my arm and says, "How did you do my homework in my handwriting and that fast?"

I say, "What, I was supposed to do it in my hand writing?"

She looks at the paper, "That is cool! How do you do that?"

"I am not real sure. Don't tell anyone I did that ok! My homework is in your book I'll get them in class. I've got to make some phone calls before five o'clock, see ya later." I trot down the hallway and into the teacher's lounge.

As I enter the teacher's lounge it is hard to believe I am in the same building. Nice Turkish carpet on the hardwood floor and beautiful landscape paintings on the wall. The walls are all mahogany with a chandelier in the center of the room. A picture of Christ on the cross is the centerpiece of the far wall. This is to help us remember our place as Christians, which we could not go to heaven if he had not died for our sins. I notice the nice black lazy boy recliner in the corner right by a table with a phone on it. *Let me take over now, you just relax for a while.* I pick up the phone and hope what everyone says about me and my father sounding alike on the phone is true, my conscience takes over talking to stock market brokers and making appointments and asking questions. I hang up the phone and I try to exit the lounge as the door opens. "Hello Mrs. Parks!"

I continue to try and walk out, but she blocks the path and says, "Excuse me, what are you doing in here?"

"I was looking for the coach and then I noticed that nice painting and was admiring it."

She looks at me wondering whether or not to trust me, "Ok, good luck tonight!"

"Thanks! See you later!" *You were doing nothing wrong; we just needed privacy to make those calls. They weren't long distant calls or any charges, so no big deal. Now what do we do for an hour before we dress for the game?*

I look around the school parking lot trying to find a ride to get something to eat. There is no one around and the place looks like a ghost town. The coach should be here by now maybe he will take a ride to the store for some food. As I walk around the deserted school I notice things I never had before. Small imperfections that never stood out to me before . . . kind of funny at a school that likes to think it is perfect. *Guess that has to do with perception on your outlook? Is the glass half empty or half full? If you are a good persuader you can make people believe anything. The glass could be empty and they will still try to drink if you are really good! Look at Shakespeare, now he was a lunatic. Because he was published, he was respected.*

I finally see the coach's truck up at the field and I walk there to see him doing final preparation to the field. "Hey Coach."

He looks at me and says, "What are you doing here so early?"

"I never left, you gave me and Kaye detention for holding hands, remember?"

"Oh yeah that's right! Help me finish the field and we'll go grab a burger before the game."

I grab the chalk duster that lines the field and start to push it. He tells me the specific way he wants it done and I take off with it. He continues grabbing more bags of chalk and when the machine would start to get low he would dump another bag into the hopper. He had them set on the side of the field at the perfect interval when I would be near empty. It was almost like he had done this before.

We finished the field and put the equipment away. He jumps in his truck and says, "Let's go! Got to get back so you can get dressed and I can meet the other team and make sure they know where to suit up."

I jump in the truck and we speed away. He looks at me as we drive and says, "What you going to be if you grow up?"

I pause for a moment and then I say, "Coach I am going to have my hand in so many barrels I'm not sure what they will call me. I just hope they look at me as the good man I want to be. Knowing my luck everyone will hate me and I will die a failure."

He can't believe what he heard and says, "That is not a very positive outlook on life!"

I ask, "Was Christ a great man?"

"Of course he was! He was the best!"

"Didn't turn out to well for him did it?"

He frowns, "That was a totally different reason!"

"Everyone has their own side of the story Coach. You know as well as I do, there are three sides to every story."

He watches the road but ask, "Three sides, what you mean by that?"

I smile and say, "Your side, my side and the truth. You can tell the exact same story but can totally change the meaning just by the perspectives being different. For example you are a country boy and I am a city boy. I tell a story about a hoe and it means something totally different to you."

He smiles, "Good point. Mind if I use that."

"Feel free just don't give me credit, I'm going to stay low profile for as long as I can."

I chuckle, "To answer your original question and not playing devil's advocate, I guess the best answer would be a business man."

He looks at me as we pull up to the drive thru window, "Why couldn't you just say that. What do you want to eat?"

I look at the menu and reach in my pocket for money, "That chicken burger please with fries and Sprite." I attempt to hand him money and continue, "That answer would have been no fun. Then you have to keep asking questions."

"Put your money away son I have got this one . . . You know you are right, too many conversations are people just asking questions."

He places our order; we get our food and head back to the school.

"Thanks for the food Coach."

"No problem Son, thanks for your help today, and the conversation."

I smile as I chew and nod in agreement. He starts talking over his game plan with me and assures me if we win this game the rest of the season will be easy. It all sounds really good to me and to be honest I enjoy hearing him rant about his team, especially since I am part of it. We pull up to the school and I jump out of the truck, "I still think you should be a preacher."

"I'll stay out of trouble so I can keep that door open Coach." He smiles and then he goes and parks his truck in his parking space.

Walking into the gym I notice a couple of people starting to gather. I sit on the bleachers and listen to people talk and wonder about their inane conversations. The gym door opens and the Knights walk in and are looking for their locker room I point them in the direction of the girl's locker room. Unfortunately it is the only other one and we are not giving them ours. They walk across our new gym floor and our coach walks in and yells, "That is a new floor Gentlemen! Please get your street shoes off of it!" They head to the sidelines of the court and tiptoe to avoid scratching the floor. "Thank you!" the coach yells. The opposing team coach points to the door, as if to say in here? Our coach nods his head in agreement. They enter and we head into our locker room to start getting dressed.

As we get dressed the coach comes in and yells words of encouragement and says we should not play like a bunch of girls tonight. That was still his favorite phrase; we were girls until we proved otherwise to him. *Tonight you will be able to show your worth but still not on a superstar level.* That sounds good to me.

We can faintly hear the other locker room chanting their school war song. The four horsemen start talking up the room. Some guys have their own rituals before a big game. Some go into meditation mode, some decide to pray, some like to hit things, some sing, and some do all the above. Chappy grabs the attention of the room as we are finally all here and almost all dressed. The coach slaps me on the pads and whispers to me, "Pay attention, in a couple of years this will be your team and your speech."

Chappy yells, "Guys when we exit this room we stay in two lines, sixteen each line nice and even and organized. We will do the beat of 'We Will Rock You' on our pads as we walk to the field. Like this . . ." He slaps his hands on his thigh leg pads twice and then claps his hands once. He then repeats this action and says, "All the way to the field. We then break into our normal exercise and stretching routine. From there we break into our offense and defensive drills. From there you return to the sidelines and we start kicking some butt all over our field! Are there any questions?"

The coach says, "Gather around and let's pray!" As we form a huge circle of people in pads we pray for our safety during this endeavor and the safety of our opponent. Then I think to myself, I wonder whose side

God is on tonight? *What do you mean by that?* Well the way I see it, we are a Christian school, and the other team is a Christian school. If we both pray for a victory, how does God choose? *The team that has the better athletes and most courage of course!* You see my point right? Is the prayer like the person filling out a lottery ticket? Please God let me win even though I don't deserve it! At that point I hear the coach say, "Amen. Now let's go show them what a real team can do!" *Let's go see whom God wants to win then.*

Chappy looks around the room and says, "Guys I am not going to lie to you, this team is going to be tough, and will be one of our hardest tests for us this year. We have practiced and worked hard. Now let's show them what it feels like to be in a dogfight with a Bulldog!" We all bark, chant and growl as he continues, "We can beat these guys and we're going to beat these guys! Are there any questions?" We all yell, "No Sir!" "Now let's go kick so butt!"

As we line up you can hear our opponents leaving their locker room. The four horsemen are up front and start the beat on their legs. You can hear our cheerleaders outside the door saying, "Go team and . . . here we go Bulldogs, here we go!" The beating of our pads gets louder as we all join in. You hear a boom-boom slap, boom-boom slap. This continues as we exit the locker room all the way to the field. You can hear the fans cheer and chant as we enter the field. The Knights try not to stare as the sound coming towards them is intimidating to hear. Now our fans joined in as well by stomping the bleachers twice and then clapping once. This was worth ten psychological points, as we glanced at the other end of the field you could see the younger guys were getting nervous.

As the game is about to start I stand on the sideline sizing up the competition. I look to the stands and see my parents nowhere. I notice my sister and her friends; I look at her as if to say . . . where are mom and dad? She shrugs and mouths the words, I'm sorry, even though the distance and crowd noise obstructed the sound. At least she made it even after she had a game earlier. I return to the task at hand, beating the Knights at football.

I watch the kickoff and notice the quickness of the runner returning the kickoff. *He's quick but we can stop him.* Our first defensive stand and I trot on to the field and assume my position on the field. I sum up the distance they need to score. They need 78 yards to score. *We let them get seventy and then take the ball from them.* Sounds good to me! The first play they gain seven of the ten yards they need for a first down. The next play they gain thirteen on a short pass to the opposite side of the field, I show up as the play is ending. The referee yells, "first down," and they mark the ball for the next play.

I go back to my position just before the play starts going. The Knights run the ball to my side of the field but the ball carrier is tackled before I can get involved in the play. This continues all the way down the field. We are now backed against our goal line and about to be scored on. I have yet to do anything but run around. *It's your turn Kid, catch the ball.* I ready myself for the upcoming play. The play begins and the receiver runs towards me, and our cornerback. The receiver turns toward the side line and Tony covers him defensively. I go towards the receiver and where I expect the ball to be thrown. The ball is thrown and as I reach for it so does the receiver. The ball bounces off his and my hands and goes out of bounds. I run past the guy as I attempt to stop running. I turn to him and say as he trots past me, "Don't try that again, next time I'll run it back for a touchdown!" Tony laughs and cheers me on as the guy smirks and continues away from us. On the next play they try a run to the other side of the field with little results. *They are coming back this way again same play as before.*

I get excited and anticipate the play, the receiver lines up and stares at me. "Hike," the quarterback yells and I slowly run to where the ball will be going as if I can see it happening in my mind. I reach out and start running at top speed. The ball lands in my hands and I am running the opposite direction of everyone else. As I run by our teams bench I hear cheers and screams, then I hear the coach and only him say, "That a boy well done, no one near you. You got it!" With that I never even try to glance behind me, which is a normal instinct when you take someone else's prize. I continue to run full steam until I get to the other end zone for a touchdown. I do no dance, I do not spike the ball in celebration, and I merely toss the ball to the referee as I pass number 82 I tell him, "I warned you." He just looks at me in disbelief. I trot to the sideline where I am pounced on by my team and given congratulations. I wave to the fans and sit on the bench for a rest, as I will soon need to return to battle.

The coach comes to me and says, "I'm putting Thomas in next series."

I look at him and say, "Bad idea coach, they will see that as weakness and try to abuse that side of the field."

"You are good to go back in then?"

Chris looks at me like I am crazy, "Let me get in there!"

"Yes Sir Coach, I'll be fine!"

He looks at the two of us, "You boys work it out!"

The coach walks away and our team kicks the ball off to the Knights. I look at Chris, "Do you trust me Buddy?"

"I thought I did until a moment ago!"

"You go out there and they are going to come to this side of the field and will score on you like a fat prom date! I'm just trying to save you from that!"

"Just let me try!"

"Ok, he is going to run a slant play right at you if you miss him he will score. And remember I tried to warn you."

Chris takes the field in my position at safety. I watch the play from the sideline and number 82 yells at me when he noticed I'm on the sideline, "Scared!"

I yell back at him, "Yeah, for you! I'm second string!" *Way to play with his brain.* I notice that comment caught him off guard and he looks at the new opposition. They run a pass play just as I warned Chris about. The receiver catches the ball and as Chris goes to attack him the receiver dispatches him to the side and runs the sideline for a touchdown. Number 82 runs back to where I am standing and offers me the ball. I say to him, "Nice work, but that is your last one tonight." I take the ball from him and say, "This was your last time touching it tonight!" He is speechless and turns and walks away. The coach looks at me, "You guys ok?" "Yeah, he is just playing the game, and now I have to hurt him."

Now with the score tied we finally get to go on the offensive. I notice Chappy acting eager to get in the game as the first quarter is almost over. After the kickoff and a meager return, our offense takes the field. I sit on the bench and the coach yells at me, "What are you doing? Get your butt up here!" I jump up and forget to ask how high. I trot over to the coach and he asks, "You rested enough?"

"Yes Sir!"

"I want you to stay at safety for the rest of the night, and go in at wide receiver right now. Next play; tell Chappy, I-22 right." I nod in understanding and wait for the opportunity to enter the game.

I run to the huddle and tell Chappy the play. He calls the play, "I-22 right on two, ready break!" I line up for the play knowing my only job is to get my cover man away from the play. I decide to have some fun with it. The ball is hiked, I stand still and turn to the quarterback who was going the opposite direction. I jumped straight up and pretended to catch the ball. This confused my defender and he watches my antics in wonder. I looked at him and laughed.

He says, "What you laughing at punk!"

I continue chuckling, "You!"

As the play comes to an end I run to the huddle and notice my replacement running in so I rush to the sidelines to avoid too many guys on the field. Coach stops me, "What was that?"

"Setting him up. Next time I go in give me a dump pass so I can take care of him."

The coach looks at the playbook and winks at me. We watch a couple of plays that have minimal gains, and then the coach grabs me and says, "Get it Dunn!"

"Yes Sir, with pleasure."

As I enter the quarter ends and we start walking to the other end of the field. I see the guy that will be covering me and I ask him, "Where is everybody going? They were going to finally give me the ball for a change."

Chappy overhears me and grabs me, "What the heck are you doing?"

We get some distance between the defender and us and I whisper to him, "Planting seeds. Next two plays, I-33 right and then next play dump pass left to yours truly. On I-33 give me a fake pump pass at the end." He smiles, "I see where you are going with this . . . You got it!"

I run to the coach, "I need two plays. Is that ok?"

He motions for me to go. Chappy gets to the huddle and explains the next two plays and I show up and he treats me like a retard and says, "Go stand over there!"

I point to my place on the field and he nods in agreement as I stand there. They run the play and I do the same thing as before, I jump as Chappy pretends to throw me the ball. The defender acts bothered by me and runs toward the play as he sees me as no threat. I stand there like I have no idea what to do as Scott gets tackled on the twenty-yard line.

We all rush to get back to our positions with no huddle. *Nice seed planting my friend.* I look to my defender and he is about five yards away from me this time instead of his normal 1 to 2 yards. I shout at him, "Don't you want to be my friend?"

He glances at me as he backs up further, "Nope!"

"Ok then, you're gonna be sorry!"

He continues to slowly get further away. Chappy yells hike as the whole team goes right and the defense follows including my defender as I stand still. Chappy stops on a dime and spins to look at me and throws the ball as hard as he can. When the ball hits me it nearly backs me up. I catch the ball standing alone with no one within fifteen yards of me and run to the end zone for the touchdown. Again no celebration I hand the ball to the referee and trot to the sideline. As I pass my defender I say, "Told you so!" He gives me a nudge as I continue to trot on past. I chuckle as the four horsemen surround him and dare him to start something.

I get to the sideline and the coach says, "Nice work, I was wondering what you were up to."

"You're welcome Sir."

As the half ends and we walk to the locker room. We sit down Chappy motions for me to sit at the end of the bench with the four horsemen. This was his way of respecting me and acknowledging me as part of the team. That is good since I had done the only scoring in the game. The coach gives his half time speech. When he is done he has another prayer.

We sit drinking water and Chappy says to me, "That was brilliant playing stupid with that guy! It worked to perfection."

They all pat me on the back and I say, "What do you mean playing stupid?"

They all start laughing. Then I say and the coach leans in to listen also, "Same type play. This time Randy stands to the outside of me. Chappy you throw it just a little in front of me, but I'm going to miss it and Randy you take only two steps forward or do a slow trot off the line. The ball will be right in your hands and you can takeoff down the sideline. I'll be there to block for you. Does that sound ok Coach?"

The coach looks at me, and the four horsemen, "Sounds like a good plan, the same scheme with everybody else going right?"

"Yes Sir, and Randy, the ball is going to be hard to see, so be ready because it may look like the ball comes right through me." He nods in understanding. The coach tells us that will be play two, and a sweep left the play before that. Coach yells, "We get the ball first, so let's kick some butt gentlemen."

Chappy looks at us and then says, "Wow! We graduated early this year! We didn't make gentlemen until the end of the season last year."

We all chuckle as the coach smiles and says, "Beat these guys and you will be gentlemen this whole season. Go get 'em guys!"

Chappy looks at me and says, "Hey Dunn, why no end zone celebration?"

I look at the four horsemen, "That is for guys that don't get there very often. I plan on being there a lot and it will get old if I do it every time I'm there."

Chappy chuckles as he nods his head at me and trots away.

We return to the battlefield with the Knights. They kick the ball to us and Scott has a great return for us as he gets to the forty yard line. The next play is the sweep the coach requested, and my defender is as close to me as he can legally get. The ball is hiked and I run directly towards him and he punches me right in the gut as I push him away from the play. He gives me an elbow and seems content hitting me instead of trying to tackle Scott. He gives me another blow to the head as Scott passes. I push him away and think this is more than a coincidence. He comes at me again and I simply step out of the way and he falls to the ground.

I look up field and Scott is pushed out of bounds, "You missed the guy with the ball!"

He looks at me and says, "I could care less about the ball. I'm just gonna make you regret me having to cover you."

"I already do, but if that is your plan you will probably watch the rest of the game from the sidelines because I am going to really embarrass you on the next play."

"You just try it buddy, I'm shutting you down!"

I trot to the line for the next play; since Scott got twenty yards we still have forty to go. I look at my defender, "Good luck with that!"

Chappy yells hike and I turn to him and jump straight up. This time the defender rushes at me trying to not get embarrassed again. The ball flies past me as my defender hits me around the legs and forces me to the ground. He stands up and points at me, "Yeah I got you Punk!"

I open my arms and show him that I do not have the ball, "Yeah but my team is scoring right now and you look stupid, again!"

I jump up and then say, "You give me one more cheap shot and you will be leaving the game, I promise!"

I run to the sideline and Randy says, "You were right, it looked like that ball came right through you."

I smile and say, "Yeah, I thought it was going to hit me also, must have missed me by only an inch."

I look across the field at the other sideline and the coach is yelling at my defender. I wanted to yell I told you so, but it would not matter at this point. Coach Bolton walks by me as I walk towards the bench, "Nice work out there, keep it up!"

"Let Chris play this first series for me on defense, I'll go back out and stop them."

He walks away and yells at Chris, "Thomas, go back in at safety and don't let them by you this time." Chris looks over at me, "Yes Sir, under control!"

As I watch the game our team puts up a great defensive stance against the Knights. *No one likes to feel like they are not needed, but sometimes you need to make sacrifices for friends.* Yeah, I know.

The Knights are unable to move the required yards for a first down and have to punt the ball. We are about to return to offense and Chappy yells to me, "Get over here!"

I look up at him, "I'm not a starter."

"You are now, we need you out there."

"Chappy, I cannot take someone else's position."

"Kid you earned that position."

"No disrespect, thanks but no thanks, I'll rotate like normal Sir."

He looks me in the eye, "As long as you help us win."

"No problem there! I'll make sure you get to state championship this year, I promise!"

Chappy and the horsemen trot out onto the field and I take my place beside the coach waiting to be sent into the game. After the fifth play of the series coach grabs me and says, "Bulldog 2!"

I run to the huddle and tell Chappy the play.

There is a protocol with sports. I don't run in and tell the guys the play. That is the quarterback's job. I am just a link in the chain. On this play three guys could receive the ball and I am one of those possibilities. My job on this play is to run out five yards and turn directly across the field and attempt to catch the ball. My defender gets in front of me and starts growling like a dog. If I was smart enough to have fear. That tactic may have worked on me. But stupid people like me fear nothing. *Like that old redneck joke . . . What is a rednecks last words? Hey y'all, watch this. Classic.* Instead I look at him and say, "Bad dog, bad dog! Sexy legs though." He stops and looks at me strangely.

Chappy yells hike and we take off. I push the defender one hard time as I am allowed and then run my route as intended. When I get to the point where the ball may be thrown to me it is right there in my grasp. I catch the ball and at the same moment feel this sharp pain in my side. I hold onto the ball as if it will save me from the pain and notice the ground rushing towards me. I hit the ground and bounce with extra weight on me. I hear the growl of the bad dog I had hoped I had left behind me. When I get up I notice my defender looking over me and taunting me. I say to him as I pat him on the shoulder pads, "Bad Dog, Bad Dog! Nice tackle!" I start to walk away and he says, "What you didn't think that was a cheap shot?" I look back at him, "Heck no, that was awesome. Hurt a bit, but good hit." I start to head to the sideline and notice no replacement for me coming into the game.

Chappy yells at me, "Come on, let's go!" I run to the huddle, and Chappy calls a screenplay to Scott. This means, all I do is block and divert players away from the play. Chappy yells hike and my bad dog was still being aggressive but not as bad. We bump a few times and then he punches me right in the stomach, just above the stomach and right under the ribs. I feel my ability to breathe stop for a moment, and everything goes into slow motion as I fall to the ground. *That's it! Now he has done it!* I suddenly feel my lungs fill with air. It was like fresh air was just put in my lungs, and I was taking my first breath. I jump up and say nothing to him and trot to the huddle. The referee looks at me as I go by and ask, "Everything ok?"

I smile and say, "Yes Sir, never better."

Chappy calls the play, which is a deep pass to me down the left side of the field. I run to my starting point for the play and never make eye contact with my foe. I hear a growl again and kind of chuckle to myself knowing his impending doom. I hear Chappy yell hike and without looking up I run straight for five yards, do a spin move which causes me to accidentally punch the defender in the face, just a little love tap. I barely am able to get my hand out of his facemask without anyone noticing. We looked like our normal hitting and pushing. I sprint down the field to the spot where Chappy should throw the ball when I get there the ball is not. I look back to see Chappy lying on the ground. He had been sacked on the play and could not release the ball. Chappy jumps up and yells at his linemen for allowing it to happen.

It is now fourth down and we are forced to punt the ball. We only have four attempts to get ten yards and we blew it this time. As I run to the sideline I notice my defender with his helmet off and holding his nose. *That's nothing wait until next time punk!*

I go back in on defense and we are able to hold them to only six yards this time, so now they must punt back to us. Chris runs the return this time and is able to gain about five yards. The offense goes in and I take my place by the coach again. They run the first two plays and then the coach sends me in with no play. He looked in my eye and knew there was something brewing. I get to the huddle, "Chappy don't get sacked this time." He understands and calls the play that had not worked before and warns his linemen to protect him this time. I run to position and my bad dog is back but not as close as before. I run the same route but refrain from punching him this time, because I want him close to me at the end of the play. While running I look to make sure the ball will make it to me this time. I look back and notice it is airborne and my defender is stride for stride with me. *Speed up!* I pick up the pace for a few feet when I hear. *Now stop, jump, turn and catch the ball!* I do as requested by my conscience and as I go up I feel a pain in my elbow. I notice the defender falling in the opposite direction as I catch the ball. *Now run!* I take off at a full sprint to the end zone for another score. Again I reverently hand the ball to the referee as I pass him.

As I head to the sideline I notice my defender on the ground. When I pass by I see blood on his face. I stop and motion for his coach to come over. All the coaches rush over and I wanted to say that is what you get, but did not say a word. I helped him get his helmet off and then the coaches take over. He had bitten his tongue, but luckily it was still intact.

He was crying and wincing in pain as they took him to the sideline where the EMT's were just arriving. The guy looks at me with fear in his eyes and I just wink at him. "Good luck to you Bad Dog." I trot away from the scene and back to my sideline.

Now comfortably ahead in the game and it being the fourth quarter, the coach uses this time to get some of the newer players some playing time. We had just scored and kicked off to the Knights and our defense is doing well. The coach comes to me as he looks at the game clock, "If we get the ball back you go in at quarterback."

Sitting by Chappy I am curious how he feels about it. The coach walks away and Chappy slaps me on the back and says, "You need to watch that right side of the line, they have been sneaking through all night. I told coach to keep Scott in for you so you don't get killed out there. Good luck Buddy!"

"Thanks Chappy."

The game is almost over and we finally get to take over on offense. We take the field and I call the play given to me by the coach in the huddle. We run the play and Scott gains about eight yards. The next play I call is a pass play. I scan the field and no one is open. I notice the linebacker bearing down on me. So I take off running towards the sidelines and feel a tug at my foot. I pull my foot towards the direction I want to go and notice there is no longer a shoe on my foot. I continue to run and manage to get out of bounds just beyond the first down marker. I look for my shoe and notice it all by itself on the field where it had been removed from my foot. I trot to pick it up and place it back on my foot.

We run a couple more small plays to run out the clock and end the game. We shake hands with the Knights and thank them for the victory as they congratulate us. Leaving the field I see the defender that I had aided in the biting of his tongue. I walk up to him and say, "Good luck with that injury, sorry it had to happen to you." I wanted to say, I told you so! I warned you! *Let's take the high road for a change! Putting people in their place always seems to backfire for some reason.* He puts his hand out for me to shake. I take his hand in mine and I feel a peace with him. As I release his hand he writes on some paper he had been given to communicate with. I look at what he was writing and I say, "Thanks! You played great as well. Probably see you at the state championship." He smiled as if in pain and waves bye as I walk away. I turn around and notice Coach Bolton standing behind me, "You are a better man than I expected, keep up the good work." Then the coach goes over to the hurt player and gives his condolences. I walk back to our side of the field where the fans are still there waiting to congratulate us as we exit the field. *That was fun wasn't it?* That was a very good day. *Don't worry kid they are only going to get better.*

Chapter 7

Let's do something; this is boring watching cartoons on a Saturday morning. Read a book, or something educational, play some basketball, anything! What? You get bored also? I look at the ceiling and think how I normally spend my weekends and mom says, "Let's go to the store and get you some new clothes."

"No thanks, I hate shopping! You know that!"

"Well you have to go, I hate buying you clothes with you not there. I have no idea what to buy."

"Is Roxanne going?"

"No she went to work at the donut shop. So let's go."

I drag my butt to mom's car and we drive off. She starts the conversation with small talk, "Sure is a nice fall day."

I look out, "Yes Ma'am sure is."

She asks, "How is school and life going?"

I look at the woman that I have told every secret since birth and realize I haven't shared the biggest secret ever with her. *But how are you going to broach this one to her? Tell her the truth; it has always worked in the past.* "Mom, why weren't you and dad at my game last night?"

"You know I am working that second job so I can keep you in that school and you can have a good life."

"What about dad?"

"He is helping his friend start a business so we can all have a better life."

"But is it worth missing my life to give me a better one? Remember that song that says, 'life is a journey, not a destination.' So don't miss out on it."

Looking at me, she realizes what I am saying and says, "It'll get better, I promise."

I watch my mother drive on the four-lane highway in the left lane. A car in front of us does not do as my Driver's Ed instructor says they should. The car stays in the left lane, which is supposed to be a passing lane. *Why won't that car move! What ever happened to driver's etiquette? Get out of the way slowpoke!* I look at my mother to make sure my outburst was only in my head. My mother passes the car in the right lane. As we pass I look at the other driver in disgust and shake my head mouthing, idiot. The driver realizes their error and changes to the right lane.

"Mom, why do people drive like that?"

Looking in the rearview mirror, "They just don't pay attention. Don't worry about it."

I look at mom and say, "It bugs me though, and it can cause accidents and make drivers angry."

Mom smiles, "You can't control idiots."

"That person would be the first to complain about some young driver though. They might actually have to pay attention to the road."

Mom taps me on the cheek, "So tell me. What is going on with you?"

"Mom, do not forget I'm a teenager and you don't want the answer to those kinds of questions."

Mom looks at me shocked, "I'm your mother and it is my job to ask you those difficult questions!"

Smiling devilishly I say, "Just remember you asked . . . production is slow, my best three drug dealers are in hiding, or jail. My girlfriends are both pregnant, my best hooker has the clap and the bank lost 20 million or is holding it under investigation. I owe my bookie three large . . ."

"Can't you just be serious?"

"About what, Mom? My life is boring, I go to a Christian school; I'm going shopping with my mom on a Saturday. I have no girlfriend I have no life! I have a father that never spends time with me unless I want to go hunting or fishing . . . in that scenario I can't talk or move for hours. Can it get any better than this?"

Mom looks at me strangely, "Well Buddy, it could be a lot worse."

"I know Ma, but I want it to be a lot better!"

"What do you suggest we do then? Your father and I are doing the best we can for you and your sister." Looking at a new building going up I say, "No Ma, what do you want?"

"I don't know? I'm happy, life is good."

There is a long pause in our conversation. I look at my mother and say, "I spoke in Chapel the other day."

"Did you get in trouble for it?"

I chuckle and say, "You don't understand. I mean I was the speaker for the service."

"How did that happen?"

I look in the mall parking lot for familiar cars, "It was a test from the coach."

"Did you pass? I heard nothing about it."

She pulls into a parking space at the mall. "Ma, it was fine and everyone seemed to like it."

My mother looks at me intently as I say, "What would you say if I told you I can make our whole family happier."

She asks, "How do you plan to do that?"

"I can do magic."

"That's great me too! I'm about to make a lot of hard earned money disappear."

I look around, "I can make it appear!"

"That's crazy!"

We get out of the car and start walking into the store. "Want to see? Look into my eyes and do your trick."

We stop at the front door of the store as she looks in my eyes, "What do you mean you make money appear?"

"I think of an amount, put my hand in my pocket and there it is."

She without blinking says, "You believe it is true, now show me."

I pull my pockets out of my jeans and hand her my wallet, "Nothing right?"

She looks at me and nods in agreement. Some people passing stare as they pass I look at them and say, "Mind your business this ain't no freak show."

They keep walking as I tuck my pockets back in and tell mom to inspect my wallet. She does and notices only one dollar and hands it back to me. I put it back in my back pocket, "Now how much money do I have Mom?"

"You have one dollar Son!"

We step away from the door as people are coming and going from the store, "How much would you like and don't get to greedy?"

She thinks for a moment, "How about a hundred?"

I reach in my pocket and there is nothing. She laughs and says, "Amazing trick Son!"

I reach for my wallet I open it up and there it is, "Told ya!"

She looks in and gasps, "How did you do that?"

"Don't know but I've been doing it all week."

"So how much do you have now?"

"This right here is all."

She is staring in my eyes as she says, "How is that possible if you have been doing that all week? You are a pack rat and save every dime."

I look around and then say, "This is the most I've done. I usually just think in twenties. I've been buying food and junk like that. I can't save it, I'm afraid it will disappear. This is still new to me."

Walking in the store I say, "Mom there is more."

She looks at me as we enter the store and she takes the hundred from me. I put the wallet away and think of another hundred. We start talking about my new voodoo or unknown magic. Just out of curiosity I look in the wallet and sure enough there is another hundred.

Mom asks, "What's in there now?" She looks at my wallet, "I sure could use that as well."

Without even thinking about it I hand it to her and she kisses me on the forehead.

Mom continues, "So what is the . . . and more you were referring to?"

"You know that voice in your head?"

"Yes, your conscience."

"Oh you know him? Is he in your head too?"

"Very funny, we all have that voice!"

"Mine is the one that taught me the money trick, and has been helping me in school also."

There is a long silence. Then she says, "What do you think of this shirt?"

"I don't like it . . . I really like those new Polo's."

"Yeah, what the heck you can afford them."

We head to what my mom calls the expensive side of the store. She goes hog wild picking out all top of the line clothes and even got my dad a very nice suit. When we go to pay for our clothes she pulls out her checkbook without even thinking about it. I say, "Mom don't you need to pay cash today?"

She looked at me shocked as the lady says, "That will be $885.87."

Mom looks at me, "That's $885 something."

The lady says, "And 87 cents."

My mom pulls out the two hundred I gave her earlier. "No mom that's alright I've got this one, put your money away."

I pull out $900 and hand it to the lady behind the counter. She changes the money as I walk off to look at a display they had nearby.

Mom takes the change and attempts to give it to me, "Keep it. All I want is to never need it."

"What do you mean? Never need it?"

I look at her as I grab the bags, "I just want to never need money. I don't need a bunch of it, just enough to survive and live well."

She smiles, "Guess I did a good job with raising you kiddo." She pats me on the head and kisses my cheek.

The lady behind the counter says, "I sure could use some."

I smile, "Unfortunately we all do," *She really does need some money badly.* "How much would you like?" She smiles sheepishly, "I was just kidding."

I use the family trick and stare into her eyes. I hear my voice say, *four hundred and fifty*. I reach for my wallet and pullout all the cash in it as I continue to stare into her eyes.

I say, "Don't tell anyone where this came from. If you have to say anything, say God supplies for the needy children and leave it at that. You owe me nothing in return but to continue living a good life. Take care of your family."

As I walk away from the counter I look down to see five, one hundred dollar bills lying there. She starts to shed tears, "Thank you . . . thank you very much!" Without turning around I give a wave and exit the store with my treasures and a good feeling in my heart.

Mom says, "What was that all about?"

I look around and say, "My voice told me she was going to steal $450 from the store today. This way she doesn't have to ruin her life because she would have gotten caught."

Mom looks shocked, "The voice told you all that."

"Yes Ma'am." We walk to the car and a bum approaches us. Before he can say a word I say, "Get a job you bum!"

"Give me one you Punk or just give me some money!"

I stop but urge mom to keep walking, "I know you are not stupid enough to try and rob me plus I see no gun, so I will let that last statement go. You need to go back to your last job and family, they still want you and you can quit drinking. You almost have as it is. Good luck to you." He yells, "You snot nose brat!" Without turning back I say, "Yeah . . . yeah I love you too!"

Catching up to mom she says, "Why did you not give him money?"

"It's not always about the money sometimes it's a push in the right direction. He's got money he just needs to go back to it and stop running."

She looks at me, "I really like your little voice."

"Me too! My turn to drive!"

"You have your permit with you right?"

"Yes Mom! You didn't see it in my wallet earlier?"

She gets in the car, "Who else knows about this voice?"

"No one! Roxanne suspects something, but not enough to bug me too much." We get in the car and drive away.

"So what are your plans for you and your little voice?"

Watching the traffic stack up as I try to drive out of the parking lot, "Not real sure! Probably something selfish . . . hey, I'm only human."

Looking at the traffic and becoming nervous knowing I am a new driver my mother says, "Ha-ha very funny. Watch that car and don't get to close!"

"If I don't let them know I'm serious about getting out of here they will let me sit here all day. Trust me."

"Yeah sure, until you get in an accident!"

"Let's look back how many of those have I had. What nothing to say now Mom?"

"Don't be a smart butt, I brought you in this world I'll take you out!"

"Now you are stealing lines from Bill Cosby mom . . . that's low."

I look at the traffic, "See this nice lady is letting me out."

Mom and I wave to the lady at the same time, "Mom, what are you doing? That was my thank you wave, not yours!"

The nice lady gives us the, you are welcome nod and mom says, "I'm just glad we lived through the experience."

I look at my mother in disgust, "If you think that was bad you should see what my life was going to be like before the voice spoke up!"

"What you saw the future?"

"No Ma'am, my voice did and said it was going to be miserable for me."

Watching the movement of the traffic mom says, "So how are you going to explain this to your father?"

I look at her thoughtfully, "Thought I'd get him fired and let him become a full time hunter. Maybe he will not even notice since he will never be around, sort of like the weekends."

"You know he loves you! Watch out for that car! Don't drive so fast!"

"What car! I think we are going to crash . . . ah!"

"Ok . . . stop it or I will drive!"

Placing my hands in my lap, "Hey, go ahead!"

"Put your hands back on the wheel!"

"You stop fussing and I will!"

"Fine, you just make me nervous!"

I put my hands back on the steering wheel, "Yeah your constant nagging seems to keep me really calm. Tell you what Mom, you watch that side of the car and I'll watch this side and let's see if we can get the old girl home . . . ok!"

"Not funny, just don't hurt my little car."

"Yes Ma'am, I promise."

Trying to relax mom ask, "So . . . about your dad?"

I think as I watch a fast car going past me and say, "Not real sure of a good way to handle him, he gets too excited and trust nothing. I think he will notice if we start spending a lot of cash. What I think we need to do is let him spend some and he will not be too jealous."

Mom smiles and says, "Good idea! How?"

"Hang on let me consult with a friend."

Mom stares at me as I talk to my conscience. She is about to speak when I give her, the silent gesture.

"Ok . . . got it. Mom what we do is when you receive your and daddy's pay you keep it in the bank. When the bills are due you and I go and pay cash."

Mom looks at me, "That sounds like it will work. But wouldn't someone notice the bank money."

"Not if we don't let it grow too fast and too big."

I can see the excitement growing in her eyes.

I continue, "And after a month or two, you will have a good buffer. I can then give you small amounts to increase it slowly. You can let daddy buy a new gun or fishing pole to keep him happy. We buy gas, food and groceries on my cash and that will never be questioned."

We pull into the driveway and I say with a smile, "Cheated death again!"

She looks at me, "You are still not funny!"

"Yes I am funny!"

"Hey look your sister is home."

"Oh hooray, I'll alert the media! And look Mommy her boyfriend is home from college."

"Stop! I like him he is a good boy."

I put the car in park and say, "Yeah, that's what I hear!"

Mom smacks me on the back of the head, "Be nice!"

I look at her annoyed and gritting my teeth I say, "Yes Ma'am!" *She took the news better than I thought she would.*

We get out of the car and mom hugs them both. I like her boyfriend also, he did teach me to play basketball. I'm not bad for a white kid from Carolina, but he is awesome. How he did not get a basketball scholarship I will never know? *Must be that small private school thing?* He is as good as that new guy at Carolina. *You mean Michael Jordan?* Yeah, that's the guy. *How much do you want to bet he helps Carolina win the Championship this year?* Really? Jordan does? Too bad I'm too young to bet on it. *Get Mike to do it for you.* Think he would? *Ask him!*

I walk over to the trunk where they are pulling out the treasures from my mother's raid on the local shops. I stick my hand out to shake his hand, "Hey Mike! How are you doing?"

We shake hands and he says, "Good, Buddy! Are you working tonight?"

I look up in wonder where this was going, "No, I quit that job, it was too demanding with my football schedule."

"You want to join me and your sis at that Japanese Restaurant where they cook on the grill right in front of you?"

The short story is, when I was younger and my sister first started dating, I was their buffer. Meaning my parents would let her go out on dates as long as I was with her. I loved it because I could go places and my parents loved it because I would keep an eye on my sister. Even though she could have gotten nude and run around, I wouldn't have noticed because I was a kid out with big kids they were my idols. These two people were gods to me. Ah . . . good times.

"Only if you guys let me pay! I owe you both from when I was younger."

Mike looks at me and says, "You don't have to do that!"

"Come on I owe you both seriously!"

"Ok, fine but we are paying for the movie. Can you get a date for tonight?"

"Not sure, do I need a chaperone? I use to be third wheel with no problem."

Roxanne walks out of the house just catching the end of the conversation, "What did I miss?"

She wraps her arms around Mike and he explains the invitation. She looks at me, "I think I know someone who might like to go with us." Now she has a big grin on her face.

I smirk, "Who? Really? She said she had a boyfriend!"

"No, that was a safety measure to see if you were crazy or what, but after your speech the other day, she is crazy over you."

Smiling at my sister, "Ok, call her for me."

"Already did, but you still need to call to seal the deal."

I look at her in disbelief, "What?"

She smiles, "Didn't want my baby brother getting shot down on his first tour of duty, so I called earlier to see what she was doing tonight. When she said nothing, I asked if she wanted to go out . . ."

I stop her, "So she wants to go out with you and I'm just tagging along that makes me look stupid!"

"No don't interrupt . . . it is rude! She asked if you were going. I said I don't know, but I would see if you would like to. Now all you have to do is call her."

"Really? You have to be the coolest sister ever. What happened to the mean ole sister I use to have?"

She smiles as she slaps me lightly on the cheek, "You did. Now hurry up . . . call her. The number is on the bedside table in my room. She should not need more than an hour. Tell her we will leave in about an hour from here."

I run towards the house, "Got it!"

I go to pick up the phone and it starts ringing. I lift the receiver, "Hello." The voice on the other end was my friend Chris, "What's up Mr. Dunn?"

"Chris it is me!"

"Man you and your pop sound just a like, scary."

"What's up?"

"Nothing want to go to the arcade tonight?"

"Not sure I can, I may have a date."

"Yeah right, with whom?"

"Leigh, but I'm not sure I have to call her and that is what I was about to do."

"That senior girl you were talking to the other day?"

"Yes!"

"Hey, way to go buddy good luck. Call me later with details. Bye!"

We hang up and before I can pick up the phone it rings again. Are you kidding me? "Hello!"

"How are you Mr. Dunn?"

"I am fine young lady, but not as fine as you Sweet thing!"

"Tommy! I am going to kick your butt!"

"This is Mr. Dunn what are you talking about?"

"Oh yeah, has your son ever told you about the time we almost . . ."

"Kaye that's just wrong!"

"I'm still kicking your butt, Buddy!"

"I've got to go jump in the shower so I can go out to eat. So what's up?"

"Just wanted to see what you are doing tonight, thought you might end up at the arcade."

"Not sure yet girl, but I might be there later. No promises though. Think I might have a date but not sure yet."

"Oh yeah, who with you slut?"

"Leigh."

"The senior? You slut! If you don't come to the arcade, I'll see you tomorrow at church. I want details! Hey, you playing ball tomorrow?"

"Yes, I play almost every Sunday afternoon, don't I?"

"Ok see you tonight or tomorrow, bye Cutie!" Kaye hangs up before I can respond.

I lower the receiver to the cradle and it rings again. I look to heaven. God do you hate me, or what? *Not this time Buddy!* I feel a relief but nervous at the same time. "Hello."

I hear the pretty voice say, "May I speak to Roxanne?"

No, don't you mean her brother, "Sure, I'll see where she is. I think she is still outside though can you hang on please. May I ask who is calling?"

"Tommy?"

"Yes!"

"I wasn't sure if it was you or your dad. This is Leigh. I didn't want your parents to think I was calling a boy."

"You want to hang up and I call you back then?"

"Would you?"

"Sure no problem! Bye"

"Bye."

I hang up the phone and it rings again, "YOU HAVE GOT TO BE KIDDING ME!"

I pick up the phone with a disgusted voice, "Hello!"

"Hey baby, what are you doing?"

"Hello Grandma, this is not a good time can we call you back?"

"Yes, tell your mom to call me. Your phone has been busy for a while now."

"I know grandma, it has been busy. Love ya!"

"Love you to Sweetie! Bye."

Mom walks in, "What is going on with the phone?"

I look at her, "Not sure, but every time I hang up it rings again. Here you take it and call Grandma. I'm going to use my phone."

I pick up the phone in my room and dial, "Hi Coach Bolton, may I speak to Leigh Ann please."

"Who is this?"

"Tommy."

"Yeah, hold on Son."

I wait for what seems to be an eternity then I hear that sweet voice again, "Hello."

"Hey Leigh, I'm sorry about it taking so long to call . . . every time I would try the phone would ring."

"That's ok, what are you doing?"

"Just got home and then my sister and her boyfriend invited me to dinner. Thought I'd invite you along, but then my phone-a-thon started."

She sighed for relief, "That is why your phone was busy. Let me ask my dad."

I start to get nervous again, "Sure."

I wait, and then I hear a man's voice on the phone, "What's going on Tommy?"

"Hey Coach. My sister and her boyfriend are going out to eat and to a movie. They invited me to go along. I was hoping your daughter could join us?"

He pauses and then says, "Where you going for dinner?"

"That Japanese place near the mall where they cook in front of you."

"What movie?"

"No idea Sir! Since I'm only 15 it can't be anything but PG."

"Tommy Dunn?"

"Yes sir."

I can hear the relief in his voice, "Yes that's fine! Just remember she is a preacher's daughter. See ya boy!"

She comes back on the phone, "What time?"

"Roxanne said we would leave here in an hour ten minutes ago. It should take 15 minutes to get there so an hour and five minutes from now, if that's ok?"

"Sounds good, see you then. Bye."

"Bye." We hang up and I run to the shower.

As I go to my room to dress for the night, I notice I already have clothes laid out on my bed. There is my new yellow button down polo, brown khakis and my new Docksider shoes. "Hey, no jeans?" My sister yells down the hall, "NO!"

I cuss under my breath like my favorite cartoon character Yosemite Sam, "Rac-n-Frac-n-dirty-rat!"

I hear two women from down the hall in unison, "I can hear you!"

"Sorry ladies!" They love to play along.

We arrive at the restaurant and we have a thirty-minute wait. Leigh looks at me, "This is a very popular restaurant!"

I smile and say, "Yes it is, but it is worth the wait! What, you have never been here?"

She looks around as if out of place, "No."

"Oh, you are going to love it! I hope! We've only been here twice because it is kind of expensive."

"So why are we here then?"

My sister leans in hoping to keep the situation from going south, "My brother owes me and he has some money that he is finally willing to spend."

Leigh looks at me in surprise, "Birthday money?"

I look at the two them and smile, "No, like money . . . money."

Mike walks back to our group and says, "Our table is finally ready."

As we walk in Mike pats me on the back and says, "You still play ball on Sunday afternoon?"

As I hear my sister tell Leigh she is having the lobster and she should not be concerned with the prices. I look at Mike, "We sure do and it is going to be good to have you back out there."

We sit down to our table. I try to be the gentleman and pretend to help Leigh with her chair. She turns and smiles. I look back to Mike as I sit, "The guys keeping getting bigger and bigger. I think the prison has some kind of day release program." They all start laughing even the people at our table not with us. These tables seat eight and we only have four. *Good you seem to be a hit keep up the good work. Women love guys that can make them laugh.* That explains a question I had about Woody Allen and a couple other comedians.

We continue with normal dinner conversation. Mike and I talk sports and fun stuff and the girls slip into their fashion world. We have our individual conversations, and then we talk together.

Mike says, "You guys need to come up skiing some weekend this winter."

Sis and me jump in and say, "Sounds good."

I look to Leigh, "Do you ski?"

She smiles blankly, "No."

"Me neither, I can't wait to learn. Would you like to?"

Still the blank expression on her gorgeous face, "Not really, I don't really like the cold."

I look into her eyes, "You look really nice tonight. You look really nice all the time . . . but tonight is different."

She smiles the biggest I have ever seen her smile, "Thank you, you do too. I really like you in yellow. I really like that book you gave me." *Look at those eyes light up. I think you found her spot. Let's talk about her and she will be happy.*

Smiling at her I say, "Glad you liked it. Anything you would like to act out later?"

Smiling she whispers, "Oh yeah, you could show me how to . . ."

The chef yells, "Good evening everybody!"

The chef pushes his cart with our food up to the table. He bows to us and begins checking our order asking, "You order steak? How you want that?" Then he would go to the next person, "You order lobster? How you doing big spender?" *Great, we get the comedian cook . . . nice!* I'm last at the table as he makes his rounds, "You order steak, you shrimp?" As everyone bust out laughing he stares at the paper again, "Sorry, you order steak and shrimp. How you want that steak?" Wanting him to know I have a sense of humor and he is allowed to jab at me I respond, "Cooked please."

Obviously gay, he smiles saying seductively, "So you want me to do it until it looks good?"

Our table still chuckling I say, "Yes please."

He says, "Don't worry I not spit on your food," then under his breath he says, "anymore."

The table erupts with laughter and he does a little yell, "Woo-Woo" and the whole restaurant responds back with, "Whoop-Whoop!" right on cue.

The chef starts putting food on the table and pulling out his knifes. People go back to their lives as he starts cooking. The cook stares at me and continues cooking, "You look familiar, you here last week?"

I say, "Nope, sorry."

"Yeah you here last week, different girl though."

The table and close by tables give the uh-oh sound and he says, "This girl much prettier than last week girl!"

Again the room laughs. "Thank you, she is very pretty!"

Now the crowd turns to my side with a big, ah! Trying to seize the moment I look at him and before he can speak I say, "Didn't you use to be Chinese? What are you doing in a Japanese Restaurant?"

Now the crowd laughs at my side of the banter. The chef gives another Woo-Woo and the crowd again answers with Whoop-Whoop!

He smiles and says quietly, "I use to be a girl also."

"Hey, I thought you still were. Hey, that's where I know you from! Sha-nay-nay! How you been girl?"

He rolls his eyes and pretends to flip imaginary hair, "Well you know, I been busy!"

We have the restaurant rolling and in tears at this point. The older lady at our table had to leave to go to the bathroom. Of course he made fun of her as she left the room, "Mommy . . . please don't go!"

And he gives another Woo-Woo!

Everyone seems to be having a great time. Our chef puts on a great show with the onion volcano, throwing shrimp in Mike's mouth, pretending to spill ketchup on me, juggling the knifes, and throwing shrimp tails in his pocket. The chef leaves as we begin to eat our meal. We give a round of applause as he makes his exit, which is the custom if they did a good job. He stares at me as he leaves as if sizing me up, "You . . . call me when you get out of prison!" He gets everyone laughing again. I give him a wink as he leaves toward the kitchen.

It was a great meal and as we finish the busboys grab our plates. The chef comes back out for the table next to us. He looks at me and says, "You still here! You got to go, this no buffet!" People start chuckling not sure what is going on, as some of the crowd is different now. I raise my hand and say, "Yeah—yeah, whatever! Just bring me more food!" He smiles and gives yet another Woo-Woo! With that out comes the waitresses and busboys over to our table singing Happy Birthday in Japanese. I look at him in shock as he points to me so the whole restaurant joins in. He pats me on the back and whispers in my ear as they put the cake down in front of me, "Thanks for playing along. That was fun! Come back sometime. The cake is a gift from me." I shake his hand as he walks back to the other table.

Leigh looks at me, "So it really is your birthday? Happy Birthday!" She gives me a big kiss, our first kiss! Wow!

"Thanks but it's not my birthday. He is just a friend of mine. I've seen his act before I was just playing along. Here have some cake it is really good."

She looks to my sister and she nods in agreement. We all grab forks and devour the cake.

"What is with all the birthday stuff? I wish it was, I would be sixteen and could drive."

Mike looks at the time and says, "We just missed the movie any ideas?"

I smile at the group, "I have an idea!"

As we get up to leave the chef yells at me, "You get out of here you eat too much!"

I wave bye and say, "See you Sha-nay-nay!"

He waves as we are almost out the door we hear one more Woo-Woo!

We leave the restaurant and head to the airport. We arrive at the little park designed to watch airplanes come and go. They have benches to sit and watch, a playground area for kids, and an airplane history area. There are about four other cars in the parking lot, two with teenagers making out and the others with people obviously having friends leaving or returning on flights.

Roxanne looks at one of the cars and sees people making out, "I see why you wanted to come here now." She gives a big smile and I say, "That is not a bad idea, but look out at the lights. It's a rainbow out there. You have your white, green, blue, amber and red lights. Then a flash of green and then a flash of white, it is amazing!"

Roxanne looks at me knowing I've never been here before but wanting to test my knowledge, "Do those flashes have any meaning or are they just pretty?"

I stare at the lights and say, "It signifies that it is a civilian airport and helps airplanes locate the airport at night or in bad weather."

Leigh says, "So what other airports could it be?"

I look at her, "Military or seaports. But if it is an airport near a city it helps it stand out better."

She looks at me in amazement, "How do you know this?"

I point at the airplane coming in for a landing, "I read it in a book the other day. If it were two white flashes and then a green flash it would be for a military airport."

We watch the airplane land and all agree it was a pretty good landing. Roxanne gets out of the car and walks through the kiddy park, which is an airplane theme. She stares off at the lights and we get out of the car and join her. As we walk up to her she says, "So do all the lights mean something?"

No one else answers so I say, "Yes! The white lights signify the runway and turn amber then red as you approach the far end. That lets you know you are at the end and better stop soon. The blue lights indicate the edge of taxiways that go from the terminal or parking to the runway. The green is the line on the taxiway that is yellow during the day to help pilots stay in the center of the taxiway so they don't hit anything as they taxi by stuff."

My sister gives me a look, "How and why do you know this?"

I look at the sky and say, "Because I am going to get my pilots license."

Leigh interjects, "I'm scared of flying. I would never get in one of those small planes."

My sister says, "How much is that going to cost?"

"Not sure exactly? You have to have fifty flying hours as a minimum to apply for a license."

My sis looks at me, "How much is that per hour?"

"Like $50/hour; $15 for instructor and $35 for plane rental."

She grabs me by the arm and pulls me away from Mike and Leigh, "What? Mom and Dad say they can't afford for me to go to Carolina, but they can afford flying lessons for you? The only way I could go to school is with a scholarship."

"Don't worry Sis! I got that part figured out with mom today ask her tomorrow at Sunday dinner if you can go to school. Now and I bet you get a different story."

She stares at my eyes, "Does this have something to do with you and your spending money?"

"Yes, but please ask no more because I'm not sure you will understand the answer."

Looking angry with me, "I want to know because I am not going to school on dirty money."

I look at her in disgust, "Hey my money is very clean and you don't mind using it for food and gas."

She grabs me again, "Just tell me."

Our friends start to look annoyed, "I will."

I start walking to Mike and Leigh, "Tomorrow! I will! I promise!"

Leigh reaches for a button on my shirt, "Everything ok?"

Mike walks over to Roxanne and I smile at Leigh and say, "Yeah, just some family business."

She and I walk over to a bench and sit down. Mike and Roxanne go and sit in the car. Leigh and I start talking about school and books she has read and I can see her starting to get a little excited. After another airplane lands I look at her and say, "Want to go for a walk?" She agrees and we get up and start walking toward the tree line.

As we get out of sight of the car she grabs my hand. At first I thought she might be nervous about being out here in the dark, but then she pulls herself towards me. She starts kissing me passionately and I try to do my best to return the affection.

She stops abruptly, "Do you want to have sex?"

I listen for the voice in my head and as if right on cue I hear. *If you do you will regret it!*

I look in her eyes, "Yes!"

She starts peeling her dress off and kissing me every time she has an opportunity. I stop her right as she pulls her panties down. *Be careful how you handle this, we don't want it to backfire.* "We can't do this here! We are standing at the edge of the woods. This is not the way I pictured my first time."

She looks at me startled and pulls her panties back up, "You are a virgin?"

I look sadly at her, "Yes!"

"So you want to go back to the car or get a hotel room?"

I look at her near nakedness, "That would be great, but are you in love with me?"

She starts getting dressed, "No! I like you, you are cute, and I admire you a lot. What's love got to do with sex?"

Smiling at her, "I want it all, love and sex. Not just love and not just sex." Oh my God, what am I saying?

She interrupts, "Good luck with that."

I continue, "And no offense but I'm not an animal and definitely don't want to have sex in the woods. You are gorgeous and if I knew you better I would enjoy having sex with you. What am I saying? I want to sex you up real bad!"

She looks at me and says, "You are a good guy and you are right. You should wait and do it the right way, don't let me corrupt you for five minutes of pleasure."

"Hey don't insult me I bet I could last at least six minutes."

We both chuckle and she kisses me and caresses my crotch as she says, "You're sweet!"

At this point we are both dressed and she says, "I understand, it makes sense. I just thought you might like to have sex for fun."

I smile at her, "You are so awesome! But I would not want to say I lost my virginity like this. How would you explain it to our kids?"

She looks disgusted, "Kids! No way, none for me thanks! I'm going to have fun!"

I stop her, "Let me get this straight. You do not like flying, skiing, or scuba diving?"

"No way and get my hair messed up!"

"So what do you do for fun?"

She looks at me, "I was trying to show you."

She starts trying to tickle me, "Not ticklish? We will have to work on that one."

We start kissing; now this is fun! *Think about that new Prince song. How many have been there before you? I don't understand? In his song 'Little Red Corvette', he says, he sees all the pictures of the jockeys that were there before him, pocket full of horses, Trojans (condoms) some of them used . . . get the picture?* Yeah, but I could be having sex right now. *Nope, you would be done by now and she would think of you like all the others. She has a bad outlook on life if you hadn't noticed.* Yeah, but I could have had sex! *Believe it or not you would regret it.* Promise! *Most definitely!* We walk back to the car and she acts as if nothing happened.

On the ride to her house we snuggle and kiss. We pull up to her house and I get out and walk her to the door. She stops me and gives me a big kiss and her house door opens. We stop and stare at the coach. He stands there looking at us; she taps me on the cheek tenderly and says, "Goodnight! I had fun." The coach stares as she enters and I say, "Goodnight." And the door shuts.

I return to the car feeling funny and my sister says, "Everything as you had hoped!"

I get in the car, "Not even close."

She smiles and turns around to look at me sitting in the backseat, "Regardless of what you think, that is why I did not want you going out with my friends. Plus, if you did go out and you two fight it puts a strain on mine and her relationship."

I look at her as she pats my hand, "I just want a girl that looks like that, but likes things I like or at least likes normal things."

"Baby brother, when you stop looking she will show up I promise."

I sit quietly for a moment and then say, "I just hope my dream girl is not like that old joke, the day my ship came in I was at the airport."

Mike chuckles, "That's a good one, humorous."

Don't worry my friend I have the perfect girl lined up for you. She will be your best friend. She will be there for your every need and will be loyal to you. That sounds familiar. *Oh yeah that joke. What joke are you talking about? God said to Adam in the Garden of Eden the same thing I just said to you. When Adam said it sounds great. What is it going to cost me? God says an arm and a leg. Adam says what can I get for a rib? The rest is history.* I begin laughing and my sister turns around to look at me, "You ok?"

I nod my head and say, "Yeah, I just had a funny thought."

"Share it with me."

"You may not see the humor like I did."

"Try me?"

I tell her the joke and her and Mike laugh as we pull into our driveway. I step out of the car and tell them goodnight and go in the house.

I walk in and mom says, "Call Kaye! She said anytime would be ok and she sounded insistent."

"Thanks Mom!"

I pick up the receiver of the phone and dial my friend, "Hello Dear I am home."

I listen to Kaye go on and on about who said what and did what at the arcade.

Then it comes, "What did you do tonight?"

"We ate and then went to the airport and watched some planes land. It was cool."

I listen to her question and then I say, "No Kaye, I did not lose my virginity. Told you I was saving that for you! Let's talk about it tomorrow I am going to bed."

I hang up the phone and sit on the bed. *That is a girl we could settle down with.* I can't control that girl and her big mouth. *But I can and she is very pretty. If I calm her down would you consider her and only her?* Why only her? Do I have to answer right now? *Only her because if you start giving yourself to a bunch of women you start losing my help, I need you to be pure. I know the answer, but I need to know if I can count on you.* I look at the ceiling and think, only one woman for life or I lose my gift? I hope it is worth it. *Trust me it will be worth it. We could go back to your other life and you will regret it I promise.* How many women do I have in the other life? *Fifty or so.* Wow, and I'm not happy with that? *Nope, not even close . . . no love.*

Chapter 8

Good morning sunshine! We have to try to explain things to your father today. Good luck with that I've been trying for 10 years now and the only time I can is if I go hunting or fishing with him. Why couldn't he have been a surf punk like I want to be? *Regardless, today we show him how to make money! So you don't have to.* My dad is a hard worker, and if you aren't, he doesn't understand you or anything you stand for. *Something smells good!* Sorry about that didn't know you could smell also. *Not that! I smell bacon and . . .* Oh yeah Sunday morning family breakfast. Got to love it! The only morning mom has time to cook breakfast.

I walk into the kitchen, "Good morning all." Mom is busy cooking and dad is grabbing coffee.

Mom yells, "It's not ready yet! I need five more minutes."

I sit down and pour myself a glass of milk, "Hey Dad, we need to talk sometime today it is important, but I know how you feel about talking business on Sunday. Could you possibly take a sick day or vacation day tomorrow?"

He looks to the ceiling then down at me, "Not sure it depends on the subject."

Mom looks at me, "Is this what we were discussing yesterday?"

"Yes Ma'am it is."

I look back at dad, "In simplest terms if you will listen to me I can work it where me and sis can both go to Carolina and you can semi retire."

He smirks, "Semi-retire? What does that mean?"

"I mean the only work you will need to do is buy and sell stocks when I tell you to. Then you just hunt and fish the rest of the time."

He smiles, "Can I get that bass boat I've always wanted?"

I smile back at him, "Most definitely! And that big truck with the duel wheels on the back to pull it around with."

"Well you have my interest."

Mom is smiling now. I look at them, "Two things are going to happen today and your answer to both has to be yes. Roxanne got accepted to Carolina with only a 25% scholarship. You tell her she can go. Uncle Glenn is going to call this evening wanting to buy your share of the family farm. Whatever he offers you take. Try to bump him up a grand or so, but that is it no more. We go down tomorrow and finish the deal. We put that money in the bank. And by the end of the year Dad, you quit work and mom starts her own business."

Dad looks dumbfounded, "What? I don't want to sell my portion of the farm, I can't quit my job! Have you gone insane?"

At that moment my sister enters the kitchen. We all go dead silent. She sits down next to me and reaches across the table to hand dad a letter, "It's an acceptance letter to Carolina. Can I go?"

She looks at me and waits for a response. Daddy opens the letter, "How much?"

She tells him a ballpark figure and then he says, "Honey we can't afford it."

Mom looks at me and is about to speak when Roxanne says, "But we can afford flying lessons for hotshot over here?"

Dad says, "We sure cannot afford that! No way!"

Mom and I look at each other and smile. Dad says, "What is with you two?"

Mom sits down with the scrambled eggs in the bowl and sits them on the table, "Your son can do quite a little magic trick with money."

My dad huffs, "Yeah but making it disappear is not a hard trick."

She smiles and says, "Would making it appear be better?"

Dad and Roxanne say in unison, "Yeah! Much better!"

Then Roxanne says, "Is that what you've been doing?"

I look at her and smirk. Dad asks, "What? What are you talking about?"

Roxanne says, "All last week he was paying for our food and gas with his money. But he quit his job."

Dad looks at me sternly, "Where have you been getting the money boy?"

"That is what I was trying to explain. Remember the two questions you had to give a yes answer to today? One you must say now."

Dad stands up and points at me, "Look here boy, you are not going to tell me what to say like some kind of puppet master. We can't afford it!"

I start to stand up and go on the defensive and I hear. *Sit your ass down! He is your dad and you will respect him!* I look up at him and say,

"Yes Sir, we can and no disrespect intended but we will! You just have to trust me."

Mom tries to calm dad down, "Trust him Honey, he has a great plan."

My father sits back down, "Let me hear it! I'm going to need some proof."

"Yes Sir! Already gave you one with your daughter. Your brother calling tonight will be another. But the big one is . . ."

I run down the hallway to my room and grab some pants and then return to the kitchen. "I've been watching the news all week to see if there has been any money missing or anything weird going on and I have seen nothing out of the ordinary."

I hand the pants to mom, "Check the pockets Mom and let whoever else wants to."

They all three feel the pants and then mom pulls out the pockets and hands them to me. I sit down at the table and hand them to Roxanne.

She looks at me oddly, "What?"

I look at her and say, "Reach into the pocket and give dad a twenty."

"Which pocket?"

She reaches in two pockets at the same time and pulls out a twenty and hands it to dad. He takes it and says, "Well there you go, and our money troubles are over." We all chuckle and he hands the money back to my sister.

I look at my sister, "That's all that is in there?"

She feels around the pants, "Yep!"

She hands me the pants. I show them my empty palms before I put my hands in the pocket and say, "Ok Dad tell me how much would you like, but be reasonable not to large."

He looks at me and says, "Give me those pants." I hand them to him and he inspects them thoroughly.

He hands me the pants, "Pull me a couple of hundred out of there." I put my hand in the pocket and pull out $200 and hand it to him. He takes the money and looks shocked, "Eat your breakfast and get ready for church. Let's pray." He says the normal blessing and we all start eating and do not say a word as you can see him trying to sort this out.

Dad eats quickly and sips his coffee, grabs the money looking at it as if it must be a fake. He walks into the living room with the money and mom follows him. They are talking for a few minutes and I hear dad ask, "What does this mean? What is going on here?"

Mom says, "I think we should trust him."

Roxanne leans over and asks, "So what's the gag? How do you do it?"

She continues eating and I say, "I really don't know. When I questioned it I was told, ask again in ten years."

She looks around as if a ghost were in the walls and whispers, "By Whom?"

I look around playing her game, "A voice in my head."

Ask her to think of a number between 1 and a 100 and if you get it right she is not allowed to ask you anymore questions. Tell her to enjoy the benefits without abusing them.

When I relay this message to her she agrees and says, "Ok I have got a number if you guess it I will leave it alone and not constantly bug you for money. One last thing, am I going to be able to go to Carolina?"

I look at her and sigh, "Ok! That number is bigger than a hundred, and that depends on your father and his willingness to cooperate with us . . . Your number is 25, no 42 and now 83 I said pick a number! Now go get ready for church so I can get in the bathroom in five minutes."

My sister looks at me in utter amazement. Then gets up and leaves the room. As she is leaving I say, "Hey! Regardless of dad's decision I will get you to Carolina one way or another, I promise."

She smiles and comes back and gives me a kiss on the forehead, "Sorry things didn't work out for you and Leigh."

"It worked out fine for me, I saw her naked."

My sister's mouth drops, "You what?"

"She offered me sex and I turned her down, but don't let her know that you know." I continue to eat and my sister leaves the kitchen.

Mom and dad came back in the kitchen and dad says, "Heard what you said. So what is the down side to all of this?"

"Dad you know that voice in your head?"

"Yes, your conscience."

I shake my head agreeing, "Mine talked to me the other day and now we talk all the time. When I read something I can actually remember every detail, even stuff I did not notice before. When I take test I remember everything I studied in one lesson, it is outrageous! The money is like a gift from my conscience. If I keep it low no one will ever notice."

He looks at me relieved and I continue, "You know the old saying it takes money to make money? That is what this money is; soon we will have our own and not need my gift anymore."

"So how do your mother and I fall into this?"

I look at the table and then them sadly, "I know you guys have had problems."

"Well Son that is not what I was asking at all."

"Sorry Dad, but it is the answer. My conscience saw our futures and is giving me the opportunity to change it."

"Tell me something that happens then."

I listen for a moment and make some faces at the statements I hear in my head. "Ok hold on! Dad you get hurt at work, Mom has a back injury and the medication they put her on makes her see demons and ghost, Me and Roxanne both have to get married due to pregnancies, and I go through two divorces and end up in jail, and Roxanne gets divorced also and you two end up hermits living in the woods."

My dad smiles, "That last part didn't seem so bad."

Mom chuckles, as she says, "Not funny!"

"Ok son, what is this plan of yours or your conscience?"

I ask mom to grab a paper and pen for us, "Let me ask you this dad? Do you ever plan to go back to the old farm? Because you always say no and you don't even like going down there."

"There is a lot of sentimental stuff there but no I could never enjoy it again."

"So there is your answer. When Uncle Glenn calls you tonight, haggle with him a bit but tell him you will sell. We go down settle it, and put the money in the bank."

"So what if he does not call tonight?"

"Then you know I am not on the level and we forget this whole ordeal ever happened."

He looks at mom just reentering the room with stationery, "Sounds fair."

"So when we put the money in the bank from selling your portion of the farm, I match it."

Mom and dad both say, "What?"

"That's right. Match it. And none is the wiser. We leave that money in the bank and continue living off my pocket money. Nothing too extravagant at first, we pay off any and all bills. Dad you will need to open a stock account. I will run this account since luckily enough everyone says we sound alike on the phone. Dad, I will need you to put money in and take money out only. In a couple of years we will be able to do it ourselves on the computer."

Dad stops me, "This is amazing! But we need to get ready for church."

"Yes Sir!

We stop talking and I run jump in the shower and get dressed as fast as I can. Tying my necktie I walk out of my room and my dad is standing there making sure I have it straight, "What do you mean I can semi-retire?"

I look at him; "Ok you work until the end of the year putting all your checks in the bank not keeping any of it. Whatever cash we need for groceries, gas etc . . . I pay."

"I see so when we start spending money it is not a question to where it came from."

"Exactly! Also the reason you are going to quit your job is financial independence. You will leave on good terms in case some unforeseen event."

Dad smiles and pats me on the back as we walk out to the car, "Ok, as a deacon it is my duty today to be an usher. If we have this new gift how much should we give the church?"

"As a deacon Dad, you know any bills or needs the church have?"

He smiles, "Yes I do!"

Before he starts listing them I stop him, "If we give too much at one time we draw attention to ourselves and we can't afford that right now."

He nods his head in agreement. I look up and say, "If we each put in a hundred in cash they will never know who it came from. That should be a good start for the church."

I reach in my pocket and pull out four hundred dollars handing one to mom, sis and two for dad. "One of those is for lunch big guy."

My sister starts putting her hands in my coat pockets, "Wish I could do that."

I think of a twenty and she pulls it out, "There you go."

She looks at it and says thanks as she puts the money in her purse.

As we arrive at church mom being on the music committee rushes into church. She checks to see if she needs to play the piano or the organ or just sit in the choir and make a joyful noise as I like to call it.

During the service I sit with my friend Kaye and she asks, "So how did last night go?" I just smile and continue singing the hymn. She continues to meddle, "You lose your virginity?" She worked it into the melody of the song. I look at her astonished and continue to sing, I can see it is starting to bug her now. "You have to give me details!" She says under her breath.

I smile, "You want the truth or what I'm going to say happened to be spread around?"

She smiles with anticipation, "The truth!"

I look at her as the song is ending I work it into the melody, "noth-ing happ-ened!"

We whisper and write notes as that morning's announcements are read. I lean over to her and say, "We made out and she wanted to go all the way, but I said no. Told her I don't love her and the first time I do it I want it to be with a person for love, not lust." She pats me on the arm and says, "Good boy." We stop talking and listen to the service.

After the service Kaye and I continue our discussion in the parking lot. She looks at me sternly, "Are you sure you didn't go all the way with her?"

I look her in the eyes, "You don't have that power, but I can teach it to you."

I grab her and say, "Stare deep into the black of my eyes. Now watch for twitches or any pattern of movement. And ask me again. You won't even have to ask out loud, that is merely a formality for onlookers. Now ask it again."

As we stare in each other's eyes I hear my voice say, *See, she is pure and sweet and she is the one for you.*

Staring deep in each other's eyes I can almost feel her sole as she asks, "Did you have sex with that girl or any other girl?"

Then we both hear *No!* She begins to back away, "Ok then, I believe you."

"Kaye you know I did not answer you right?"

"Yes you did, I heard you say No and saw no movement what so ever in your eyes."

My father grabs us by the arms, "You teaching her my lie detector trick?"

She quickly hugs my dad, "How are you doing Sir."

During their embrace he winks at me, "I like this one Son."

"Me too Dad. That's why she is my friend."

He looks at her as they stop hugging, "You eating lunch with us today?"

She looks at me, as if to say, what do you think. I nod yes and she says, "Let me check with my parents."

She runs off and dad says, "That's not the one you supposedly get pregnant is it?"

"That's hard to answer."

He looks at the church and then back at me, "I think we are far enough away from the church."

"It's not that. She is the one the voice says I should marry and have lots of kids with. Not the one I did marry in that parallel life."

He looks confused and we start walking towards the car. "Hey dad, I like your suit by the way."

He pats the tie on his chest, "Yes it is very nice! Did you do this?" I nod yes and he says, "Well, I don't like it then." He laughs and gives me a hug.

Kaye comes toward the car with a bag of clothes in her hand and says, "I was planning on going to a friend's after church today, I just didn't know which one."

We all chuckle as my sister and Mike approach.

My Dad shakes Mike's hand and my sister asks where we are eating lunch.

They look at me and I say, "I feel like eating steak." They all nod in agreement.

Then dad says, "The place right before our neighborhood."

Mike says, "I know the place, but I'll just wait and follow you guys."

Sis and Mike head to his car and Kaye and I get in the back seat of our family car.

My father says, "I hate waiting on your mother!"

My mother is the type that has to talk to everyone and then take request for the songs for the next service. She is almost always the last to leave the church.

We eat lunch at Dad's favorite steak house where the waitresses always flirt with him and me. Must be something about the blond hair they can't resist. After eating we head home to relax for a while before Mike and I head to the courts for some B-ball. We all sit around the living room talking about what we would do if we were rich and I take mental notes. We joke and have a good time enjoying each other's company.

I look at Dad and say, "Dad what do you plan to do when you retire?"

We all listen for his response, "I would like to have a house in the mountains, one at the beach, but I would live on my game land full of deer and other wild game for people to come and hunt with me."

We all smile and I say, "Sounds good. Where is this game land going to be?"

He looks at me like are you serious, "Not real sure! Depends on what I can afford?"

"Should be good land near the coast, but not right on the coast." He smiles, "I like the sound of that."

I look to Roxanne, "Sis can you miss school tomorrow?"

"I think so. Why?"

"A couple of reasons actually, dad needs some research done on how much land is available for sale in a couple of Counties. If you and mom can get the documents you need; I want y'all to set up our stock market account while we go and settle the farm."

"Sure I can miss school then. What are you and dad doing?"

"Going to sell Dad's portion of the farm and see Uncle Glenn. Beyond that it gets too complicated and we have guest. I'll get you up to speed tonight before bed."

"Give me those Counties you want researched."

"I will tonight I promise."

Kaye and Mike look as if they are in the twilight zone. I grab Kaye by the hand and say, "Let's take a walk?"

She gets up and says, "Let's go."

We get outside and I start talking immediately, "Got to let you in on some insane stuff, maybe. Mike I'll see you at the court in about twenty to thirty minutes?" He nods as he looks at the clock.

Kaye and I walk outside and I say, "Kaye, I need to ask you some serious questions before I let you in on some secrets."

She says, "Ok shoot!"

"How long have you liked me and how serious are you?"

She stops in her tracks, "What? I don't like you like that!"

"Really?"

"Yes really!"

"So if I kiss you here in the middle of the street it won't affect you?"

"Nope not a bit!"

I grab her and kiss her as firm, lovingly, and passionately as I can. The type of kiss you see in the movies where the girl's leg goes up in the air. I stop and she is like melting butter in my arms.

"Now look me in the eyes and tell me you don't like me!"

She huffs as her eyes are still closed, "Easy, I don't . . ."

"Kaye you have to open your eyes to look me in the eyes."

She opens her eyes and says, "I don't like you and you know why?" She stops and then says, "Because I have been in love with you since the moment I met you . . . you ass!" And she grabs me and starts kissing me very passionately.

I push her off of me, "Kaye please! We are in the middle of the street. What are the neighbors going to say?"

She smiles and hugs me, "That the good guy finally wins and he gets to keep the prize."

I hug her and pull her to the side of the street. "If we are going to make this work we have to get some things straight between us."

"I bet you want to get things straight between us." I laugh at her tease about us having sex as she reaches for my crotch.

I stop her hand and say, "Yeah we need to discuss that as well."

She starts to look concerned, "Ok, what do we need to discuss?"

"Kaye I don't want to date, whore around or any of that, I want one woman. And if you think you can be her then I want you to be her. If not then no hard feelings we will always be friends."

"Are you being serious?"

"I've never been more!"

I look at her as we start walking toward the basketball courts, "I'm going big, and in a few years I'm going to be nationwide, if you want to be along for the ride you have to step up now. I will make you happy and give you everything you could need or want, but there is going to be a lot of trust involved. I want you to be there with me, but I have some things you have to commit to before we proceed."

Looking me in the eyes she says, "Go ahead I'm listening."

"Remember I don't need an answer today but definitely before we move our relationship any further." She smirks, "Ok, let's hear it!"

"I want a woman to love me no matter what I say or do; a woman to back me up and be on my side no matter what the argument is. I would never do anything to hurt my woman. I want a woman who trusts me and I can trust with everything. I want a woman that is not scared of anything. For instance and these are must have conditions; surfs with me, flies with me, skis with me, rides any ride at an amusement park with me, scuba dives with me, goes on my boat with no problem and pretty much anything I do. I want my woman to be my best friend and that will go anywhere with me. How are you doing so far?"

She sighs and says, "It sounds like I have a lot of fears to overcome. Does this work both ways?"

"Yes it most certainly does. I fear shopping but am willing to do that with you. I will even buy you your own store if you want. I want a woman that acts like a lady and lets me treat her like one; allows me to open doors for her, and pull out her chair . . . You know, I want it all . . . A lady in the street, but a freak in the bed."

We sit down on a bench at the park. My friends on the court start yelling to me, "You got next?"

I yell back, "Yeah, I got next!"

They continue playing basketball and we go back to our conversation, "Kaye, I know this is a lot to process . . ."

She stops me, "Do I have to be good at all those things or enjoy it?"

"If you can't, then we will never work. Because that is the stuff I will be doing and I want my wife right there beside me. Now, what do you want out of life?"

"I want a loving husband who will take care of me and my kids. Any idea how many you want?"

I look at the ground, "It's no fair asking me. I know how many kids we have if you say you want to be with me."

"Oh yeah! How many?"

"Are you sure you want to know?"

She nods her head yes. I look in her eyes and say, "It's two more than you think you want."

Mike shows up and I stand up, "I'm going to play basketball now!"

In shock she waves bye. I lean over and give her a kiss on the cheek, "I love you too!"

I trot to the court and start a game with my friends. She watches and tries to absorb it all. My sister walks up to her, "You ok? You look like you have seen a ghost."

Kaye looks at her, "I am so in love with your brother right now, but he needs stuff from me I'm not sure I can do?"

"Like what?"

"Surfing, flying, skiing and stuff like that!"

"Oh good I was afraid you were going to drag me into some weird sex world or something."

My sister hugs Kaye and Kaye says, "You know you are right, he would not let anything bad happen to me he just wants a fun girlfriend or wife, right?"

Roxanne looks at her funny and thinks did she say wife, "Yeah a fun friend, that's what he needs."

They hug and Kaye yells at me, "You got it Buddy, I am there for you!"

I am dribbling the ball and I pass it to a wide-open player on my team and he dunks it. I walk over to the court side, "What?"

She smiles, "I will be that friend for you, I'm yours."

"Ok Honey, but I'm kind of busy right now. Love you too!"

"No, I love you!" I run back to the court action and she hugs my sister.

My sister and Kaye watch us play three games and then we take a break and get some water. My sis calls me over, "Hear you and Kaye are an item now."

Kaye smiles waiting for my response, "Not yet! We have some details to work out and if we both agree to the facts of our discussion and she still wants to be a couple. Then we will be an item!"

She smiles and says, "I already agreed to those terms so we are an item!"

I kiss her and then say, "I've got one more game to play. Then we will talk."

I head to the court and I hear her say, "Not going to change my mind!"

I keep walking and then turn around and say, "Good!" She smiles and hugs my sister again.

After the game my sister walks over to where all the guys are congratulating each other and saying our goodbyes. "See ya next week guys."

Kaye hugs me and says, "You did great out there Honey!"

"Thanks Dear!"

My friend Marvin walks by and looks Kaye up and down, "This you?"

"Yes Marvin, this is my girl Kaye."

She shakes his hand and he says, "Good on you Buddy. I saw her during the game and was going to talk to her. Since she is spoken for I will back off. Hey girl, he don't treat you right . . . call me!"

He finally releases her hand and I say, "Get you butt back to jail before they know you are gone!"

He laughs, "Yeah-yeah you know I got parole!"

"See ya Buddy!"

Trotting away he says, "You too! Work on that jump shot or I'm going to knock your stuff off my court!" I laugh and say, "This is my neighborhood and my court and always will be!"

He walks to his car, "Next week my friend, Peace! I got to get back to the real hood before it gets dark." He waves and gets in his car.

Kaye looks at me, "You two always like that?"

I look at her and grab Mike's basketball, "Yeah! I don't think we have ever had a real conversation. We just trash talk each other all the time. He's cool, fun to be around!"

"Was he really in jail?"

"Yes!"

We start walking towards the house. She stops and says, "For what?"

"I really don't know or care."

"Don't you think you should find out?"

"Why?"

"He could be dangerous!"

I look at her as Mike and Roxanne listen in, "Everyone is dangerous at some point in their life, some get caught some don't, what's the big deal? I am not going to judge him because he got caught, just if he sucks at basketball." We start to chuckle.

Roxanne says, "You guys want to ride to the house with us or are you going to walk?"

I grab Kaye's hand, "We'll walk thanks."

As we walk, we talk about my and her expectations of each other. We cover friends, her being obnoxious, my arrogance, and our feelings toward each other.

She says, "How do you feel about sex?"

We sit down on the hill in my parent's front yard and I say, "I really want to, but don't think we are ready yet. How do you feel?"

She smiles, "The same. I don't want to be some kind of slut. When I do it I want it to be for love and hopefully the person I am meant to spend the rest of my life with."

"That's good. I know it doesn't sound like most guys, but that is all I want too. Like a wise person told me once. You don't need a bunch of girls for sex because you can't beat the feeling of having it for the right reason."

She looks at me, "I want to right now!"

"Me too but we need to wait we are too young. Not that we would get pregnant, but how would you feel if our kids were our age and doing it."

"I'd be mad!"

"Me too and I am no hypocrite!"

Kaye looks at the ground, "Yeah you are right. Don't get to use to me saying that though."

"Oh you will say it a lot! I'll make it look like your idea though and never make you look stupid, because I love you girl."

I lean in and give her a passionate kiss. We embrace for what seems like hours; kissing, touching, caressing and I think to myself *if sex is better than this I can't wait.*

She says, "Yeah me too!"

We stop kissing and I say, "What did you say?"

She looks as if she just came back to reality, "Not sure, thought you said something?"

"How? My tongue was in your mouth!"

"I have no idea, shut up and kiss me."

She closes her eyes and starts kissing me again. I look at the darkness around us, "Can't Babe, I have to go in the house my uncle is going to call soon and I need to talk to my dad real quick. Come on let's go!"

We dart into the house and I see my dad on the couch watching TV. He looks up at me, "You ok Son?"

"Yes Sir. Just need to talk to you before Uncle Glenn calls."

We walk back to the bedroom area and into my room. Mom heard us and joins us.

I look at them, "Ok, when he offers you money for your portion of the farm. You say it is an answer to prayer. He will bump it up an extra grand at best, thank him and tell him we will be down tomorrow to close the deal. Dad, just swallow some pride here, when you are rich I promise he will be kissing your butt. Not begging money kissing butt, but a real respect kind of kissing butt. The kind of relationship you wanted with your brother. I promise it will be good."

Dad looks at the floor, "When do I get my bass boat?"

I smile, "You already have one picked out or do you have to order it?"

Chuckling he says, "Both!"

"I say the one you have to order we do tomorrow on the way home, as long as it won't be here until next year or at least until Christmas."

Mom chimes in, "And when do I get my new car?"

"That is between you and dad." We do a group hug and the phone rings.

I say, "Dad you're on. You want me nearby or out of the way?"

"On the other phone so you can hear."

"Yes Sir," I run to the kitchen for the other phone.

We both pick up the phone at the same time and dad does all the talking. The plan goes perfect and almost word for word as we had rehearsed. The money is actually agreeable to dad and the fact he is getting twice the amount helps out a bit.

Dad says, "Ok we will see you tomorrow."

Uncle Glenn says, "We?"

"Yeah Tommy is coming with me."

"Great! See you guys tomorrow around three at the bank."

"Sounds good, we'll see you then."

Dad gives him his car phone number just in case. I know these two though; they will be talking to each other on their CB radios as soon as they get close enough to talk to each other. They hang up the phones and dad starts explaining everything said to mom.

Kaye comes looking for me and says, "What's going on?"

I look at her and say, "Family business. When I put a ring on that pretty little finger of yours you will be privy to all family matters, but not until then."

She smiles and kisses me, "I got it tough guy. I need to go home."

I smirk at her, "Then you had better get walking it's a long ways."

She smacks my butt, "Not funny!"

I yell down the hall, "Mom I need to get Kaye home. Any suggestions?"

Mom yells back to us, "She had better start walking then."

We laugh out of courtesy and Kaye says, "I see where you get it from now."

Mom says, "I can ride with you."

I whisper to Kaye, "Watch this!"

I lean out of my bedroom, "Thanks Mommy dearest!"

Mom yells, "Boy I am going to kick your butt!"

Dad can be heard laughing from down the hall and mom says, "Don't encourage him!"

Kaye asks, "I don't get it?"

"Family business Honey! Just kidding, you know that movie 'Mommy Dearest'? My mom hates it and gets mad when I call her that."

Kaye smiles and grabs her stuff; "Oh I get it!"

We walk out of the house and I say to mom, "I can tell dad really likes my plans."

Mom nods and says, "Yeah I think you are right."

Dad sticks his head out the back door as we are getting in the car, "Stop and grab some burgers or chicken on the way home."

I give him thumbs up and back down the driveway.

As we drive Kaye rubs my neck and plays with my hair and I am really enjoying it. My mom notices what she is doing and says, "Kaye Honey please don't do that."

She stops immediately like a scolded dog and I say, "What you can't stand for me to be happy!"

"Not that. I just want you to stay awake while you are driving." She goes on to explain, "When he was little and would not sit still in church, I would rub his head and he would fall asleep. It relaxes him too much! So if you want him to calm down."

Kaye smiles at her, "Got it!"

Mom says, "You can watch his eyes twitch right before he falls asleep."

I decide to put a stop to this, "Ok mom, enough. Don't give away all my secrets! We just started dating."

Kaye and mom smile at each other and mom says, "Then I definitely won't tell her to kiss your belly!" Mom whispers, "He can't stand it!"

Kaye is howling in laughter and I say, "Ok Mother! Don't make me pull this car over!"

She looks around, "Why? You are sitting at a stop light."

I smile at them and say, "I just always wanted to be able to say that!"

We get to Kaye's house and I walk her to the door and kiss her goodnight. She says, "I guess you won't be at school tomorrow?"

"Yeah that's right family business."

We say good night and I return to the car and mom says, "I like her."

"Good she is going to be your daughter-in-law."

"Really when?"

"In about nine months. There is something I need to tell you Mom!"

She smacks me in the back of the head, "What?"

I rub my head, "No Mom, just kidding! In about four years or so."

She does the math as I pull out of the driveway. Mom looks disappointed, "So you are not going to finish college first?"

"Nope."

She still does not understand, "Are you going to at least finish college?"

"Yes I am! But I can't give you the whole story now or you won't buy the book."

"You are so not funny sometimes!"

"Hey I could say the same thing! What was that kiss him on the belly stuff? You should try to keep girls away, not tell them my weaknesses!"

"Yeah I guess you're right. But it sure was funny."

"Hey we need to start working on dad for the Bahamas for Christmas break."

"Why then? Why there?"

"You only have to be 18 to get into the casino and that's when dad's going to win enough money to quit his day job."

"You are not eighteen!"

I smile, "I will have an ID that says so."

"Why not Las Vegas?"

"Vegas age is 21 and I could never pull that off with this baby face."

"Got it, but Christmas still has to be at Grandma's."

I look at her, "New Year's week then at Freeport, Bahamas. I've got a plan that will allow us to say we won even if we don't. It will be great!"

Chapter 9

I know what you are thinking and I don't recommend it! Oh come on why not? *I'm really going to have to sit you down and explain this parallel universe if you don't just shut up and color.* I think you should do that soon, ok? *Sure, not today but I promise soon. Sisters are not toys.* Yes they are! I reach over and grab the toilet handle and flush the toilet and run out of the bathroom. I wait outside the door for the blood-curdling scream; I start my count down 3, 2 . . . "Ahhh crap! That is hot! I'm going to kill you!"

As I'm laughing I say, "What! Mama did it!"

I feel and hear a smack on the back of my neck, "No lying in my house mister!"

I turn as I rub my burning neck, "Yes Mama, sorry!"

She yells through the door, "I got the little punk for you!"

"Thanks Mom!"

She looks at me sternly, "Go get dressed before I smack you again!"

"I'm not scared of you Mama. All you can do is that little sucker punch anyway."

Daddy comes out of the bedroom reaching for his belt, "Bet I got something you are scared of!"

"Yes Sir, going! Love you guys, you too Sis!"

Roxanne yells from the shower, "What?"

At breakfast dad says, "Ok, Roxanne goes to the records department downtown and explains to them how she has a school real estate paper due for economics and finds out what land is available. Look for stuff that could get grants for having game land and those kinds of details."

My sister nods in understanding and says, "I can handle that."

Mom dials the school on the phone, "Yes. Good morning to you also. This is Mrs. Dunn, I was going to send you a note Friday but it totally slipped my mind. Tommy and Roxanne will not be at school today." There is a pause in the conversation then mom says, "Thank you very much and if things go as planned they should be back tomorrow. Bye."

As mom wraps it up on the phone, I lean over to Roxanne, "You like doing research on properties?"

She smiles, "That is what I want to do after college."

"See what commercial property is available here in town as well. Or property that can be made into commercial properties, I've got an idea."

I reach in my pocket and pull out some cash and start handing her twenties, "Here's eighty bucks. Have a good lunch, bribe money if you need it and get mom something nice. You've got dad's number if you need us."

Mom looks at my father and starts playing with his hair. She looks at him as if they were still seventeen and still so much in love. I want that. A woman that loves me like mom loves dad! I just sit and watch and smile at them.

My sister nudges me, "The land in town? Where do you want me to look?"

"The new part of the interstate is going to be finished in a couple of weeks. There are two spots I have in mind but I need a map to show you." She reaches in her bag and hands me a notebook. I smile, "You are good! When we hit the big time are you gonna stick around or hit the road?"

She smiles as she keeps taking notes, "If you hit the big time little brother, I'm going to be right there cheering you on and running the family business."

"Any chance of getting some law classes there at Carolina?"

"You pay for it and I will!"

"Excellent!" I draw a map and explain details of the city lay out future and present.

Dad and I head to the car as mom and Roxanne get in mom's car. Dad looks around as we get in the car, "Sure is a nice day."

"It will always seem like this from now on. No worries coming our way. I hope."

On our drive down to the farm we look at different properties that are nothing now but in a few years will be hot spots. I explain to my dad about my voice in my head and how I've gotten smarter due to my being able to retain things better. He is amazed by my story. I keep giving him tidbits of proof, just to keep him interested. We have the best discussion ever about life and consequences of our actions. Some of what I say, he does not agree with, and some is hard for him to believe. On some points we actually see eye to eye on, and he has that look in his eyes like, that explains it, and now he understands.

"Hey Dad, we need to go and buy some property at the beach."

"That sounds like a good idea, but I am just afraid this gift of yours may end badly."

There is a silence in the car then I say, "I think I know why I was given this gift Dad. To fix you and mom and to give us a better life."

He rubs my head and says, "I may not say it enough Son, but I love you and am very proud of you!"

I blush and smack him in the stomach, which is still rock hard. He still has the body of a twenty year old and he is close to forty. "Careful Son, don't make us crash." We both laugh and then we both stare down the road.

Dad looks over at me and says, "What now? Are your mother and I going to be ok?"

"You are going to be better than ok. You need to be there for her. Listen to her and talk to her."

We arrive at the old farm and look around. Dad says, "Hey they cut some trees down and I did not see a dime from that."

"Well you are about to see a lot of dimes and you don't even like this place and said you'd be glad when you don't have to come back here."

He looks sad at the old house, "Yeah, but I grew up here."

I put my hand on his shoulder, "We can live in emotions and be poor or look forward and be rich, your choice." He says nothing.

We drive to grandma's house over the river and through woods. Hey that is ironic. I mention it to my father and he is not amused. As we drive the phone rings dad looks at the time and says, "Who could that be?" I look at him, "It's Roxanne!" I answer the phone, "Hey girl what's up?" I listen to her and decide the best way to handle it. "Ok we are headed to Grandma's house we have thirty minutes before we are supposed to meet Uncle Glenn. That sounds good. How about that other property?"

We pull into Grandma's driveway. Grandma is in her garden working away. I continue to listen to my sister as dad leaves the vehicle running so I can use the phone. I interrupt her, "Sis that is great, you are doing wonderful. Talk to dad a moment let me say hi to grandma. I will tell her for you." I hand dad the phone and say to him, "Good land available, listen to see if you recognize any of it, I'll be right back."

I step out of the car and run to give grandma a hug. I tell her the short story of why we are there.

She hugs me again and says, "Did you boys get a chance to eat? I have some pastry on the stove."

"That sounds good Grandma I'd love some and I'm sure dad would too."

Grandma waves to my dad and goes into the house and starts warming her pastry for us. Her pastry is so awesome! Some people refer to it as chicken and dumplings and some call it chicken and pastry, at grandma's house it is simply pastry, the chicken is just understood. I call it good stuff.

I look at the car and dad motions for me to come back to the car. When I open the door he hands me the phone, "Yes! I'm getting some pastry!"

I listen to her and then say, "That sounds good see if we can build an island there and if so how far out. Yes I will bring you some pastry."

I listen and then say, "Call us when you get good info. We will see you in about three hours. Everything sounds right in line with our plans."

I look at dad and say, "Let's go eat!"

We eat and talk with grandma about what was going on. Dad looks at the time and reminds me we have an appointment. We run to the car as if we just robbed a bank. Dad drives at speeds over a hundred and grabs his CB radio mike and says, "Big Bro you out there!"

"Yeah, you got me little Bro, I'll be there in about five."

I look at the speedometer and dad does not slow down. "Dad didn't we just pass the bank."

"Yes we did, at about 110 mph. Glenn wasn't there we'll go down here and wait for him."

I know that look in his eyes. That means, wait so they can race. These country roads are so far from real roads and rarely see law enforcement that these rednecks still like to play on them. Guess I should be glad they are paved roads.

My father stares down the road, "Did I tell you the stories about this road?"

"Some, but I'm sure there are a lot."

"Oh yeah, good times!"

I look down this perfectly straight ten miles stretch of road and say, "Tell me one Dad!"

Still staring down the road like he is in his own little world, "Ok, one time on a moonlit night when I was about eighteen, a buddy and me were riding this road and decided to ride with the headlights off. I did it for almost a mile when all of a sudden; I hear this crash and feel the car shake a bit. I slam on brakes and turn back on the lights. I look in the side rearview mirror and see nothing. I turn around to look behind me and see brake lights. I back up to see what had happened, the other car was doing the same. We park near each other on the side of the road, and guess who it was?"

I look at him, "Billy Bob?"

"Your uncle! He was doing the same thing in the opposite direction and our side mirrors hit as we passed each other. We were both pretty lucky."

Laughing I say, "Is that back when you use to run moonshine for Uncle Jessie?"

"Ha-ha very funny! We were lucky more than once. Guess we all are."

We hear over the radio, "That you in the middle of the road lil brother?" He pulls up next to us, "When did you get that junk heap?" They have a huge rivalry over their cars and always have.

I pullout a hundred dollar bill and say, "Hey Uncle Glenn, to the bank for a hundred!"

He smiles, "Hey Buddy, you're getting big! Is that parked or past the bank?"

"Past!"

"Let's go!"

They sit side-by-side revving their engines. I hated to piss on the fire but sometimes you do what you have to do!

I grab the mike for the CB radio and turn the channel to PA or Public Announcement, "Good luck Dad" Pressing the mike key I say, "Ready, Set, GO!"

They both leave black marks on the pavement and a cloud of smoke. They stay side-by-side until they hit 120 mph and then my uncle starts pulling away. Not to the point that we saw tail lights but enough that you knew who won. We pass the bank at 135 mph in a losing effort; it was still worth the ride to watch these brothers playing together again. They have so many family quarrels that I lost count. We slow down and then they turn around and head back to the bank.

At the bank we get out of the car and I go over and hug my uncle and try to give him the hundred he just won off of me. "Boy, I ain't going to take your money; we were just having some fun!" Then the brothers shake hands. He hands my dad the papers for the release of ownership to the family farm, and a check. As Dad reads the papers, my uncle and me catch up with what is going on in my life. Dad looks at the check, "This is not the amount we discussed."

"I know Bro, we have to go into the bank so I can get the rest out of this account or you can just move it into your account."

My dad smiles and says, "Ok let's go."

Walking into the bank the one teller sits upright in her chair. The little old lady sees my dad and his brother and says, "Oh no! You boys aren't here to rob the bank are you?"

My dad laughs, "You sweet talker you!"

She laughs obnoxiously, "Boy you stole my heart years ago, so I figure now you are back for my money!"

She comes around the counter and hugs my dad and then my uncle.

She looks at me and says, "Who is this? Not little Tommy? Oh my goodness boy you have gotten so big! I have a daughter for you!"

I look at her shyly as she hugs me, "But I didn't get you anything."

She laughs very loud again and then I say, "She's not a cousin is she?"

They all start laughing and she says, "And you have that family wit! Wow, you look just like your grandfather! Cute as the devil himself!"

"Yeah wish I could have known the man better."

They all get quiet and then the lady says, "What can I do for you boys today?"

She pats me on the cheek and walks back around the counter. My dad and uncle tell her they need her to notarize the papers and give my dad the rest of the money. They do the paper work and I sit on the one sofa at the bank.

An old man walks into the bank, must be the rush hour here in this one horse town. He looks at my dad and uncle, "I thought I smelt trouble roll back in town, or was that just all the smoke you left in front of my house." The old man hugs the brothers and I sit and watch.

Then he starts again, "Is it an anniversary or something? I remember about twenty years ago you boys had a near miss in that same spot you started your race a little while ago. I'm surprised you miracle babies are still alive."

The man turns around and looks at me like he sees a ghost, "Gabriel is that you?"

My dad jumps in as I shake the man's hand, "Mr. Langdon this is my son Tommy."

He stares at me, "He's your Dad reincarnated!"

The lady behind the counter says, "Isn't it scary how much he looks like Gabe!"

The man finally releases my hand, "Eerie! What cha boys doing here?"

My uncle speaks up, "Robbing the place just like old times so if you need money you need to talk to my baby brother, he is keeping the money from this load."

The old man hands my dad the check, "Could I get that in tens and twenties please."

He then sticks his hands up like it is a real stick up. They all start laughing and hugging again.

The old man says, "It sure is good to see you boys again!"

The lady hands them the papers and takes the check from my dad. She makes the deposit slip and asks, "Is that going to do it today for you boys?"

My dad looks at me and has a look like is that it. I stand back up, "No Ma'am I have to go to the car."

I point to the old man, "Could you please help this gentleman and I'll be right back."

I motion for dad to come over and whisper to him to help clear out the bank so there are not as many witnesses. My dad nods in agreement and I go outside to get the money. When I come back in, I place the backpack on the counter. I notice my dad leading the old man and his brother out the door. I say to the lady, "So tell me about this daughter of yours, is she as pretty as you?"

She starts giggling like a schoolgirl and I start stacking the money on the counter. I hand her old bank statements and tell her I want the money distributed between the accounts. I tell her how much to put in my sisters account, mom and dads, and mine. I can see the lady is curious about the extra money, but she does not question it.

I watch the brothers as they talk on the front stoop of the bank. I see the brothers hug and I hear in my head *that is one mended fence . . . couple more to go!* Grandpa Gabe, is that you in there? No answer. Then I hear. *That's right kid! Just you, no grandpa in here it's just you and me. Now that you made that deposit your money is untraceable and untouchable.* I thank the lady and walk out of the bank; I join in my father and uncle.

Glenn says, "You get everything straight in there?"

"Yes Sir, you gonna give me a chance to get my money back?"

"What money boy? I just gave your dad all the money I have!"

I look at the ground and kick up some dust, "That hundred I owe you."

He smiles, "Then you will just owe me two if we keep this up."

"Dad's gonna let me drive and I won't let you win like he did."

He laughs and I can tell he did not like the thought of, being let win.

I say, "See it is not my car and I don't care if I blow it up, unlike my dad."

Dad jumps in the conversation, "But I care if you blow it up!"

My uncle smiles at me and says, "Let's go, but this time it's not a straight drag. Three times around the bank and then to where your dad and I started, then to my house, first one on the couch holding the remote to the T.V. wins."

"Wins what?"

He thinks for a moment, "Double or nothing!"

"That's not fair! How am I supposed to get in the house?"

"Door is open like always."

I smile at him, "Yeah, but Aunt Becky will want a hug and I'll never make it to the couch."

"She's in the garden."

I look at dad, "Get in Dad, ready, set . . . go!"

We all take off running to the cars. Dad says, "See this is why I always back into a parking space!"

We jump in and start the car. I throw the car in drive and spin out of the space. On my first lap around the bank I notice the back end of Uncle Glenn's car just getting his first lap going. I stomp the accelerator harder. My dad says, "We are trying to beat him not kill him! Don't hurt my car!"

"I'll buy you a new one that he would be scared to race."

As my dad tries to hold on and not get thrown from the car he says, "Hurt my car I don't give a damn!" Then he does his best redneck yell. I finish my third lap and am comfortably ahead. I get out on the road and floor the accelerator. I look in the rearview mirror and notice my uncle fly out of the parking lot sideways and smoke billowing all around his vehicle. Looks like a cop in hot pursuit.

I seem to have no more power and I notice my uncle is steadily catching up to me. I look at the speedometer as we reach 125 mph and my dad says, "You better get off of it your turn is coming up!"

I jam on the brakes and swing the car right to make it easier to make the left turn. I nearly flip the car and my dad just smiles at me and says, "Nice recovery!" I look in the rearview mirror again and notice my uncle maneuvered the turn perfectly and is only inches from my bumper and waving at me. I punch the accelerator again and our distance does not change. I look at the speedometer again and am closing in on a hundred but have to slow down for turns because this road is not as straight as the first.

I glance in the mirror again and he is gone, I look to the sides and he is not there either. I look in the rearview and notice dust at a road we had just crossed. "Where did he go dad?" My dad looks back and thinks for a moment then says, "Crap! You better go hard he took a new short cut! Guess that's his way of saying you don't come down here enough and you can't beat me in my backyard."

I push the car as hard as I can without killing us. About that time Uncle Glenn slides right in front of us about ten car lengths. As he maneuvers to get his car straight again I pull up on his left and smile at him. He points ahead to a car headed towards us. He goes right and I go to the left shoulder to give the car room to pass between us. They blow the horn as they pass between us and are obviously upset. My dad just laughs and then says, "Slow down, the house is right after this sharp turn."

I take the turn at max speed and almost hit my uncle's car, but manage to hold it off. I pull into the first driveway and he hits the second one. I throw the car in park and run into the garage thru the kitchen and dive for the couch. I begin looking around for the remote. It is not on any of the tables or couches or chairs. I look on the floor and under both couches. I check on the TV and it's not there either. My dad and uncle walk in. I check the cushions of the couch and find it. I hold it up in victory and my uncle takes it from me and sits on the couch and says, "I win."

"No you didn't, I won!"

He looks at me and says, "Are you sitting on the couch with the remote?"

I look at him in disbelief, "You have got to be kidding me!"

He and my dad start laughing and my uncle says, "Thanks though, I can never find the remote."

I grab my uncle by the ankles, "Well then if that is your rules the race is still going."

I pull his legs and off the couch he comes, he hits the floor and I go to grab the remote as he curls into a ball. I reach for the remote and miss but I did catch a punch meant for my head right in the shoulder.

"Oh the gloves are off now old man!"

I grab him by the shoulders and head butt him, but he still does not relinquish the remote. We both fight for the remote and I finally wrestle it from his grip and jump on the couch, "I win!"

He gets up and goes to the fridge, "You guys want something to drink?"

He gets everyone a soda, and says to me, "You didn't win, we said first on the couch with the remote not second or last."

I ponder the conversation in my mind. *He is right!* My dad sips his soda and says to me, "See what I've dealt with my entire life."

My aunt comes in and hugs my father and me, we sit and talk with my aunt and uncle for about thirty minutes and I look at the time, "Dad we had better get going."

He looks at the clock, "Oh yeah you are right, let's go!"

We give hugs and say goodbye. They try to get us to stay and we say our apologies but we have to go.

"Can we stop and pick up some Barbeque to take home?" Dad nods yes.

I wish we had an interstate instead of these little country roads. These roads are protected by those Barney Phife type cops from Mayberry, that hope you try to speed through their little redneck town. They sit at the city limit sign with a radar gun and watch you like vultures. *Speak of the devil!*

I slow the car down and pullover, "Hey dad, I'll be right back."

"Is everything all right?"

"Yes Sir."

I walk over to the police car, probably the only one this town has. He watches me and not sure of my approach he gets out of his car, "Yes Sir, may I help you?"

"How fast was I going?"

He proudly says, "Clocked you at 35. Is there a problem?"

Not wanting to get him angry I try to show the proper respect for authority, "No Sir, on the contrary. I wanted to commend you on a job well done."

He gives a curious smile at me, "Well thanks Son."

"No Sir, thank you! I bet you have no crime in this town because you are out here stopping the dangerous speeders."

"Is there a problem Son?"

"No Sir, none at all! Wait a minute I am sorry I lied to you! There is a problem! It bugs me to see you out here pointing that radar gun at people hoping for the chance to bust somebody. Yes there are some speeders out there, but we don't endanger people its people like you that do. Get a life and stop messing with people!"

He starts walking towards me as I turn and walk back to my car and he starts choking. *Go save his life!* Got it! I run to him and he is on all fours beside his car hacking and gasping for air. I grab him from behind and stand him up. I grab him and squeeze his chest by giving him a hug and begin giving him the Heimlich maneuver. He coughs up a huge glob of sunflower seeds and I notice my father getting out of the car and coming towards us. I look in the officer's car and see a water bottle. I rest him against the car and reach in and grab the water bottle and then I hand it to him. "Thanks buddy, guess I owe you one." *Hey there is an idea, get on the good side of the law and they can never catch you or would they want to.* I smile at him and say, "No problem, hope you would do the same for me." He smiles and takes another sip of water, "That is kind of my job you know."

"Hey you want to catch a speeder you need to go to the next county."

My dad stands next to us curious of what was happening, "Everything all right?"

I look up at him, "Yes Sir, we were talking and he started to choke. We're good now."

I look back at the officer and he says, "Yeah we are good."

He looks at my dad and says, "You look familiar?"

My dad's fear of cops leads him back towards the car, "You must know my brother. Hey Son, your sister just called a moment ago we need to get going." Dad chuckles and continues to walk away.

Stop the cop from talking right now or I will make him choke again.

The cop points at my dad and I say, "Sir did you drop this bottle of water over here?"

He spins to look at me, and then the water bottle on the ground, "Yeah I guess I did. Thanks! I wouldn't want to have to right myself a ticket. Your dad looks like the guy who called me and told me to watch for speeders in the next hour. He said some hot foot would be coming through here." I !ook and notice dad getting in the driver seat of the car. *So much for that mended fence!* I know my dad and my uncle look a lot like, but I don't think my uncle would try to set me up.

"Anyway, my name is Tommy Dunn and I hope we can be friends Officer Jones?"

The officer realized what was going on and says, "Yeah Son no problem and thank you for . . . you know!"

I wave to him and go to the car.

I get in the car and ask dad, "What is it with you and cops?"

He starts the car and drives away, "Goes back to my younger days. It is a good feeling to out run the cops, but when they wait at your house until you get home it kind of takes the fun out of it. People see a police car in your driveway and it sends a signal to the neighbors unless you are a cop."

I look at the floor of the car, "Makes sense, but I am going to embrace them, not run from them."

He looks at me and says, "Just keep me out of it. I cause them no problem and I expect the same from them."

We sit in silence as he drives back to the big city where speed limits are a good idea with thousands of cars on the road. *Don't worry, I will take care of your uncle and humble him a bit.*

Chapter 10

My last regular season football game of the year. We have had an incredible year undefeated and now it appears we have college scouts in the crowd, even my parents were able to show up. I don't think I have ever seen them so in love or happier. Mom looks great and dad is a new man as well, attitude wise. Could it be because their money worries are over? *Could be.*

Coach Bolton walks up and says, "You ready Buddy?"

"Yes Sir!"

"You are going to be defense only tonight until the second half, unless we get behind."

I look to the stands where the scouts are and he says, "Is that a problem Son?"

"No Sir . . . yes Sir! I want to play more than just defense in college."

"Don't worry these guys have seen your abilities and you have two seasons left. We are going to make it to the state finals and you can show off then if you want to. I need to get these senior stats up to ensure college for some of them."

He is right you know and he will use you some, I promise let him stay in charge. "Yes Sir, I am here for whatever you need." He smacks me on the shoulder pads, and walks away.

Chappy walks over, "How you feeling Buddy?"

I look up at him, "Hey, I'm fine. You?"

He looks across the field, "Nervous? You ever get that feeling that something is not right?"

"Only when I'm awake." He chuckles as he looks at me and I say, "You have any request?"

"I would like a long offensive stand for this game, so I can build my stats. My scout is here."

I look to the stands, "You got it Buddy!"

The rest of the four horsemen walk over and try to pep me up for the game. We all stop for the opening kickoff and watch in reverence. The Raiders return the ball to the thirty-yard line and I put on my helmet and take the field. I stop and go back to the sidelines, "Chappy, where do you want the ball?" He looks at the field and shrugs, "Just get the ball!"

"You got it!"

I run to my position and await the snap of the ball. *It's going to be a running play opposite side of the field.* I line up and warn Tony that the play is going that way. Tony looks back at me, "You hit him high, I'll hit him low!" I nod in agreement as they hike the ball. I run toward the location where the guy is headed and Tony pushes blockers out of the way. The runner is now in our path and Tony dives for his legs and I dive at the runner's chest. While in the air I hear the grunt from the impact from Tony and I notice the ball right in front of me. I reach for it and it falls out of bounds.

Everyone is cheering and I can hear the roar of the crowd again as the world speeds up again. We get up from the collision of bodies and Tony is hitting me on the helmet saying, "Nice job, we showed him." We trot back to our positions and Tony is still pumped up from the play. My voice is telling me where to stand and I move five feet left and then two feet forward. *When they hike the ball back up five steps and the ball will come straight at you.*

I look to the sidelines, and when I see Chappy, I point to him. He recognizes this as a signal and puts on his helmet and gathers the four horsemen for a game plan session. The ball is hiked and I start back peddling to get in the position to catch the ball. As the ball comes to me I catch it and am instantly hit by the intended receiver. *Guess that had something to do with that physics thing about matter being in the same place at the same time.*

I hit the ground and the intended receiver lands on me and starts cursing his little head off. Woo thought we were playing another Christian school what's up with the mouth, "Kiss your mom with that mouth!" I stand up and he realizes where he is and the referee walks up and says, "Watch the language Son!" He looks at me and apologizes. I trot towards our sidelines and notice the crowd going crazy as the four horsemen take the field. They come at me jogging in a straight line and give me high fives as I exit and they enter the field.

The coach hugs me and says nice work. I look to the stands and see my father and his friend standing up clapping for me. I point to them and give a wink. They both point at me and then clap again. I notice a new face next to my dad's friend; this is significant due to my dad's friend being a Carolina Alumni. I try not to notice and grab a cup of water and sit on the bench. Chris sits next to me and says, "Coach says check with you to see if I can play next series."

I listen for a moment then say; "Four plays unless you can get the ball before then."

"Thanks Buddy, I'll try!"

We sit watching the game and at that moment Chappy throws a beautiful touchdown pass. We jump up cheering and hopping up and down. The guys come to the sidelines and we give them low fives. This is more of a respect thing, as we appear to be bowing down to their greatness.

The next defensive series starts and I remain on the bench. The Raiders are moving the ball very well down the field. Chappy notices I am on the bench and yells, "Why are you here, I need you out there!" I point to the coach and Chappy walks over to him and they appear to be arguing, I jump off the bench, don my helmet and run between them as I take the field and motion for Chris to exit between plays. I get in position and hear in my head what I need to do.

We have our backs to the goal line and I am actually standing in the end zone. I hear *go now!* I sprint towards the offense and around the linemen and straight towards the quarterback. I dive for him just as he sets to throw the ball. I hit him right in the middle of his back and the ball falls to the ground followed by me holding on to the quarterback like a life preserver. I watch the ball bounce away out of my grasp and one of our linemen falls on the ball. *We did it nice work.* I stand up and the quarterback pushes me and I turn around and smile at him as I trot to the sideline. The referee almost steps in but notices we need no assistance.

I pass Chappy and the boys again, but this time the whole offense files in to give me high fives as we pass. I yell, "Get 'em boys!" The offense only run six plays and then is forced to punt. Chris looks at me, "Four plays again!" I hold up my hand and show him five fingers and our defense takes the field as I continue sitting the bench.

Chappy comes and sits next to me, "What the hell is going on? Why are you not playing?"

"I am playing, but it is senior night and . . ."

"That loser replacing you is not a senior!"

"Yeah but he needs experience and confidence for next year. I will need him for the next two years. I promise Chappy, I won't let you lose this game." I look at the ground and say, "As far as what's happening with you, you're rushing the ball. Settle down in the pocket, you have plenty of time. Don't throw to far ahead of Randy he doesn't have the speed." I look at the field, "Got to go, where do you want the ball?" Chappy looks at the position of the ball, "Right there is good!"

I point at Chris and motion again for him to exit. I walk over to Tony, "You go for the ball, I've got your back, the ball should be coming right in this area after the hike maybe go three steps left and one back." Tony looks at me strangely as I continue, "Trust me Tony if I'm wrong I'll take the blame and if I'm right you are the hero."

He smiles and says, "You got it!"

I look at Chappy and he motions as if to say, should he put on his helmet. I give him the thumbs up and I pretend to run away from Tony, and then slowly creep back as they hike the ball. Tony is almost where I told him to stand as the ball comes toward him. The ball bounces off his hand and right into the hands of the receiver. I rush over and grab the receiver and as I throw him to the ground I see the ball just there for the taking. I decide to take it from him, as I pull it from his grasp and turn to run, the Raiders fullback attacks me. I fall to the ground and manage to hold on to the ball in front of our bench. My team pulls the guy off of me and then they attack me, ouch love hurts.

Our offense has a more successful attempt this time and score. They start playing like pros and we end up winning the game by a score of 35-0. As we shake hands with our opponent at the end of the game I am approached by the receiver I took the ball away from at the beginning of the game. He shakes my hand and says, "Sorry about the language earlier. You are good and I was just angry." In shock I don't know what to say which is unusual for me. He smiles and smacks me on the shoulder pads; "See you on the court in a couple of months during basketball, I'm Jimmy."

"Tommy. Yeah I'll see you then." He walks away and I head towards our bench.

I see my dad, his friend, and a man I do not know. As I walk to them my dad hugs me and picks me up, he introduces me to Mr. Johnson. I shake his hand and then hands with my dad's friend Mr. Woods. He gives me a one arm hug as he shakes my hand and says, "Nice job out there Buddy, and you have yet to put on a bad show. My favorite though was when you played the Knights and you ran right out of your shoes."

I say, "Hey, if that tackle wouldn't have tried to shoestring tackle me, I would not have to leave those shoes behind."

"Guess that guy liked your shoes more than you did." The big man that is an alumnus of the school I wish to attend laughs loud and says, "Let me take you out to eat."

As we stand in a circle talking an announcement about the State playoffs is announced over the PA giving the details to the fans for the next weekend. "Mr. Woods I'd love to eat with you guys, but I promised my girlfriend I'd do something with her."

"Bring her along Son, Mr. Johnson here wants to talk to you about maybe attending Carolina."

I smile a big smile as he introduces us. Kaye runs up to me and hugs me. She says, "Didn't get to see the game, but the word is, you're awesome!"

I look at her, "What do you mean you missed it? You were with my family the whole time."

"Oh, so you did notice!"

"Kaye, did you meet these gentlemen?"

"Yes, they sat with us as I bragged on you the whole game."

"They want us to eat with them after I shower and change. What do you think about that?"

The cheerleaders see me and attack our group, they hug me and congratulate me and beg me to go for pizza with them. Kaye pushes in as politely as she can and says, "Sorry girls he has plans with his father and father's friends." They walk away and Leigh the head cheerleader says, "If you change your mind you know where we will be."

"Thanks I'll keep that in mind."

The coach walks up to us and hits me on the pads, "Nice work Son! Next week I am going to need more time from you, it won't be as easy as tonight."

"Yes Sir I look forward to it,"

I introduce him to everyone. The coach looks at Mr. Johnson and points at him, "Did I speak to you earlier this year? You are from Carolina correct?"

He smiles, "Yes, I saw your game against the Knights and was impressed. My friend here is a friend of your rising star. Small world. Would you care to join us for dinner?"

The coach looks at me and says, "No thanks, maybe next time. I'll see you guys later."

He points at me, "I'll see you Sunday," waving as he leaves.

"Yes Sir!"

My dad looks at me, "Sunday, what's that about?"

I look around to see who might be listening, "His church is having youth Sunday and he asked me to speak."

They all looked humbled as Mr. Woods asks, "What will be the subject? How to kick butt on the football field?"

"Barabbas . . . and how Christ saving him from the cross is symbolic of saving us from our sins. Gentlemen I'm going to grab a quick shower." Walking away from them I feel a reverent vibe from the crowd.

As I walk toward the locker room Kaye joins me and wraps her arm around mine, "You know we need to let people know we are exclusive."

"Kaye have we slept together?"

"No!"

"Have we said I do?"

"No!"

"Then what makes us exclusive?"

She stops as she is holding on to me, "Do you want me to sleep with you before we are exclusive?"

"No! I'm just saying what would make us exclusive. I'm not going to jump from woman to woman. I just want one that will love and honor me and allow me to do the same, and will be there for me no matter what. Me announcing my allegiance to you now is not going to ensure that. When you say, 'I do' then I will be yours with no doubt to a soul on this planet or elsewhere."

She starts walking with me again, "You need a shower."

She kisses my cheek, "You make a very good argument . . . you are right! We have nothing to prove to anyone right now. A relationship should be about the couple not the people viewing the couple."

"That's my girl. While we are on relationships can I ask you a stupid question?"

She looks at me and says, "How will it be different from your regular questions?"

She starts laughing and I smile at her attempt at humor, "What is with Billy and Sarah? They have an anniversary every week? I thought anniversary meant annual? Either they have never been good at commitments or they love celebrations of any sort."

"See, now who is watching other relationships!"

"Because they keep it in everyone's face and it is annoying. That is what I want to avoid."

I huff and say, "I'm going to take a shower see you in a minute."

Walking through the gym with Chappy and the four horsemen I see a crowd of people in the gym. They swarm us and give us well wishes for the championship next week and more than once I had my butt grabbed. We manage to get thru the crowd and Chappy asks me where I plan to attend college. I look at him not wanting to give away too much yet, "Not sure yet, how about you?"

"After tonight and if we can win State I should get a full ride to Liberty."

I smile and say, "Is that what you want?"

He looks down at me, "No, but you need to know getting a scholarship coming out of this school is damn near impossible. You need to take what you can."

We continue walking and I say, "So where would you want to go then if the big schools wanted you?" We continue walking to the parking lot and I see my dad's group. I steer us in that direction as Chappy says, "Ideally Carolina or State, but they would never come to one of our games or even give me a partial scholarship."

"I'm not so sure about that. Dad, Mr. Woods, Mr. Johnson this is our quarterback Mike Chapman. We all refer to him as Chappy."

They all smile at him and tell him it is nice to meet him and that he did a wonderful job on the field. Mr. Johnson asks, "What is your grade point average Son?"

Chappy looks at me curiously and I say, "Mr. Johnson is a scout for Carolina."

Chappy looks at him and says, "3.45 and 1445 on the SAT the coach could probably give you a stat sheet."

Mr. Johnson holds up a sheet of paper and says, "Already got it and I'm impressed, that is why I was asking about grades. I wonder if you would care to join us for dinner. I would like to talk about a future at Carolina with you."

Chappy has his mouth open and I say, "Hey I have a solid 2.0!"

They all chuckle and Chappy now has a chance to gain his composure and says, "I have been offered a full ride to Liberty, but I have made no commitment yet. My parents and I would love to hear what you have to say Sir. Um, would it be ok if my dad joins us?"

Mr. Johnson looks at the other men in the group and says, "I have no problem with that." The rest of the men shrug as no objection. Chappy looks at me and grabs me and hugs me, "Thanks man!"

He runs over to his father's car and tells him what is going on. My dad tells me, "Go tell him where we are going and to meet us there, let's go."

"Yes Sir!"

We show up at my father's favorite steak house, as we walk in the restaurant personnel see my father and get excited as their favorite patron has returned. While they are seating us my father puts his arm around me and says, "This meeting was supposed to be about you. What are you doing?"

I look up at him, "Planting seeds."

He looks at me curiously, "You are smarter than you look!"

"I sure hope so!"

As we sit down my mom finally has an opportunity to give me a hug and tell me she is proud of me. During dinner some questions are directed at me, but the majority goes to Chappy and his parents. Mr. Johnson looks at me, "So how would you feel about attending Carolina?"

I chew the bite I had just taken and notice I have the entire tables attention, "I might like it if they could get in Championship contention for football. Basketball program is awesome, but football is lacking. That is why I was hoping you would take Chappy and get them on track so when I show up in two years we could compete for a title." My dad smiles as he now understands my plan.

Chappy smiles real big and then Mr. Johnson ask, "How do you mean?"

I look around the table and say, "Look at your non-conference schedule. We need to play some ranked teams if we are ever going to get a shot at the title and that could take two or three years. For instance if my freshman year we go undefeated the best bowl we could get is Peach or Gator with no shot at Sugar due to our weak schedule? By my senior year we are finally taken seriously and then it may be too late. So you guys take Chappy and the team beefs up the schedule, by the time I show up we could be title contenders my sophomore year and start a dynasty like the basketball dynasty you already embrace."

I look around the table and they are in shock and Mr. Johnson says, "The reason for our schedule is our talent level. Due to our strict academic program a lot of the more talented kids do not want to attend Carolina."

"I understand Sir, but I am offering you the chance to get the talent and the brains required to attend such a great university."

Mr. Johnson says, "I'm impressed with your play on the field and your discussion. Would you be interested in talking to our athletic director?"

"If you will speak to him about Chappy attending I would gladly have an audience with him."

Mr. Johnson looks around at the faces at the table, "You guys win State and you will be offered a meeting with him I guarantee you that."

I look at him, "Not fair and no deal," the group looks at me in shock as I continue with, "State is a tough enough task, we do not need added pressure."

He looks at me, "You are correct and I apologize. I merely meant after your season is finished we will have a meeting with the director."

"Thank you Sir, we would like the opportunity to speak with him."

He reaches over to shake my hand and says, "Then it is a deal."

I stand up and walk over to him so we do not reach across the table and shake his hand. I lean to him and whisper, "I would guarantee State but I don't want added pressure on Chappy." *Don't say that!*

He looks at me and then Chappy and says, "I understand. Thank you for your time and honesty."

"No Sir, thank you!"

Kaye walks over to me, "Nice job Honey. So you are going to Carolina? You know I want to go to State. So we will have to be enemies."

I smile at her, "I don't think that is the way it will turn out. I'm betting you will be right there beside me at Carolina. Unless you want to be a vet you don't need to go to State."

Frowning at me she says, "My parents could never afford Carolina."

"Kaye you let me worry about that kind of stuff, you worry about looking good and making me look good by just being here for me."

She smiles, "Are you proposing to me?"

"Not even close! When I do, you will not need to ask if it is what I am asking, you will know for sure. There will be no question what I am asking at that time."

She holds my hand and stands beside me in utter reverence. *See I told you she is the one, she just needs to mature and you are helping her with that by giving her confidence. You may have screwed up promising a State Championship. I see a lot but that is not a definite yet.*

I look at Kaye and kiss her on the cheek and then walk over to the group of men preparing to leave. My mom walks over to Kaye, "You are very good for him, but it is our job to protect him from himself."

Not sure exactly what my mother means she looks at my mom and mom says, "You will understand later, just know he loves you very much and will always look out for you and this family."

"Yes Ma'am."

Mom continues, "You may not always understand what is going on, but it will be explained to you. Do not force him or be too eager for him to share information and he will as soon as he can."

Kaye not sure what this is all about but listens intently to her as mom goes on about love and trust. Mom stops talking and they watch us conclude our meeting.

My dad looks to me, "Son did you know that Mr. Chapman owns a construction company?"

"Really, that is interesting. We are looking for someone to clear some land for us and build some properties. What a lucky coincidence."

Mr. Chapman hands my dad his business card and says, "You get my boy into Carolina and we should be able to help you with your construction needs. Goodnight gentlemen."

Everyone leaves and we are still in the restaurant when dad says, "You plan all that?"

"Oddly, it just fell into place, but I did see some opportunities. I just hope Chappy can perform at the college level."

"But you knew about his dad?"

"Oh yeah Dad, of course I did. That part was for us, you know you wash my back I wash yours type thing. It is good to have friends."

Dad looks at me and puts his arm around my shoulders, "You are good my Son!"

Chapter 11

"Wake up Son you have half an hour to get out the door!"

"I'm up Mom."

I stand up and head for the kitchen and as I pass the bathroom it is surprisingly not occupied. I walk into the kitchen and Roxanne is cooking and my dad is still home, "Dad what are you still doing here?"

He looks at me strangely, "Where should I be on Sunday morning Son?"

"Oh I was thinking it was Monday for some reason."

I sit down at the table, "Then Mom, what was with the thirty minute wake up thing about?"

My sister sets a plate of food in front of me and rubs my head or hits it I'm not too sure which it was. Mom walks in and sits down and says, "The blessing please."

We all bow our head as dad asks the blessing over our food. Then everyone starts eating and mom says, "That seems to be a motivator for you now, so I go with what works."

I smirk, "Love you too!"

She smiles and takes a bite of bacon, "I know! How long is it going to take to get to that church today?"

"It's about five miles on the other side of the school. So I guess about twenty minutes, but we need to stop and pick up Kaye on the way." They all look at the clock, and decide what time we need to leave.

"Sis, can I ride with you?"

Mom says, "No you drive with me and your father, we don't know where that church is."

Roxanne says, "Mike is picking me up anyway."

I look at my sister, "So which church are you going to today?"

"My brother, I would never miss your first sermon in a real church."

I look at my eggs, "I never really thought of it that way."

My dad looks at me, "You ok Son?"

"I hate public speaking! What was I thinking? Maybe nobody will show up today!"

My dad tries to help, "It is probably a small country church, and how many could be there anyway?"

"That's right a small gathering of friends no problem."

My sister tries to change the subject, looking at me she says, "Hey Mom, when did you and Tommy want to open your shop?"

Mom looks at me, "I'm not sure we mentioned the end of the year?"

I start eating faster and they all stare at me and I look up, "What? Oh about that, I was just kidding we are not smart enough to pull off something like that. I changed my mind I'm too scared to try it." They all look at me angrily.

"What I can't change my mind?" dad starts to get worried, "Son do you realize how many lives you affect by making changes to your plans."

"Yes Sir, that is why I got scared. I don't want to ruin a bunch of lives if this fails."

I look at my family and they look very sad and let down, so I say, "I would never do that. Tell me what the rent is Sis."

Roxanne looks at me, "Don't do that it creeps me out. The rent is 400 a month and that includes utilities and waste."

I look over at dad, "We don't need a store we need a mall. Four hundred a month, you get a hundred stores in a mall and that's $40,000 a month."

My dad adds in his head then says, "You borrow $500,000 and you could almost pay it off in one year."

I look at my sister, "Put that on our list of things to own. Half a million income a year is not bad, but after expenses we are probably looking at half of that."

Dad says, "That's still not bad."

"Hey Dad, when can we start building your dream house on that lot you supposedly bought for me?"

"Let's ride by there today after church and look at it, and we can see what needs to be done."

Dad looks at the time, "Ok people let's get moving."

On the way to pick up Kaye my dad tries to keep me calm by telling me funny stories about public speaking hoping I wouldn't make those kinds of mistakes. We pull up to Kaye's house and she comes out the door as we stop the car. My dad says, "A woman you don't have to wait on! You'd better marry that girl!" My mom chuckles as he gets out of the car to let her in the back seat. She hugs my dad as she gets in the car and she pats my shoulder as she sits down in the back next to my mother. She gives me a kiss on the cheek, "Good morning!"

"Hey girl!"

"I know that voice. Don't be nervous you are going to be fine!"

My dad gets back in the car, "He is a little nervous."

Kaye looks at me as I back out of her driveway, "Just do what you did that day at school and you will be fine. I know you know what you are going to say."

Kaye looks at my mom and says, "We went over it last night."

Then my mom says, "You have done this before? Why did I never hear about it?"

I look in the rearview mirror, "I told you after the fact. Coach wasn't feeling well one day and asked me to do his speech in Chapel. That was how he and I mended our fence from last year."

"I was wondering about that. I thought he would never let you play after the trouble you two had."

Kaye says, "Oh, there is a history there I am not aware of?"

"Kaye, you remember last year don't you? All that scolding I got by Bolton for standing up to him." She says, "I remember one time you fell asleep in his bible class and you . . . yeah I remember now."

"I'm not saying I didn't deserve a butt whopping but it still caused friction between us."

Kaye looks at me, "So you are doing this to make it up to him or you trying to prove something."

I think for a moment, "Yes."

They all wait for more as I pull into the church parking lot and I say, "Both, to prove him wrong about what he thought I was going to be and to thank him for making me what I am going to be."

My dad looks proud, "A preacher?"

"No Sir, a prophet, and a saint!"

We get out of the car and I look at the church, "Wow, this is a big church!"

Kaye grabs my arm and my dad grabs the other, "You are going to be fine!"

We walk in the church and it looks as if it was even bigger from the inside and it is packed with people. Coach Bolton sees me and walks up to me and sticks his hand out, "Good morning Pastor."

I look at him, "I don't think I can do this."

The coach looks at me curiously, "Sure you can. You possess the courage of a veteran pastor and the skill of a traveling evangelist."

"What? You trying to hypnotize me coach?"

He laughs and says, "Yeah, did it work?"

"Almost, I think I'll be fine."

Chappy walks up the isle toward me and shakes my hand, "You are one brave dude!"

"I didn't know you went to this church Chappy?"

"I don't I go to First Baptist, but the coach asked us to support you today and the whole team is here."

"Oh great, hope I don't screw this up!"

"You won't, just do what you did before and you will be fine. He slaps me on the back and walks back to his seat. Coach leads me to the front row of the church and we sit down.

The entire service is being done by the youth of the church; the choir director, the choir, and the ushers. I feel like I just landed in the Land of Oz and the munchkins are running the show. As they take the offering I drop a hundred dollars in the plate as what has become usual at my church. I look at the coach and he notices my generous donation. He leans to me, "You don't have to give that much. Do you even have a job?" When he said that I knew I was busted, "My dad has always let me put the money in the offering plate for the family, even as a small kid." *Nice recovery! I'll get you through this relax and enjoy it.* Coach Bolton or today I guess it would be Pastor Bolton walks up to the podium and introduces me. I walk up and there is a reverent applause from the audience, which would not have been allowed or at least frowned upon in the church I normally attend. I stand in front of what had to be a thousand people and think what am I doing here? I've got to be nuts!

"A wise man once told me. It is better for you to remain quiet and let people think you are stupid than to open your mouth and remove all doubt." The crowd chuckles at my opening line. "Well I don't have that option today. I am here to speak and remove all doubt." They continue chuckling and smiling at me. I tell them my joke about Adam and God talking about creating Eve, and most laugh hysterically. *All right you got them warmed up I'll take over now.* As the laughter slows I begin speaking, "Thank you for inviting me to speak to you today on this youth Sunday. I would like to speak today about a man named Barabbas. What did he say mommy? Barabbas, I thought we came here to hear about Jesus!" The crowd smile at me again as I see the youth sit up like, what is he saying, this is not what we are used to hearing. I go on with the story I had read in a book in the library a couple of weeks ago. It was about how Barabbas was saved from the cross and how his life had changed because of it. Much like a person gets saved today. So in essence he was the first real Christian, even though it was not really his choice. I told the story of this man's life after Christ died for him. I explain the way a person should live after being saved and how to get to heaven. The crowd was intrigued by my sermon and the kids seemed to enjoy it as well.

At the end I call Pastor Bolton back to the podium and he does the alter call or benediction and there was an empting of the pews. People were coming forward to rededicate their lives and people actually wanting to get saved. It is a preacher's dreams come true; to actually say something that leads someone to heaven. It was a great feeling to make a difference in someone's life. At that moment someone softly grabbed my hand. I turned to look and Leigh smiles at me. She looks up at me as the majority of the church has their heads bowed in reverence and says, "You are awesome, wish we could have worked out." She kisses me on the cheek, and then walks over to the altar and drops to her knees and starts to pray.

I watch her and wonder what it would have been like. *She would have died in two years of an over dose because of a fight you would have had over her being promiscuous. Now she lives to be an old lady and she will have better morals. She will eventually marry a preacher. We did well!* Great, that you can tell me, but you won't say who wins State next week.

Now I feel another hand in mine and this one feels familiar and comforting as the persons other hand caress mine. I look and it is my Kaye. She puts her head on my shoulder and whispers, "Never thought I'd marry a preacher."

"You are? Good luck with that. Do I know him?"

She smiles at me, "Whatever you are, I'm happy to be there for you."

That's my girl! I hope so.

We leave the sanctuary area of the church and head to the huge dining hall, people shake my hand saying thank you for speaking today and how moving it was in their life. I thank them and continue to grab a plate for lunch in the huge buffet style line. I walk between my football team members and family members, and as I approach the service line Pastor Bolton gets the crowd's attention and says the blessing of the food. Little old ladies are begging me to try their casseroles and other dishes they prepared for the feast. Since I was the speaker today I am ushered to the front of the line. I grab Kaye's hand and pull her with me.

After selecting our food we sit down and start eating. People still walk by and pat me on the back saying nice job. Coach Bolton walks over and sits down across from Kaye and I, "Are you sure I can't talk you into going to Bible College?"

"I am not rejecting the idea but it is not really what I have in mind for my life."

"Sometimes life is about what God wants and not what we want."

I stop eating and say, "Sir, I feel what God wants in our life is going to happen whether we want it or not. I like to think of the story of Jonah when it comes to our lives."

He smiles at me, "You don't really need Bible College, but it sure could use you!"

"Thank you Sir. Like I said, it is still an option."

He looks at Kaye, "You with this guy?"

She looks at me, "Yes Sir and I hope I always will be."

He points at me, "You are a good kid and young lady I want you to help keep him out of trouble."

"I will do my best Sir."

The coach stands up just as my parents and sister come over to sit with us. My sister grabs my head and kisses my forehead. Chappy walks up and says, "Roxanne, you know this guy?"

She smiles boldly, "This is my baby brother!"

He looks at the two of us, "I never knew that!"

I look at them, "I'm her best kept secret."

Smiling boldly Roxanne says, "Not anymore because now I am very proud of you."

Chappy looks around and says, "I'm proud of you too, nice job up there. Is there anything you can't do?" I smile and say, "I hope not!"

The people around us laugh as they sit down and start eating. I look at Mike sit beside Roxanne and I say, "Two hours! The court?"

Chappy ask, "What court? Basketball?"

Mike looks at the time, "Yeah no problem."

"Yeah Chappy, we have two courts in my neighborhood and every Sunday we get pickup games going."

"Is it open to anyone?"

"Yeah, but it helps if you have a criminal record. You can show up if you want."

"Cool I'll be there."

Chapter 12

That afternoon we go to the courts and play basketball. I look over at Kaye as she watches me and reads a book. After the second game, which my team lost, I go and sit next to her and she hands me a bottle of Mountain Dew.

"Thank you Dear."

"Have you read this yet?"

I look at the cover, "The Red Badge of Courage, Not just no, but heck no!"

She gasp at me, "You know that the book report is due tomorrow?"

"Oh it is? Written or oral?"

"Both!"

A scream comes from court 2, "Hey little white boy get your white butt over here!"

I wave at my friend Marvin and stand up and say to Kaye, "Honey it is on my desk in my room. You can go get it if you want or I will go with you in about twenty minutes."

I kiss her and trot over to court 2 and say to Marvin, "This ain't going to be like a prison love scene or anything is it?"

He laughs and hugs me with one arm, "More like a prison riot! I need a token."

I look on the court and there is one white guy on the other team. By court rules I am needed to balance the teams on this court, "I'm your man then, let's roll cause they don't get much whiter than me." The court laughs and they check the ball to start the game.

Marvin walks up to me, "I see you are still with my girl! Your game on or off today?"

I look over at Kaye no longer reading, "On, but last game they would not get me the ball."

"No worries my friend I'll feed you, because I can't hit shit today! Let's go!"

He passes the ball to the offense and we start on defense. On the first pass they attempt a pass to the guy I am defending. I intercept the ball and toss it to Marvin for a slam dunk. We get back on defense and they pass the ball around and a guy pulls up to shoot and he misses. I see Marvin jump for the rebound, so I run towards our goal and he passes it to me and I do a layup and make the shot. This type play continues until we are up 5-0. A guy from the other team gets right in my face, "This ain't fair! He ain't white!" Marvin yells, "What are you talking about of course he's white!"

I stop him, "He's half right!"

They all stop and look at me and one of the guys says, "Whatcha mean white boy? Half right!"

I smile, "Well if the myth is true, I must be black from the waist down!" They all fall out laughing. Marvin gives me a high five and says, "Please don't make him prove it! That's my bitch right there!"

We continue the game and end up winning 10-2.

"Marvin this next one is going to have to be my last."

He looks at me walking to Kaye, "Cool Buddy I have to get also."

I look over at court 1 as I sip on my soda. Kaye grabs my shirttail and flips it up and down in an attempt to cool me down. I watch the game for a moment and notice Chappy and Mike on the court. Chappy gets the ball and dunks it, on the way down he collides with a teammate and rolls to the ground. He rolls around on the ground in pain as he grabs his ankle.

I look at this in shock, "Crap! There goes the State Championship next weekend!"

We run over to him as he is trying to get up. I try to help him and he puts his weight on Mike and me. We take him over to the bench and set him down. My sister takes some ice out of the cooler sitting on the bench and begins holding it on his ankle. These two have gone to school together since first grade and have always been friends but never dated. Mike still looks at them curiously.

"The other side please . . . that's it right there. Thank you!"

Marvin walks over, "You alright Bro?"

Chappy looks at him, "I think so?"

"Good, I need to steal my boy away."

He grabs me by the shoulders and says, "He's in good hands, come on."

We start our next game and I can't help but wonder what our football games will be like next weekend. *He is going to be fine just twisted his ankle it is not even sprained.* Good I don't think I am ready to take the team all the way yet and I'd like to see him go to Carolina.

As Marvin passes me the ball he says, "I need you here Buddy."

I look at him and start to dribble the ball, "I'm back! What's the score?"

The other team yells, "0-0 white boy!"

I dribble towards the guy that made the comment, "Don't you mean 1-0 black boy!"

I jump as high as my legs will carry me right in front of him and shoot over his out stretched hand. The ball goes in without hitting anything but the bottom of the net. They all scream in shock and awe and point to the initial teaser as Marvin yells, "That white boy showed you!"

He looks at the ground and says, "He won't do that again!"

They pass the ball inbounds to this guy and I run over and take the ball away from him and do a nice easy layup.

"What? You think you can shut me down? Many have tried, so don't be embarrassed when it doesn't happen."

I walk over to him, as my team is going crazy and say, "Don't rely on your blackness to win the game . . . rely on your skills. One more thing! This is my court and don't you forget it."

We continue the game and my team beats them badly. Marvin runs over and hugs me as he picks me up and says, "That's why I love you man. You are awesome!"

We all shake hands as the games break up. And the guy at the end of the game walks up to me, "You are good, I'm sure we will see each other again."

We shake hands and I say, "I look forward to it."

I walk over and check on Chappy and he is walking gingerly on his foot.

"Are you ok there, Boss?"

"Yeah it is feeling better, not a word to the coach!"

I raise my hands as if he is holding a gun on me, "Whatever you say."

Chappy looks around, "Can I talk to you in private?"

"Sure."

We sit on the bench as people scatter from around us and he says, "You really think I can play college level ball?"

I look at the ground, "I sure hope so, because I am counting on you."

"Why are you counting on me?"

"Remember what I said the other night?"

He thinks for a moment, "Not really I was excited about going to a real college."

"I need you to help build up their players. You are a motivator type person. That is what they need. I put in a word for you and if you don't deliver it makes me look bad. You just need to do like you did in high school. Surround yourself with your key players and learn how they operate on and off the field. You are a motivator and it will be easy your first year but your second year they are going to rely on you and you will have to step it up at that point."

Chappy looks around, "I wish you were going to be there also."

"I will be your junior year for your first title. Your job is to make the team look good so they can get some strong recruits. Concentrate on your linemen for protection the rest will fall into place."

He looks at me oddly, "Can you see the future or something?"

Kaye walks up and says, "I'm riding to the house with your sister so I can start that project."

"Ok, I'll be right there."

She kisses me, "Don't rush on my account, I have to read some anyway."

Kaye walks away and Chappy says, "Nice girl, cute too. Didn't know you were going out with her?"

"Nobody knows. That's what I explained to her. If she is going to be with me she needs to learn how to control peer pressure and gossip. I don't want people talking about us so we stay out of the spot light and off the radar."

"That's smart then you don't have her friends telling her what she should and should not do, cause they have no clue."

I point at him, "Exactly and I told her if that kind of crap starts we are done. I explained to her I will give her the world if she will just trust me."

"Good luck with that."

I smile, "Yeah, back to you. Are you going to be ok this weekend?"

"I hope so! I am really starting to get nervous about scouts being there."

I look at the ground, "Would you rather know now if they wanted you before or after the game?"

He thinks for a moment and then says, "I'd rather know now and I could play better . . . you know not so nervous."

I look at him; "Don't be nervous then and that is all I am going to say."

He looks at me, "Are you serious! That's awesome!"

I stand up and help him to his feet, "Now let's just have some fun next weekend. You know Coach Bolton is going to try and switch things up, due to the fact that two of the teams in the tourney have already played us." Chappy looks at me and says, "Still my favorite play is when you say throw it hard down the right side and I'll do the rest."

He hugs me and then starts hobbling to his car. "See you tomorrow Chappy!"

He waves and gets in his car, as he drives away I think about Kaye and how she might need some help with our English assignment and I start jogging to the house. I walk in the house and my mom and dad meet me at the door.

Dad says, "I've got an idea!"

I look at him oddly, "Did it hurt?"

He smiles "A little but I'll be all right, thanks for caring. That land we bought going out of town?"

"Yes Sir?"

"What did you have in mind for that?" Before I can explain he says, "That mall idea you had this morning!"

"Yes but it is not big enough for a mall, maybe a mall parking lot."

"Stay with me now Son. I was talking to your mom earlier and she says we have nowhere to put anything. She wishes we had more room."

I look at them, "Ok I'm listening."

"When we were growing up we stored stuff in the barn, attic or in the shed. Here in the city there are no barns and nobody wants a shed in their yard, because they're an eyesore and they don't protect that well. So we build a shed mall and call it the Attic?"

He is correct, and that is what that area would be perfect for, and people will love it.

"Guys I love it! How many units do you think we could have?"

Dad pulls out this crude drawing and says, "I think about a 1000 units at $35 each month."

"Dad I don't think the lot is big enough for a thousand units. That would be nice, but why don't we make different sizes and charge by the square foot. We could even put climate control in some and charge for that as well."

Dad smiles, "I like it! We could build an apartment on the front of it, and get a homeless guy to stay there and watch the place for us. He stays rent free and we pay him minimum wage."

We do the math and figure our expenses at $2000 a month and our income to be around 35,000 per month with 500 units. We are all getting excited now as we think about somewhere around a thirty thousand dollar profit per month.

My dad says, "I am taking off tomorrow to see what I can find out about the cost of building and clearing the land and advertising."

Mom looks at me, "When do I quit my job?"

Roxanne walks in the back door and I ask her, "Where have you been young lady?"

She smiles and pats my head, "What's up?"

"Your mother wants to quit her job. Mom, to answer your question . . . as soon as we have at least $100,000 in the bank and we have our new house finished . . . you can quit." Mom gets up and leaves the room.

Dad looks at my sister and says, "That property going out of town. Is there any building restrictions on it?"

"No Sir, but it is zoned commercial. I thought we were going to build on that other property?"

Mom walks back in the room with the bank statement and hands it to me and says, "We have double that amount." I look at the bank statement and can't believe it.

Mom says, "That is from selling your dads portion of the farm and our last two months of pay. Since you were taking care of the bills it added up fast didn't it."

Dad says to the girls, "Sit down so we can bring Roxanne up to speed."

He explains the layout to her and what we hope to do.

She smiles and says, "Just an idea for advertising. We go after people with cars in their yards that don't run, garage bands, and people with too many toys! We have some units with electricity and charge more for those."

I stop them as they are getting more and more excited, "We need a contract to protect us and them. About storms, flooding, stuff they store that may be hazardous, hours and nonpayment." They all smile and agree with me.

"Mom, I say leave your job tomorrow, but leave on good terms; we may need those people for help in the future."

She smiles and looks at my dad, "So when can I get my new car?"

My dad says, "You don't!"

We all start laughing and he gives her a kiss and then he says to me, "Can we get it for her tomorrow, she already has it picked out?"

I look at the bank statement and say, "Yes, but let me give you the down payment. How much is the car?" Dad looks at mom and then says, "I think we can get it down to $25,000."

I look at them in shock, "What are you buying a Cadillac?"

They look at each other and then me, as my dad says, "Yes, we thought you knew that. Your mom has always wanted one."

I think for a moment, "Dad you have to keep working until the end of the year then or until this storage idea is making money, so we can show some income. Take vacation this week if you can so you can get this stuff going and buy mom's car."

We all hug and mom says, "I'm going to go get some KFC for dinner I'm too excited to cook."

I look at her and say, "You need money?"

She looks in her purse, "No just someone to ride with me."

"I've got Kaye here and I need to help her finish her project."

Dad starts drawing on a new sheet of paper how the storage should be laid out.

My sister stands up, "I'll go with you mom."

Dad stops Roxanne, "How many acres is that land? And is the land around it available?"

She looks at dad and says, "Ten acres and yes some of it is available."

I walk back to my bedroom and Kaye is sitting at my desk writing away. I kiss her like I had just won her in a race.

She smiles, "Thank you! What was all that in the kitchen?"

I look at her as I fall on the bed, "Family business! When you are family I will let you know about the families business but not until you say I do."

She stands up and comes and lies on top of me and kisses me, "I do, and I do!"

"Very funny! Get off me you harlot!"

She tries to get up and I kiss her and hold her tight.

The phone rings and I hear my dad answer it, "Kaye Honey, phone." She pulls away from me but I do not release her.

She kisses me and says, "That might be my boyfriend, let me go!"

I release her and say, "Tell him I love him too!"

She jumps up and is walking out the door and I say, "Kaye, I love you!"

She turns and smiles, "Sure you do!"

She runs down the hall and picks up the phone receiver. She talks for a moment then looks down the hall at me, "She wants to talk to you and you are in trouble Buddy!"

I walk to the phone and put it to my ear, "Yes Ma'am?"

"So you love my daughter huh?"

I look at Kaye and say, "Where did you hear such a thing?"

"Your phone picks up a lot of back ground noise when it is off the hook. I heard you say it!"

"Yes Ma'am I do love her."

"Ok good, then she is not wasting her time with you. When is she coming home or when do we need to come and get her?"

"After dinner I guess we will take her home. I am waiting for her to finish her English . . ."

She grabs the phone from me, "He's joking I'm helping him finish. I should be home in about an hour. Love you Mom, bye."

She hangs up the phone and glares at me, "I had to tell her I finished that project so I could hang out with you all day." I kiss her and say, "That would have been good information for me to have known. Don't cha think?" She takes my hand and drags me down the hallway.

We return back to my room she hands me some paper and a pen and I begin kissing her. She says, "You've got to stop kissing me like that, because all I can think about is sleeping with you when you do that."

"Well we can arrange that!"

"Don't play with me, because I will rape you right here, right now!"

I stop and think, we are too young for this, and we had better cool down.

I say, "Kaye what do you want in your future?"

"I thought we were talking about sex?"

"I'm trying to see if we did, would we regret it or would we be happy we did."

She thinks for a moment and then says as she sits down at my desk, "I want to be in love like I hope we are right now forever. I want the nice things life has to offer, but will not be sad if I don't, as long as I have love. I would like kids . . ."

I stop her, "How many kids?"

"Not sure. At least two kids, but no more than six. I would like as many as I could afford comfortably. I want to go to college with you; I want to be with you, I just want you. All of my thoughts are of you. What do you want?"

I sit on my bed, "I want you to finish your English paper!"

She smiles and kisses me and starts writing. I look at the paper she handed me, "What am I supposed to do with this?"

She looks back at me, "Do that thing you did that day where you did my homework for me in my hand writing. How do you do that by the way?"

I look up at her, "You would not believe me. I'll explain it to you when it is time. I need to know what to write Honey. Where are you?"

I look over her shoulder to see what she is doing. She looks up at me, "Quit cheating off my paper!"

"Get up Babe; let me finish this for you real quick."

I sit down and start writing at break neck speed and tell her about the book that she only skim read. Kaye watches in amazement as she lies on my bed.

Looking at my wall she says, "Sometimes I feel if I don't sleep with you I will lose you. I'm not ready and you say you are not ready, but I still feel I'm going to lose you to some whore who will."

Without looking up I say, "I'm not going to lie to you. I am curious, but not enough to jeopardize our future. Plus lose the trust of your parents and mine. We can wait, there is no rush and I promise I will not go out with some whore who will."

My dad clears his throat, "You think you could miss school tomorrow Son?"

Not sure what he had heard I get nervous, "No Sir, not in the morning. I have two tests and then this English paper to turn in. I'm free for the afternoon and no football practice. I could say I have a doctor appointment at noon."

I can see in his eyes that he heard our conversation and is not sure what to say about it.

He smiles and says, "That sounds good write the note and I'll sign it. Oh and by the way I am proud of you guys and love you both." He turns and walks away as my mom and sister enter the back door of the house.

Kaye looks at me, "Wholly crap he heard us! I am so embarrassed!"

"Don't be Kaye we can use this to our advantage."

"What do you mean?"

"Think about what he heard, two teenagers agreeing not to have sex and why. We are golden, someone could tell him they saw us having sex and he would never believe it. We have earned my father's trust and that is a big deal."

Kaye replays the conversation in her head and smiles, "You are right, we said nothing bad. If I overheard it I would feel good about it as well."

"And now my father is bragging to my mother about how good we are and we can do no wrong right now." *You are welcome! Your dad is still wondering why he felt the need to come down the hallway. Trust is hard to get but easy to lose so be careful!*

I finish Kaye's paper and hand it to her as my mom yells dinner is ready, come and get it.

Kaye looks at the paper in amazement and says, "I hope you really love me, because I am going to be very hard for you to get rid of." She kisses me and walks down the hallway. *You are welcome! I told you she was the one.*

During dinner my dad is asking questions about the land. He is really getting worked up about it.

"Your mom will pick you two up from school tomorrow at noon so you guys can go to the doctor."

Kaye looks at me, "Why what is wrong with you guys?"

Roxanne looks confused, "Yeah. What's that about?"

I look around the table and say, "I think my spleen fell out and Roxanne keeps blowing stuff out her colon." The table erupts with laughter and Roxanne says, "Ha-ha very funny! I'm going to blow you out my colon. Really what is going on?"

"Dad wants our help tomorrow and I can only leave right before lunch."

"I have nothing tomorrow so I'll just stay home and help dad."

Dad looks at her, "That sounds good."

Roxanne starts again, "May I run for the county beauty queen? The winner gets a five hundred dollar scholarship and a chance to go to state finals in the spring."

Mom and dad look at each other, and then at me as I say, "What are you going to do for talent, that colon thing?"

The table erupts with laughter again. Mom takes charge of the situation, "Of course you may, what does it cost to enter?"

Kaye and I finish eating and Kaye taps my hand and points at the clock. "Can someone ride with Kaye and me to her house?"

Roxanne says, "You pay my entry to the contest and I'll take her."

"Kaye, call a cab that will be cheaper than $25." Kaye gets up and picks up the phone.

My sister says, "Kaye put the phone down, we are just kidding. Go grab your stuff I'll take you home."

Kaye leaves the kitchen and I hand my sister twenty-five dollars, "Please don't do that kind of stuff in public or mixed company. I don't want anyone else to start to expect money from me. I told you I would take care of your reasonable request, didn't I?"

"Sorry! I understand it won't happen again."

Kaye comes back with her stuff and says to me, "You are going with us aren't you?"

"Sure I don't have anything better to do."

Kaye says, "You are not very funny Mr. Dunn!"

"I think I'm hilarious you should hear all the laughter in my head."

My sister drives us to Kaye's house and Kaye and I sit in the backseat making out all the way there. As we drive into the driveway I kiss her one more time. I walk her to the door and am greeted by her parents. Her father says, "Kaye, go on in the house!"

"Yes Sir. Goodnight Tommy."

I say goodnight as she walks through the door.

Her mother barks, "What are your intentions with our daughter?"

"This conversation is a bit premature isn't it?"

"We don't think so!"

"Do I need a lawyer or my parents or some help?"

"Please just answer the question."

"At this point I have no idea. I know a part of me tells me I would like to spend the rest of my life with her, but then again I'm only fifteen."

Her mother says, "And that part between your legs? What does it want?"

I look at them and try and decide how to handle this.

I continue by saying, "There are times like now I wish I did not know her."

They look at each other and her mom says, "You wish you didn't know her because we question your intentions?"

"Again, still a kid in a very awkward situation. I understand where you are coming from with you being concerned about your daughter, but please put yourself in my situation."

They look at each other and decide they approached me wrong, and then back at me.

"I care for your daughter a great deal and would never do anything to hurt her or you guys."

They look at each other and then at me, and her mom hugs me and says, "I'm sorry! I heard you tell her you love her and it made me crazy. I just worry about her. She is my baby."

Her dad looks at me, "So you honestly think the two of you might have a future together?"

I look up at him, "That is up to you Sir. If you don't want me in her life I can just leave her alone. If you like me and want me to be a part of her life I would like to give it a shot."

He looks at his wife, who is still holding onto me and crying.

He says, "I say if you make my little girl happy, then I'm happy. You hurt her and I hurt you!"

He sticks his hand out to shake my hand and I say, "That sounds fair." As I shake his hand.

As I return to the car and my sister asks, "What was that all about?"

"You don't want to know. Let me explain what is going on tomorrow so you know what to do."

I tell her what we have in mind and the money we should make off the deal. She smiles and then says, "What do you expect our unit load to be? Full or half-full?"

"I expect full, but would be happy with half as long as we clear $2500 a month it will be profitable."

She smiles and says, "So we start that and our new house and buy mom a car. When do we pick you up?"

"After fourth period, I will be finished so have mom or dad there then. Plus we need a good contract lawyer."

"Why not me pick you up?"

"Um, I don't know, I thought you were sick or blowing something out your colon."

She chuckles, "Oh yeah, I don't feel so good!" As she does her fake cough.

Chapter 13

"What is Kaye doing here this morning?"

I look out the back door, "I have no idea?"

I open the door, "Good morning ladies. What's up?"

Kaye steps out of her sisters Mustang, "I thought you might need a ride to school since your sister is sick."

"Oh thanks, I'll be right there. Mom I'll see you at 11:35."

I run out of the house and get in the car with Kaye and her sister. My mom sticks her head out the door and yells, "Thanks girls."

Kaye looks at me in the backseat and asks, "What did you say to my parents last night?"

"I'm not sure. Why?"

She smiles and says, "Because evidentially we are golden at my house also."

I smile at her comment, "That is good, one less headache."

Her sister looks in the rearview mirror at me, "What's this I hear about you being a pastor now."

"Oh that. I was just doing that for fun, I'm no pastor."

"I hear you did very well."

I pat Kaye on the shoulder, "You can't believe everything you hear, and Kaye is biased anyway. I think she must like me or something."

"I didn't hear it from Kaye. I heard it from my friends; Chappy, Leigh and Sarah. I heard ten people got saved and twenty rededicated their lives to Christ. That is not too shabby my friend."

I look at her and realize she is a senior also, "Yeah, I guess so."

We get to school and Kaye says to me, "So where are we in our relationship at school?"

"Kaye it's not like we can hold hands or make out, we are friends here and everywhere. I am not going to go out with anyone else and I expect the same from you, but at the same time I am not putting up billboards announcing our love. That belongs to us not these people."

She smiles and says, "Got it, here it is business as usual. What do I say if someone asks if we are going out?"

I look at her disappointed and stop walking, "Kaye I know we are in high school and you need acceptance from your peers, but I don't! Say whatever you want. I am yours and you are mine and that should be the end of it."

"So I can say yes if someone asks?"

"Sure, whatever you want as soon as we sleep together!"

She looks around, "Let's go back to the car then!"

"Kaye stop being silly!"

We walk through the auditorium to get to the locker area and everyone is sitting around in the gathering area. This is where we wait for the first bell so we can go to homeroom. As we walk through they stare at us as if we were the ones who shot Kennedy. I walk to the school office and Kaye waits for me in the hallway. I give the secretary the doctor note from my mom and she stamps it and makes a note in her book and returns it to me. As I walk out she says, "You did great yesterday. Have a nice day!"

I turn back and look at her, "Thank you."

"Kaye Honey, I think the whole world must have been there yesterday or at least heard about it."

"You did do a great job yesterday if I didn't say it earlier. Very informative, I liked the relationship you did with Christians and Barabbas. I never thought of it that way."

At that moment the teacher's lounge door opens and the teachers flow out like lava from a volcano. They see me standing in the hallway and start clapping and congratulating me on my performance from yesterday.

Kaye leans in and says, "I think you are golden here also!"

"It would appear that way wouldn't it."

We walk to our lockers as the bell rings and Chris catches up to us and says, "Why didn't you tell me? I would have been there and maybe I could have gotten saved also."

"I don't think we can save you Buddy!"

He laughs and Kaye and I chuckle. "So you two are going together now huh?"

I look at Kaye, "That was fast! Where did you hear that?"

"Nowhere, I just made it up, but I guess I am right, huh?"

Kaye smirks and looks at me and before I can answer Chris says, "You might as well admit it I'm already telling everyone you are anyway!"

"Why would you do that Chris?"

"With you off the market it increases my chances with the ladies around campus. I hear after your speech yesterday you could have your pick around here."

Kaye smiles and I say, "Then in that case, yes I am off the market!"

"Hear that ladies? He is officially off the market until Thursday!"

"Thursday, what happens Thursday?"

Chris smiles and points at a poster, "You know the fundraiser for the tourney, the slave auction for the football team and cheerleaders. We are put up for bidding at a pep rally Thursday and the student or teacher that pays the most for you gets to be your master all day Friday until we get on the bus to go to the tournament." Chris leans into me and says, "I just made your stock go down. Heck, one girl wanted to pay twenty-five bucks for you."

Chris walks away and a cheerleader puts up another poster next to us saying the info he had just given us. The cheerleader winks at me and says, "Nice job yesterday!"

"Thanks you were there too huh?"

"Yeah that is my church."

She points to the poster, "The pollsters are saying you, and Chappy, Lisa and Leigh will go for the most money. This is good because we need a lot for this trip."

I laugh and look at Kaye, "Oh did they now? That is interesting!"

The peppy cheerleader runs done the hall to put up more posters.

I look at Kaye, "You want everyone to know I'm yours?"

She looks around, "Yes!"

I look around and then at her, "Here is your chance."

I point at the poster, "Win me in the auction and we will then let everyone know."

She looks at the poster, "I only have twenty-five dollars and it sounds like you will be out of my price range."

"Tell you what my love, you bid whatever you want or need to win me and I will give you the money to cover it. There is a catch though; you can't say anything to anyone about us going out until after the auction. Then you can tell the world or I will if you want."

Kaye studies me for a moment, "Why do you want to do all this?"

"Two reasons I don't want to be the lowest bid guy at the auction. If everybody knows we are going out no one will bid against you. The other reason I want to test you and see if you can keep from being a blabbermouth about us. A trust tests if you will. You say nothing good about me or bad about me."

Her friend Amy walks up to us as Kaye says, "So can I do these kind of test on you?"

"Of course as long as I know the rules and that I am being tested."

"Ok you too are being tested then until Thursday. We are broken up and you have to flirt with as many girls as you can."

I look at her strangely and so does her friend, "Rule one you are not allowed to kiss them touch them or be out of public with them. Number two you are not allowed to date them either. Number three you have to call me every night this week and talk for at least thirty minutes with no complaining."

I look at Amy and she says, "Nice job yesterday! So you two are broke up? That's too bad, you lasted a whole day or two? Going for some kind of record or something?"

Kaye smiles as they turn and walk away. Chris returns with three girls in tow and says, "Where is the wife Buddy?"

I point to Kaye walking away, "We got divorced! Good morning ladies."

I walk to my homeroom. This should make for an interesting day. Kaye and I finally get together and now we fake a breakup. I sit in homeroom watching her talk with her girlfriends or the posse as they are commonly refereed too. The bell rings and everyone departs and I see Christy walking in front of Kaye and I say, "Christy you look lovely today."

She stops and says "I hear you did an awesome job yesterday."

"Thank you. It was nothing just making amends with Coach Bolton."

She smiles and walks back to her group with Kaye stewing already. Yeah, this should be very interesting.

I head to bible class where my first challenge of the day is, a bible test that closes out our first report card. I sit down and Coach Bolton says to me, "Your sister ok?"

"She'll be fine, some girl stuff I think?"

He smiles and says, "Take these papers for her please."

He hands them to me and then begins handing out the test. I look at the test, um, wish I studied for this. *Why? I know this stuff cold. Number 1 B, 2 C, 3 A . . .* This goes on through the entire test. I look around when I'm finished to see if I am the only one done and the Coach notices me, and motions for me to come to the front. I walk up and remember our past; he would be accusing me of cheating for looking around. I hand him my test, "Yes Sir?"

"I thought you might be done. Look at those plays there and see what you think."

He grades my test as I sit down and look at his playbook for the tournament. He tosses my test back at me and quietly says, "Nice job, today and yesterday."

I look at the paper and it has a 106 on it. I whisper back to him, "Thank you Sir."

I look at the plays and they are very similar to what we have but spruced up a bit. He walks over and says quietly, "What do you think?"

Pointing at a play I say, "I like it, but when I'm in the play can I run the route this way since they will be pulling everyone that way."

He looks at it, "When you are in they will most likely double cover you."

He looks at me as if he just discovered fire and says, "That's what I was going for, so this side would be wide open the first time and next time they will leave you open. Genius! You saw that without needing it explained. I'm glad you are on our side."

Looking at me for a moment and then he says, "I have some game videos I want you to see also."

"Coach I have to leave at 11:30 today for an appointment."

"Then you can take the videos home with you, I need you to look at their offense."

Looking at the floor, "Coach I have no VCR at home."

"You have me for health next period right?"

"Yes Sir, but don't we have a test in there today?"

"I think I should know if you are fit or not I'm your coach."

He reaches in his pocket and hands me his keys to his office and starts writing a note, "The videos are on top of the TV and one game is in the machine already watch what you can until I get there and then we will watch together."

"Yes Sir."

I stand up and walk to my seat to grab my stuff. I walk by Hope and give her a wink in passing; she smiles and then continues with her test. That is another girl I wish I could be with, she would be fun to play with, and she is gorgeous. As I walk by Chris he raises his hand and the Coach says, "Yes Mr. Thomas?"

"Tommy is looking at my test!"

Everybody chuckles as the coach says, "Good maybe he will help you pass."

I walk out of the room and walk towards the coach's office. Half way down the staircase a teacher stops me. I reach for the hall pass I had put in my pocket when he says, "Nice job yesterday, I was impressed with the way you tied it all together. I can't wait until next year to get you in my philosophy class." He continues up the stairs and I watch in amazement. Have they all gone mad, I was a target last year at this school? Anything went wrong and I was a prime suspect, always in the line up being asked questions. I shrug and continue to the coach's office. As I unlock the door a junior stops me and ask what I am doing?

"Oh hey Jimmy, what are you doing?"

"That is what I was asking you?"

I hand him the note, "What, you a hall monitor now?"

He reads the note, "Actually, I am."

I walk into the office and set my stuff down.

I turn on the TV, "Hey Jimmy you know how to work this thing?"

"Sure don't you have one yet?"

"Nope, my dad is trying to wait to see who will win the VCR war; beta or VHS. He says we are not getting one and then it just go out of style the next week!"

We laugh and Jimmy says, "I think they will both be around for a long time. We have both and that stupid big laser disc thing."

He turns it on and I watch to make sure I can do it again later if I need to. He sees it is the game between two of our rivals that will be in the tournament against us. He sits down on the desk, "Think the coach would mind if I watch?"

"No I think he wants us all to watch it. I have to leave early today, so he sent me here to watch it for the next two periods." We watch the homemade movie of the game and I start to notice details in the way they line up. Jimmy points at the TV, "That was the play they just ran two plays ago!"

"I thought so too. Hey Jimmy hand me that pad of paper over there. And rewind it to the beginning."

He does and I write the plays as we watch. Before I would only watch the game but now I see the pattern of plays they are running. I notice the way they line up gives away what they are going to do.

"Hey Jimmy take this pen and paper and write the defensive schemes for both teams as I do the offense for both teams."

He smiles like a kid in a candy store, "You got it. You want to rewind or go from here?"

"Here is good. I am more concerned with the offense, but want to see if we can find holes in the defenses as well."

As we continue watching we can guess the play before it happens. We give high fives and chant, as we now know how to stop the plays by looking at their setup. The school bell rings and we keep watching, "Hey Jimmy isn't your dad a cop?"

"Yeah, for about ten years now, he is trying to make detective."

"Tell him good luck for me."

"I will, he liked your sermon yesterday he told me to tell you if I saw you today."

"Thanks, I'd like to meet your dad sometime."

"He will be at the Tournament. I'll introduce you to him then."

"Cool!"

We keep watching the game and the coach walks in, "My two star defenders! What are you boys doing in my office?"

I hand the coach my paper and Jimmy hands him his paper. The coach looks at them and I say, "See a pattern there coach?"

He looks closer and says, "Yes I do!"

Jimmy excuses himself and runs out of the office to his next class. Coach smiles and says, "This is why I wanted you to look at these films because you see stuff normal people take for granted."

He points at the paper and says, "I like what you did here about the key players. Ok start with this tape here."

He changes the tape and presses the play button. Ted our tight-end walks by the office and the coach yells at him to come in the office. "Son, would you rather take my test now or watch this game film and make a 91 on the test?"

He looks at the coach, "Films! I can live with a 91."

"Good! Sit down here and write the defensive set up for both teams for me. Thank you boys I have to go give a test now."

He leaves the office and I say, "Why a 91? You should have fought for a 93!"

He looks at me, "Hey an A is an A!"

"Look Ted, I know you just came from public school, but we are on a seven point grade scale not a ten." He looks at me with no understanding of what I am saying. "He is not giving you an A; he is giving you a B+."

Still looking clueless he says, "That is my average so no big deal either way. You got any drugs?"

I look shocked and say, "Hell no! Do you?"

"No, but I need to find some, I'm losing my buzz!"

He looks at me, "You're cool right? You aren't going to squeal on me are you?"

I plant a seed, "I won't have to squeal on you. Didn't you know the coach bugs his office for just this kind of thing?"

Paranoia is a killer for drug addicts. He starts looking around the office in wonder. I watch the tape and continue writing patterns and telltale signs for the teams we will meet this weekend. Ted's paranoia is getting the best of him as he says, "You know I was just joking right?"

"Sure I do Ted, I just hope the coach does."

"Don't rat me out man!"

Getting annoyed of his antics now I say, "Tell you what Ted, you do your job by watching the tape and we will pretend nothing was ever said."

He stares at the TV and starts writing and continues to look around the office between plays.

Just before the bell rings the coach comes back in the office and Ted looks nervous. We hand him our papers and he looks very pleased. Ted walks out and the coach starts talking to me about the games. He looks at me and says, "You found out about Ted's drug problem didn't you?"

"Yes Sir I did, unfortunately."

The coach closes and locks his office door, "He got kicked out of public school and we are trying to help him get back on track. Hopefully we can save him, it may be too late."

"That is weird. My parents send me here to keep me off drugs and away from people like him. He comes here trying to score drugs off me. It is a funny world isn't it?"

The coach sees me getting upset, "Calm down you need to learn to channel that anger, remember last year you punched that kid in the throat and almost killed him."

"He was robbing me!"

"Still . . ."

"Sorry Coach maybe I should do like Ted and take some happy pills so I don't lose my buzz!"

In hopes to calm me down, "Why did you punch that guy anyway? He was twice your size!"

I look at the coach and say, "I don't do well with bullies! Drug addicts that ask someone like me if I have anything makes me just as mad. Do I look like a pusher or drug dealer?"

The coach shrugs, "Don't know, maybe you do to him. So what do you think we should do with him?"

"I just don't like being made to feel like I'm not cool because he has a problem!"

The coach smiles and says, "So kicking his butt going to make you cool?"

I finally come back to reality, "No Sir, you are right I need to deal with this differently. I need to ease him into false sense of security and then show him what drugs can do to him. Kicking his butt would only make me feel good and he would need more drugs to recover from that."

The coach chuckles, "Strange way to say it, but you're correct. Show him the error of his ways."

"No Coach, we need to strangle his source and find out what is making him resort to drugs. Most likely a bad home life, I know I almost started drugs for that reason. Now my home life is getting better and so is my real life."

The coach smiles at me, "There you go! Feel better?"

"Yes Sir, I have to get rid of that instinct to just kill my enemies and learn to deal with them."

"Yes, unfortunately there is good and bad in the world, and we have to deal with all of it. Neither will ever go away, and they need each other to balance things out."

"And you say I have a weird way of looking at things. I say we crush evil and take over the world!"

"Then someone somewhere would consider you the evil one and themselves the good one and it would be another vicious cycle."

I look at him in amazement, "Now that Sir is good! I like how you did that thing there. Just so you know Ted thinks you might have your office bugged and he is very paranoid right now."

He smiles at me, "Aw the teacher becomes the student, very wise my Boy. You feel better now?"

"Yes Sir, I think I know how to handle the situation."

He raises one eyebrow as he writes me a note. He hands me the note and says, "Thanks for the help and talk. Get to class you drug dealer!" I laugh and run down the hall.

The coach closes the door and sits at his desk. For a moment he watches the game on the TV and then he reaches in his desk drawer and pushes the stop button on his tape recorder. He presses the rewind button and continues watching the game and making notes.

I walk into English class and hand Mrs. Williams the note, "Sorry I'm late."

"Are you ready to give your presentation?"

"No Ma'am."

She looks at me shocked as I say, "I thought it was a silly assignment and did not feel like wasting my time on it."

She is speechless and her mouth is wide open from shock. I look at the room and it is the same on everyone's face. I look back at Mrs. Williams and hand her my report. I walk to the class podium and say, "This book was like that for me. It was a struggle . . ." my mind takes over and I look at the room as they hang onto my every word. I look over to Mrs. Williams and give her a wink. She blushes and at the same time I can see her relief that she does not have to flunk me. The bad thing about this is we all are giving the same report on the same book, so I decided to spice it up a bit. Still looking at the faces in the room, I would say it was a success. "And that is how I felt about this book and what it meant to me. Thank you for your time."

I walk towards my seat and the class starts clapping and giving me a standing ovation. The teacher tries to regain order of the class and the Principal walks in the room and everyone instantly sits down. "Is there a problem in here Mrs. Williams?"

"No Sir the class just became over jubilant over Mr. Dunn's oration of our book."

He glares around the room, "But that was yesterday, why the joy today and so loud?"

Walking towards the Principal she says, "No Sir, the one he just did for our class. It was unconventional but very good."

The Principal locates me in the room and says, "A word . . . outside please."

I stand up and walk outside as the Principal says to the class, "Now keep the noise level down to a dull roar."

They scoff at his attempt at humor as he closes the door and they make a low roaring noise.

"Everything ok?"

Not sure where he was going with this I say, "Sir?"

"You ok? I saw you have a doctor appointment today."

"Yes, my dad wants us tested to make sure if someone in our family needs a kidney or something that we know who can and who can't."

"That is interesting, hope that everything is ok with your family. I've seen your grades for this reporting period, I've seen you on the football field and I heard you speak yesterday. This is not the same student from last year that almost killed a bully." What is going on here? *Ah man we are busted. Say we hid the drugs and he'll never find them and he can't make you talk, where is our attorney. Say the dog made you do it and you ate your homework! Say the maid did it with the candlestick in the library.*

I say nothing as the Principal looks at me as if wondering what to say, "I don't know what you did over the summer but I have to say, I like the change. Would you like to date my daughter?" *Wow he is offering us his first-born take her we can use her for bait!* We laugh as he puts his arm around my shoulders, "Nice job all around, but help us keep order here will ya?"

"Thank you Sir, I'll do my best."

He walks away, "I don't doubt that for a moment."

He waves as he walks back in his office next door to our English class.

I walk back in the classroom and Kaye is giving her speech and when she sees me she stops talking. I look at her and Mrs. Williams as I take my seat, "Sorry for the interruption."

Kaye starts reading her notes again and sounds very strained and nervous. I look at Amy as I sit down and she hands me a note. I read it, and I nod yes to her. As the bell rings and the teacher says to Kaye, "And in conclusion?" Kaye gives a quick synopsis and says, "The End."

"Very good Dear, we will start back with someone else tomorrow."

Everyone stands up and begins leaving the room. Kaye walks up behind me and says, "I could have done better if someone hadn't used up all the time!"

I look at her and as I am about to speak she says, "May I speak to you alone for a moment?"

The few people around us walk away as she says, "We may be broke up, but . . ." she looks as the last person leaves the room. She says much quieter, "I still love you! You are awesome. Any problem with the Principal?"

"No, he just wants me to date his daughter because he is very proud of me."

Kaye thinks for a moment, "I'm sure this could be used to our advantage, but I got nothing right now. You be good today. I want you so bad right now. When can we have sex?"

I look at her and say, "The same time you would want our daughters to have sex."

She looks to heaven, "I hope I can last that long! Can I borrow five bucks for lunch?"

I reach in my pocket and hand her a five, "I'll call you tonight."

She walks out of the room pretending to cry. I walk down to the office and there is my mom smiling at me ear to ear. She hugs me and sees Kaye crying and says, "What is wrong with Kaye?"

I look behind me, "I'll explain in the car."

We walk to the parking lot and mom walks up to her new white Cadillac, "What do you think?"

I look at it and my dad is sitting in the front seat smiling. "I like it Mom! It looks perfect for you, I like this size of car. Can I drive it?"

"No! It's my new car!"

"Which you wouldn't have if it weren't for me!"

She looks sad, "I guess you are right."

She goes to hand me the keys and I say as I get in the backseat, "Mom I'm just playing, you enjoy your new car. Dad where are we? Do we have any progress?" He turns around to look at me and begins explaining as mom starts the car and drives away.

We go to our lot for our new house first, because it is the closest to where we are, only five minutes from the school. As we look at the land and the trees my dad points out where the house will be. I am in shock about the different look of the land, "So when can we start building?"

My dad smiles, "Tomorrow! Can I quit my job and let your mom keep hers?"

I look at him, "What?"

"I want to be a part of the building and I could never go back to work now I am too excited about these projects!"

"How did you get it going so fast?"

"I called Chappy's dad and he was between projects so he came out first thing. He is at the other lot right now clearing the entire lot. The only payment he wants right now is the trees on the land. Are you sure you can get Chappy in Carolina? I think he is counting on that." We get back in the car and mom starts driving to the other lot. *Tell your dad he can quit his job, but to use all his vacation and sick days first. By then you will have the Attic finished and profitable by Christmas.*

Dad looks at me, "What's wrong Son?"

Mom says, "You are not going to be sick in my new car are you?"

"No Mom, it is very nice by the way." She smiles in agreement.

"Dad, when is our house going to be done? When can we move into it?"

"If I quit work, before Christmas. If I keep working, it might be Valentine's day."

"How about the Attic lot?"

"That could be finished in a couple of weeks. We got all the work permits for both this morning, plus we got a tax break for the first year for improving the property so fast."

Mom says, "I quit my job today, and they said I did not need to give a two week notice, because they had girls waiting for jobs in the secretarial pool."

"Too much information I'm getting full again. Where is my sister?"

"The mall looking at that store space we were talking about renting."

We pull up to the lot for the Attic and my eyes grow big at the sight, "Wow it looks a lot bigger with no trees."

My dad and I step out of the car and look around. Mr. Chapman sees us and walks over, "Hey guys how you doing?"

"Good. How is Mike? I noticed he was not at school today."

"He is fine, just soaking the ankle today so he will be ready for this weekend. Really think he can get into Carolina?"

"Yes Sir I do and I have a lot riding on it."

"You do that for me Son and my bill will be very small for this job."

"Oh yeah how small?"

"Your dad helps out like he and I were talking about, and it may be nonexistent."

I smile, "What were you guys talking about, I'm sorry, but I missed that part?"

"He was saying, he wanted to oversee the two projects and I would not need to be here, just my guys. We sell these trees for today's payment and if Mike gets into Carolina we are finished financially. If he doesn't, I send a bill only for my cost. I make no money."

My dad looks at me as I say to Mr. Chapman, "You Sir, have a deal."

We all shake hands and I walk to the car. Mom looks at me as I get in the car, "You ok Babe?"

"Oh yes Ma'am, I just got a taste of how business works and I like it! It's not always about money sometimes it is faith and helping each other out. They don't teach you that in school."

"They do indirectly. Be kind to your neighbor."

I smile at her as my dad gets in the car, "The concrete will be laid tomorrow morning and the frames will be here the next day."

"Dad when do you see this part being ready so we can open for business?"

"If we stay on schedule a week tops. The fence company will be here tomorrow also to put the poles in, so we can concrete around them for added security."

"Ok here is what you do dad. Use your sick days and vacation and then quit. Once the new house is finished we rent the old house, not sell it. We need to go to the mall now to look at this shop for mom's store."

Mom drives away and looks at me in the mirror, "How do you like my car? We only had to pay $23,000 since we paid cash for it."

I look at it, "Very nice Mom. They did not question the cash?"

"Nope. Just got me to do the paper work."

"Pull in somewhere I'm hungry."

"You are not eating in my new car! Wait until we get to the mall and get something there, we need to eat also."

We get to the mall and there is Roxanne standing in the food court on the pay phone. I walk up behind her, "Hello."

She starts talking as if I had answered the phone at the other end. I start to answer her and she turns around and jumps from being startled. "You are bad and not funny!"

"Really, I think I am quite funny!"

"You guys eat yet? I am starving!"

We go over to the pizza place where you can order by the slice and each get our personal favorites. We sit down and eat as Roxanne explains the layout of the store and how she got the rent down to $350 per month.

Dad looks at me, "How long before that is profitable?"

They all look at me and I listen to my conscience and then say, "About a month. This won't make a lot until prom and wedding season. I didn't want my sister to know this yet, but now is a good of time as any. Mom's first big dress will be your pageant dress. If you win it will make the store flourish."

Roxanne and my mom get excited and both give me hugs.

Roxanne says, "When can we open?"

"Let's go talk to the mall manager." My sister runs to the office for the mall to fetch the lady as the rest of us stroll to the store.

Dad says, "You are good boy and I love you!"

"Thanks Pop! I love you too! That sermon must have been good yesterday, because that is all I've heard today."

Dad puts his arm around me as we walk to the store, "It was very moving, but I just thought I was prejudice because you are mine."

We arrive in front of the vacant store and the lady unlocks the huge steel gate in front of the store. We walk in as she walks to the back to turn on the lights. We look around and the lady comes back to where we are.

She points at me, "It's you!"

My dad automatically remembers my past and is about to apologize for me when she says, "You spoke at my church yesterday."

I smile and say, "Did I? That is one big church."

"You were awesome! My little girl got saved, thank you so much! My husband went and he said he would start going back to church! He had no idea our youth were so stoutly religious."

"Thank you Ma'am, I am glad I could help."

She smiles at me and hugs me and then backs up.

She says, "So you want this place?"

I look around, "I want it for my mom and sister. It is going to be their dress shop."

The lady just stares at me as my dad says, "Can we add walls?"

Without looking away from me, "Yes Sir, it just has to be returned to this condition if you move out. Anything removed that is here now needs to be cleared with the mall first."

Mom grabs my arm and says, "I like it and want it."

"Yes Ma'am."

I look at the lady that has not stopped staring at me, "I'm sorry I did not catch your name?"

"Deloris."

"Deloris, my sister explained a bit to me, but could we talk about the rent and any clauses we should know about?"

My father comes in close to hear the details. She looks around, "Tell you what. We had discussed $350/month, but I did not know it was for you. Your first two months are free so January 1st the $300 a month will be due. Your sister has a copy of the contract."

My father and I look at each other, "Dad I like it. What do you think?"

"I like it Son and it sounds like a great deal."

Deloris smiles, "Great! Shall we sign the contract? How old are you Tommy, 15?"

"Yes Ma'am good guess."

"I have a daughter your age. If you would care to meet her I could introduce you."

"That sounds great, but only if she is as nice as you, then I'd love to meet her."

She giggles as her and my father sign the papers. "The only thing I need from you Mr. Dunn is five hundred dollar deposit."

I look at dad and point to mom, "Son, please get your mothers checkbook for . . ."

I walk over to mom, "Pretend you are looking for your checkbook."

I reach in my pocket and pull out five hundred dollars. I turn back to Deloris, "Is cash ok?"

"We prefer a check. It has an address on it."

Mom starts writing the check, "Five hundred you said?"

"Yes Ma'am."

I stop mom from writing the check and look at the nice lady, "Deloris do you have any food court slots available? I was thinking of opening a Delicatessen or a sandwich shop."

She smiles, "I have one available with a cooler but no freezer would you like to see it?"

"Any chance the same deal as this store?"

"Nope sorry, that one is cheaper. Two hundred a month and I can only give you one free month."

I smile, "Well let's look at it anyway."

We walk down to the food court and it is small but perfect for a deli shop and there are no other deli shops so it should do well. *It will do very well, get it!* We look around and I say, "The deposit the same?" Deloris nods in agreement and mom writes the check. Deloris hands us the keys to both shops and hugs me one more time as she shakes hands with the rest of the family.

"Deloris, do we need to pay by check each month or is cash ok?"

She looks at me, "Either way is fine. Thank you and I will see you around the mall." She waves as she exits.

My sister walks into the music store across from the food court. She sits down and starts playing a baby grand piano. The rest of us follow her in, "Dad I wish I could remember how to play after all those lessons I had!"

"Sit down and try you might remember some." *I will help you!*

"Alright I'll give it a shot."

I sit down at the upright piano next to my sister and stretch my fingers as my favorite cartoon character, 'Buggs Bunny' would do. I watch my sister's hand movements and time it beautifully as I join in with her. We play in unison and I have no idea what song we are playing. We must be doing well, I look around and a crowd is growing. We get to the end of the song and applause erupts in the store. My sister curtsies and I take a seated bow.

I start playing again and Roxanne joins back in. We are doing a duet in dueling banjo style. At the end the crowd again goes wild. The manager walks over and shakes my hand, "That was awesome! You play the piano, preach, and play a good game of football."

My sister continues playing and my dad walks over to the piano.

Smiling at the man I say, "Do I know you?"

"No, but I think this whole town knows you. My name is Sammy. My daughter goes to your school and you spoke at our church yesterday. Nice job by the way, not many your age have that kind of power and drive in their speeches."

"Thanks!"

Smiling at me, "Can I help you with something or are you just playing around."

"My parents are opening a Deli over there, and a dress shop down the mall a couple of stores away. I wanted to get a grand piano for the dress shop. You know in the front window to class it up a bit. Also my sister can practice for an upcoming pageant she is going to be in."

He smiles, "Maybe we can work out a deal. I will loan you that baby grand for as long as you want, just advertise for me in the pageant and in your store window, with a small classy sign on the piano."

Dad calls Roxanne over, "Honey would you want to put that piano in the front window of your dress shop?"

She looks at us in shock, "I would love to, that would look awesome and class up the joint!"

I look at him, "And if later we decide to buy it?"

"Well it would be a used piano, so I'd have to discount it accordingly."

My sister jumps up and down for joy and hugs all of us.

Sammy says, "When you guys open the store let me know and I'll push it down there."

"Thank you!"

My sister yells in joy.

Hugging dad and me, Roxanne says, "You guys are awesome!"

She looks at me and hits my arm, "And you have been holding out, you still remember how to play! Very impressive!"

We walk out of the store and Sammy from the music store chases us down, as we walk away, "Mr. Dunn two small requests and this will not affect our deal. Could you say hello to my daughter Shelly at school one day, which would mean a lot to her? And could some Saturday after you open your store maybe come and play that duet thing again. That was awesome! That got people in the store."

"Sure thing we would love to play for you sometime. What does your daughter look like?"

He pulls out his wallet and shows me a picture. "No problem if I see her tomorrow I will say hello."

"Thanks, I will see you later."

I catch up to my family as they stop in front of the new store. I hug my mom and she says, "I assume you have a plan for all this because now I am nervous."

"Mom you know what happens when you assume you make an a . . ."

"Yeah I know. Seriously, it is going to be ok?"

"Yes Ma'am, better than ok! This celebrity status is really paying off; maybe I should be a preacher?" Dad says, "That would be great!"

"I'm scared I'd be like that Jim Jones character or some cult leader and it would go to my head and I'd go crazy like they did."

We look around the store and I say, "Let's get out of here for a while."

Mom looks at me, "How do you like my new car?"

I smile, "Can I drive it?"

"No!"

"Mom didn't we already do this?"

On the way home dad shows me another property with a big billboard on it. Dad says, "It too can be used for a storage mall, and this is on the other side of town." *He's right, one store or office and people are skeptical, they see more than one and they think it must be good and safe, everyone is doing it. People are such sheep!* "That's great Dad, I think you should call the guy right now and see what he wants for the land." He picks up his car phone and dials the number. While speaking with the guy I hear my dad say, "That sounds good when could we meet and look at it and discuss all the particulars about it?" Listening to the man on the phone my dad then says, "That sounds good I'll see you in one hour."

My dad hangs up the phone and says to my mom, "Let's get to the court house and find out all we can about this property. We drive away and my sister looks in a portfolio she has started about the most available properties in the area.

She pulls out a sheet of paper, "Here Dad, I got it right here."

He smiles, "How did you get this?"

"A couple of weeks ago, Tommy told me certain areas to find out info on. This was one of them." She showed what the guy was asking for the property and the value of the land and tax value.

"There are no leans or mortgages and there seems to be no neighbor problems, land locks, or easements."

Mom stops her, "What is a land lock?"

"You know, like any blocks for you buying the land around it or not being able to build on it or you can't access it. It also is tied in to city water and has a well, so you could go either way."

I say, "I vote we use the well. It's less expense!"

Dad says, "We let it be our option. We don't use the city water, we don't pay. We shouldn't need much water there anyway."

I shrug, "I just feel we are moving too fast right now. We have a lot of money going out and none coming in yet."

My dad turns around and says, "We strike while the iron is hot. Hey, let's head over to the hardware store I need to place an order for the house."

Mom says, "Yeah I need to go to that fabric store that is in that strip mall and order some cloth for the store."

I nudge my sister, "You go with mom and I'll stick with dad."

She nods in agreement, "I'll see who the wholesaler is and get mom to just get the essentials for now. Hey we could use some of our storage containers for the store also right?"

Dad turns back to us, "Yeah, that storeroom was not that big was it?"

We arrive at the stores and my father and I go into the hardware store and mom and Roxanne go in the fabric store. I have never seen my father in action like this before. He is ordering lumber, nails, plywood and bricks like a pro.

The salesman says, "Sir how long would you like the 2x4's?"

My dad looks at me and then back at the clerk, "I'd like them for a long time, I'm building a house."

My dad laughs like it is the funniest thing he had ever said. The clerk and I smile at each other hoping he would stop soon.

Dad looks at him and says, "Three skids of eight foot long and one skid of ten foot please."

"Dad doesn't Mr. Chapman supply this stuff?"

"No just the storage buildings he has a wholesaler for that stuff, he is giving us some things for the house. We have to do the majority of the house. He is supplying seven guys to help me with the house. We have to pay them in cash. Is that a problem?"

"No Sir, that is actually good."

"You are going to help me also right?"

I smile at him, "Yes Sir!"

"Good, that's my boy!"

The clerk looks at me strangely, "Hey I know you! You are that little preacher boy from yesterday!"

I smile and my dad says, "Wow that was a big church."

"Yes Sir that was me." I reach to shake his hand and he slaps it away and grabs me and starts hugging me. "I got saved yesterday thanks to you! You helped me see the error of my ways!"

He starts crying as he hugs me again.

My dad smiles and pats us both on the back.

The man finally releases me and I say, "Thank you! I am glad I could be of service. I wish you the best with the rest of your life."

He smiles at me like I was a movie star, "No, I thank you Sir!"

He looks at the bill for our building supplies, "I would just give you this stuff but that would be stealing from my company and I can't do that. Do you guys have a company by any chance?"

My dad says, "Yes we do, The Dunn Group."

The man pulls out a store card from under the counter and writes the name on it. He hands it to my dad, "This will give you 20% off any purchase in any of our stores any time. I will even include free delivery for you guys."

My dad takes the card, "Thank you . . ."

"Bob Lowe."

"Thank you Bob."

"No the pleasure is all mine Sir! You have a great kid there."

"Thank you Bob, I feel the same way."

"You guys have a great day and I will have this delivered first thing in the morning."

I wave as I walk away, "Thank you Mr. Lowe, it was nice to meet you."

"You too Son, we will see you later."

Walking out of the store my dad says, "Your being a celebrity is really paying off!"

"It is weird though. I have been offered peoples daughters and gifts from everywhere."

"Enjoy it while it last, it will fade. When I played high school baseball I wanted to go pro, but I could not handle being a celebrity. I am way to shy and stupid."

"Pop you are not stupid by any stretch of the imagination. You just do things different than other people."

"Well a lot of people consider that stupid when they don't understand it."

"Yeah perception is a funny thing."

We walk to the fabric store and see my mom and my sister still in the store. "You know your mother could stay in there all day if we let her."

"Then let's do that. We take the car, meet the gentleman and then come back and pick them up."

"Son she is not going to let us drive her new car." We walk in the store and they are looking at sewing machines and thread and patterns for clothing. "Mom we need to go! Would you like to go or stay here and we could come back for you?"

She hands me the keys, "Love ya, and see you when you get back."

"Yes Ma'am in about an hour then."

She looks at her watch and waves bye and says "Hey what's our budget for now?"

"That cash I gave you earlier enough?"

"These two sewing machines cost that much!"

The sales lady comes from the backroom and looks at me like she had seen a ghost, "It's you! What are you doing in my store?" I smile thinking my celebrity is about to kick in again. "You get out of here you little womanizer!"

"Excuse me!"

"You broke my little girl's heart!"

I think for a moment, oh crap Tammy's mom. "Yes Ma'am, sorry!"

"You should have said that last year!"

"I'm going!" I walk out of the store and mom continues talking to the lady. My dad and I walk to the car and he says, "Let me drive," and he takes the keys from me.

As we drive away dad asks, "What was that all about Son?"

"Remember that girl Tammy I use to see, but we broke up because I would not have sex with her. That was her mom."

"You mean the girl I caught you about to have sex with and I made you break up with her?"

I look sheepishly at him, "There is that perception thing again, Dad!"

We pull up to the lot and the man is sitting in his pickup truck. We walk over and shake hands and my dad and the man start small talk and introductions.

I walk onto the land and I yell back to them, "How many acres?"

The man yells, "Five and a quarter acres."

I look around at the land and there is scattered debris and trash everywhere. I walk back to them, "This use to be a land fill or something?"

My dad looks shocked from the question. The man looks at me, "No Son, but I have had homeless people camping out here and that is why I want to sell it."

"Can we keep the people? Like livestock, they are on the land when we buy it and they become ours?"

"That's funny Son."

He looks at my father, "What do you plan to do with the land Sir?"

"We plan to make it storage or warehouse type area for my wife's dress shop in the mall."

"That sounds nice."

My dad asks, "We know what you want for the land, and we know what the land is worth and the tax value. But what can we both settle on?"

The man looks to heaven and then at me, "Tell you what, give me $5000 and the property is yours."

I look at my father and then the man, "I say $4500 cash!"

He looks at me, "Who am I dealing with?"

"My father is Mr. Dunn and I am the group. Is that an acceptable offer or not?"

He looks pleased and shakes our hands, "That sounds fine to me, let's go to the court house and sign the papers."

We get back in our vehicles and drive downtown. My dad says, "I could have gotten him to $4000."

"I know, but I wanted to give him the extra $500. He could use it."

My dad looks at me with question in his eyes. I say, "He is going through a divorce and is selling everything to survive. He has a moving van for sell also, we should buy it."

"How do you know that?"

"Dad I can't read minds, but I pick up clues from people sometimes, it's weird."

We park at the courthouse and we start to get out of the car and I give dad the cash.

"Don't offer him more money or give him more, he will think it is charity and get upset. He will ask if you need a truck and you say maybe let's look at it. Same deal for the truck we offer five hundred less than he is asking. In both cases he is getting five hundred more than he thought he would get, and five hundred more than he will claim he got."

My dad agrees and we get out of the car and walk in the courthouse together.

After we are finished with the paperwork we walk out of the building and he says, "You guys wouldn't happen to need a big moving van would you? It has a lift on it and comes with a moving dolly."

My dad smiles at me and says to the man, "Maybe? When can we see it?"

"We can go right now to my house. You said you were getting in the storage business and if you do that you will need a big truck for moving stuff."

"We need to pick up my wife and daughter and then we can come over if that is ok?"

"Sounds great, I'll see you there." He gives us the address and directions and then gets in his truck and drives away. We get back to the fabric store and my sister and mother get in the car. Mom turns around, "I fixed it! I told Tammy's mom it was your father's fault that you broke up with her and she is fine now. Go in the store and get that box of stuff we bought."

I look at dad and he is not fine with that. I go in and the lady points at the box by the door. I pick it up and put the box in the trunk of the car. Dad drives the car in the direction the man had given us for the truck. Mom rubs my dad's head and explains why she did and said what she did. He calms down as mom says; "We need a truck to move our stuff and store things until we have space."

Dad looks at her, "You are in luck." We pull into the farmhouse driveway and see the truck being washed by the man and his young son. My sister and I sit in the car as the adults discuss the truck and my dad inspects it.

Roxanne smiles at me, "What do you think of mom's new car?"

"I like it. What do you think of your dress shop?"

"I like it, thank you for the piano deal you made. I haven't seen you practice in a while, so how did you do that?"

I smile, "It's a gift. My whole life I fought things I did not like or think was cool. Now I am trying a new approach, embrace and not fight. All my lessons just came back to me."

The car door opens and dad leans in and says, "He would like a check for $9,000 and $1,500 cash."

I start laughing as my dad and sister look at me thinking I'm crazy, "He's good! Dad you did like we discussed right?"

"Yeah I talked him down five hundred like we said."

"Excellent! Here you go." I hand my father $1500 in one hundred dollar bills.

"Hey dad, go back to the hardware store and get three of those dining room tables we saw on display and bring them to the store in your new truck."

Dad asks, "Just the tables?"

"No Sir, I think those tables would make nice display tables and grab some yellow paint and supplies also . . . and twenty-five of those full length mirrors."

He smiles, "Need anything else?"

"Whatever you see you think we might need. I'll get us some help for the store and we will see you there."

He reaches in the backseat and kisses my sister and me on the forehead, "Just like when you guys were babies."

We chuckle as he trots over to mom and the guy and hands the money to him and the checkbook to mom.

My sister nudges me as I chuckle, "What was so funny?"

"Oh nothing. I got shotgun!" I get out of the backseat and sit in the front seat.

Not letting it go she says, "Come on share."

"Earlier when we paid for the land we gave him cash he put down an amount less than we paid on the courthouse paper. Now he sells the truck and wants a check for a certain amount and cash for the rest."

"Ok big deal."

"He is going through a divorce and is selling stuff cheap, claiming he sold it cheaper and pocketing some of the cash."

"I'm still not following?" I turn around to explain when she says, "Oh I get it!"

Dad drives the truck past us as mom gets in the car and she says, "So what do you think of my new car?" I look at her as I am getting annoyed with the same question, "You got a new car? Where is it? Can I drive it?"

She chuckles, "Fine, I'll stop asking, but if I haven't said it yet thanks for making all this happen."

"I love you guys and want the best for you, you are welcome Mom."

She smiles and says, "Where to now?"

"Back to the mall, we have some work to do."

I look at the time and say, "We need some help."

I pick up my dad's car phone and begin to dial, "Wouldn't it be cool if one day we could have our own mobile phones . . . Hey Kaye how you doing my girl?"

I listen to how the rest of her day went and I stop her, "Honey I need some help. My mom and sister got their shop in the mall today and we need a hand fixing it up, would you and your sister mind helping?"

I listen again and say, "Bring your homework and mine and we'll do it there. Tell your parents just until nine. Hey get your dad to come also if he is not too busy. My dad wants to ask for his help with a project."

She speaks and then I say, "You will, ok great. I'll see you there, bye."

Mom just looks at me as she drives. I say nothing and she says, "Ok what now?"

"Her dad lost his job the other day and I want dad to let him help with the house and other jobs as well."

"That is sweet Honey. What does he do?"

"He is a Plummer."

"That's what your dad did before he took that supervisor job."

"I know, I thought they might start a plumbing company together."

"That sounds like a good idea."

We arrive at the mall and my mom asks, "Anyone know how to get to our service entrance?"

We direct her and we pull up to what we think should be our door. I get out of the car with our keys to the building. Just as I attempt the key in the door it opens.

The prettiest girl I had ever seen in person opens it and says, "Oh sorry! May I help you?"

I look at her as if I had just seen an angel, "um key work door . . ."

She smiles at me, "What? This door is for Gap employees only!"

She has magnificent legs, a nice rear end and the finest breast I have ever seen in a sweater, "Sorry, I was trying to open my door but not sure which one it is."

She points at the door next to hers, "That store is vacant. Is that it?"

"I hope so!"

I walk to the door and open it and my sister and mother step out of the car. The girl sees them and says, "Nice car! My dad has a black one just like it."

Mom smiles at her, "Thank you Sweetie, what's your name?"

"Debra!"

"Hi Debra, I'm Mrs. Dunn and this is my daughter Roxanne and you met my son Tommy. This is going to be my dress boutique."

"What are you calling it or is it a franchise like ours?"

"I'm going to call it Roxanne's."

"That's cute. I go to State and I will need a formal dress in the spring. Do you do specialty dresses?"

"Honey, that is going to be our main market. Specialty dresses are what we do."

Debra lights a cigarette and says, "Great slogan. We will need to talk then."

"I look forward to it my dear, now if you will excuse me I need to get this baby rolling so we can open soon."

"Good luck Ma'am!"

"Thank you!"

We walk into the back entrance of the store and I look for the light switch. My sister hits the switch and I return to the car, hoping the smoking demon is still out there smoking, so I can gawk at her again. I see a puff of smoke and I walk to the car and open the trunk.

She walks closer to me and says, "Why do you look so familiar to me?"

Hoping she did not go to that church also, "Maybe earlier here at the mall?"

Church this girl would have no clue. She looks like one of those things my school warns you about. She looked like a nymph straight from Satan's lair, an evil temptress that would lure me straight to the gates of hell.

"No, that's not it. Did we ever sleep together?"

"Now that I hope you would remember? I know I would."

"Sorry no! I got it you are someone famous some local big shot!"

"I don't think so!" I lift the box from the trunk and head to the building.

"Yes you are you were in the paper this weekend some football guy?"

I place the box on the floor inside the building. I come back outside and say, "Yes I do play football, but I don't think I was in the paper."

"Yes, that was you my boyfriend and his buddies were talking about. They hope you come to State in the future. So you are what a senior in high school."

She says it like I was scum and I see an opportunity to get out of this, "Much worse a sophomore at a Christian school!"

She looks at me and says, "Well you are cute. You still a virgin?"

Shocked at her boldness I reply, "Yes I am!"

Putting out her cigarette she says, "When you want to change that give me a call." She spins and walks back into her store.

I walk into our store and my mother says, "Stay away from that girl she is trouble!"

"But Mom, what about our love child we have together?"

She looks at me in shock as I say, "I just got her pregnant on the top of your new car. Yeah your new car, I like it by the way! I just lost my virginity with that super slut."

Not taking me seriously at all, "Boy I'm warning you! I can sense things about people."

"I know Mom. You have nothing to worry about."

I look to the front of the store and Kaye and her sister are standing there.

"The Calvary is here mom." I take the keys off the counter and trot to the huge gate blocking the store from the mall.

As I open it I say, "Welcome to Roxanne's ladies!"

They walk in and Kaye says, "Oh I love what you did with the place." "Where's your dad?"

"Getting some drinks, he'll be here in a moment."

She hugs my mom and sister and they look around.

A strange lady tries to walk in the store, "Excuse me Ma'am we are not open yet!"

"Just looking sonny, keep your pants on!"

She turns and walks out. The girls chuckle as she leaves.

Kaye's dad walks in with drinks for everybody and I shut the gate so we have no more people walking in. Kaye walks over to me, "Everyone thinks we are broke up and I heard talk about girls pooling their money together to buy you for Friday. So you may need to cover me for quite a bit of money. I am bidding until I win. We both got A's in English today. You are a tough act to follow." She gives me a quick peck on the lips.

I smile at her and say, "Let me show you the store and what we have in mind! Here in the front window we are going to have a baby grand piano, courtesy of the music shop down the mall. Beside it, here against the wall we will have dressing rooms. Here in the middle of the store we will have a runway for models."

Mom stops me, "A what?"

"Runways like models use to prance on. We can let girls try on outfits and pretend to be models; it will be great for business."

My sister says, "It's like a dream come true, my own runway. We could have actual little beauty pageants for little kids."

I jump back in, "Exactly! And the back of the store is going to be storage for materials. Over there we are going to build mom a booth that she can sew and watch the store or pull her blinds and block out the world. That side of the store will be displays and racks of clothing. Any questions?"

My sister walks over and hugs me as Kaye says, "Can I work here?"

My mom hugs her, "You sure can Dear."

I hear a truck pull up and I say, "Someone needs to show dad where we are."

Mom goes to the back door to let him in.

I say, "Mr. Lewis I was hoping you could look at our bathroom situation. We have one but I want two or maybe three if it is possible. One with a shower and we can't dig, so we will have to lay the pipes on top of our existing floor back there." He nods in agreement and goes to survey the situation.

"Tonight we paint and plan, that's it. Any questions?"

My dad walks in, "Send someone for a pizza or something quick and easy so we can get to work. Come help unload this truck."

I give my sister money, "Get food please!"

I walk outside and start grabbing paint cans and mirrors. Then my father and I grab the boxes with the tables in them, "Hope you brought some tools, so we can put these together?"

"Yes, they gave me a small set for using my company card."

"Nice!"

While moving the stuff Debra comes back out to smoke another cigarette and waves at my dad and me. We walk in the store and as he is about to say something I say, "I know mom has already warned me!"

"Good I hate I had to be so stern with you!"

"Thanks Pop!"

I look at the store and the girls are halfway done with the first wall. I grab a roller and begin painting. I look back at dad and Mr. Lewis shaking hands and think so far so good. My sister walks in with two pizzas and she yells, "Come and get it! Nice color I like it."

We gather at the counter and say a quick prayer and then grab slices. I notice the dads sitting together on the floor.

I wink at Kaye and we go sit next to them. "Dad, Mr. Lewis is a plumber and carpenter and I asked him if he would add some bathrooms for us here. They would have to be able to be removed if necessary."

My dad says to Mr. Lewis, "That sounds great! How often are you available? After work and weekends?" He looks at my dad and takes a bite of pizza, "Anytime is good for me."

Dad looks suspicious at him, "That's great! I just quit my job also. If you will help me Bob we can have this place and the Deli up and running by the weekend."

Kaye looks at me, "What Deli?"

"We rented a place in the food court as well."

Kaye smiles, "You're going for broke? Can I work there too?"

My dad says, "Of course you can, Honey!"

I explain the layout again to my father and my mom continues painting while we eat. After the girls finish eating, they jump up and start painting. Mom finally takes a break and grabs some pizza and looks at us talking on the floor. I show the two dads what I want it to look like and draw design of the rooms we need to add.

Mom looks at me as the dad's talk, "What do I do for inventory until I get enough dresses to fill the shop?"

I smile at my mother and say, "I'll take care of it for you tomorrow. Roxanne knows a wholesaler that should be able to get you about fifty dresses and some blouses until you are up and running. You are going to run like a specialty store though, someone walks in and you make his or her request. Take the picture off the patterns you have and put them in a photo album type thing so they can browse the book and the store. After you make whatever, they can walk the runway like a fashion show."

My mom tells me to stand up and as she hugs me she says, "I love you, this is like a dream come true."

"I love you too. Now make me some money to pay for all of this. The first thing you need to do is create Roxanne's gown for her pageant. That will be good publicity for this place."

"I need my sewing machine from home."

"Roxanne, that wholesaler, do they have sewing machines and fabric and stuff?"

"I will find one tomorrow."

"Also we need to find signs for both shops and the Attics."

Dad says, "I'll take that one first thing in the morning, I know the place. Just give me designs and what each says."

Kaye's dad speaks up, "What do you want me to do tomorrow and at what time?"

I look at dad and he says, "We can go get the stuff we need for here, bathroom stuff, a runway and walls. Is 8 am good for you?"

Kaye's dad says, "Perfect we can take my truck, I'll just come and pick you up in the morning."

"Sounds good."

The two men put the tables together and we finish painting. Not a bad day's work.

Kaye and I walk down to the Deli and look around. We go in the back and start making out when she stops me and says, "We can't be doing this."

"You are right; there is probably some kind of health code or something."

"Not that reason. We broke up remember?"

"Oh yeah, then get off me you slut!"

"Never Mister you are mine."

We laugh and walk to the front. My mom is standing out there looking around, "Thought you two broke up? You don't act like it!"

"We are just doing that for show Ma, I explained that to you."

"Back in my day, if you liked someone you showed it, but not in public."

"So how is that different from what we are doing?"

"Every girl knew not to mess with your dad."

"Mom isn't that back when they thought the world was flat and they dragged the women by their hair?"

"You better be glad you are my favorite or I would bop your ears."

"I love you too Mom!"

Kaye kisses my mom on the cheek, "Me too!"

We close up the Deli and mom says, "You want me to do anything with this tomorrow?"

"Look at it and make a list of what we need, thanks. I'm tired can I go home yet?"

As we walk by the Gap I notice Debra looking out at us as I put my arm around Kaye's neck. Kaye puts her arm around my waist as we walk. I smile at Debra and she winks at me like I could have you if I wanted you.

Mom says, "Yes we are done! Let's get out of here."

"Mom, any idea how much money we spent today?"

She chuckles, "I don't want to think about it!"

She thinks for a moment and says, "We spent more today than me and your father made last year."

Kaye and I stop walking and I say, "You scared yet?"

Mom looks at the two of us, "No I trust you! For the first time in my life I really feel happy and carefree. Ride home with your sister I want to talk with your dad for a while."

I go over to my sister, "You ready to go?"

She smiles at me and says, "This place is going to be awesome. Any chance we can fly to NYC to get some clothes to deck this place out?"

Kaye and her sister anxiously await my reply as well. I look at them and say, "Not this weekend I have a big weekend planned already, and I need you all there."

Kaye's sister Kim says, "You want me too?"

"You are optional, these two I want there."

My sister says, "The next weekend then?"

"I'm in if you can get mom and dad to go along with it."

She looks over at them, "No problem I may need help with mom though she is tough."

Kaye tugs at my shirttail and says, "Can you ride with us you said you would help with my homework?"

"Sure, I can do that. Bye Sis."

On the ride home Kaye and I ride in the backseat. I write as fast as I can for her and for me, she sucks and kisses on my neck and grabs my crotch. I look up and notice her sister watching in the rearview mirror.

I say, "Hard to believe we broke up this morning isn't it."

Realizing that I see her looking, she quickly looks back at the road, "At least you guys made up and got back together."

Kaye stops and says, "No we didn't we are still broke up! He's got till the end of the week and then I might take him back."

Kim looks in the mirror, "Can I have him then?"

I start laughing as the sisters start arguing. As we pull into my driveway I still have two more problems to do for the homework assignment. "Ladies come in the house so I can finish."

We walk in the house and I sit at the kitchen table and keep writing answers to questions. Kaye excuses herself and leaves the room for the bathroom. Kim puts her hand in my crotch and whispers in my ear, "Seriously if she doesn't want you I will take you anytime, anywhere," and she kisses and licks my ear. As she pulls away I keep writing. Not sure what to say to Kim, Kaye enters the room saving me from any embarrassment.

The sisters start talking about the shop and what they would like to do there. I finish the homework and close the books. I look at the two of them and say, "All done. Put out or get out!"

They both look at me and Kaye says, "Same time or who goes first?"

"You ladies figure that out."

Kim laughs and says, "Goodnight Cutie!"

She leans over and kisses my cheek almost on my lips and whispers, "Anywhere, Anytime!"

She walks out the door and I look at Kaye, "She is totally hitting on me right in front of you."

"I trust you Honey. You have will power or we would have done it by now. She . . . cannot be trusted though."

Kaye looks at her sister getting in her car and then back to me, "We can have sex right now if you want?" I look deep in her eyes, "Don't tempt me Honey!"

"Tempt shmempt, let's go right now!"

I stand up and kiss her, "I love you too. Now go home."

Kaye kisses me, and as she presses against me she starts laughing, "I can tell you do love me! Seriously let's go to your room right now." I almost start walking that way and I hear, *you will both regret it and you two will be over, and that other life will creep in.*

"Not yet Honey, we need to wait. But I don't want to wait! You better go; I will see you in the morning I have to go take a cold shower."

She kisses me one more time, "I love you!"

She runs out the door and hops in the car with her sister. I wave bye to them and they drive away.

My sister drives up and parks her car as I sit down on the back steps.

She walks up, "Problem?"

I say nothing and she says, "Oh, you have a woman problem!"

I look at her strangely and she continues, "Yes my brother, I can do some of the tricks you can do. Watch and learn." She sits down next to me and grabs my hand. She closes her eyes and says, "Yuck! Quit thinking about that! Gross . . . both of them? They are sisters and that is gross!"

I chuckle, "What? I was in the middle! They started it!"

She throws my hand down and says, "You are sick little brother!"

"What do I do Sis? I have women throwing themselves at me left and right, and men offering me their daughters. I want the women and it is getting harder and harder to say no!"

"You have to be strong Buddy. If you give in now you may lose your girlfriend and a lot more. You never know? You have a lot riding on this now and a lot of people relying on you. Not just our family anymore."

"Wait a minute, who else is relying on me?"

"Seriously?"

She looks at me and says, "Think outside the box! The box being your world and outside is everyone else's. People at the mall are counting on our money for a living, your football team, Chappy is really counting on you, our family, Kaye's family, people you help find the Lord yesterday and a bunch of people I don't know that you touch their life just by walking past them."

I look at the ground, "Nice analogy with the box there, Pal."

She hits my shoulder, "Trust your conscience. It seems to be working for you so far."

"Yeah you're right. It would be easier if I wasn't so cute and loveable though."

She pulls away from me and says, "Waa-boo-hoo! You poor baby! You're not that cute! Sorry but we are cursed with good looks, embrace it don't run from it!"

We laugh and start talking about the day's events and get our game plan ready for the rest of the week. I told her about the slave auction and my plan with Kaye.

"Hey get me in on that!"

"What do you mean?"

"I will put you out of the bidding for anyone but her. If someone is bidding against her I will bid higher so only she and I will be bidding."

"Yeah, but my sister bidding on me?"

"I'll get Leigh then or I could just say I was doing it so I could boss you around."

"Hey that would work! Thanks Sis! I am going to go take a shower now. Do you have a good grasp of what we want to do for the shops? I've got football the rest of the week."

"Got it covered Bro, but I'll keep you informed. I'll have to pick you up from practice anyway, you non-driver."

"Hey, I'll see about a new car for you for Christmas."

I walk into the house and leave my sister outside. That should keep her on my side for a while longer. *What you think she is a donkey or something.* Actually that is very close to what I think she is. *No, I mean you dangle a carrot in front of her to get her to pull your cart down the road like a donkey.* Actually that is exactly what I was going for; I still have a hard time getting over that State Fair incident two years ago. *Let it go she is on your side now and is going to stay there from now on.* If you say so, she is just hard to trust. Why has she always hated me so much? *You stole her thunder and for that you must pay.* I never stole anything from her or anybody else! *Before you were born she was the princess of the castle and she got all the attention. Then this little toad moved in and tried to take her space and breathe her air. You had no right to do that to her. Her first words when she saw you were, I don't like it take it back.* That sounds like the sister I know and adore. *Like I said you no longer have to worry about her, she is on your side.*

Standing in my room I watch my sister walk down the hall towards me, "How did you read my mind while ago?"

Looking at me oddly she says, "I didn't . . ."

She looks around like, where am I and then she says, "Dirty little minds are easy to read," and she walks into her room.

I hear mom and dad walk in the back door as I try to figure out what is going on. Mom sees me in my doorway and says, "You ok?"

I look at her, "Yes Ma'am . . . I am ok how are you?"

I close my door and wonder what is happening to my sister. She has no power or abilities I need to worry about does she? *No, that was a fluke she just guessed right, that's all.*

Chapter 14

Thanks for coming guys. That is all you should say! I walk out of the locker room and see my family and friends and say, "Thanks for coming, it means a lot for you all to be here with me." They all hug me and pat me on the back saying you can't win them all. I look to the field we had just lost our championship game on, and then at the scoreboard that still showed the score 28-34. My dad places a hand on my shoulder and says, "You guys played hard, the other guys just played harder." Kaye comes over and kisses my cheek, "Come on slave let's go home."

I smile and say, "Kaye, the slave thing is over! Lincoln died so I could be free."

The family laughs and we leave the field and Kaye says, "I sure hope Scott is ok!"

I reply, "He'll be fine but his pride is going to hurt for a while."

Kaye holds my hand as we walk, "Did you see his leg break? I bet it was gross?"

"No I missed it when that big guy knocked me on my butt, but I heard it. Bones snapping is a sound I won't soon forget either."

We get into my father's new suburban truck that he bought two days ago. Kaye and I crawl in the very back so we can talk and play around on the two-hour ride home. Kaye sees I am disappointed, "Don't be sad Honey you have two more years to win The State Championship."

"I know, but coming from a small school I will have to win all the games if I am going to make my plan work."

"What plan is that?"

"To conquer the world!"

"What do you want the world for? You will only have headaches then."

"I want to make everyone's life better."

Kaye scoffs at me, "I thought you were smart!"

Our parent's turn to look at us, and Kaye's mom says, "Everything ok back there?"

"Yes Ma'am we are fine." Under my breath I say, mind your own business.

"So I am not smart for wanting to make the world a better place?"

Kaye chuckles and says, "Yes, it is just impossible!"

"Why do you say that?"

"Imagine two children at your side and you can only give one a lollipop? What do you do?"

"I get more lollipops."

"Ok let's say you give both of them one and another child walks up and then another and so on. It never ends and the world is over a billion lollipops."

I smile, "See Honey that is my plan. They will never know where the lollipops are coming from."

She looks at me like I am crazy, "Not every kid is going to take a lollipop that they do not know where it came from. And one kid will try to find the source, so they don't have to rely on you for your secret lollipops."

"Yeah you are right, maybe I need to move out in the woods and shut off the whole world. Or we could do my plan where we give out as many lollipops as we can and make as many happy kids as we can."

Kaye kisses my neck and mumbles, "We will try it your way, if it doesn't work out, I will say I told you so and we will move our six kids to the beach and become sand crabs."

I grab her hand and shake it, "It's a deal!"

My dad hears me, "What was that? You want to stop for food?"

Knowing my father, I know that means he is hungry and wants to stop for food, "Yes please!"

He points at the next exit and in his best caveman imitation he says, "Um steakhouse good. Ugh they burn meat for us!" We all laugh out of courtesy and I say, "Ugh! Good!" Mike is driving behind us with my sister in his car and they exit the interstate with us.

After eating we return to our vehicle and Kaye and I return to the backseat. It started raining while we were eating and this means we will need to drive slower. As we sit down and get cozy and comfortable I whisper to her, "Take your pants off." She loosens her belt and unzips her pants and I put my hand on her hands, "Baby stop, I was just kidding."

She looks at me and then grabs my head and pulls me to her and whispers in my ear as she licks it, "Do you understand my level of commitment to you?"

I nod my head yes as I reach down and slowly and quietly zip her pants up. Kaye whispers, "My mother is less than a foot from us and I would do it right here, right now."

She continues licking my ear as I say, "I know, and I'm sorry. I just like to test my power sometimes."

Our parents talk in front of us about the businesses and what they will do and need to do. I watch them and listen as Kaye has turned into a cat and gives me a tongue bath. "Kaye, how do you feel about our fathers working together?"

She looks up at them, "I think it is great, they have similar interest and they both love building things."

"Do you think it will cause problems for us?"

"I don't think so? I hope not!"

I look at them, and then at her and say, "You're right it will be fine."

We start kissing and I drift into her mind. *Wow! This girl loves you more than I could have imagined. You are welcome by the way.* Kaye and I continue talking and I rub her temples and say, "Let's try a trick."

"Ok what?"

"I am going to try and talk to you without using my mouth."

Can you hear me?

She looks at me and says, "Do that again!"

Our moms turn around and look at us. *Only if you will calm down. We can't let anyone know we can do this or they will lock us up and throw away the key.* She puts her head on my chest and I rub her head. *Honey if you can hear me nod your pretty little head.* She nods yes and starts caressing my chest. *Would you like to hear a story of today's game or the slave auction and yesterday's events?* She thinks for a moment and then says, "The latter! That is so cool!" Our moms turn around again and her mom says, "Yes Dear?"

"Nothing I was just talking to Tommy. Can you hear him?"

"No Dear, just you."

Smiling at her mom, "I'm going to sleep. You know how I am about driving in the rain."

Our moms go back to their sewing and fabric conversation. I continue rubbing Kaye's head and I whisper to her, "You really going to sleep?"

"You tell me the story, now Slave." *Yes Dear, here we go, welcome to your journey inside my head. One time in an enchanted land far away I kicked your butt!* She giggles and I now tell the real story from my prospective.

You are getting better with these public appearances aren't you? I really wasn't given a lot of options. I have kind of been thrown to the wolves and it has been eat or be eaten. I sit on stage waiting for the bidding to start on me. As I wait I wonder why my name has not been called yet all of the sophomores on the football team have been bid on and half of the juniors as well. Maybe because the four horsemen made me sit with them, they have made me a silent partner in their little group. I sense some jealousy from friends my age, but that is natural. I try to keep the whole thing under control but that is impossible. I can't please everyone all the time.

The guys before me have made very little money during the auction. Chris went for ten bucks and a couple of the other guys went for as low as five. I look at my friend Chappy and wonder what he will go for? I listen to the auction and hear our first big bid. This guy is what girls like to look at and he has a nice car. A bid comes from the back of the auditorium, where the seniors are sitting for $27.50. The crowd is really starting to get into it and have a better understanding of what is going on. The auctioneer yells, "Going once, twice, and sold for $27.50" Everyone starts clapping as the new slave walks to his new master.

"Our next slave for auction is our defensive safety and wide receiver, Tommy Dunn!" The crowd goes wild as I move to the front of the stage. It is a challenge due to the mock chains and cuffs that they have shackled us in. I stand there in my number thirteen jersey hoping no one offers too little for me, or my worse fear, nobody wanting me at all. That fear goes away pretty fast when my sister stands up and says, "Five dollars and thirteen cents!" That got a laugh from the crowd. Then a small voice from the elementary side of the room says, "Eight dollars!" I look over as everyone cheers for the little girl that might have been in the fifth or sixth grade.

The bidding continues to increase and we are now up to thirty-seven dollars. I am happy and ready for this to end, and Kaye says, "I'll give you two dollars for him!" The auctioneer says, "Ma'am the bid is at forty!" Everyone around her is chuckling and she says, "But I know what he is worth, we are getting robbed here!" The crowd erupts with laughter and when they calm down she says, "I'll give you forty-five dollars and thirteen cents, since it is for a good cause." I look at her and mouth the words to her, I will get you. Kaye sits down and winks at me and blows a kiss. This activity awoke the rich girls and you can see them pooling their money together. It turns into a bidding war between Kaye, the cheerleading squad, and the rich girls. My thinking turns to what are the other girls doing? I know they don't want to rape me, but a guy can hope. *They're trying to piss off Kaye and get more money for the auction at the same time.*

Kaye is starting to get aggravated and decides to end this game and says, "$125"

There is a hush over the crowd and no other bids are given. The auctioneer says, "Going once . . ."

"$130," Comes from the back of the room. Everyone turns and sees my sister holding up her hand.

"Kaye holds up her hand "$131.13!"

My sister does not say a word. The auctioneer says, "Going once, twice . . . sold for $131.13!"

The crowd starts cheering as I walk down to Kaye and she grabs my chains and pulls me along. We get to the table where the money has to be paid and Kaye sets the money on the table and the teachers look shocked that she actually has the money. They thank her for her donation as they takeoff the pretend chains and cuffs from me.

Kaye and I start to walk away when the Principal ask to see us in the hallway. As we walk out Kaye and I look at each other like what could this be about? He stops in the hallway and says, "That was quite the show in there. Where did you get that much money young lady?"

"I am working for Tommy's mom at the mall. Why?"

"Your parents missed their last month's school tuition payment and we were wondering since we haven't heard from them what kind of arrangements they were planning to make?"

Kaye and I look bewildered at each other and Kaye says, "I had no idea. Would you like me to get my money back and pay some of it?"

"No Dear, please tell them to contact us or send payment by you or your sister."

The Principal opens the door to the auditorium and motions for us to enter. We walk in and sit with our classmates. *He stole the thunder from our fun didn't he?* As I sit next to Kaye we both cross our arms across our chest like pouting children. Not that we were pouting, it was just an easy way for us to conceal the fact that we were actually holding hands under our arms. I lean over to her as the bidding on Chappy gets loud, "Don't worry Honey, I'll take care of it for you." She smiles at me and says nothing. Chappy goes for seventy-five dollars and Kaye says to me, "You going to do that the rest of my life?"

I clap for Chappy and say to her, "If you play by my rules, yes I will!"

With tears in her eyes she says, "You gonna let me see these rules, or are you just going to make them up as we go?"

We cheer for Scott, as he is the last slave on stage and I say to Kaye, "Both! Because I love you."

Friday morning and school is a joke due to all the activities going on today in preparation of The State Championship. I don't have to attend classes today due to my slavery. I was bought by Kaye, meaning I will be in her classes for the day, most are mine anyway. In class, if Kaye is called on I have to give the answer. We have some fun with the situation but try and keep it civil, since slavery was a cruel stupid issue anyway. I can't imagine living in those times. I would not want to be a slave, own a slave, or even sell a slave. *Wonder what level of hell you go to for that? Never mind you don't want to know! Humans are funny animals aren't they?*

I carry Kaye's books to class and treat her like royalty.

We get to her locker and I say, "Kaye Honey!"

"Yes my Slave?"

"Remember those rules we were talking about?"

She looks around, "Yes, what about them? What did I do wrong?"

I look at her sternly and in a muffled voice I say, "Look, it is not always about you!"

I watch some seniors walk by and say, "You know the way I am treating you today?"

"Yes, am I being to mean?"

"No Honey, please hear me out and please listen to me!"

Kaye looks at me humbly as I say, "What I was trying to say is, the way I am treating you today is how I want to treat you the rest of my life. I want to love and honor you and respect you. Not to grovel at your feet, but to look up to you. I want you to feel the same way for me."

She looks at me and then smiles as she says, "I do feel that way for you. I just don't show it, because I don't want you to get a big head or take advantage of me."

The bell rings, "We are late let's go. Come on Slave, let's go."

We walk fast to our next class and due to today's activities it was not noticed that we are late. We walk in and the four horsemen are doing a cheer routine mocking the cheerleaders. Something their masters, the cheerleaders put them up to. They motion for me to join them. I don't want to, but Kaye waves me in that direction. My girl loves a good laugh, and we making fools of ourselves will give her that. I go up to join them and help make us look stupid. The class laughs and cheers as we finish. The teacher motions that we have done enough damage and that it is time for us to go. As we are led out the door I tell Kaye I will be right back. "Come on Tommy, we have to hit one more class and we are done."

We walk into my sister's senior Economics class. We do our cheer, a show that our cheerleaders normally do for us. As we finish the seniors stand and clap for us and my sister gives me a hug, "That's my baby brother right there." The four horsemen thank me for my help and I leave the room as they stay in their class.

I walk to the school office and see it is only the school secretary in the office. She notices me and says, "May I help you Dear?"

"Yes Ma'am, I have a delicate situation and I was hoping you could help me, discretely."

She smiles and looks around, "What is it Dear?"

"My friends Kaye and Kim Lewis' dad and my dad just started a business together. The money is kind of tight right now for them and I was wondering. Actually, my father was wondering if we could pay their school tuition for them and when they get back on their feet . . . well my dad and her dad will work out those details."

"Sure, that would be great. Are her parents going to know about this?"

"Her dad will, but not Kaye, her sister, or mom. My concern is if their mom tries to pay some of the bill you could give it to me until their father can explain it and he can save face with his girls."

The secretary says, "Yes, I could do that. How much are you paying today?"

"All of it, for the whole year."

She smiles at me and says, "That sounds good."

She grabs the file and tells me the amount and I pull out the money from my pocket and hand it to her. "Can't believe you walk around with that much money in your pocket?"

"I know. I'll feel more comfortable in a minute I need to pay ours also . . . Good thing this is a Christian School and my chances of getting mugged is not that great." She laughs as she takes in the money and gives me a paid receipt. After taking the money for mine and my sister, she writes up another receipt as she hands it to me she says, "Thank you! Anybody else you would like to pay for?"

"Sorry, no more cash."

Kaye sits up and says, "You paid our school bill?"

My father looks in the rearview mirror at us, "Is there a problem kids?"

I look in Kaye's eyes and say to my father, "No Sir, no problem we're good, just talking."

I hold her face with a hand on each cheek and say, "Kaye, that was one of the things we talked about that you need to learn to control. If you're going to be with me for life you are going to be shocked a lot. You have to learn to control your outburst a lot better."

Kaye looks around the car and then back at me, "Sorry Honey, I will try to work on it."

"Hey Dad, you know we were talking about going to the Bahamas the day after Christmas?"

"Yes Son, I remember that discussion."

I wait for more from him and nothing ever comes so I say, "And . . ."

He laughs and says, "It will have to be your Christmas present."

"No Sir!"

He looks at me in the mirror, "What?"

"No, for my present I want the Lewis' to go with us! Please!"

My dad looks to his new friend Bob and says, "What do you say Bob a couple of days in the Bahamas after Christmas? New Year's day in the Bahamas?"

He looks to his wife and says, "What do you think Honey?"

Kaye's mom says, "Sounds great to me, but we can't really afford it right now."

I excitedly say, "My sister found a great travel package and it will be our gift from our family to yours. It is a larger discount the more people we have, so we need you to go."

Kaye waits anxiously and is gripping my leg really tight while hoping they say yes. Her parent's smile at each other and her dad then says to my dad, "Well, since you are my new boss, I guess it will be fine. Can I have that week off?"

They chuckle at the joke and my dad says, "Sounds like a good idea to me."

Kaye screams in happiness and hugs me.

My dad says to Bob, "Hey, we are partners and we are both the boss of the plumbing company."

Our dads start talking about their company and our moms return to their conversation as well. Kaye starts kissing me and then sucks on my neck.

Her mom watches her and smacks her on the butt, "Kaye calm down!"

"Sorry Mom!"

Kaye looks at me and says softly, "Can I lose my virginity in the Bahamas?"

I look at her, "Not this trip. In about ten years we will take care of that for you."

"I'll be twenty-five? I'll be an old maid and you had better had married me by then."

I laugh and she joins in.

Kaye kisses me and then says, "So what do we tell my parents about the money for the school?"

I look at them and then back at Kaye, "How do they normally make the school payments?"

"They give me or my sister the cash or a check each month."

"Cash is better; you and your sister could just split that. Checks you will just have to misplace or tear up. The problem there is your parents will notice the checks haven't been cashed and question it. But that will actually give us a couple of months."

Kaye says, "You don't want us to pay you back?"

"No! They already paid me by giving me you."

Kaye starts taking off her pants again, "Kaye, stop playing!"

She smiles at me, "I'm not playing!"

She buttons her pants back, "But you really do want to have sex with me someday, right?"

"Girl, once I do, it is going to be hard to get me to stop. I will be like one of those Ford engines that need a tune up. You shut the car off and the engine tries to keep running."

She laughs and says, "Well, I'm waiting on you whenever you want to!"

We think for a moment and Kaye says, "We could say we won a scholarship?"

I point at her, "That's it! We can make up a fake scholarship! This year you guys already won it. I could give one away every year. I will talk to Coach Bolton I think he will help with the teacher side. I will explain to him the situation this year and let the teachers pick a needy family for next year and we can say it is from a nearby church that wishes to remain anonymous."

She smiles, "It could work."

"It will work!"

She kisses me and her mom says to my mom, "Think we need to separate those two?"

My mom looks back at us as we stop kissing, "I think they are ok, they have good restraint for kids their age."

They go back to their conversation. Kaye lays her head in my lap, "Finish your story, I will shut up." Before I can add a smart comment she points at me, "Don't say it!" I chuckle and think. *Ok back to the story.*

Later that afternoon I go to football practice. You watch me as if you are my slave instead of the way it was supposed to be. "Hey you're my slave!"

I look down at her, "Am I telling this story or are you?"

She puts her hand to her lips and makes a zipping motion across her lips. I smile at her and just as I start again she does the motion in reverse and says, "It is so cool how you do that!"

She then motions the zip again. I lay my hand on her chest and say, "Are you going to be a good girl? Or do I need to twist one of these real hard?" She gives a devilish smile and nods yes and places her hand on mine.

Ok, let's try this again! She smiles at me even bigger as she closes her eyes. *Nothing out of the ordinary happens at practice other than you staring at my butt the whole time.* She opens her eyes and says, "Not the whole time!" She remembers she was trying to be quiet and closes her eyes and mouth very quickly. *I love your pretty green eyes.* She opens her eyes and looks at me like an adoring child. *I look in your eyes and I can see your soul. So sweet, pure and innocent, are you sure you want to be with me?* Looking up at me she nods her head yes again. *Ok then ten or twenty years down the road don't blame me, you made a conscious decision Pal.* She is about to speak and I put my finger over her lips and shake my head no. *Not everything needs a response my dear.*

Now back to the story. I almost forgot to tell you about what happened in the lunchroom. After being at the school office I come back to class and listen to the rest of the lecture with you. When the bell rings we go to lunch. In the lunch line I am getting our food when the cheerleaders approach me. The head cheerleader says, "You had better be glad your girlfriend bought you in the auction, or we would have taken you and had unspeakable fun with you!" I wanted to say it's not too late. Take me, rape me; choose me, abuse me. But I am content with the woman I have. *Sex is fine. Without love it just leaves you wanting.* I smile at the girls and let them cut in front of me in line. I thought that might be the end of it as long as I just smiled and said nothing.

Later on the bus to the tournament they start again and this time you are not there to protect me. I do not want them not to like me, but at the same time I don't want them to like me too much. I won't cheat on a friend that will one day be much more to me. I decide to act like my friend Billy, interested but aloof. I watch him and he attracts girls like flies and shoo them away like a horse would in a pasture, gentle and like they do not even bother him. I sit with my buddy Chris for protection and he is a good companion and excellent repellent for women. He chases them so hard that they just run from him naturally. We talk about the task at hand as the girls continue picking at me for costing so much in the auction. They were curious what I did to cost that much and joked about wishing they could afford me.

As they go on about the auction, I flashback to ninth grade when I bought a cheerleader for five bucks. She was a gorgeous blond junior that had to hang out with a ninth grader for the whole day. I was in heaven and I am sure she felt she was in hell. She was very nice about the whole ordeal, she did my homework and carried my books it was great.

Two weeks later she died in a car accident. We had just gotten in the car in the parking lot at school. I see this awful car wreck in my mind. I tell my sister not to turn on the car, because I just saw this terrible accident in my head and am afraid it is about to happen to us. Like a premonition or something, she looks at me curiously. She tells me that I cannot see the future and starts the car and starts to pull out of the space and the traffic is not moving at all. I close my eyes and discover I had not seen the future but an accident happening. I saw my slave girl die in a car wreck.

I tell my sister her friend has just died in a car wreck just outside the school parking lot. A very big truck had crushed her car. My sister does not want to believe what I am saying and neither do I. As we see people running towards the intersection I tell my sister you don't want to go up there it is bad. She does not listen and she parks the car and goes anyway I follow because I know she is going to be upset when she sees the destruction. When I catch up to my sister she is already crying her eyes out. I hug my sister and try to comfort her as the police and medics show up. Most of the school is witnessing this terrible event and trying to figure out how it could have happened. A bunch of my sister's friends gather around us and hope and pray that by some chance everyone is ok. I know this is not the case. If I say anything about seeing it happen they will think I am crazy, so I will keep my mouth shut and try not to cry as I watch the workers try to find survivors.

Thinking of that day made me wonder what my voice told me about balance in the universe. Was that to be my fate as well, do I only have two weeks to live? Was it a premonition of things to come for me? As I sit there on the bus I begin to get nervous and wonder what I should do. My voice comes to me *don't worry about death. It happens to everyone sometime, you should just live everyday like it is your last. No one is promised tomorrow and you can't live in fear of the future or you won't live at all and you will already be dead.* A calm and understanding came over me then that I had never felt before. Then my conscience said to me. *I showed you that accident that day because I know she meant a lot to you. I was testing you that day to see how you handled things back then, and you handled it well. That is when I decided to give you the gift. And here we are today, riding a bus to the state championship.* Why did you wait a year to contact me? *I had been trying, but you would always ignore me like most humans do.*

I look down at Kaye and she appears to be asleep and I decide to keep going on with the details of the weekend in my head anyway.

Friday night we play one game and win with no problem. That night at the hotel I discover that half the team are freaks and are in a Christian School, because they need or have to be. Some are drinking booze, smoking, and crushing aspirin and snorting them through a dollar bill. They don't act like this in school, but get them away from mommy and daddy and they go crazy.

Saturday morning we prepare for our game that night. The coach has the fear that we might be getting cocky as he runs us through our plays and timing. He tries to calm us down but he is excited as well.

That night at the big game we have a tough battle on our hands, the toughest of the season. The game is a rematch with the Knights. We are tied with two minutes to go. We have the ball and are about to score. I had just gone into the game when the play started. I block my guy as Scott comes towards me. Another guy hits me and I go down with my defender on top of me. I lie on the ground and hear a snap and then a blood-curdling scream. And then several more screams as I roll over and see Scott on the ground next to me. He is holding his leg and wincing in pain. I stand up and look down the field as the opposing team scores. I walk over to Scott and see the bone sticking out of the skin and his pads. I have to look away to keep from vomiting. I attempt to help him as the coach comes running to him. As gentle as I can I remove his helmet. The coaches wrap towels around his leg as the rest of the four horsemen gather around him trying to help their fallen comrade. I back away to let them help and I watch to make sure they do not require any more assistance.

After getting him off the field we are pretty much done, finished, defeated. We worry about our friend as the ambulance takes him away and we try to regain our composure to finish the task at hand. The Knights miss the field goal so we just need to score and kick the field goal to win, with a minute and thirty seconds to go.

We get a pep talk from the coach and go and attempt to win the game. Chris takes the kickoff and returns the ball to the thirty-yard line and we only have a minute twenty left to score. We do a quick toss to me and I get about ten yards and run out of bounds to stop the clock. The next play Randy drops the ball on a pass play. Next play Chappy tries to run but gets only five yards and you can see the fear in his eyes as the guy that broke Scott's leg approaches him.

The clock continues to run as we set up for the next play. Chappy throws the ball to Randy again and he catches it and we get another first down, but the clock continues to run. The coach calls a timeout and we head to the sideline to discuss our next four plays.

We return to the field and I can still see Chappy is shaken up. "Relax Chappy, you're going to be fine! Hit me down the right side in the back of the end zone!" He nods his head in agreement. We go to the line, as Chappy yells hike the clock starts ticking again. I run my route and as I turn for the ball I notice it is in the air. I run and jump for it, but it is just out of my reach. I stretch as far as I can and the ball hits the goal post and bounces right into the hands of the defender behind me. My body hits the ground and I try to change the direction I was running so I can tackle the guy. He falls to the ground and curls up in a ball. We all watch in shock knowing there is now no possible way for us to win or go to the Nationals now. And just like that our season ends. The opposing team and fans go crazy in joy at their accomplishment and their revenge from losing to us earlier in the season. That was the only interception that Chappy had thrown for the year. He should still be able to go to Carolina, I hope. My bad bog from the first game of the season approaches me, "Remember me?"

I smile at him, "Sure I do. I hope there are no hard feelings?"

He laughs and says, "Only when I try to speak." He winks at me and slaps my back, "Good game out there. Knew I'd get even with you somehow."

"So, we are even? Good to know. Congratulations, nice game. Good luck at Nationals." Bad dog walks away and I shake my head in disbelief. Guess it could've been worse; he could've tried to bite my tongue off.

As we pass the city limits sign I look at my Kaye lying in my lap fast asleep. I tap her mom on the shoulder, "What is the best way to wake her up?"

"By not doing it."

She laughs at her own joke and I smile. She touches Kaye's head and says, "Honey, it is time to wake up."

Kaye sits up and says, "I'm up!"

She looks around trying to realize where she is. She sees me and puts her arms around my neck and says softly, "Hey you!"

I kiss her cheek, "Hey you."

She says, "That was a real sad story about the cheerleader. I really liked hearing your side of the game though that was interesting. I felt like I was there."

"Um Honey, you were there? I thought you were asleep during those stories."

"I think I was! It was weird."

We pull into Kaye's driveway. I look down the street, "I just thought of something. When we finish our new house we will only be a half a mile away from each other."

Kaye says, "You just realized that? I have already walked over there twice to see how long it takes to walk it."

I look at her and act retarded, "Hey, no picking on the slow kids, we can't help it!"

The parents laugh at us as Kaye waves bye to me and says, "See you tomorrow, Slave."

We all say our goodbyes and I shut the suburban door as I sit upfront.

My dad backs out of the driveway and I say, "Dad, what did Mr. Johnson say about Chappy?"

Dad looks at me, "Looks like he will be offered a seventy-five percent scholarship not a full ride, so I guess we will owe some money for that stuff his dad did."

I look out the side window of the car, "His dad said if we get him in, not a full ride scholarship. But at least we should get a discount, right?"

"I hope so, but I am not going to count on it."

"Let's ride by the storage lot, please."

My dad says, "It's dark and you won't be able to see anything."

"I just want to see if we have any standing water after that rain we had."

My dad raises his eyebrow, "Good point."

We drive over and pull up to the gate. We look around and everything looks good as my dad says, "I don't have the keys on me."

We look around and I say, "How many units?"

My dad smiles as he backs away from the gate, "We got six hundred and fifty here and five hundred at our other location. This one has more parking area than the other as well. That is 1150 units; if we can get them all full then that is a nice chunk of change every month."

My dad gives me the prices per units on the different sizes and I do the math. I look at him, "Dad that is a profit of around eighty thousand per month very close to a million per year. When do we open for business?"

He laughs and says, "I know, but I am only figuring on thirty to fifty thousand per month and we open next week."

"Still that is awesome! Why didn't we do this years ago?"

My mom leans forward, "Because you didn't give him the idea until this year."

My dad says, "Thanks for my new truck by the way! I'm sorry you guys lost, but it was a great game you guys just caught a bad break."

"Unfortunately Scott did."

Mom says as we pull in our driveway, "I'll send him a gift basket tomorrow!"

"Thanks Mom! That will be nice."

"Where is he going to college?"

I step out of the vehicle and say, "He's not, he is joining the Marines the last time I heard anything."

My sister and Mike come out the back door and she says to me, "Hey loser!"

She hugs me and I know she is joking. She is happy because her volleyball squad won state and now might get more recognition since the mighty football team went down in flames.

My mom yells at her, "That is not nice or called for young lady!"

I look at my sister and Mike puts his hand out for me to shake. As I take his hand he says, "Nice job out there Buddy I thought you were going to pull it out there at the end. Tough break!"

I look at the two of them, "Thanks Mike. Next year I will be in charge and I will take us to Nationals I promise."

My sister says, "Good luck with that baby brother. I will be at Carolina!"

She holds up a letter as we walk in the house. She says, "It came this weekend while we were gone." Mom takes the letter and starts reading it, "A twenty-five percent scholarship for volleyball! That is great Sweetie!" Mom and Roxanne hug, and then my dad joins the hug with them.

Roxanne walks over to me and hugs me and whispers in my ear, "Did you have anything to do with this?"

I look at her and shake my head no, "I mentioned you played and wanted to go to Carolina to Mr. Johnson, but that was it."

She realizes she did it on her own merits and is now even happier. She looks at mom and dad and says, "Can you guys handle paying the rest?"

I wink at my dad and he says, "I don't know? That pageant you are supposed to be in . . . how much does that pay?"

Roxanne looks back at me snickering and she says, "You guys are bad!"

She hits my arm as I say, "Now who's the loser baby!"

Dad hugs her and says, "Of course we will take care of it. Do you think you are smart enough for that school?"

He starts laughing and she says, "You guys are mean!"

I pat her on the back as I walk out of the kitchen, "Congrats Sis!"

Mike announces he is going home and hugs my sister and leaves. Dad follows me down the hall and says, "You really did nothing for her on that scholarship?"

"No Sir, like I said and that was it, goodnight Pop!"

That is mighty big of you not trying to take credit for your sister's scholarship. You might be a bigger man than I had hoped you would be. Goodnight.

Chapter 15

Christmas morning one of the happiest times of the year, the family is together and everyone is happy. It would be better if we could have been in the new house but a couple more weeks won't be too bad. I know but it would be better if it could have been this year. I hear my parents come in the back door and my sister saying, "Where have you guys been?" I sit up in bed and listen to my sister.

She looks in the backyard at the misty foggy morning with no snow on the ground and sees her new Mustang with a big ribbon and bow on it. She screams and hugs mom and dad and then she runs in my room and jumps on my bed, "Get your lazy butt up and look at my new car!"

"That's not yours it's mine!"

"Shut-up before I kiss your entire face! You are not even old enough to drive!"

"Ok, I'll shut-up just get off me you bully!"

Roxanne runs to her room and starts getting dressed and says, "Let's go for a ride!"

I stand up and put on some jeans. My sister comes back in my room, "Come on let's go!"

She runs down the hall to the kitchen and asks for the keys. My dad plays along and says, "Honey, I am not giving you the keys to your brother's car."

She does a pouting face and I walk in the kitchen as my dad says, "But maybe Honey, if you open some of your presents you might find something just as good."

I smile and try not to laugh and mom starts cooking breakfast. Roxanne looks around at each of us and says, "It is really not mine?"

Mom joins in, "Go open your presents I got you something just as good as a smelly old car."

As we enter the living room, I flashback to my sisters thirteenth birthday. We had not said happy birthday to her all day and made no big deal over her at all. That night before we gave her cake and her presents, she was sitting in the living room crying. We come in and ask, what is wrong and she says, "I can't believe you forgot my birthday?" She is sitting right beside her presents we had sat under the living room coffee table. We bring out the cake that was on top of the fridge and sing Happy Birthday to her. This Christmas is a lot like that birthday.

We open presents as mom opens something and then returns to the kitchen to flip bacon and check on biscuits. I get the box that should have my sister's keys to her new car and toss it to her, "This got in my pile of gifts somehow!" She looks like she had forgotten about the car and opens the box. She opens it and it is a key ring with a Mustang emblem on it, but no key attached. She holds it up and says, "Thanks a lot!" My parents look confused and say, "Is that all that was in there?" She looks again and says yes. I point at the Christmas tree as my dad is giving me the evil eye. He looks and sees the key hanging less than a foot from my sister's head.

My dad puts a hand on her shoulder, "Honey sometimes if we look hard enough we might see the thing we really want in life."

She looks sad and dad says, "Sometimes dear you just need to turn your head to the right and look about a foot away from you."

She turns her head and sees the keys hanging on the tree. My parents say, "Merry Christmas Sweetie!" She picks up the keys and says, "Thank you!"

And then she looks in my direction like she had just beaten me in a race and tackles me and starts hitting me in the gut and back. "You are not funny!" She screams repeatedly as she hits me.

My parents and I laugh and I protect my head with my arms and say, "Ok let's go for a ride!"

We take the bow off of her car and my dad steps out and says, "Get in the back Son. I'm going also."

We ride around the block and my dad says, "Be careful Sweetie, this car has more power than the one you use to have."

"What do you mean?"

"Your old Mustang was a six cylinder engine and this one has eight. So when you step on the gas you will have more power."

She stops the car and says, "Oh yeah!"

She stomps on the gas and the tires spin and she makes a cloud of smoke behind us.

I look at her and say, "Now that was cool Sis!"

She smiles, "Whoever I have to blame for this car, thank you very much!"

I say, "Santa Clause!"

She chuckles as dad and I smile at each other and he says, "Let's get home and eat some breakfast."

My sister spins the tires again and races toward the house.

At breakfast I explain to mom and dad about my sister and my fake ID's and how we plan to use them for gambling. My conscience explains to them how to gamble and how not to gamble, when to hold 'em and when to fold 'em type gambling. I get more excited over the trip than over Christmas. I got a new dirt bike motorcycle, but it is too cold to ride it. My sister tells us about the rooms for the Lewis' and us in the Bahamas.

My parent's look at each other and my dad says, "I trust both you kids, but since you both want your friends there I think we need to have the talk."

We both grunt and I say, "No Dad, we already had, the talk!"

"Not this one!"

My sister and I listen intently to him, "First of all we are not going down there to baby sit you and your friends. Secondly if we pretend not to know you then keep walking. Third of all we are going to have a goodtime and I don't want to worry about you sneaking off and getting pregnant. Are we clear?"

We look at each other and both say, "Yes Sir!"

My dad and I go in the backyard and play with my dirt bike and he tells me how to clean it when I'm done. As we look at the bike I explain how roulette is played and explain the odds to him. We crank the bike and my dad rides it around to check it out as he calls it. He finally brings it back to me and I ride it around the yard and then down the street and back. Some of the neighborhood kids come out and watch me ride by. I begin getting cold and call it quits.

I walk in and mom says, "Kaye called and wants you to call when you get back in."

I am not a dog on a leash. The phone rings and I think if that is her calling I will kick her butt next time I see her.

"Hello!" as I listen to the caller I think, good she is not getting too controlling, "Merry Christmas Aunt Nette. Sure just come on over, we will see you in a bit."

"Mom Aunt Nette is on the way over."

"Honey you are grown now you really need to try and call her Aunt Annette."

"Sorry Mom. I can't and won't do it. It's too hard. I got away with the Aunt Nette thing for too long, so now she is stuck with it. I'm going to take a shower. I'll be out in a minute if Kaye calls back, but she better not."

"Are you mad at her?"

"No Ma'am, but I will be if she calls back."

I get out of the shower and get dressed just as my cousins and aunt walk in the house. They see all our new stuff and brag on the stuff they got as well. I talk with them a few minutes and then excuse myself to call Kaye back. I dial her and my little cousin walks in my room as I say to Kaye, "Merry Christmas Babe!"

My cousin being the kid he is says, "Oh, you have a girlfriend!" I ignore him and continue talking with Kaye.

We talk for a while and I try to entertain my 10-year-old cousin at the same time. "I will see you tomorrow glad you got all the stuff you wanted, bye girl."

As I hang up the phone my cousin breaks my model airplane, "Merry Christmas Buddy, you can have that now!"

He looks at it and says, "I don't want it. It is broken."

"Let's get out of my room before everything is."

We walk in the living room and talk about our upcoming trip.

My dad says, "I just asked your uncle to work for mine and Mr. Lewis' company Son. What do you think?"

"I look at my father's expression and say, "That sounds great."

"I was just telling your dad the plumbing company I work for is not doing anything right now and I only get paid when I work."

I look at my dad and say, "The plumbing on the new house is finished isn't it?"

Dad nods in agreement, "Finished it last week and after New Year we get the carpet and tile floors down we can move in."

My uncle asks, "What are you going to do with this house?"

My dad looks over at him, "We are going to rent it and if that is too much of a hassle we are going to sell it."

"Hey Dad, we still need some help at the Attic storage."

My dad looks at my uncle, "We need someone to rent storage sheds and watch the place for us if you would like to do that until we get some plumbing work?"

"I could do that for you until your plumbing company gets busier."

My dad says, "Great!"

Mom calls me from the kitchen, "Tommy could you come in here please?"

I get off the couch and step into the kitchen, "Give me a hundred bucks Honey!"

I reach in my pocket and pullout two hundred and my mom takes both and kisses me on the cheek, "Thanks Honey!"

She places the two bills in a card and then slides it in an envelope.

We walk back into the living room and my mom hands her sister the envelope, "Merry Christmas Sis!" They hug and she thanks my mom without even opening it, "So how are your shops doing at the mall?" My mom sits back down in her favorite chair and says, "Good! We actually made a profit last month and we should be good for this month also."

She looks at me, "How is Tommy's Deli doing?"

"I should have been named Tony and it would be doing better!"

They all laugh and I say, "Everyone eats and we have been profitable since we opened. I've got some good people working there."

My aunt looks at me, "You need anymore?"

I look at my mom and then back at her, "I thought you were going to help mom at the dress shop?"

My mom looks over at her, "Yeah wouldn't you rather work with me a couple nights a week?"

"Why not both. Maybe a couple of nights and every other weekend or something like that."

I look at mom and say, "I could use her on the weekends no problem."

My mom says, "Then I could use her during the week, especially this coming spring, with all the proms and weddings coming up."

My sister says from the back of the house, ". . . and pageants!" Everyone laughs at my sister.

My uncle says to my dad, "So, how many of those units you have rented out so far?"

My dad looks at me and says, "One location is half full and the other is about seventy-five percent full." He nods at my dad, "After only two months, that's not bad!"

"No, it isn't. My son had a good idea on that one." I smile as they all turn to me.

My aunt looks at me and says, "So what are your future plans there Buddy? Are you going off to college also or you just going to take over the family business?"

"Both! I hope to go to Carolina and then let my parents retire!"

"My aunt looks at my mom, "You going to retire in six years Sis?"

"If my son finds someone to run my shop I sure will!" They laugh and I hear the phone ring once and that was all.

My sister yells, "Mom can Tommy and I go to the Lewis' house for a while?"

"For an hour or two and then you need to come home and pack we leave early tomorrow."

I look at my mom, "I'm packed Mom just so you know. Aunt Nette can you work the Deli tomorrow and this weekend?"

"Sure I'd love to, thanks."

"No. Thank you, I only have one guy for tomorrow and they could use you with all those people returning gifts tomorrow."

My sister walks in the room with my cousin and says, "You ready Bro?"

"Let me get some shoes on and make a quick call." As I stand up my aunt hugs me, "Thank you Sweetie."

"Sure no problem, thank you!"

I go in my room and dial the phone, "Johnny, this is Tommy, Merry Christmas! I am sending you help tomorrow. She will be there at eleven tomorrow. If you have any questions call me later today. I will be leaving town tomorrow morning. See ya!"

I hang up the phone, "I hate answering machines."

I walk towards the kitchen and say into the living room, "Aunt Nette, they will be expecting you at eleven tomorrow. Bye y'all!" Roxanne and I walk out the door and get in her new car.

My sister says, "That was nice of you Bro."

I chuckle and look at my sister, "It actually worked to my advantage I had forgotten Johnny said he needed some help during Christmas break. I guess in my mind I planned to be there so I just didn't think about it."

She stomps on the gas pedal and says, "It worked out good for everybody then didn't it?"

You are welcome Pal! Thank you my friend, now keep my sister from killing me.

We arrive at Kaye's house and Kim and Kaye run out of the house, I open the door and they jump in the backseat. My sister starts the girl talk with them and Kaye rubs my head, so I just ignore them and enjoy the Christmas music on the radio.

"Roxanne, I love your car! You all packed Tommy?"

I look at my girlfriend's sister, "Yes Kim, are you?"

"No, I like to wait until the last moment. Kaye is ready to go."

I smile and say, "That's why she is my girl!"

She smiles and says, "Where are we staying down there?"

My sister stops for a red light and says, "The Bahamas Princess Hotel and Casino! My brother is giving me a thousand dollars to gamble with and hopefully I can double it."

Kaye taps my head, "You going to give me some to gamble with rich guy?"

Kim says, "Me too!"

I look in the backseat, "When did I become responsible for you girls?"

Kaye says, "In about two to four years I hope!"

"Kaye you are already gambling by dating me."

The girl's chuckle and I notice Kim sitting back shyly. "Kim, how old are you?"

"Old enough to know better, but not do better."

The girls laugh again and then she answers, "I just turned eighteen a month ago."

"Ok, I will make a deal with you. You are old enough to drink and gamble down there. I will give you one hundred, and whatever you win over that amount you have to split with me."

She sits up and says, "I like that deal! What if I lose?"

I give her a devilish smile, "Then we will have to take it out in trade."

Kaye slaps my head, "You won't sleep with me, but you will sleep with my sister?"

My sister looks at us in shock and I say, "But she is of age!"

My sister and Kim start laughing as I try to calm Kaye down, "Honey I was just playing! I won't sleep with her again!"

The two older girls laugh harder and louder at this and Kaye starts hitting me like a punching bag. *That will calm her down for a while. She was going to try and sleep with you on this trip, but I think you fixed that.*

Kaye calms down as we drive to my family's new house. We go in and look around the two story four bedroom, five and a half bath house and it is looking really good. The pool area is very nice. The back yard is nothing but a huge deck, and a pool with a waterfall at one end and a Jacuzzi at the other. A barbeque stone grill, and a cast iron and glass patio table with umbrella is against the back wall. I show them the two car garage with an exercise room above it. We look around inside the house and show off the house to our friends.

Kim looks to my sister, "When are you guys going to be able to move in?"

"The week after we get back from our trip."

"You guys excited?"

I look at my sister and smile as she says, "I think grateful is a better word! We may not deserve it but we are sure going to enjoy it."

My sister hugs me and whispers to me, "Wish you could have pulled this off two years ago!"

I chuckle, "Me too!"

We get back in the car and Kaye and I jump in the backseat. She tries to still play like she is mad at me but can't be. She starts kissing my neck and nibbling my ear and she says, "I really like your cologne!"

"Really, my girlfriend must also, because she gave it to me for Christmas." She bites my neck hard enough to get my attention but not enough to hurt.

I start laughing and she says, "Yes she does!"

I tickle her and she releases me. As we pull into their driveway a phone rings. My sister looks around, "Did dad leave his car phone in here?"

"No Sis, that was a present from dad, I guess he forgot to mention it."

She answers her new car phone very excitedly, "Hello!"

"Yes Mom, we are on the way home in about ten minutes . . . yes Ma'am. Bye!"

She looks at us, "We have to go home so we can only stay for a few minutes."

We walk in the house, "Merry Christmas everyone!"

I hand Kaye's dad an envelope, "This is from my dad and he says you are not to save a dime of this. It is to be used in the Bahamas gambling or having fun. If you use it or lose it, it is no consequence as long as you and your girls have a good time. I think that is the way he said it. Anyway it is a bonus for your help. Thank you for your hard work!" I hug him and then Kaye's mom, I grab a handful of cashews from a bowl on the counter. I sit at the bar as her dad looks in the envelope and says, "Thank you very much. Merry Christmas." I nod to him as Kaye starts showing me the gifts she received for Christmas. I try to pretend to be caring and enthusiastic as I can. *Getting sick yet? This is the way she feels over things that matter to you Bud, so suck it up, because she is willing for you.* I decide to spice it up as a gay friend. "Girl that is going to look so fabulous with that beige skirt I bought you, um huh! You got to work it girl, accessorize that outfit!" Her family and my sister start laughing at my antics.

I eat another cashew and say, "It is all very nice! I was just playing. We have to go we will see you here at 6 am."

Her dad says, "You're going to pick us up?"

"Yes Sir, at six. Pack one bag for each of you and a carry on."

"We have never done this before what do we need to pack? For cold, warm, or hot weather?"

"If I were you and this is the way I do it. Put your toiletries and a change of clothes in your carry on. I am taking one suit if we need a fancy night out and the rest beach clothes. What we don't have we can buy there. The weather will be warm with cool evenings."

They look fine by my explanation and I head toward the door, "See you in the morning."

Kaye follows me out and grabs the shirttail of my sweater and she says, "Incase I forget to say it, thank you and I love you!"

I hug her and kiss her, "I know Honey, but you need to get use to this, I am going to do this for you the rest of your life if you trust me and listen to me." She nods in agreement and kisses me.

I say as we stop kissing, "Hey give me your driving permit just for tonight." She runs in and grabs her purse. She digs and then hands it to me. *Total trust she is getting good!*

"Now get your narrow butt back in the house before you get sick!"

I walk to the car and get in. Roxanne looks at me, "She going to be eighteen also?" I nod yes to her question.

We pull out on the main highway and a corvette pulls up next to us and begins to taunt my sister and looking to race. We have to stop for a red light and my sister plays along revving her Mustangs 5.0. *Man, I wish you were driving this car!* "Sis you know how you like to spin the tires on this thing?"

"Yes!"

"Don't this time; get on it, but a bit easier. Don't let the tires break traction and you will get a huge jump on this guy. The light is about to change, get ready!"

She watches the stoplight and puts the car in first gear. The light changes and the corvettes wheels scream and smoke billows from the tires. My sister presses on the accelerator just like I instructed and pulls away from the stoplight like a pro as the corvette spins it wheels and sits in one spot. My sister pulls two car lengths ahead of the guy in the corvette. He starts to creep up on us as she slams her shifter into fifth gear. A rookie mistake, but just at the right time. *Stop! There is a cop up here a half a mile away!* I lean over and say, "Cop in front of us slow down fast!" She drops the car into third gear and presses firmly on the brake. The corvette flashes past us at what had to be in excess of a hundred miles per hour, and showed no sign of slowing down. My sister gets the cars speed to forty-five and the cop pulls out in front of us to chase the corvette.

As the cop turns on the blue light my sister looks at me and says, "Good call, baby brother on the cop thing!" As she turns into our neighborhood we can just barely see the police and the corvette on the side of the road.

"I'd say I won. What do you think?"

"I would have to agree! That was an excellent takeoff on the start by the way. You are a bit like your dad there Sis!" She smiles and pulls into the driveway.

"Should we tell mom and dad about the race?"

"Not if you want to keep your car. That is an over dinner story in the Bahamas when there is a crowd around for a buffer for you."

She smiles and says, "You are right."

She kisses my cheek, "Thanks for everything Baby Bro!"

We spend the evening with just the four of us telling stories about life and our hopes and dreams. My dad tells a story about racing and my sister can't resist telling the corvette story. I chuckle as she is told she can't drive for one week. When we head to bed I say to her, "Good thing we are going to be gone for a week eh?" She smiles and goes to bed.

Once I get in bed my dad comes in my room and lies down beside me. This will be the first time any of us have been outside the country. He asks how to handle different situations and how much to tip and double-checks with me on gambling procedures. My mom walks in and sits on the end of my bed. I tell my dad how much we are going to win and no more. My father has always been a worrier especially about money, but I slowly see that anxiety lifting.

"You gave Bob that money right?"

"Yes Sir, it is going to be good, relax and enjoy it!" He kisses my forehead and says, "Good night Son." He walks out and my mom pats my foot and says, "Your plan seems to be working Honey! Keep up the good work, I love you!"

She stands up and walks to my head and hugs me and kisses my cheek. "Thanks Mom I love you too!" She stands over me in my dark room, "You and Kaye haven't had sex yet have you?"

"No Ma'am!"

"You have any plans for that on this trip?"

"No Ma'am. I think Kaye was planning something but I fixed that today. She will wait for a while before she tries anything. I am not going to try for a couple of years so don't worry."

My mom stands over me for a moment, "I trust you then, and I am not going to be worried about you the whole trip then."

"Thanks Mom, I won't let you down. Mom when we come home I want a beach house."

"Goodnight my boy!"

I watch my parents exit my room holding hands like teenagers still in love. *I told you I would fix them for you. Isn't that better than the screaming you use to have to fall asleep to?* I smile and look at the ceiling and listen to the clock radio playing Christmas songs and I think to myself. Much better, thanks for everything.

Chapter 16

"Good morning my Son, the car will be here in a half hour, go take a shower."

I jump out of bed and head to the bathroom as my sister walks out, "Good morning brother of mine."

"Stay off drugs Pal!"

I walk in and shut the door to the bathroom and turn on the shower. I look in the mirror, no need to shave with this baby face. I'm done in five minutes and return to my room to get dressed.

"Car! Mom, what car did you mean?"

I walk to the living room with my bags and look out the front door and see a stretch white limo sitting there, "Oh that car! Nice touch Sis!"

She walks by me, "You're welcome. This is going to be a fun trip!"

Mike maneuvers his car around the limo and parks in the backyard. I grab some bags and head to the car. I arrive at the car the same time as Mike and we greet each other in our normal fashion, handshake and half hug at the same time. I run towards the house, "Mom I'm hungry when do we eat?"

She has Tupperware containers with her homemade sausage biscuits and one with mixed fruit. "Right now if you want."

"Dad you need me to do anything?" He shakes his head no so I jump in the car with the food.

"Wow this is nice!"

I play with the radio and get some good music going as everyone else climbs in, "Sis, you did good! Is the whole trip going to be like this?"

"I sure hope so!"

We drive away and everyone waits as dad says a prayer for our safety and the food we are about to eat. We start eating and enjoying the moment and my dad looks at my sister and me, "You got the tickets right?"

"No Sir."

Dad is about to tell the driver to turn around when my sister says, "We don't need tickets."

Everyone looks confused and I say, "Then what airline are we on?"

"We are not. I rented a small jet. It was cheaper than 9 first class tickets and we can pick the time we want to travel."

My dad says, "Then why the hell are we up so early?"

We all laugh and she says, "For our check in time and it is what was suggested. Plus I knew we would all be up early and eager to go."

"I was just kidding Sweetie."

We pull up to the Lewis' house and I see their mouths drop when they see the limo as they come out of the door of their house. I hug Kaye and say, "Now how is this for sweet?"

"Not bad, but I am nervous I have never flown before."

"I haven't since I was a kid when my mom would take us to New York to see her family and friends up there. Here is your driving permit."

She takes it and says, "Why did you need it?"

"Look at your birthday!" She smiles and says, "You are bad!"

We get in the car and get comfortable and her family joins in eating biscuits and fruit with us."

We arrive at the airport and see the jet and the two pilots waiting for us. Everyone smiles in anticipation of our flight. The driver says, "Sit tight everyone while we load your luggage. We will come and get you when we are ready for you."

He steps out of the car and they load the plane and I say, "I feel like a rock star, but without the hangover." Everyone laughs at me and makes their little jokes.

The car door opens and the driver says, "This way please."

We step on the aircraft and I think to myself I want one of these. *Yeah me too, someday my friend we will!* I count the ten-first class seats and I ask if anyone has a preference to a seat and the pilot says, "I call the front seat!" and the copilot yells, "Shotgun!" Everyone laughs at the pilot's humor. Kaye and I sit next to each other, well across the isles from each other facing the rear of the plane. And our mothers sit in front of us facing forward towards Kaye and me.

Kaye leans over, "Your mom worried about us?"

"Yes yours?"

Kaye nods yes and I say, "Let's not make them worry on this trip. We will not sneak off; we will use this trip to gain their trust."

Kaye smiles and says, "Ok, but we will have some time just for the two of us, right?"

"Of course we will!"

The copilot explains the emergency procedures and asks for questions. I raise my hand and the copilot says, "No one. Are you sure?"

I look around as my hand is still in the air and he repeats, "No one at all?"

We start to chuckle and I just ask, "Can I fly the plane?" As soon as I said it I thought; may I, not can I.

He says, "Don't know if you can or not. You may be able to. Are you a licensed pilot?"

"Um, no I am only fifteen and to obtain a private pilot's license you must be sixteen by FAA regulation." He recognizes I have some aviation knowledge and decides to test me. "Tell you what Buddy, if you can answer some questions I might let you sit up front for a moment in flight." *Don't worry I got you!*

"Sure I will risk it to sit up front if only for a moment."

"Can you tell me the difference between IFR and VFR flight?"

"Sure it is two types of weather flying, the V signifies Visual Flight Reference and the I signifies Instrument Flight Reference." The families look impressed and so do the pilots.

"Very good, what are we right now?" I look out the window and find the tower and see the beacon rotating above the tower.

"I would have to say IFR."

He is surprised that I answered correctly, "Why do you say that?"

"From what I have read if the beacon is going during the daytime IFR conditions exist or either someone forgot to turn it off. It looks pretty cloudy to me, so I am guessing IFR."

He is impressed and says, "One last question, what makes an airplane fly?"

I am about to say lift over weight and thrust over drag when I think of the pilot's humor before. I look at the pilot and then the copilot and smile, "Money!"

The pilots laugh and walk to the cockpit. The copilot says, "I will come and get you in a bit and let you fly this bird Sir."

I smile as big as I think I ever had, "Thank you!"

We takeoff and the aircraft goes into the clouds and we can see nothing through the windows as the plane climbs. I am very excited to be in the air and I look at Kaye cringing in fear. My mother leans forward and touches my hand, "How did you know the answers to those questions?"

"I have been studying. I told you I want to start flying this spring."

"I didn't know you were serious!"

"Yeah and I am going to buy a plane and let the school rent it to pay for my lessons."

"You have this planned out don't you?"

We rise above the clouds and there is that big orange ball in the sky that we haven't seen for a couple of days. As I put on my sunglasses I reply, "Yes Ma'am I do."

I look out the window at the white fluffy clouds that we just came through and am amazed by the beauty of it all. I look over to my Kaye and she is nervously reading a book, she won't even look out the window.

I lean across the aisle, "Baby you ok?"

"I don't like flying!"

"Why? It is awesome and beautiful, just look out the window."

She looks and says; "I can see clouds from the ground."

"But it would take you hours to make this trip on the ground and water. We will be there in less than two hours."

"I just don't like it, it is not natural."

"Kaye I guess we are not going to be able to be together in the future then if you feel that strong about it. I am going to see the world and if you can't and don't want to fly we better call it quits before we start and we can still be friends."

"Are you serious? You would break up with me over something like flying?"

"More like your close mindedness. You are flying right now and yet still fear it. Remember the rules we discussed? Well this one is going to be a big one. I am going to be a pilot someday and my wife will be with me not at home wondering where I am."

"I will do this for you, but it will take me a while to get comfortable with it, but I love you and will do anything for you."

"I believe that now more than ever!"

I kiss Kaye and now think to myself. If I hadn't sworn to my mom I would not have sex with her this week, I would have to prove my love to her. Kaye looks out the window and I can see her comfort level increase. My dad points to the cockpit and I turn around and notice the cockpit door has opened. The copilot motions for me to come up; I release my seatbelt and walk to the cockpit. As I enter I see the view in front of the plane for the first time and am utterly amazed. I kneel down and the copilot says, "Any of those ladies available?" I look to the back and think for a moment I point to Kim and she waves at me, "That girl waving is the only unattached one here." The copilot says, "Take my seat I am going to go check on the passengers." He stands up and I sit in his seat. He walks to the back and checks to make sure everyone is ok and enjoying the flight.

I look at all the gauges and controls and switches and am about to get overwhelmed as the pilot says, "You don't need them all at the same time, but they all do something you need." He saw my eyes and knew what I was thinking. I touch nothing and I watch him as he gets a radio call. He points to the headset and motions for me to put it on my head. I do as the pilot request and the sound of the engines almost disappears. He smiles and says, "It makes it easier to talk and to hear the radios." He points to the radio stack and says, "Could you change that one to read 129.75?" I do and he says, "Jacksonville center 38 Alpha Juliet with you flight level 2-5-0."

He looks at me, "That is probably the worst part of the job, talking on those radios. When you planning to start your training?"

I look at him, "Just started."

He laughs, "I like you Buddy, you're funny and smart."

We look back at the copilot and he is talking to Kim. The captain explains the movement of the flight yoke and rudders and gauges to watch and what to expect from different movements of the airplane. My father walks to the cockpit and observes my lesson in the Gulf Stream aircraft. The captain says into the headset, "That your dad?"

I nod yes, "He ok with this?"

"Sure, he is all for it." We both look at him and he smiles and gives us a thumbs up signal. The captain introduces himself as Jerry and then goes back to our lesson and says, "Ok you ready?"

"Ready for what?"

"I am going to turn off the autopilot and you are going to fly."

"I have been ready for that since I sat down."

The pilot presses the button to shutoff the autopilot and I feel the controls and try to maintain the flight level and attitude he told me to maintain. "Make small corrections on the yoke or your need for correction will become larger and you will have a porpoise effect."

I fly the aircraft with small touches to the control as the pilot explains again. "If you correct too fast or too often your oscillations will become larger and larger and the airplane will be like a dolphin jumping out of the water in front of a boat."

"Gotcha, small corrections. How am I doing?"

He looks at the gauges and then out the window, "Looking real nice, just keep doing what you are doing." My father taps me on the shoulder, "Don't crash Boy!"

"Yes Sir, that is on my to do list. Not crashing." My dad returns to his seat and leaves us to our work.

The pilot chuckles and answers another radio call. When he finishes he points to the heading indicator and says, "We now get to test your turning ability. Turn right to heading 1-8-0."

I look at the indicator and we are currently heading 155, "Going to one eight zero."

He watches me to make sure I do it correctly by not turning to hard or too easy and I start the turn.

"When you get close turn the opposite direction to get the wings level again. It is a finesse thing not too fast and not to slow."

I almost turn too much but I can feel him bump the controls a bit so I am aware he is there for me and will fix it if I screw up. I level the wings and the new heading reads 181. He points to the indicator and says, "Now give it a little rudder to fix that problem."

I do as I am instructed and then say, "Does one degree matter that much?"

He smiles at me, "Not on a short flight, but when you fly a long distance one degree can put you a mile off course and you may not find the airport."

"Good point."

"Hand me that chart next to you there."

I look beside me and see a map, "This map?"

"Yes, but in aviation we call them charts. Maps are for explorers not pilots."

He adjusts the knobs on the autopilot and presses the button. I notice a difference in the controls and I look over at him folding the chart. "The autopilot is back on I want to show you something."

I look at the chart and he shows me how to look at it. He shows me airways (highways in the sky), airspace around different airports and then says, "Using this chart, if you take off from this airport and fly 2000 miles due south or 1-8-0 degrees. Where would we end up? Mexico, Atlantic Ocean, Gulf of Mexico, Ecuador or Pacific Ocean." I look at the chart and find the airport and then make an imaginary line due south. My first guess is the Gulf of Mexico, but as look, I can't be sure without a measuring device. The pilot hands me a ruler but instead of inches on it there are miles. I hold the measuring device known as a plotter to the chart and follow it down for 2000 miles and end up in the Pacific Ocean. That can't be right, I started on the east coast and went south. *That's right he was trying to trick you because it doesn't seem logical.* I look at the pilot and he says, "What did you come up with?"

"I thought it would be the Gulf of Mexico, but if I did it correctly, I came up with the Pacific Ocean."

He looks shocked and says, "Nice work! You're right, it does not seem logical. Let me show you what being off one degree can do to you." He takes the chart and draws three lines one for 181, 180 and 179 degrees. I look at it and notice how, over a large distance the lines get further apart. "You see what one degree can do to your course?" I nod in agreement as he answers another radio call. He continues saying, "Notice here at our departure point there is no change for about ten miles, but 2000 miles away I could end up in three different places." He points to the autopilot between us, "Change that heading to 1-3-0 please." I turn the knob in the wrong direction at first and then the correct way and I feel the aircraft lean right and then to the left. The pilot looks at me without raising his head, "Left for left and right for right."

"Sorry."

The pilot sticks his hand out for me to shake and says, "It has been a pleasure, but we are getting close and you need to return to your seat."

I shake his hand, "Thank you for your time Sir, I really enjoyed it."

He smiles and says, "You are welcome. We will try again on your return flight home."

I turn towards the door and I notice the copilot headed towards me, "Did you have fun, or was he trying to teach you the whole time?"

"Both, it was very nice. Thanks for giving up your seat!"

"No problem Sir, glad you enjoyed it."

I return to my seat and talk to Kaye and our moms about me flying the plane. They are excited for me as I go on and on about my experience and the things I learned. We start our descent into Freeport and I am like a little kid again staring out the window. Kaye taps me on the shoulder, "So you are going to start flying lessons when we get home?"

"Yes I am! I love it Honey, I really do, almost as much as you!" She smiles at me and I say, "How are you doing? You feel better about flying yet?"

"It is getting better, but I am still nervous."

"Why? You aren't scared of dying are you?"

"Yeah, aren't you?"

I take off my seatbelt and sit in her chair with her. I unfasten her seatbelt and put it around the two of us as I hug her I say, "No, and I am not scared to fall asleep or to wake up either."

We snuggle and I can now see out of the window, "What is that supposed to mean?"

Looking out the window I see only water and it gets closer and closer, "Honey I look at death as inevitable as waking up every day. It will happen sometime and fearing it is not going to change that." She whispers in my ear as our mothers are watching us, "At the same time you should respect it."

"I do, I am not going to play Russian roulette or lock myself in a closet and hide from it either."

The wheels of the plane screech as they touch the ground and I say, "See, nothing to fear. What means the most to you in your life?"

She smiles at me and says, "You and shopping!"

"What if I said you can't have me or go shopping ever again because I fear those things?"

She laughs, "You're scared of yourself?"

"You know what I mean!"

Kaye pats my hand, "If it means that much I will endure it for you!"

"Not trying to be selfish here Kaye, but I really want someone in my life that will enjoy things as much as I do, not just endure it for me. I hope you can because I really would like to enjoy life with you."

Our moms look at the two of us and sit up.

My mom says, "Baby, did you just propose to Kaye?"

"No Ma'am, just explaining that if I do someday, we need to have an understanding between us."

Our moms look at each other and not sure what to say. The aircraft pulls up to the parking area and comes to a stop. The engines shut off and the door opens. The weather appears perfect as we look out the window. My dad unbuckles his seatbelt and stands up. He looks at Kaye, and I as the cockpit door opens, "That must have been one ruff landing if they ended up in the same seat!" Everyone chuckles at my father's joke and we all unbuckle our seatbelts.

As we step off the plane the pilots shake my hand and say, "See you in a couple of days!"

"Thanks for the ride. So you guys are coming back to get us?"

"Unless there is a shift in our schedule we should be the ones who pick you up."

"Great I'll see you then. Maybe I can fly home."

The copilot hands me five dollars and says, "Sir could you get one of your parents to bet this on twelve for me on any roulette table?"

"Sure Buddy, I will see that it happens for you. And if you win?"

"Then I would appreciate you give me the winnings."

"How about this, if it wins I keep half and then gamble the other half for you, and see what I can build it up to. Does that sound ok?"

"That sounds great!" I wave bye to him.

Walking to our ride Kaye is holding my arm and says, "I will be that girl for you. You are going to protect me and keep me safe, right?"

"I will do everything within my power for you."

She looks around before we step in the car, "Then give me a hundred bucks so I can shop down here without having to beg my parents for money all the time."

"Where is your money from your job?"

"I am saving that for a car when I turn sixteen."

I reach in my pocket, "In that case here have two and have some fun girl." She hugs me and steps in the car.

The parents get in the other car and it is just the kids in this one. The car drives away and goes to the hotel. I sit in the crowded Crown Victoria next to Kaye and the door. I look at my sister sitting on Mike's lap and I say, "I liked our ride to the airport better." Roxanne smiles and says, "Me too. Sir how far is it to the hotel?" The driver turns around, "About five minutes my little lady."

I start laughing as we hit the main road. "What is so funny!" ask Kaye.

"He is driving on the wrong side of the road."

My sister says, "The islands are still under British rule so they drive on the left here."

I smile at her, "I was not aware of that, thanks for sharing."

She punches me in the arm as she says, "You are such a smart ass sometimes."

"No, I was being serious I feel stupid for not knowing that."

I reach in my pocket and pullout four hundred dollars, "Ok girls and boy, here is the deal."

I hand them each a hundred dollar bill, "You gamble with this money only, no buying clothes, or food, just gambling. If you lose it that's fine, if you win you must split the winnings with me."

They all agree and the driver says, "Can I get in on that deal, Mate!"

"No sorry!"

He says, "What if I bet you ten bucks that I know where you got those shoes?" *It's a scam, but do it he needs the money.* Kaye looks at my shoes as I think of his possible responses, because I don't even know where I bought them.

I pull out ten bucks and hand it to Kaye, "Ok Buddy, go ahead work your magic. Ten bucks says you can't tell me where I got my shoes."

He looks back at me and smiles as he says, "On your feet Man!"

We all start laughing and Kaye hands him the ten bucks.

We arrive at the hotel and I look around the lobby area, "Where is the casino?"

The lady at the counter points down the long hallway, "But you need to be eighteen to enter."

I look at my dad, "Sorry Pop, you are too old!"

He makes a pouting face and we chuckle as the lady says, "I'm sorry, at least eighteen to enter."

My dad smiles, "That's better, because I am twice that age now!"

We walk up to the rooms and the four rooms are all together, two adjoining rooms on each side of the hallway. The moms look at the rooms and decide the girls would share the adjoining room with the Lewis' and Mike and I would be connected with my parents. I look at the rooms and say, "Dad we need suites instead of these rooms." My sister tells me the price difference in the rooms and I say, "These rooms will be fine." Roxanne tells me that if you win a lot of money they upgrade your room for you.

"Then let's hit the casino then and get bigger rooms!" We change our clothes and head to the casino. The moms decide they are going shopping at the street market they saw when we pulled into the hotel. As the rest of us walk to the casino I catch up to my dad, "The plan has changed. You will win a lot today so we can get the suites."

"Just point me in the right direction my Son."

I pat him on the back, "Yes Sir! Make sure you listen to me and we will kick butt."

We walk to the casino entrance and I see all the lights and get excited it reminds me of the midway at the state fair. I show the security guard my ID and he motions me in. The girls just walk right in without showing an ID, sexist guards. They do pretty the place up though.

"Dad what do you want to do first?"

He looks around, "I know blackjack let's give that a shot."

"Yes Sir, let's go lose some money."

"What do you mean?"

"The house wins that game the majority of the time, but let's go it will be good to warm up on that."

I sit down with my father, Mr. Lewis and Mike. My dad hands us each twenty in chips and says, "Compliments of the hotel." I look at the sign on the table and the minimum bet is five dollars and the max is five hundred. We all place a five in the square for our bet and the dealer begins dealing out the cards. Mr. Lewis gets a blackjack dealt to him and the rest of us get crap. We all end up winning the hand as the dealer bust. I lean over to my dad and whisper, "Dad if I tap your leg bet all your money. Once you get above five hundred just bet that because that is the max bet." To cover up for the cameras and whoever else might be watching dad says, "I love you to Son, but I'm not giving you anymore money right now."

Our plan works to perfection; we win some and lose some. My dad has turned his twenty bucks into just over three thousand. The pit boss and I are the only ones privy to that information, as the chips lie scattered not stacked in front of my dad. The rest of us have been winning but my dad is the leader.

We have all had a drink from the bar, but just one each. The pit boss has the girl come by way to often and it is getting annoying. They are trying to break the rhythm or card counting ability by distractions. I decide to change it up a bit. I bet the max and get my stack of chips up and between my dad and I, we have over five grand. Kaye comes over and sees we are doing well and I stop playing and watch a couple of hands. Mike wins two big ones back to back and then I get back in. I scan our chips and count the dealers. We have been through four dealers now and the house is getting nervous. With what the dealer is missing in chips since we sat down and what I can count of our chips we are up to around eight thousand.

I look at my dad and say, "I'm getting bored with this. Let's do something different."

My dad says, "I'm happy here, you go ahead if you want."

"Thought we discussed your problem before we came, Dad?"

He looks at me sadly as other people start sitting at our table thinking the table is good for players right now. "Don't you think it is starting to get crowded?"

He looks around the table, "No not too bad. We all bet five hundred this time and if we all lose then we change games."

I look at the crowd building and dad says, "You have a deal!"

The dealer deals the cards and it looks good for us but the dealer has a ten showing. He goes around the table asking each player if they want a hit or hold. The little old lady in the first spot hits sixteen and bust. I start picking up my chips and getting ready to go I hand Kaye my chips and I stay on 12. Mike takes a hit and bust, my dad says, "What are you doing? Where are you going?"

"I already told you it is time to move plus the dealer has blackjack."

The dealer flips his card and says, "Blackjack!" Kaye and I walk away from the table and I see a roulette table with only one guy sitting at it and head in that direction.

Kaye tries to counts the chips, "How much is here?"

"Just over $2500, let's sit at this table Honey."

"How much did our dads win?"

"Your dad won about two hundred and my dad won over five thousand but if he stays there he will lose it all." I look at the board to see the last twelve numbers that came up as winners at the table. I put five dollars on thirteen, five in each corner and twenty on black.

Kaye looks and says, "You going to throw it all away in one try?"

I smile at her as the dealer spins the ball my father comes over and watches the ball fall on thirteen black. I stand up and say, "Thank you!"

Kaye claps and cheers as the dealer pays me $375 and says, "Congratulation Sir! Nice play."

My dad says, "This game is not bad." In my excitement I forget to remove my chips still on the table from my last bet and the dealer says, "No more bets."

We look at the table and the ball bounces around and lands on sixteen red. I luckily have a chip on two of the corners, which makes me win $80, since I left all the other chips on the table I lost the other chips. I quickly pull my $60 profit towards my stack of chips.

"Dad thanks for getting up, didn't you see what was going on there?"

"No, I saw money and when you left I lost a thousand pretty quickly. So what was going on over there that made you want to leave?"

I continue making small bets at the table winning twenty or twenty-five each time and Kaye loves it. "Hey can I try?"

"Sure girl, go ahead and win me some money."

I look over my dad's shoulder and say into his ear, "That little old lady is a casino winner killer!"

"A what?"

"While we are here at this casino watch and see how many times she shows up. She is a cooler, she cools down winning streaks. Plus the cameras watch if you stay in one place to long. Did you notice the drink girl kept coming by more and more frequent? These are warning signs, the casino is trying to change your luck or make sure you are not cheating."

My dad gives me a look of understanding, "So help me with this game."

"Just watch or bet small your choice."

At that moment Kaye jumps up, "I won, I won!"

She hugs me and then she picks up the winnings. I laugh at her excitement and place a couple of bets. I win nothing but on the next try I win twenty bucks.

My dad says, "So I can bet one five dollar chip or five hundred and win how much?"

"Whatever you bet is multiplied by the odds for that space you placed it on."

"So if you and I both bet on seven and the ball lands on seven, who wins?"

"We both do, we all play against the casino."

"I get it now!"

I push a chip on thirteen again and the guy says, "No more bets . . ." the ball bounces and stops in ". . . thirteen black."

My dad looks at the money being pushed to me, "How much did you win Son?"

"One hundred and seventy-five dollars."

Kaye says, "But I lost that time."

I kiss her cheek, "It happens Babe, and we can't win 'em all."

I notice my dad holding a coin cup for the slot machines with chips in it. I watch as he fishes around in the cup and he pulls out a hundred dollar chip, "What is the max at this table Son?"

I point to the sign on the table, "$500 Pop. You put $5000 in a cup?"

"Yeah, what was I supposed to do with it?"

The guy that had been sitting at the table lost all his money and gets up and leaves and Kaye is still just betting small amounts. My sister and Mike sit down and join in the fun. My dad holds up the one hundred, "Where do you think Son?"

"Black."

He places it on the black and so does my sister, Mike and Kaye.

The croupier says, "twenty-six black!" They are all excited until they see their payout.

I say, "What? You just doubled your money. The outside bet is a one to one bet. The big money is when you bet on the number, that pays 35-1."

They smile and Kaye says, "Ok which number?"

"When is your birthday Honey?"

She looks at me, "July 30th you know that!"

"Then bet on seven and thirty."

She does and wins nothing and I shrug, "Hey, it was a gamble."

My dad says, "Let me try that," he puts a hundred on 29 and 12.

The guy says, "Twenty-nine black! Winner!"

We all cheer at my dad's luck. He just won $3500 in one roll.

I hug my dad and say, "Now that is what I like to see!"

Mom walks in and witnesses us going crazy.

My mother says, "What did we miss?"

I look at her and say, "Your husband is on a hot streak!"

I hug her and whisper to her, "He is going to have one more big win, and then we need to get him out of here to make my plan work."

She looks at me, "Well it is lunch time."

"You're good Mom, that's why I pay you the big bucks."

She winks at me and walks over to my dad and hugs him, "Let's take a break and get some lunch."

He looks at me, "Ok, one more and we go eat."

"Hey Dad, bet my birthday."

Roxanne yells, "Mine too!"

My dad puts a hundred on 1, 26, 29, and 3 for all of our birthdays and one more hundred he tosses on the table and it lands between 13 and 14.

The croupier says, "No more bets," as the ball falls. It bounces for what seems to be an eternity. It finally comes to rest on the number one.

I raise both hands in victory, "That's my birthday just like I said!" We all cheer and hug my dad. He now has won over twelve thousand and has not even touched his own money. *This is working lovely and the manager is on the way over here.*

When we calm down the manager says, "Congratulations Sir, we are very impressed by your play. Would you like to play in the high roller area?"

My dad looks around and finds me, "Well we were going to eat right now, maybe when I come back. I would like that."

"Sir have you just arrived? Where are you staying?"

"We got here a couple of hours ago and we are staying here at the hotel for the week."

"Sir, are you a Princess Casino member?"

"No, this is my first time in a casino!"

"Sir, are you currently in a suite or stateroom?"

"No, we are in regular rooms on the third floor."

"We would like to give you a suite Sir, and your lunch today is on us in our restaurant."

"Thank you for the lunch, but I have these people with me, so I would need four suites unfortunately."

He looks at the rest of us and says, "Sir that is no problem."

He writes some info on a card and hands it to my father. "Can we do anything else for you Sir?"

My dad smiles at me and says, "I would like to bet five hundred on one number, would that be possible?"

"Yes Sir, at that table you were playing or a high roller tables, your choice."

My father looks at me and walks over, "Which?"

I say, "This one, but I want you to bet whatever number you want the first time act disappointed and say one more time and that one you bet 13 and you will win I promise."

My dad looks at the manager, "This table has been good I will stay here for this one."

My dad walks over to the table and puts five hundred on number 34. After the roll the ball stops on 25 black. We all sigh and say it's ok, dad. He takes five hundred more and places it on 13 black.

"Dad, I will join you on that one that is my lucky number!" I put a hundred on it as well and my sister bets five dollars on her birthday and Kaye does the same for hers. We all watch anxiously for the ball to stop. When it does the croupier says, "Thirteen black, winner!" We all jump and hug for joy; my dad just won over $17,000 in one roll bringing his total to over $29,000. I had just gone over ten thousand dollars and no one hardly even noticed, or at least I thought.

My dad wants his chips he won and I explain it is more than they care to hand out. The manager comes over and congratulates my dad again, and explains his chips would be kept on a marker. He explains my dad would be given the amount at the cashier cage when he wanted it or could use it to gamble some more later.

My dad looks at his chips in his cup and says, "Let's go cash in."

I laugh and say, "Dad that is, cash out."

We all chuckle as the manager walks to the cage with us. I whisper to my dad, "Put all yours on the marker and I will cash mine. Yours keeps us in the suites and mine covers expenses."

He winks at me and I say to the manager, "May I put my winnings on my father's marker and use it just like him?"

"You can do that or have your own it looks like you have done very well also."

We give the girl in the cage my father's chips and card from the table and she adds up the amounts as the manager explains what to do.

"Sir, that puts your total at $29,720. Do you need any cash, or put it all on the marker?"

"Let me put my son's chips on the marker also."

I set my chips on the counter also. She adds up the total and says, "That brings the total to $39,445."

Dad says, "Let me have the $445 please and the rest on the marker."

"Yes Sir, no problem." She flips out the cash and begins talking to the manager as she hands my father the marker card. We walk to the family and lead them towards the restaurant.

"Dad next time I won't help you, but lose no more than five thousand. If you win that's fine, but when you lose five you stop."

Dad smiles and says, "Got it, let's eat I'm starving!"

We eat a wonderful buffet that the casino restaurant has. Kaye and I walk up to the buffet and look at the selection of food. Salad bar that has almost every vegetable imaginable, the meat selection has roast beef, lobster, steak, shrimp, shark, chicken six different ways, fish, etc. It is a very well stocked buffet and our family and friends are very happy. The casino manager comes and checks on us to kiss up and to make sure his money is not going anywhere. He is very nice to us and after he leaves I explain to my dad how he needs to work his winning and losing to our benefit.

Kaye looks at me and says, "I want to try those slot machines! How do they work?"

I look at her and say, "You put money in pull the handle and hope! There different ways to play I will show you after we are done."

My sister, Kim and our moms say, "Show us too!"

A waitress walks by and my dad says, "Excuse me, do we get a bill or need to sign anything?"

She smiles and says, "No Sir, the manager has already signed your bill. Do you need anything else?"

My dad looks at the dessert bar, "More pie!"

As he stands up she says, "What kind Sir? I can get it for you."

"Thanks Sweetie, but I will probably sample more than one." She laughs and walks away and my dad and Mr. Lewis walk to the dessert bar.

Our dads come back to the table and I pull out a roll of quarters, "Dad, I am going to show the ladies the joy of slot machines."

We all stand up as our dads sit down and my dad says, "We'll come and find you when we're done, so we can go change our rooms." I wave to him in agreement as we leave for the casino.

I will tell you the machine to use. That's the one right there with the frogs on it.

I stop and say, "This one requires only one coin and one chance to win. Some machines you can put in more coins to double your odds or some with more than one way to win. Just read whatever machine you sit at." They all seem content with my explanation, but even happier when the machine I just played gives me twenty quarters.

They all sit at machines and my sister walks up to me and puts her hand out, "Give me a quarter please!"

"Hold on," I trot over to the change cage and give the lady a fifty, "Five rolls please."

The lady looks at the bill and then gives me five rolls of quarters.

I walk back over to the girls, "Here you go ladies, quarters for everyone."

My sister looks at me and says, "Lead me to a good machine!"

I look around and say, "You got it girl!"

The rest of the girls have already picked machines and I lead my sister to what should be a good one. "Sis, play the max amount in about twenty pulls to win the big pay out. Before that you will win some small payouts, but wait for the big one."

"Ok, I got it." She puts a coin in and wins three on the first try; I wink at her and go back to Kaye.

"Hey Kaye my sister is about to win six hundred coins want to watch?"

She watches her machine as she loses again, "Sure I'm not winning here!"

We stand up and walk over to my sister. *Three more pulls and she wins.* My sister only has about ten coins left and is not looking too thrilled with her luck.

"Hey Sis, play the max this spin!"

She looks at her coins, "I need one more coin."

Kaye hands it to her and she drops it in the slot and pulls the handle. The wheels spin as my dad and everyone in our group walks up and watches. The tumblers fall one at a time and the bells and whistles go off as the lights flash. We all jump up and down with excitement as the coin girl walks over to congratulate her. The girl writes down the machine number and amount. My sister looks at the paper in confusion, "What's this?"

"Sorry Ma'am, but the machine does not payout amounts larger than five hundred coins."

"But I want to hear it fall in the coin drop."

"Sorry Ma'am."

I take the paper from my sister and drop it in the coin drop and make the sound, "Chink, chink . . ."

The rest of our group laughs and makes similar noises as we hug her.

My sister says, "Whatever! I just won fifteen hundred dollars!"

I look at the machine and say, "No Sweetie, you just won fifteen hundred quarters. That is $375 which is still very good!"

She looks at the machine and says, "Oh yeah, it is quarters not dollars. Still I won!"

My mom hugs her, "Yes you did Honey! You did very well!"

My dad says, "Let's go change our rooms before they change their minds."

My sister runs to the cashier's cage to receive her money. She runs to us and shows us her winnings as we are walking to the exit.

She flashes the money in my face and I say, "Now you can pay me back the money you owe me."

She pulls the money away and then realizes I am correct about owing me money. She starts to hand it to me and I hug her around her neck, "I was just kidding! We are even now, you owe me nothing but respect."

She smiles, "Can't I just give you the money?"

The group laughs and she kisses my cheek, "Thanks Bro!"

We walk out of the casino and I take my mother by the arm and stop walking. She turns and looks at me, "What's wrong Baby!"

I point to the huge slot machine in the entranceway of the casino, "Mom that machine is going to payout in five hundred and twenty pulls."

She looks at the massive machine and says, "You want me to put five hundred and twenty dollars in it?"

"Not right now, but you will win that $100,000 before we leave here. For now, go put a dollar in it." Mom walks over to the slot machine and looks like a little doll next to the huge machine. She puts her dollar in as a security guard watches her as she loses. She throws her hands up and walks back to me. We wave to the security guard and then walk fast to catch up to our group.

As we enter the hotel lobby we meander around while my dad hands the receptionist the paper given to him by the casino manager. The receptionist calls the bellman to the desk and says to him, "These people are moving to bungalows 3-6, please assist them in moving their luggage please." She types in her computer and he walks over and grabs a cart.

My dad says, "I just want to verify, who is paying for these rooms?"

"Sir your rooms are compliments of the casino and there will be no charges for the mini bars. The only expense will be if you use the phone."

"Thank you."

The bellman heads toward the elevator and presses the call elevator button. I follow him and I walk up to my mother and say, "Looking good Mom!"

"Thanks Honey, I am going to the pool after we change rooms care to join me?"

"Oh yeah, that reminds me!"

I walk over to the receptionist and my dad, "Excuse me where is the beach and how do we get there?" The lady hands my father our new room keys and says, "Here you go Sir, enjoy your stay. When you finish with the old rooms just give the key to the bellman." She looks at me and says, "Sir the beach is five minutes away, you can ride our complimentary bus that departs every thirty minutes or take a cab, scooters, or rent a jeep, it is your choice."

My dad and I look at each other and then back at her, "Thank you!"

Back at our unused rooms the mothers gather our luggage that had not even been unpacked and give it to the bellman. Dad and I go to the suites and look around. This time our rooms are all poolside and right beside each other. My dad wants to go back to the casino, but I am able to talk him out of it. "Dad you need to pace yourself. Don't let them think you are going to give the money back to soon or we will lose our perks." He agrees and the rest of our group shows up. My mother and Kaye's mother look at all the rooms and decide that the best idea is for the adults to have the two center rooms, the girls then choose their room and leave the other end room for Mike and me.

We move into our new suite and it is much better than our rooms from before. Mike and I notice girls at the pool and we do some innocent watching of the pool area. There is a knock at our door and Mike answers it. The girls walk in as I grab a soda from the mini fridge. Kaye takes the can as I sit it on the counter and takes a sip.

"Anybody else want a soda or beer?"

Kaye says, "Yeah, give me one of those!"

I hand her a beer and say, "If you get drunk I am cutting you off right after I rape you."

Everybody laughs and Kaye says, "Rape me now so I can enjoy it!"

We laugh and I pretend to attack her. She sips the beer and there is another knock at the door. Kaye hides the beer and sips my soda to cover any smell. Mike opens the door and it is my mom.

She is dressed for the pool and says, "Come on let's hit the pool! Ok, who is drinking in here?"

I look around the room and everyone looks away, "That would be me Mom, sorry."

"Don't be sorry, get your mom one!"

I reach in the fridge and pull out another one for her, "Here you go Mom."

I hold up the beer Kaye had sipped and say, "Cheers mom!"

We slap our cans together and take a drink, "If you kids drink down here you have to play by the rules."

There is another knock at the door and I say, "What is this grand central station today?"

Mike opens the door and the rest of the parents walk in and see my mother sipping a beer with me. My mother says, "I was just telling my kids if they are going to drink it will be responsibly."

She points at Mike and says, "You are one of my kids this week."

"Yes Ma'am I am."

"If any of you start feeling light headed or doing stupid things you stop drinking booze and drink water. Alcohol will dehydrate your body and the water keeps that from happening. Rule number one if you drink you guys cannot be alone, no sneaking off and having sex. Number two, no driving mopeds or cars or any vehicles. Number three, you look out for each other. Do you have any questions? Kaye and Kim, it is up to your parents about you guys."

I hold my can up, "Cheers Mom, I will abide by your rules!"

My dad says, "Toss me one of those beers Son."

I look in the fridge, "Sorry dad all gone, we only had two in there. Give me your key and I'll get one from your room."

He hands me his key and I look around the room, "Anybody else?"

Mike raises his hand and so do Kaye and Mr. Lewis.

Kaye's mom says in shock, "Bob are you going to let your girls drink?"

"Pat, if they follow the rules I don't have a problem and I trust the judgment of our girls and the Dunn's. If the Dunn's think they can trust their kids then I feel we should trust ours."

Kaye's mom says to Bob, "If that is the way you feel I agree, but if my girls mess up I will kick their butts all the way back home!"

My dad says, "Give me my key back. We can just go to the pool and get drinks there."

My dad points at the bar at the pool and says, "Let's go!"

I grab a bathing suit and go in the bathroom and change; the girls go to their room to change.

I walk out of the bathroom and grab my beer and walk out to the pool where the two dads and Mike are sitting at a table. I look in the pool and see my mother already swimming laps. She always did like the water, which must be why I am like a fish. The waitress brings flowery looking drinks and sets them in front of the men as I set my beer on their table. I take a sip of my father's drink and then jump in the pool. I swim around and try to stay underwater as long as I can. As I come out of the water for air the girls show up.

My mom says to me, "Let's race!"

We are at the edge of the pool and we look across the pool and my mom says, "Down and back any style. Ready, Go!"

She splashes water in my face and takes off swimming as hard as she can. I shake my head in disbelief and then I take off after her. I swim as hard as I can and with each stroke I close the gap between us. As I make the turn I notice my mother passing me in the opposite direction. I attempt to pull myself through the water with greater force, but I cannot seem to catch her. She has always been a good swimmer. As I reach the edge of the pool and raise my head out of the water my mom is leaning against the wall, "What took you so long?"

"It didn't take me long! I just got beat by a superior swimmer."

She grabs me by the head and kisses my wet head, "Good try Babe. You need to use your legs more and not so much upper body."

Dad pats the seat of the chair beside him as he looks at me. I jump out of the pool and sit next to him as mom goes back to swimming laps. The girls order drinks as my dad says, "I trust you and you have never given me reason not to, but please don't get drunk or sleep with your girlfriend as a favor to your parents during this trip!"

"Yes Sir, I promise, but can we promise no sex instead of no sleeping together."

My dad looks at me curiously, "That sounds . . . ok I guess."

My mom sits next to me and orders a drink and I say, "Mom that slot machine we spoke of earlier? Play it every day sometimes twice I will let you know when it is getting close."

Mom nods in agreement as my dad says, "What slot machine? You mean that big one in the front that says giant jackpot $100,000?"

"Yes Sir, mom is going to win it if I time it right."

He smiles and says to my mother, "Nice Honey, good job!"

She smiles and says, "Say that after I win."

"Sounds like you already have, so I was just getting it out of the way."

We sit and enjoy the pool and drinks and I start to feel funny. "Mom, when you am drunk do you know?" Smirking at me and now aware of how drunk I am, "Yes Dear, you are!"

She orders a glass of water for me and takes away my beer. I jump in the pool and come up for air. Mom yells at me, "What are you doing?"

"I thought I'd get hydrated quicker this way."

They laugh at me and my mom tosses me a bottle of water. I sip it and let it float next to me. Mom tries to be funny, "How many fingers do you see?"

I look and she has the peace or victory sign up in the air to me with all her fingers exposed to me.

"All of them! Two up and three down." I go under the water and swim back to the pool edge.

We have a nice afternoon by the pool. I return to my room and sit down in the lazy boy recliner and stare at the TV. A knock at the door startles me, "It is open, come on in!"

Kaye walks in the door and tries to disguise her voice, "You need a massage Sir?"

With my back to her and without looking at her, "That would be nice, but no special massage . . . I'm all sexed out Babe!"

I almost start laughing as a pillow hits me in the face from over my head. Kaye starts hitting me over and over with the pillow. We wrestle on the floor and I pin her so she cannot move. I kiss her neck and ears as she slowly calms down.

"Tomorrow I want to go to the beach . . ." I kiss her lips, ". . . I want to jet ski, snorkel, and parasail. You will do all of these things with me because you love me! Right?"

"Can I lose my virginity also?"

"No, I promised my parents we would be good this trip."

She looks upset and says, "Ok, but if we are going to do all that we have to do some things I like as well."

"I do not have a problem with that at all."

"What are you wearing to dinner?"

"The only suit I brought, dad wants that fancy Chinese place in the lobby. Did you bring that sequined dress my mom made for you that I requested you bring?"

"Of course I did! I have never had Chinese food before, what do they have?"

"Excellent wear that please, I love that dress! The food . . . I have no idea Honey. I've never had it before either. Whatever it is, you have to do me a favor and this is one of those tests we spoke of. You and I must try everything, if you don't like it you never have to try it again and I will never ask you to try it again."

"I don't want to."

"I'm serious I will not ask you to eat anything bad or gross. We only eat normal stuff, but if you try it I have to and vice versa. Deal?"

She looks concerned as I let her up, "I will try my best! Will you take me dancing after that?"

"Yes whatever you want!"

She stands up, "I am going to get dressed, see you in a few minutes." She kisses me and runs out of the room.

Mike walks out of his bedroom, "That is one cool girl you got Buddy!"

"Yeah I know, she is awesome and she makes me happy."

After getting dressed I walk out and Mike and Roxanne are sitting on our couch drinking beer. "You guys are going to ruin your appetite!"

My sister says, "Don't think so, I hear after eating Chinese food you are still hungry." We chuckle and there is a knock at the door. I open it and it is my parents dressed like they are going to the opera with the Lewis' looking just as nice. I kiss the hands of the ladies and shake the men's hand as they enter. Kim walks in behind her parents, "Where is my Kaye?"

"She is ready she just wants you to pick her up like a date."

I look around the room, "Well this would be like our first real date. Excuse me everyone I need to get my date and I will return."

I step into the hallway and walk to her room, as I knock on the door I get a bit nervous. She opens the door and I am not prepared for the beautiful sight I see before me. This vision of loveliness was wearing a strapless white body tight glittery sequin gown, with a split up the side, just above her knee that shows her every luscious curve. My mouth drops as I notice her long blond hair pinned up gorgeously and she says, "So what do you think?"

"I can't! You are so beautiful! You look like an angel my darling! Wow!"

She laughs and says, "Can you tell I am not wearing panties?"

"Oh my God Kaye! I didn't need that in my head! I already want to rape you right here and now!"

"Good now you know how I feel every day!"

Kaye walks out of the room, "Where are our parents?"

"Waiting in my room."

I take her hand and I feel like I just handed her my heart.

At my door I stop her, "Kaye, stay here for a moment I want to announce you as your loveliness dictates. People need to be warned when such beauty enters a room so they don't stare or at least they can and get away with it."

She giggles as I open the door, "Ladies and gentlemen my date for the evening, the lovely Ms. Kaye Lewis," She enters the room and everyone is in awe of her beauty, much like I was. They hug her and tell her how lovely the dress is. She blushes and thanks them as we all exit the room.

My parents leave the room arm in arm followed by the Lewis' and then Mike and Roxanne in the same fashion. I look at my lovely date and her dateless sister. I spin and put my back to them, I put out both elbows so they can latch onto me. They both take an arm and we exit the room and try to catch up to our party. "Kim you want a boy toy for the rest of the trip?"

She smiles at me sheepishly, "Yes please."

"I will find you one tonight while we are out. You want long or short term?"

"Yes please."

I smile at her and kiss her cheek, "We will take care of you girl."

We enter the restaurant and they immediately seat us at our table. The little Chinese lady is about to hand out menus and I say, "No menus please." She looks at me oddly as I continue, "We would like family style everything. Like a sampler for all, but nothing to exotic please. This is the first time any of us are having Chinese and some are scared and some are skeptical so please make it lovely for us." She bows

MY CONSCIENCE

and says, "Drinks?" Everyone places an order for a drink and the lady disappears.

I sit between my father and my Kaye. One squeamish and one who will eat anything and I am there to keep them both straight and out of trouble. My father leans over, "Thanks for doing that Son, you did a great job."

He pats my knee and I say, "Sure Dad, no problem. Did you go back to the casino today?"

"Yes, I won a thousand and then lost two."

I smile at him, "Excellent Dad!"

Dad smiles at me and notices the casino's manager walking over to our table. My father stands and shakes the man's hand.

The manager says to our table, "I trust your rooms are satisfactory?"

We all nod in agreement and say, "Thank you."

He looks at my father and says, "I am at the end of my shift, but we hope they will see you in the casino tonight?"

Dad says, "Most definitely! But I'll try to leave you some money."

"Thank you Sir, and to show I am a good sport your dinner is on me."

We all give our small golf clap and say thank you, "Excuse me Sir? Is there a good club we can go to later tonight?"

"My name is John, and I will put your name on the guest list at the best club on the island. You need anything else?"

"No John, nothing else. That would be very nice, thank you very much."

He leaves the table and my dad sits down just as they bring our drinks and appetizers or as I like to say appe-teasers.

We eat our meal and Kaye does exactly as I requested. She and I tried everything they brought and discovered things we liked and things we thought were disgusting. It was wonderful sharing this moment together and it drew us even closer together. At the end of the meal I could not keep my hands off of her and felt I was in trouble. *I told you she was your girl!* I want her now can I marry her tonight! *No you must wait; it will be worth the wait I promise!*

Leaving the restaurant my dad says, "Come here Son."

I walk over to him as my mom and Kaye's mom play the big slot machine.

"Yes Sir?"

"Are you going to be alright, Son?"

"Sure Dad. What do you mean?"

He looks around and finds Kaye and points my body in her direction, "Don't let the dress mess up your mind. You promised you would wait and I expect nothing less."

"Yes Sir, I'll be good I promise!"

"Good boy, now come help me win some more money before you go."

He drags me into the casino and I ask, "How is Mr. Lewis doing money wise?"

"Good, he says he is up one thousand and that seems about right."

We walk up to a roulette table with two guys sitting there that look to be about twenty and with very little cash in front of them.

"Sit here Dad." Bob follows him and they reach for their wallets.

"Guys what are you doing? Don't use your money use the marker."

The croupier calls the pit boss, "Marker!"

The pit boss walks over and I say, "Good evening Mr. Dunn here would like one thousand for himself and one thousand for his friend."

The pit boss checks his list and he verifies our ID and says, "Yes Sir, no problem!"

The pit boss motions the croupier to hand out the chips.

One of the guys at the end of the table says, "We are friends too! Where is ours?"

"Follow their bets and you will win back your own money."

The guy smiles at me and winks knowingly. My dad and Bob place small bets around the table and the two guys watch.

Kaye and Kim walk up and Kaye says, "Baby, how long are you going to be?"

I lean over and whisper to her, "Think your sister would like one of those guys at the end of the table? My conscience told me they are good clean boys ages twenty and twenty-one."

Kaye turns to her sister and does sister talk. I watch as our dads win about thirty dollars each. The guys decide to follow their bets.

Kaye whispers to me, "The one on the left."

I don't even look at her I just watch the guy.

I whisper between the two dads, "Bet 33 and two other numbers."

They do and the guys on the end of the table do the same. They all win and my dad is starting to act like an old pro as the guys on the end jump up and down over their $350 win.

They thank the dads for letting them tag along for the win and then they notice Kaye's dress. The guy Kim said would be good for her says, "Nice dress you going to the ball Cinderella?"

They laugh and I say, "That is a nice dress, but it is spoken for."

"Hey, no offense Dude!"

"None taken, it is a wonderful dress and that is why I bought it for her."

He realizes I am secure about Kaye and he starts betting again.

They win again and get excited again, "You guys are good luck we were almost done here."

They notice three girls standing loyally behind me, "All those gorgeous girls with you Buddy?"

"Yes and they are these gentlemen's daughters."

I introduce everyone as they continue gambling and we meet Jim and Steve.

They continue gambling and Jim and Steve appear to be up to around five hundred dollars each.

"Dad, put a hundred on my jersey number."

Dad places the chip on thirteen and everyone follows his placement. Dad places some smaller bets to distract like I taught him.

The croupier yells, "Thirteen Black, Winner!"

They win again and Steve and Jim hug me and shake hands with our dads.

Mike walks up, "I have us a cab."

He takes my sister by the hand and Roxanne kisses her daddy on the cheek and leaves.

I look at our new friends, "Jim and Steve we are going to the club down the street care to join us?"

They look at each other and then at me and Jim says, "I'm staying here. Steve you go I'll catch up when I win our money back."

Steve walks over to us and says to his friend, "Cool, see you later Dude."

I lean over and kiss my dad on the forehead, "Love ya, Pop!"

"You too Boy!"

I whisper in his ear, "After three rolls the next two numbers will be 0 and then 13, see ya."

Dad hands me five hundred in chips, "Cash that on your way out. Check in at midnight."

I take Kaye by the hand and walk towards the cashier cage and lean to Steve and say, "If I were you I would take half that money now and cash it in."

He thinks about it for a moment and heads back to the table. I cash in my chips and Steve trots over with six hundred in chips in his hand, "He just won again! Your dads are awesome!"

Kim says, "We know! Thanks for noticing."

After he cashes in, we go to the cab with my sister and Mike already in it. I walk past my mom at a slot machine and kiss her, "The big machine is at 380 pulls you should win it tomorrow morning."

I point her to a machine closer to dad, "Keep an eye on dad, if he wins too much or loses too much get him to stop . . . it is all about timing. That machine right there will give you a couple of hundred."

She kisses me and then Kaye, "You guys be good and be safe, I love you both!"

On the cab ride we introduce Mike and Steve and find out that Steve and Jim come over to the island almost every weekend to gamble. They own a restaurant in Florida together. They moved from Ohio after high school and have loved the south much better than the north.

We get to the club and Steve says, "Are you sure you can get in this place? It is real exclusive!"

We walk to the door and the bouncer looks at us and I say, "The Dunn party from the Bahama Princess." He looks at his list, "May I see some ID please?"

I hand him my ID and he says, "Welcome Mr. Dunn let me get your hostess."

He leans inside and this beauty walks out to us and removes the velvet rope from the entrance.

"Follow me please."

I walk past the big security man at the door and I shake his hand and slip him a hundred, "We will be here all week, hope to see you again."

"Yes Sir, it will be a pleasure!"

The girl leads us to our table and takes our drink order and explains that John already paid for our first two rounds.

She leaves and Steve says, "How did you do this? Jim and I have been trying for months to get in here?"

"Not real sure Steve, my sister has a lot of pull though."

He looks over at her and says, "Thanks for getting me in here with you guys. Next time you are at Daytona Beach you come to my restaurant and eat for free."

Our drinks arrive at the table and we all hold them up and say, "Cheers!"

We all start talking to our girls. Kim and Steve start talking and Roxanne and Mike begin cuddling. Kaye looks me in the eye, "Did I do ok at dinner?"

"Kaye you were awesome, I couldn't be prouder of you! You also look so beautiful, in case I forgot to mention it." She blushes and looks around as the club begins getting busier.

"You say our relationship is give and take no questions or complaining if I want to be with you, right?"

"I did say that Honey and by your tone I'd say you have something in mind for me?"

She smiles, "Yes I do, and you have to do the same without complaining or questioning it, if you want me to do the same for you!"

"Name it, no problem I care that much for you! Whatever you request my lady!"

"I liked the dancing in Saturday Night Fever. You have to do the solo routine that John Travolta did in that movie." She smiles and giggles.

The fear strikes me and I wonder if I can even dance, I have never done it in public before. *I will take care of this for you.*

I say to Kaye, "If you can get the DJ to play it I will dance it for you. If it happens you must slow dance with me after that."

She stands up, "You can't make all the deals! I will decide if I want to dance with you or not."

Kaye looks at the DJ booth, "This dress will get him to play it!"

She kisses me and says, "Thanks for the dress by the way."

She gets her sister to go to the DJ booth with her.

The dance floor is empty still and Steve says, "Kim is nice thanks man. What is going on by the way?"

"Oh Kaye and I made a deal tonight at the restaurant."

The music stops as the DJ begins speaking over the PA.

I tell Steve, "I made her eat some food she said she didn't like and now I have to dance for her and make a fool of myself."

"You guys are fun!"

The DJ says, "I need Tommy Dunn on the Dance floor!"

I stand up, "Wish me luck!"

"Break a leg my new friend!"

I go down the steps to the dance floor and point at my beautiful girlfriend. The music starts from the movie and I think to myself take over please. *I got this Buddy don't worry!* I walk on the dance floor like a man possessed by John Travolta himself. Everyone starts clapping and cheering as I dance like I have been doing it since birth. At the end of the song I dance up the stairs to my girl and lead her to the dance floor. As everyone goes crazy the music changes to a slow song and I do a seductive slow dance right in front of Kaye. She melts like butter in my arms and the dance floor fills up with people. Roxanne and Mike are next to us and then I see Steve and Kim across the floor. Kim is smiling and so is Roxanne, I can feel Kaye bursting with pride and she says, "Is there anything you can't do?"

A couple dance up behind us and pat me on the back, "Nice job Sir!"

"Thanks!"

I look at my Kaye, "Lord I hope not! Did I prove my loyalty to you?"

"Yes you most certainly did, I love you!"

"I know but something you should know, I love you more!"

"I loved you first!"

I stare at her, as she looks at me like, what are you going to say now. I snuggle into her and whisper into her ear, "You win!"

Back at the table we drink and talk and I look at the time 11:45.

"We have to go, I promised dad midnight!"

We all stand up, but Steve and Kim stay seated. Kaye tells her to come on and she does not budge. I lean over to Steve, "My dad is a powerful man, and if we disappoint him he gets angry. If we do like he says he gives us more freedom, please help us get her out of here. You can stay if you want, but we have to go."

I whisper in his ear, "She is a virgin and looking to change that also."

He stands up, "Ok girl let's go!"

She says in a drunken slur, "But I don't want to!"

"None of us do girl, but we have to go!"

We make it to the parking lot and a cab pulls up to the door and the bouncer opens the door for us, "We going to see you later?"

"Most definitely my friend!" I shake his hand and get in the car.

We arrive at the casino at 11:55 as I walk in I look for my dad. Security stops me and wants to see my ID. When they are satisfied, I smile at them and walk away. Where is he? *Back right corner.* I go back and he is betting on this mechanical horse racing game. He sees us walking towards him and my mom standing beside him looks at his watch. Mom says as we approach, "Beautiful, right on time. Thanks guys!"

Your mom needs to get to the big slot machine it is down to thirty pulls! "What?"

Everybody looks at me, "Sorry! Mom, a word please!"

She walks over to me, "What's wrong Baby?"

"You need to get to the big slot machine, now!"

"I need cash!"

I give her ten ones, "Let's go! Come on Kaye this is going to be fun!"

We walk my mother to the front of the casino and tell her about our night. When we get to the machine a little old lady is playing it. We pretend not to be interested and a waitress walks by and my mom requests a drink as we talk. *Twenty more pulls and someone is going to win the jackpot!* I look at the lady playing and say, "Are you going to do it Sweetie?"

"I don't think so I'm out of money! I've got one more pull wish me luck!" *Don't do it!* I watch silently and it comes up nothing.

"Oh, too bad! Let me have a try."

I put a one-dollar bill in and I win another pull. I pull the handle and nothing happens.

The old lady walks away and my mom walks over, "My turn?"

"Yes Ma'am, have fun."

She puts all the ones in that I had given her at one time. She pulls the handle and wins another turn. Kaye comes over to me and puts her arms around my neck and kisses my cheek. "I'm tired Baby, and want to go to bed."

"Eight more tries and then we will go."

We watch and Kaye has no idea what is about to happen. My mom wins ten more chances. My sister gets into it and the crowd is starting to form around us. My mom looks at me and smiles, the waitress hands her the drink she ordered.

"I got it Mom, you go ahead."

I hand the girl five dollars and mom says, "I thought the drinks were free?"

"They are but if you want to see a waitress again you need to tip her."

I look at the waitress, "Has she been stiffing you all night?"

The lady nods yes and smiles as I give her a twenty, "Thanks Sweetie!"

"She is new to this she meant no harm."

"That's ok; I'll look after her for you."

"Thanks!" *Winning pull right here!* My dad and Mr. Lewis walk up and dad says, "She winning or losing?"

The lights and bells and whistles go off, "You tell me, Pop!"

Mom looks shocked at her victory, while everyone around is cheering and clapping. My mom hugs my dad and then me and Kaye at the same time and then she hugs Mike and Roxanne. The night manager comes over and congratulates mom and gets the information and puts the winnings on our marker. My parents walk over to the cashier cage with the manager.

Kaye and I walk over to her dad and we hug him.

Kaye says, "Where is mom? Sleeping?"

He nods yes and I say to him, "How have you done tonight Sir?"

"I'm still up but not as much as your parents!"

"You want a big win?"

"Sure who wouldn't?"

I look around and point to a table, "Go to that roulette table and bet five hundred on the number 36."

"The max now is a thousand."

"Then bet a thousand, but if you win you have to buy our Kaye a car for her birthday. No make that red seven."

He walks over and places a thousand on seven.

Kaye says, "Is he going to win?"

A security guard is eavesdropping on us, "I have no idea Honey, and I just wanted to get rid of your old man so I could grope you!"

I start tickling her and kissing her neck.

Her father yells and I say to Kaye, "I think you are getting a car for your birthday Honey!"

Kaye runs over to her daddy, "No way, you won!" They start hugging and bouncing together.

The guard looks at me suspiciously and I say to him, "How you doing Sir?"

He nods and walks away. I walk over to Mr. Lewis and he looks at me, "Boy, I love you like a son!"

"Can I have your daughter then?"

"She is yours!"

Kaye looks confused but happy, "So where do I sleep tonight?"

He looks at her, "Wherever you want girl, that's your man as far as I am concerned."

She smiles at me, "Ok no sex, but I am sleeping in your bed tonight."

We leave the casino and everybody is happy.

My mom walks up to me, "Honey I am sorry!"

"For what Mom!"

Dad joins us, "Did you tell him?"

"Not yet give me a minute. Son our new balance after my win is $262,500."

I stop walking and my sister says, "No way!"

Everyone is happy except for me, "Crap! What happened to our plan? This is not good!"

Everyone looks at me like I am crazy, as I feel right now.

We are in front of our suites. "Goodnight everybody, see you in the morning. Mom, Dad, and Roxanne, we need to have a family meeting please."

My dad opens his suite and we walk in. "Tomorrow we need to lose twenty thousand dollars!"

Roxanne says, "Why we won that money fair and square?"

"Whom did you win it from?"

"A casino."

"Here is a news flash Sweetie! They don't like losing and don't play fair. Sis, how much have you won and how much of their money would you say you have?"

She pulls out her money. "I won like five hundred and still have four hundred." *She is lying.*

"Mom how about you?"

"Before the jackpot, I won like six hundred and lost it all."

"Good girl Mom!" She smiles with pride.

"Here is the new plan. I wanted to spend the day at the beach tomorrow doing all the fun stuff like Jet Ski, and etc. First thing after breakfast, we go in the casino and lose twenty thousand. You girls shop in the hotel stores and spend the casino money so they can see they are getting their money back. Then we go to the beach and have a nice day. Tomorrow evening we lose about ten thousand more and stop for the day. The casino will be happy and not worried about us. Any questions? No, good I am going to bed!"

Mom says, "How much can we spend in the stores? They had some nice jewelry down there."

"I'd say no more than ten thousand!"

Mom and Roxanne smile, "We can deal with that amount."

We all hug and I leave the room, "Goodnight!"

I walk into my room and Mike is watching TV. "You mind if your sister comes over for a bit?"

"No, why would I mind?"

"Just wanted to make sure you wouldn't tell your folks anything."

"Just don't let me hear or see anything and we will be fine."

"Same for you, Buddy."

"What? I am going to sleep; it has been a long day."

I open my bedroom door and walk in the dark room. I see a lump on the floor and a lump in the bed. I turn on the light switch and see Kaye lying in my bed and her sequin dress on the floor. I look at the dress in a ball on the floor, "So much for that theory!"

I shut the door and walk over to the bed.

Kaye questions me, "What theory are you talking about?"

I pick up her thousand-dollar dress, "Ever heard a guy trying to get a girl out of her dress and say that stupid line? 'That dress would look better on my floor'."

She chuckles, "Yeah, I have heard that one in a movie."

I go to the closet and hang up the dress, "Honey in your case it is not true!" She starts to look offended as I continue, "This dress looked awesome hanging on you tonight!"

Now she is blushing and smiling, "Thank you! Now come to bed and let me rub your head. I won't try to rape you; I will just cuddle you and rub your head I promise!"

I take off my suit and grab a tee shirt and put it on. I walk back to the bed and notice she also has on a shirt of mine.

She looks at the shirt after seeing me look at it, "Is it a problem with me wearing your clothes?"

I walk over and turn out the light, "No actually it has never looked better! Just wish it looked that good on me."

She giggles and the room goes dark. I climb into bed and I feel her snuggling into me and her hand begins caressing my head. She cranes her neck to kiss me and I reach down to return the affection. She pulls away and says, "Goodnight my darling!"

I rest my head to the pillow and that is the last I remember as her fingers claw through my hair slightly.

Chapter 17

I wake up to my mother standing over me yelling, "I thought you made a promise buddy! Do your promises mean nothing?" As we all love our mothers, them yelling at us is not the thing most of us love. I look and see Kaye lying in the bed beside me waking up slowly.

Mom continues, "What do you two have to say for yourself?"

"What would you believe? The look on your face tells me the truth is not going to be believable to you at this point?"

Kaye wakes up and sits up, "Nothing happened! I rubbed his head and he fell asleep just like you said he would. My father said it was ok . . ."

My mother looks at her, "So nothing happened?"

I jump in, "No mother, we are both still virgins I promise you. We are going to stay that way for a while." Kaye says, "Seriously we told you we wouldn't do anything and we will not lie to you!"

My mom looks in my eyes and grabs my chin, "Did you guys sleep together?"

"Yes Ma'am, we did!"

"I mean did you have sex or anything close to that?"

"No Ma'am!"

"Did Kaye's father really say this was ok with him?"

"Yes Ma'am, last night leaving the casino."

She releases my face knowing I am not lying to her. "I will talk to her father this morning. I don't like you sleeping in the same bed it opens up to much temptation."

My mother looks around the room as if looking for condoms or any other evidence of us having sex.

Walking towards the door she says, "Get your little butts up and down to my room for breakfast in five minutes!"

She storms out of the room. "Mom!"

She stops and looks back in the room at us as I say, "Good morning we love you too! We would not do anything to lose your respect, we promise."

She leaves the room and Kaye says, "Is she always like that in the morning?"

"Yes, but only this bad when she thinks we lied to her or betrayed her trust." I get out of bed and put on my bathing suit and I am ready to go.

"Give me a pair of shorts so I can go to my room."

I point to my bag and she digs until she pulls out a pair that have elastic and will not fall off of her too easy. She slides them on and releases them and they fall to the floor. I laugh as I stare at her naked butt and say, "Just a bit too big eh?"

She flashes her butt at me as she pulls them back up. Kaye kisses me and leaves to get ready for breakfast with the parents. That should be fun, plenty of fireworks I bet!

I walk out of the room and Mike and Roxanne are sitting there watching me. "Sorry Bro?"

"It will be fine you know mom."

Mike says, "We passed out here last night on the couch and she was hot over that before she found you guys."

I laugh, "Oh, this is great no wonder she is pissed, both her good kids messed up on the first night. This should be a fun breakfast. What did you guys tell her?"

"The truth!"

I look around the room, "Why does she want to believe we are sluts? I know how to handle this! I will take care of it! There will be no breakfast inquisition!"

I walk out of our patio poolside door and walk to the pool. I stretch and look around. No one else is an early riser around here huh? Or they are still at the casino that never closes. I dive in the pool and start swimming laps. As I reach the end of the pool I notice my mom helping the wait staff set up our breakfast. She looks over at me and I motion for her to come over to the pool. She walks over and sits at the pool edge and puts her feet in the water.

"Mom what are you scared of with Kaye and I?"

"I don't want you getting pregnant and ruining your life like I did!"

"If I can promise you that won't happen will you stop these rants of yours?"

"How can you promise that?"

I look at her and raise my eyebrows at her, "Have I not proven anything to you?"

She smiles and says, "Yeah I keep forgetting about that. You two just can't flaunt your sins though."

"Mom I slept with her in the car before on football trips and nothing happened and you said nothing."

"That was different!"

"How was that different?"

She thinks for a moment, "So what are you saying? I should let you do as you please!"

"No, just trust me! I will not embarrass you or let you down I promise! My conscience has showed me the consequences if I have sex with her or anybody, believe me I don't want that life."

"So you have this situation under control and I never have to say another word?"

I smile at her as she slips into the water and I say, "You think you can handle the future if I share it with you?"

"No! That scares me; don't do that I will just trust you."

"Mom, I promise I will not have sex until I can support a family on my own."

Mom begins to swim and I join her for a lap.

We finish our lap and mom says, "Can you see and protect your sister's future also?"

"No, but she is a good girl. If you keep pushing her, she will go the wrong way just to spite you. Let her know you are concerned and care, leave it at that. She likes our future outlook and does not want to screw that up."

"I will trust you and calm down. Did Kaye's dad really say you could sleep in the same bed?"

"Not in those words, but he said she was mine as far as he was concerned, and made it clear he wants us to be together forever. Could have been the fact I just helped him win $35,000."

Mom laughs as we get out of the pool, "Yeah I'm thinking that might have something to do with it."

We sit at the table and begin eating fruit as everyone else slowly shows up. I pile eggs and bacon on my plate and sit down as my father walks by and slaps me on the head, "Good morning my favorite son!"

"That's only son, Dad!"

"That's why you are my favorite!"

The girls all come out of their room together and I think they are thinking safety in numbers. My father hugs all the girls and tells them good morning. My sister looks at me sheepishly and I give her a wink and thumbs-up. My mother hands my father a cup of coffee and kisses his cheek. The Lewis' come out of their room, grab some coffee, and join us. Kaye sits across from me due to fear of what might happen with my mother.

I say to Kaye, "You want coffee or juice?"

She looks at me, "Juice please."

I go to stand up and my mother says, "I got it, sit down Son."

"Roxanne, Kim, what would you girls like?"

They both say coffee and mom pours it and takes it to them. She sets the drinks in front of them and as she sets the juice in front of Kaye, she hugs her around the neck and says softly, "Sorry Dear for jumping to conclusions, I love you!"

Kaye starts tearing up and says softly, "I love you too Mom. I will not disrespect you or your wishes for us."

Kaye stands up and they hug as I look over at my sister and wink. She looks at me in amazement and holds her cup up to me in a salute type fashion and winks.

"Not the breakfast I expected Bro, nice work!"

We both drink and start eating.

Dad looks around, "Where is Mike?"

"I'll check on him dad."

I walk in our room, "Come on buddy the coast is clear. I calmed the beast, just act normal and we will be fine."

We walk out and I say, "He fell back to sleep."

We sit down and eat and the little old lady from last night walks over to our beverage table and pours herself a cup of coffee. She looks at us and says, "Good morning!"

We all return the greeting and she walks away. We start chuckling realizing she thought it was for anyone not our private use.

I rub my foot on Kaye's thigh, "Mom, when you and Roxanne go to look at that jewelry, will you pick something out for my girlfriend?"

The people sitting at the table look at me like, who is he talking about.

Mom tries to play along, "Why don't I take Kaye with me, she could probably find something for her better than I."

I look at Kaye as she smiles at me, "Kaye would you mind?"

"I've got a busy morning planned with my boyfriend, but I think I can work some time in to help you guys out."

The rest of our crowd is confused by our conversation and Kaye rubs my foot with her hand.

"So Kaye, this boyfriend you speak of, is he good to you?"

She smiles and says, "He is very good to me."

"So what are these big plans you guys have today?"

"He is taking me to the beach and we are going snorkeling and jet skiing and maybe parasailing as well."

"That sounds like fun. Very interesting my girlfriend and I are doing something very similar. The only difference is my girlfriend wants me to take her shopping after we do all that."

"Sounds like that girl is a gold digger maybe you should dump her and find someone else."

"Really, someone like you maybe?"

"Sorry I am spoken for!"

"Maybe me and my girlfriend will see you there?"

"Not if we see you first!"

The table applauds our playful banter and appreciates our little show and she mouths to me, I love you. I wink at her and I stand up and head towards the pool.

My mom yells, "No swimming for forty-five minutes after you eat or you will get cramps."

I look back at her, "Minstrel or regular cramps!" and I jump in the pool.

I swim around for a while and Mike joins me, and then the girls join us. My mom walks out of her room towards us and I say, "Hey guys when she gets here act like you have a cramp."

My sister says, "Minstrel or regular?"

We chuckle and mom steps to the side of the pool and says, "You guys ready to get going?"

We all grab different parts of our bodies and say, "Oh cramp! Ouch, cramp! Help Mom!"

She does not look amused and says, "Ha-ha very funny let's go! You children are now known as the children that cried cramp! So don't call me when you really do have one."

As I walk towards the room my dad still sitting at the table with Bob says, "What time does the casino open?"

I walk over to the gentlemen sitting and drinking coffee and I say, "It doesn't, because it never closes."

"What do we need to wear?"

"Are you going to the beach with us afterward?"

"Sure we might as well."

"Then wear whatever you are going to wear to the beach."

I look to the pool entrance and notice Steve and Jim walking in and looking around. They see us and walk over to us, "Good morning guys!"

"Hey guys what is going on?"

They shake hands with us and begin thanking us for helping them win their money back last night.

"So how did you boys do last night?"

Steve smiles and says, "I did very well last night!"

He realizes Kim's father is sitting right there with us and Jim says, "I won over five thousand. How did you guys end up?"

My dad smiles, "We are a bit ahead of how we started out and that's all I'm going to say!"

I look at them getting more curious, "He is very superstitious!"

They nod in agreement, "We understand!"

Kim walks out and sees the two guys and hugs them both. "Dad may I go out with Steve and Jim today?" He looks at me and I look at the three of them, "Why don't you guys come with us today? We are going to have fun on the beach."

The guys look at each other and then us, "We could start out with you guys, but we didn't want to impose on your week here."

Bob pats Jim on the shoulder, "Don't worry Son, you are not imposing, and we'll have a good time."

I walk in my room and my sister and Mike are sitting on the couch together and she says, "Thanks for straightening out that mess this morning!"

"No problem, that's what I do! Hey guys I don't know what you guys are doing sexually and really don't want to, but if you are please be careful I told mom you guys would not be stupid."

They look like they have no idea how to respond and my sister says, "Ok Bro, we understand and don't worry."

"Thank you!"

Kaye walks in with our mothers and she sits on my lap.

My mom says, "Girls are you ready to go?"

Kaye whispers in my ear, "Do I have a limit I can spend?"

"No, but use your good judgment you will be with my mom, follow her lead. If you see something you want that is real expensive, tell me and I will get it for you later." She kisses me and jumps up.

Mom leans over to me, "What were you thinking for Kaye?"

"A ring, tennis bracelet, or something like that. Hey, if they are not too expensive see if you can get a good deal on some stuff to sale in your shop; necklaces, bracelets and so on."

Mom smiles, "Good idea Son."

My dad walks in the other door, "Ready Son?"

I stand up, "Yes Sir! You?"

"Ready as I am going to be to lose that much money."

Mike says, "What are you talking about?"

My dad looks at him, "Nothing Son, we need to go."

My father and I walk into the casino, and when the manager sees us he rushes towards us, "Good morning gentlemen! Welcome back! How would you like to start this morning?"

My dad looks around the casino, "Which table is giving away the most money?"

We all chuckle and I say, "Any chance we could get a craps table to ourselves? I would like to teach my dad craps."

"Sure thing, right this way gentlemen. Would you like to play for money or just play to learn the game?"

"Money please, if we lose we will learn quicker!"

The manager takes us into the high roller area and summons his dealers, "Good luck gentlemen!"

"Thank you!"

I point at the areas on the table for my father and explain the rolls as the dealer pushes eight dice to me. The dealer explains the payouts and common misconceptions. I pick two dice and the dealer says, "How much money Sir?"

I look at my father and say, "Twenty thousand please."

They count out the chips and say, "Hundreds ok?"

"No, half hundred and half quarters please."

They give me the stack of chips and I place my bets.

I toss the dealer a hundred, "This is for you, Gentlemen."

"Thank you, good luck Sir!"

I shake the dice and roll a nine. I won twenty-five dollars on the field and let it ride, next roll is a ten and I win again.

"This game looks easy. How do you lose?"

"Watch this next roll and I'll show you."

I pull all the bets that I can and bet $100 on the seven. Bob and Mike walk up and join us, I roll the dice, and a seven comes up. The dealer pulls in the dice, pays my winning bets, and pulls my losing bets.

"See Dad, in three rolls I made $750."

The dealer says, "Next shooter."

He pushes the dice to my dad and he chooses two from the bunch.

I split the money with my father and give the $750 I just won to Mike, "Bet it if you want or hold on to it."

I place some bets and my dad rolls the dice.

We continue betting, not really winning, we are around the same amount as we started and it has taken us a half hour already.

The manager comes over, "Sir your wife is in the jewelry shop in our lobby. She would like to make a purchase of $20,554 against your marker is that ok with you?"

He looks to the front of the casino pretending to look for mom, "Yeah that is fine. It's her money anyway."

"Yes Sir!"

The manager seems pleased that the casino is getting their money back one way or another.

"Maximum bet?"

"There is no max Sir, this is your table do what you want."

"Dad, hold on just a minute."

I look at the manager, "How do I bet it all on seven?"

Mom and the girls walk over. The dealer marks my chips and puts a single chip the same color on the seven.

"Sorry Dad, go ahead."

He looks at his money and shifts some bets and Mike puts all his on the seven. Dad rolls and we all eagerly await the result.

The dealer yells, "Seven!"

Kaye comes over and says, "Baby what is going on?"

"My ten thousand just turned into seventy thousand!"

She jumps up and down and hugs me tight. "Kaye it's about to get real big!"

The dealer looks at me, "Push or let it ride Sir?"

I point at him, "Let it ride my good man!"

I look at my dad, "Roll me another one of those please Sir, and I'll have close to half a million."

Kaye looks at me, "No way!"

The manager comes over to me, "So how was the club last night?"

I shake his hand, "That place was awesome, thank you very much!"

My dad rolls the dice and seven comes up again. I can see the dealers cringe as if they were expecting to be fired any moment. We all go nuts over me winning $490,000. My dad has almost lost his stack and Mike's is growing. My dad smiles and comes over to me.

He whispers as he hugs me, "What the hell are you doing Son?"

"It's more dramatic this way. I'll be able to say I lost a half a million in one roll of the dice."

I make some smaller bets and I now have a half a million dollars. I look at the dealers as they push me the dice.

I throw them a $1000 tip and say, "Thanks for being there boys. All my money on number seven, please." They all smile and say thank you. They pull my chips to ensure the amount.

My dad pushes his chips in as well, "Me too!"

Mike holds his chips and acts as if there is no way he is doing it, as he is up to twenty-five hundred dollars. I pick up the dice and begin to shake them and Kaye says, "I can't watch!"

The drama is intense at this point. I toss the dice and they appear to be in slow motion. The dice fall and tumble, but bounce funny and do not reach the wall and a seven comes up. My family goes crazy and my dad and I shake our head in disbelief. The family sees daddy and I are not happy and calm down.

Mom says, "What's wrong?"

The dealer says, "Sorry it must hit the wall."

I look at the dice, "I'm sorry everybody, guess I am too weak to complete the roll."

As I pick up the dice, Kaye kisses me, "Good luck Honey!"

I look at her as I shake the dice and my sister walks over to her and starts hugging her knowing what is about to happen. I throw the dice and this time it hits the wall and bounces off and an 11 is showing. Everyone is sad and inside I am laughing at the drama that just unfolded. I pretend to be disappointed and then smile at everyone. I wish I could have sold tickets to that show.

Kaye hugs me, "It's all right Baby. You will get them next time."

The dealers shake my hand and say nice try sir. My dad hugs me and we walk away and John the manager follows us, "You guys aren't done are you? You can't let one bad roll beat you!"

My dad smiles at him, "No John, we are not done. We are just going to take the girls to the beach and relax for a while. We will be back this evening to win our money back."

"The beach! Do you want jeeps or scooters? Or would you like both?"

"What do you mean John? Isn't there a bus?"

"We take care of our high rollers Sir, and we would like to rent for you your choice of jeeps or scooters so you could tour the island in style. I could also give you drivers if you prefer."

My dad says, "How about a jeep for the adults and scooters for the kids John?"

"No problem Sir, they will be waiting out front when you are ready to go."

"Thank you John!"

Kaye smiles, "I cannot believe you lost half a million dollars!"

"I know, wasn't that cool! Kaye, stop hitting me!"

"Sorry, but that is more than I will probably see in a life time!"

We walk to the lobby to pick up our scooters.

She says, "If that first roll would have counted, how much would you have won?"

"Baby you don't want to know!"

"Yes I do!"

"Don't hit me when I tell you."

She nods in agreement and my sister stands between us as a buffer.

"Sure you can handle it? Three point five million."

All the girls turn and start slapping me, and yelling at me as my father laughs at us.

The jeep pulls up and Mike, myself and the girls all jump on scooters. The rental guy says, "Remember to drive on the left side of the road!"

He gives us directions to the beach and we drive away. When we get there, we are not impressed by the beach area, but are amused by the festivities that the big bulletin board says will be going on. It is like a big beach party, and I am in trouble because there are fine women everywhere. Half of them have bathing suits that the back is up their butt cracks. I point this out to Kaye and she says, "It is a new style and is called a thong."

"Where is yours?"

"Ha-ha! I wouldn't wear that. Don't want guys like you staring at my butt."

I laugh and we get towels and chairs set up on the beach and prepare for fun in the sun.

The waitress comes over to take our order and I say, "Ok Mom how does the drinking work since we all drove?"

She looks around, "One drink and no more for you guys."

She looks at my dad and then she says, "One for you as well."

We start ordering and the waitress recognizes me, "He disco dude! You did a wonderful job last night! First round is on me!"

"Thank you!"

"Sure thing Babe, you need to sign up for the beach dance contest you will kick butt and win some cool prizes."

"Sure thanks."

I lean over to Kaye, "See what you started!"

She smiles at me, "But you still love me don't you poor boy?"

"That I do!"

My sister and Kaye look at the list of prizes for the contest and I say, "Kaye let's go parasailing!"

"I'm scared of heights!"

"Me too, let's go conquer that fear together."

"No thanks."

"Remember our deal?"

"That was before you lost three million dollars."

"3.5 Honey! But a deal is a deal or do I need to find someone else to go with me?"

She looks around and sees I have plenty of other options available, "Tell you what . . . Me first today! You win this contest and I'll do whatever you want to do on the beach!"

The parents watch us as we talk and my mom says, "You can't dance baby don't make that bet!"

"Reverse psychology, nice Mom I didn't know you would resort to that!"

I say, "Kaye my Dear, you have a deal."

"Good because we already signed your cute butt up!"

The contest sets up, I find out it is Kaye, and I verses two other couples. I talk Kaye's parents into joining us and my sister and Mike as well. First, we have a freestyle dance, then we do the shag dance, and then we have to do beach blanket dance routines. We do well but it is down to three couples Kaye and I, her parents, and a sweet old couple. They tell us we have to do a waltz and Kaye's parents sit down saying they have no idea how to do it. I explain the steps to Kaye and tell her to stare into my eyes and I will do the rest. The music starts and Kaye and I wait but the old couple starts right away. I step on the first high tempo I hear and we flow perfectly with the music. Kaye stares intently into my eyes and we move as one body around the sandy wooden deck. The older couple gets into a better flow and seems to glide with us and that is when I start to show off. The crowd goes wild over our moves as Kaye smiles, but still stares into my eyes. The music stops and I bow and Kaye does a wonderful curtsey. We exit the dance floor and our family cheers and hug us.

The beach crowd votes on the winner and a line forms around the bar to cast their vote. We rest and sip our drinks and I ask Kaye, "Ready to go parasailing?"

Kaye looks at me and then at the line, "Do we have time?"

"The DJ said they would announce the winner in thirty minutes."

She stands up, "It should only last how long up there, five minutes?"

"I think that is right. Wouldn't it be cool if they announced the winner was us and we landed on the stage in a parachute?"

She laughs, "Delusions of Grandeur Dear?"

I smile and say, "No, but very James Bond wouldn't you say? Let's go!"

We walk over to the guy at the boat and are about to pay for our ride when he says, "No worries! This ride is on me." We look at him confused as he continues, "That was some awesome dancing out there! I could already tell you that you won and there is a coupon for a free ride in that packet." He leads us to the boat and tells us to have fun.

We ride the boat out to the platform for our departure. Stepping on the platform, I notice Kaye getting nervous and our guy says, "You guys together or separate?"

Kaye says very quickly, "Together!"

The guy hands us our harness and we put them on. We are standing on the platform ready for takeoff and Kaye says, "If we die, will I see you in our next life?"

The boat pulls away and we are professionally lifted into the air. By talking to me, she hardly even knew we were airborne. I look around, "Wow this is awesome, and look there is our hotel!"

Kaye looks and says nothing she looks straight down and says, "What is that black thing in the water?"

I look down and see what she is referring to, "It is a school of fish. Look you can see a reef over there!"

I am like a kid in a candy store or a dirty old man in a strip club. I smile from ear to ear, as Kaye still looks uncomfortable. The boat turns and we both get nervous. We feel the parachute start to sink a small bit but not very dramatic. As the boat picks up speed, we feel the lift again. I go back to sightseeing and enjoying the view. We see our family and friends on the beach waving at us as we pass by about a hundred feet above them.

The boat turns again and prepares to bring us down, "No! We just got started! Kaye Honey I could stay up here all day!"

She looks around, "It is nicer than I expected."

"See you open your mind and you can enjoy life!"

"Speaking of enjoying life, I love the bracelet you bought me it is beautiful!"

"Glad you like it! How much did I pay for it?"

She blushes as we sink back to earth gracefully, "It was on sale for $550 and was normally $735."

She was expecting me to be upset at the cost as I say, "You ready for the landing?"

She clamps on to me, "Yeah!"

She lifts her legs and wraps them around me and I watch the guys on the platform guide our towline into a piece of metal designed to help us land on the platform. We land as easy as we took off and Kaye cheers over our safe return to earth. The boat pulls over to the platform to return us to shore.

I look at the distance and it is half a football field length, "Would it be ok if we swim back?"

"Sure Sir, that is no problem at all."

Kaye looks disgruntled at me and says, "I don't need exercise. I need rest!"

"You have to get in shape, when we get home we are going to take karate lessons."

She smiles and says as she runs to the edge of the platform, "Race ya to the beach!"

She dives in and I watch her swim, "Uh oh, she is fast I'd better go!"

The guys on the platform laugh as I dive in. I swim and my conscience says. *How is she working out for you? She everything as I promised?* I swim and notice I am slowly catching up to her. *Make it close but let her win.* I am right beside her and she stands up and is laughing and running the final distance to the beach. Kaye and I stand up in the water and jog to the dry sand. My sister and Mike run over to us, "How was it up there?"

I start to say but Kaye beats me, "It was great, you definitely need to try it!"

We walk up to where our parents are as they sit enjoying the sun and my dad says, "We need to do this every year! I bet it is about ten degrees at home today."

We all chuckle and I say, "Dad are you going to become a migratory bird?"

The chuckles become laughs and the beach DJ says, "It is now time to announce our beach dance winners. Third place goes to Mike and Roxanne!" The crowd cheers and claps as my sister and Mike go and receive their little trophy and gift bag. "And now the winner of our beach blanket dance contest. Let's hear it for that lovely couple . . . Kaye and Tommy!" The crowd applauds as the older couple walks up with us to receive their prize for second place as well. We wave to the crowd in appreciation as we walk away from the DJ booth and he begins playing beach music. Kaye looks through the bag and finds gift certificates and shopping sprees all over the island. She locates the tickets for the entire beach festivities; parasailing, snorkeling, free drinks and jet skis.

My sister comes over with a new volleyball and points to the court, "Let's go baby Brother, time for me to tattoo Spalding on your back as you duck in fear!"

"Hey!" I stand in her face, "It won't be on my back, it will be on my forehead just like last time!"

The family laughs and she bounces the ball off my head.

I grab my sister's arm and whisper, "Hey don't let people see how good you are for the first game. Let's not scare anyone off too quick." She nods in agreement and we walk over to the court and start volleying the ball around. A group of girls with two guys come over and ask to play. We now have enough for six on six and we begin. My sister has to keep herself calm, as we don't play at her level. Two of the girls on the other team are obviously very good, which frustrates Roxanne because she promised not to play hard.

We win the first game but just barely by a score of 15-13. My sister says to our team, "Ok team! No mercy this time! We are going to kick their butts this game! Are you with me?" We look at each other and try to remember it was for fun at first, but now it is a blood sport. We return to the court and a small crowd starts to build around the court. My sister gets into the game and the rest of us just try to hit the ball to her. We win, but now it has become about her and the two girls on the other team. They challenge her to a two-on-two match-up. I sit down with Kaye and hope she does not pick me for her partner. She points to me and says, "He plays like a boy, but I'll take him!"

The two girls look at me and say, "He's too cute for a volleyball court. He should be on some cheerleader's bed with the rest of the cute stuffed animals!"

The girls laugh and Kaye wants to say something to her but I stop her, "Honey there will be no cat fights out here over me." *What are you saying? Girls wrestling in the sand!* I thought you wanted me to stay a virgin? *Good point!*

Roxanne walks over to me, "Come on tough guy, I need you!"

I stand up and walk on the sand court, "Tattoo that mouthy blond so I don't have to marry her!" Everyone watching laughs as my sister walks back to serve the ball, I walk to the net and playfully kick sand under the net at the two girls. Everyone chuckles at my humor and Kaye yells, "Get 'em Honey!"

Just before my sister serves I yell, "Time!"

I trot over to my sister, "This is your time to shine girl! I will just make you look good, let's have some fun!"

I run back to the net, "Kaye, get me another drink please!"

My sister serves a hot one, it lands in the sand, and I say, "What's wrong ladies weren't you ready? She is going to do that the entire game so be ready!"

They say nothing and both get their game face on. The next serve they get under the ball, but it flies off the girls arm.

I can't help but laugh and I say, "Thought you were going to kick my cute butt ladies?"

"Don't worry its coming! We are just giving you a false sense of security!"

The crowd chuckles at us being playful. The next serve the girl gets under the ball and they hit the ball back to us. I bump the ball up and my sister jumps like a gazelle and spikes the ball right between the two girls. I yell and say, "It's like she is on fire!"

The DJ notices the crowd building around the volleyball court and plays music that is more appropriate. The next serve is another ace, but the next is returned to us and we actually get a good volley going. They hit the ball to my side of the court. I have to dive for the ball and as I make contact with the ball, but I can do nothing but let it hit my hand. The ball bounces very lightly and rolls down my back as I lay face down in the sand.

My sister yells, "Good try! Now get your butt on defense!"

I stand up and get in the position my sister points to. The ball is served to me and it bounces off of my arm into the net. My sister hits it straight up after it comes off the net. I jump and spike the ball and it hits one of the girls and bounces off her and out of bounds. Now I have to serve the ball and I am good at placement of the ball as long as I can serve under handed. I jokingly put a finger up to test the wind. The crowd chuckles and I serve the ball very high. The girls think it will land out of bounds so they make no attempt at the ball and the ball lands just inside the line. I throw my arms in the air as if I had just won the game and they look at the ball in shock.

They toss me the ball for my next serve and I say, "Here we go again same spot!"

I hit the ball and this time I hit it harder and it should go out of bounds, but the girl goes after it this time not wanting to be embraced twice. She hits the ball and trips over the rope that marks the out of bounds. Her teammate hits the ball high to give her time to return to the game. The girl returns after her fall and jumps and spikes the ball into the block my sister had put up, unfortunately the ball goes out of bounds on our side and we lose the serve back to the other team. This type play continues back and forth.

After a half hour we finally beat the girls 15-10.

We shake hands with the girls and they still make smart comments, "He would still look cute next to Pooh and Muffin on my bed!"

The other girl gives me a half hug and handshake as she says, "Go back to your girlfriend before we rock your world and then you won't go back to her!"

Two girls at onetime I thought that crazy stuff only happened in the movies. *More trouble than you want my friend, believe me!* The two girls walk away from me, and wink as they notice Kaye approaching. "What did they say to you Honey? And don't say you don't want to know because I do, I really do!"

"Well not in so many words, but if it weren't for you they would tag team my butt until I couldn't walk straight. It was something close to that, but I don't really remember because my mind went blank at their suggestion."

She chuckles at me, "You don't have to lie to me Honey. Let's go eat some lunch."

She knows you are telling the truth just let her save face right now.

"Yeah sure girl, I could go for a burger right about now."

My sister and Mike eat lunch with the girls and Kaye and I decide to join them. We find out that the girls are from Florida and are on Christmas break as well. They talk about college, where they go to school, and where my sister hopes to go. The girls and my sister make dinner plans and the girls leave. They both rub my head as they leave and say silly things like, he is so cute. Kaye just grits her teeth and says nothing.

I look at her and say, "Thanks for not going crazy!"

She watches them leave, "Well they weren't wrong and if I had to fight off every girl that flirts with you I will be fighting all the time. The other week in the mall I had to listen to these girls going on and on about the cute guy in the deli shop. I wanted to say stay away from my boyfriend, but then they would leave the dress shop mad and they would not come back. They would tell their friends not to come back either."

I smile, "Thanks for doing that, but if it is any consolation to you I've had to bite my lip about you a few times as well, but people mostly know you are mine and leave you alone."

My sister is talking to Mike and I make it aware that I need her attention by tapping her foot.

"Yes my Brother. What do you want?"

"You were really awesome out there. If I can get Carolina to give you a better scholarship, will that be ok?"

"That sounds good to me."

"I will fix it then."

She goes back to talking to Mike and I return to Kaye as mom and dad walk up, "Who's up for jet skis?"

We all raise our hands and head to the beach. After an hour of fun on the jet skis, we return to the beach to relax for a while.

Kaye places her hand on mine, "You having a good time? Am I doing a good job being your girlfriend as requested?"

I look around to see who might be listening, "I am having a great time and I enjoy your company!"

She looks around as I did, "And the girlfriend thing?"

"Let's take a walk down the beach."

We start walking and I say, "I have some request."

"Yes go ahead."

"I think I have proved I will do anything for you. But I don't want our relationship to be tit for tat."

She looks at her chest, "What's wrong with my tits?"

"Ha-ha! No, I mean I don't want to have to do something in return every time I ask you to do something with me. I want you to want to do things with me. Not make me do things so you will do stuff with me."

She looks up the beach, "Then I don't understand how this is supposed to work?"

"Kaye I will learn the things you like and just do them for you. That is why we date to learn each other before we get married. You have to want to learn the things I like as well."

"But what if I don't like jumping out of airplanes?"

"How do you know until you try it? It's like the food; you have to try it to be able to say you don't like it."

"So I can't ask you to do things for me?"

"Yes you can, but you can't say I will do this if you do that every time, I want us to do something. It takes some of the fun away if I feel I am only getting you to do things as a payment."

There is a long pause in our conversation as we walk.

Kaye stops, "Let me see if I have this straight? You want me to do things you like such as surfing, swimming, parasailing, and skydiving without asking for stuff in return. No questions asked? At the same time if I want you to go shopping, to a fashion show, a play, or opera, you will go with me no questions asked?"

I look at the sand and then her, "I think you are finally getting it! That is the kind of friendship I want. I like the way the coach said it, 'a marriage is a friendship that got out of hand'."

Kaye starts walking again, "We are to just expect things of each other not request things?"

"Yes and no, that is one of those situations where there may be problems. For instance, you make reservations at a nice dinner somewhere without telling me and I planned for us to go to a business meeting. We have to pick what is important and maybe incorporate the two. We must have give and take and an understanding in our relationship. I don't want it to be all about me or all about you, and I definitely have a problem with, I will only do that if you do this."

She smiles and puts her arm in mine and we head back to our seats and family, "I get it. We should want to do what the other wants and trust each other completely without question, and we should want to spend all the time possible with each other. Does that sound right?"

I kick sand on her foot, "That sounds perfect!"

"Maybe that should be in our wedding vowels."

"I like it!! So we are in understanding?"

She smiles, "Yes, it is crystal clear my love. Can I lose my virginity now or at least take yours?"

I wonder if that is even possible to do one without the other happening, "If we do that, it will change our future and I don't like that other road it would put us on. By the way did you know your sister slept with both Steve and Jim last night?"

Chapter 18

The week continues the same every day, but tomorrow is New Year's Eve. Kaye and I cuddle up and watch the tiny waves roll in on the beach. My sister's friends from Florida head out for a stroll on the beach, "Hey Cutie!"

Kaye says, "Hi Ladies! How are you tonight?"

They wave and say, "You get tired of that boy, you send him to us ok?"

"Will do!"

Kaye watches them stroll down the beach and says, "You know they are Lesbians don't you?"

"No! I thought they said they were from Florida."

Kaye looks at me and says, "Not Lebanese from Lebanon, lesbians from Carpetmunch!"

I look at her pretending not to know the difference. She gets frustrated, "Carpet Muncher, girl on girl, gay!"

"Oh, then what would they need me for? I'm no girl!"

Kaye lays her head on my chest, "Thanks for playing. That was fun."

I rub her head and say, "Anytime my Dear!"

The girls come back and say, "What party are you guys going to tomorrow night?"

Kaye looks at me and I say, "Not sure but we will probably hit all of them."

"We will make sure you are on the list. Be here before midnight ok?"

Kaye smiles and says, "Why here at midnight?"

"We just want a big crowd here at the Xanadu."

Kaye looks at me, "Ok we will plan to be here then."

"Cool see you then if not before! Goodnight."

Still rubbing Kaye's head I say, "Hey girl, where you going to sleep tonight?"

"Same place I have all week, why?"

"Just making sure because that is where I'm headed."

Kaye taps my leg and says, "Life is going to be very different when we get back home."

"What do you mean?"

"We won't be able to sleep together anymore except in English class. We have to go back to being fifteen. Can't we just stay here?"

"In a couple of years this will be a, remember when memory."

"A what?"

I chuckle and say, "Haven't you ever heard anyone say, remember when we were kids and we did that thing with those people in that place?"

She stands up, "Let's go you're tired and silly."

We walk to the only jeep in the parking lot and jump in.

I look over at Kaye, "Hey Honey, how much is your dad up to money wise now?"

"Not real sure, but I am getting a car for my birthday."

"Yeah, it's going to suck going back to the real world where we actually have to spend money."

Kaye looks at me as I drive down the narrow road, "How much have we spent on this trip?"

I tally the amount in my head, "The plane ride here and home will cost seven thousand. The hotel has still only charged us for our regular rooms and that comes to around fourteen hundred. We have either been given food or paid for food and shopping with money won from the casino."

"So, around ten thousand for the week?"

I pull into the parking lot at our hotel, "That's close but we have won way more than I planned. If my math is correct, your parents have won around $55,000 and have lost close to $38,000. My family has won $900,000 and still has $325,000."

Kaye smiles as we step out of the vehicle, "We are rich!"

My sister is waiting for us in the lobby with Mike and walk towards us.

I fear something has gone wrong as my sister says, "Can we take that jeep to the beach?"

I breathe a sigh of relief hand Mike the keys, "Goodnight guys, I'm going to bed."

My sister hugs me, "Goodnight Babe, did you see Trish and Lindsey down there?"

Kaye says, "Yes and they want us to be there tomorrow at midnight."

Roxanne laughs and jumps in the jeep, "Oh they want to kiss my brother!"

I turn to look at her, "What?"

Mike says, "Yeah at midnight everyone kisses everyone to bring in the New Year! Oh yeah, this is really your first time as grownups! Goodnight!"

They drive away and Kaye looks at me, "No lesbian is putting her gay tongue down my boyfriend's throat! She might turn you gay!" I point at Kaye and almost say something but she stops me as she says, "I know that made no sense, let's find our parents and tell them goodnight."

I walk in the casino with Kaye following me and holding my hand. I see our mothers playing slots and they seem to be doing very well and having a good time. I hug Kaye's mother around the neck and kiss her cheek, "Mom do you trust me?"

"Sure I do Sweetie!"

"That big machine is going to pay someone $50,000 in about 30 more tries. Do you have thirty dollars?" She opens her purse, "I sure do Honey, here you go."

Kaye asks, "Why is my mother handing my boyfriend money?"

I look at Mrs. Lewis, "No, you have to win it, not me. When you win . . . I told you nothing." She stands up as the man playing the big machine walks away. She loads the machine with three tens and starts pulling the handle.

"Mommy dearest, I am going to bed! That snorkeling today wore me out."

My mother hugs me and punches my back while hugging me, "Don't call me that! How much is Pat about to win?"

I say, "Fifty thousand. Love ya, Mom see you for breakfast."

"Goodnight my baby. Update. Your dad has lost about twenty thousand and I've won about three thousand. I'm going to watch Pat win, watch my money."

"Mom! I'm going to bed!"

She walks away anyway. I see our dads coming towards us thank God! I walk to them and hug them, "Goodnight gentlemen! My mom has money in this machine and she went to watch Mrs. Lewis win fifty thousand on the big slot machine. Please watch this machine so I can go to bed!"

My father sits at the machine, "I lost fifty thousand tonight!"

"Good, thank you!"

Kaye talks to her father and I say to her, "You guys may want to watch your mom Kaye!"

They walk over to the big slot machine as my dad pulls me close to him and whispers to me, "I thought the plan was to win!"

"I told you Dad around $200,000 with what you told me you are still around three hundred thousand correct?"

"Yes, that is correct."

"Don't get greedy Pop! We had a fun free week plus they are giving us a bunch of their money to take home."

"You're right Son, but how are we going to take it home? Won't customs say something with that much money?"

"You get a check for half and the rest in cash. I think that is why my sister hired a private plane instead of the airline."

Dad smiles, "Now it makes sense. You had this planned didn't you?"

"Yes Sir, I did. You need to claim the check as gambling money to the bank and set aside about fifty thousand for taxes."

I tell my father the rest of the plan as Kaye's mom hits the partial jackpot for $50,000. As Mrs. Lewis looks for me, runs and hugs me and I say in her ear, "Mom you won! That is great. It had nothing to do with me!"

She pulls away from me, smiles and says, "Ok!"

She runs back to the machine to claim her prize. Kaye runs over to me and says, "Did you tell her . . ."

"Kaye, you have to make sure your mom says nothing about me telling her anything! Go baby!"

Kaye runs back to her mom to keep us all out of trouble and out of the spotlight.

The bedroom door opens and Kaye's mom walks in and sees Kaye spooning me. "Wake up my little ones!" I hear this and a hand hits Kaye's butt, she jumps and I feel her recoil from the blow. "Breakfast is in five minutes! Get up!" Then her mom leans over the bed and kisses me on the head, and then she kisses Kaye. "See you outside in five!" She walks out of the room and I say to Kaye. "Is that the way she wakes you up all the time?"

"Pretty much, why?"

"Same as my mom. Wonder if they were in the military together?"

Kaye chuckles and rolls out of bed. "Hey, let's take a shower together!"

"Kaye, have you lost your mind? If we did that I would have a very hard time staying a virgin!"

She smiles a devilish smile at me and walks into the bathroom. I walk out of the room wanting to go into the bathroom so bad. Why does she keep tempting me? Doesn't she know that could ruin what we have going on? *That is her bad side talking; you are supposed to be tempted. You are going to be given all kinds of temptations in life and it is still your job to make the right choices. It is my job to tell you the good from the bad.* Nevertheless, I want to be with her so bad! *She knows that, but her insecurity makes her think that if you sleep together it will keep you from being with someone else.*

I run and jump in the pool and begin swimming laps and try to get rid of my sexual frustration. My dad jumps in the pool with me and swims laps with me as the two moms set up breakfast again. We stop at the far end of the pool and my father asks, "What's wrong Son?"

"Nothing Sir."

My father treads water over to me, looks in my eyes, and asks, "It's a woman problem!"

He's good! He continues, "Well you are still a virgin, so it is most likely sexual frustration." *He is real good!* I look at my father in shock. "How did you . . ."

"I have it too Son, but have just recently realized how to use it when I started talking with you about it."

I smile at him and he says, "You want to get rid of the frustration and stay a virgin?"

"I'm not that interested in staying a virgin though."

"You said your life would change for the bad if you did though?"

"I know, but I don't know what I want anymore. The temptation is too great!"

Mom yells, "Breakfast gentlemen!"

My dad holds up one finger to my mother and then says to me, "You want the temptation to stop?"

"Yes Sir I do!"

He looks around and sees Kaye coming out to the patio area, "Then stop sleeping in the same bed with the girl Son. That is a stronger temptation than most men can handle!"

"I think that is what I am supposed to prove, that I am strong enough."

My dad smirks at me, "Race you to the other side!"

He takes off swimming and I jump to catch up and paddle with my arms as hard as I can. We reach the other end of the pool and my dad touches just before I do, "The old man has still got it!"

"Yeah Dad, but aren't you use to gators chasing you?"

"That's what I thought you were splashing around back there!"

We get out of the pool and walk over to the breakfast table, "Dad does your voice tell you stuff also?"

"I have no voice Son. I can just look at people and tell if they are lying or not."

"How did you do that thing in the pool while ago?"

"You are my son and I can read your thoughts. Especially when I was your age I had the same thoughts."

"Then do it again!"

He looks in my eyes, "Bacon and waffles, no cereal! Not real sure, what that's about Son?"

We all sit down and start eating after Bob says the blessing. Kaye waits on me like a good wife and I am as gracious as possible to her. The parents watch us and wonder if we have crossed the point we assured them we would not. My dad says, "Last full day here what are the plans?" No one says anything and we all seem content. The Lewis' say they are finished gambling, and they are content with their eighty thousand. We have all done enough gambling and gone to the same beach every day. I look around the table and say, "My suggestion is we get three jeeps and go to the north end of the island and have a picnic on the beach. John said it was 90 kilometers up there and it is nice and serene." They all look around and decide it is a good idea. The little old woman from earlier in the week walks toward our coffee urn again. As she pours herself a cup my mom stands up and says, "Ma'am would you care to join us?"

She looks around at us as if she did not even know we were there, "Thank you Dear, I would love to."

My mother gets her a chair and she sits down, "That casino has been kicking my butt! I have lost way too much and can't seem to get my money back."

I look at Kaye and whisper to her, "Go get my wallet off the dresser Honey."

Kaye stands up and walks in my room as the old lady begins telling us her life story. Kaye returns and sits down and the lady says, "That's why I am glad the hotel has this free coffee out here every morning. It gives me a chance to clear my head out here by the pool. You guys must like it too, I see you out here almost every morning."

We smile at her and my dad says, "Yes it is good coffee, and a relaxing atmosphere also, like you said." She smiles at us and says, "How much longer are you guys staying?"

My dad says, "We have to leave tomorrow morning. What about you?"

"I leave here in a couple of hours."

I lean over the table, "Ma'am can I ask a favor of you?"

She looks at me, "I guess so Sonny, but I have no money."

I hand her a ten-dollar bill, "This is my lucky ten dollars. I was only going to spend it if I needed to, but my parents have won enough that I don't need to have it anymore. I would like you to have it and if you use it on the big slot machine I am willing to bet you win your money back."

She takes the money and says, "Thank you Sonny, I'll go give it a try right now. Whatever I win I will split it with you."

"Thanks, but that will not be necessary you keep it all. Just remember my kind act. That will be my share of our winnings."

She stands up, walks around the table, hugs me, and whispers in my ear, "I knew I made the right choice by helping you. Listen to your voice. You are a good boy stay on the road you are traveling on my friend and you will have a good life."

She releases me and I stare at her in shock as if I had just seen a ghost. She kisses my cheek and waves to everyone as she walks away. I stare as she walks out of sight and my voice says. *I see you met Angel! She checks up on us from time to time. If she finds you undeserving of the gift she can take it away. Did I forget to tell you that part? She is why Kaye keeps tempting and testing you.* So this is some kind of game in the spiritual world? *Sort of, if you want to look at it that way. If you want it to stop, just say the word. Things can go back, as it would have been.*

Kaye stands in front of me, "You ok, Babe?"

I look at her and then our family staring at me as I tremble, "Yeah! I am fine I just realized I know that woman from back home. Her name is Miss Devine."

My dad says, "Small world huh? Let's get going that may be a long drive up the coast."

I think that my small world is going to get smaller all the time.

We drive up the coast to the beach looking at the land along the way and I see some places that look trashy and unattractive and some that are very nice. I guess no place is perfect, wonder if the real paradise will have trashy areas. *Yeah but you will never see them.* We get to the beach and set up a canopy that the hotel loaned us, to provide some shade. My mom looks around at the area, "Good call Son, this is really lovely up here." I smile at my mother setting up lunch and say to Kaye, "Kaye, do want to swim?"

"With you, I don't think so!" She laughs and peels her clothes off to reveal her hot pink bathing suit and we run to the ocean. When we get in the water, we see jellyfish and Kaye screams. I show her how to avoid them so we do not get stung as we play in the water. We swim and play and our sisters and friends join us.

We look up at the beach and a convoy of Rolls Royce's pull up and unload teenage boys that look Arab. We watch them cautiously at first, and then just continue talking and wading in the water. We walk out of the water and towards the canopy to eat lunch with our parents.

I walk past one of the older boys and say, "Speak English?"

"Of course I do! Do you speak Arabic?"

"Not yet, I am one of the stupid American children that think the whole world should speak English."

He chuckles at me and I say, "You and your friends need to be careful we saw some jellyfish out there earlier."

"Thank you I will watch out for my brothers."

"Those are all your brothers?"

He looks out at the water, "Yes they are my brother's, some have different mothers, but we have the same father."

"Interesting, my name is Tommy."

"My name is . . ." He thinks of what he wants to say, "My name is Turkihe."

He is a prince! Down the line, but he is still a prince. He listens to his conscience as well and he knows you do too.

We shake hands and I say, "Nice to meet you Sir!"

"You too! Are those your wives?"

I look to my sister and Kaye approaching, "No, my sister and my girlfriend."

"Please stop them from approaching or I must leave you!"

I put my hand up to the girls and wave for them to go back, "I'll be there in a minute."

They walk backwards to our picnic area and do not understand the situation, but do as instructed.

He looks to the sea and says, "Sorry for that! My customs do not allow me to talk with unwed women or women in general conversation. I realize we are not in Saudi but I must respect my training."

"I understand!"

"So, how much for your sister or for your girlfriend? I will give you ten thousand camels for them both."

"Now see that is the point in my culture I am now allowed to kick your butt for making such an offer."

"I know. I was just testing your character. By your dialect I thought we might already be fighting by now."

"Do you want to fight me? Because I am not too dumb to know that you just called me a redneck!"

My dad and Mike start coming toward us. "I don't need to fight you today, but after you have had some training I would like to spar with you. One day we will fight and one day we will fight together. I would like to remain your sadeqi, oh sorry your friend, we will need each other one day!"

"I am not sure I understand?"

"It will be explained to you. When you gain more control in your country we will become better friends. We will have a common enemy one day and I will need your assistance."

He places his hand out for me to shake, "Until then my friend!"

As we shake hands, we both use the firmest grip possible. "Masalama Prince."

"You are getting better as we speak, good bye Sadeqi."

He releases my hand at the same time as I do and he returns to his brothers and yells, "Mashena!"

My dad and Mike walk up as Turkihe trots off and his brothers run to him like trained pets.

Dad says, "What was that about Son?"

I guess mashena means come here or let's go. "Oh, just some hot shot Prince of Persia that I am going to have to put in his proper place someday. Hey Dad, I need to start taking karate again when we get home. The Prince seems to think I need more training before I kick his ass."

"That sounds good to me. We will both start back next week. But right now let's eat."

Mike and my dad walk towards the picnic area and I stare at the Prince.

Kaye comes over and takes my hand, "What's going on Babe?"

"Today keeps getting weirder and weirder Kaye! That lady from this morning was not what she seemed and that guy is some weird Prince that wanted to buy you for ten thousand camels. When I offered to kick his ass for free he said I needed more training first and that someday we would have a common enemy."

I point to the water, "Look at these guys picking up jelly fish and throwing them. What kind of person does that?"

She looks at me and smiles, "That is strange. What does your conscience say about it?"

"Nothing yet! Guess I need some alone time."

"Come eat and then I will rub your head so you can take a nap and possibly find out."

We eat lunch and as I finish the Prince approaches, but stops a safe distance from the women.

I walk over to him and he says, "I want to make sure we are going to be friends. I meant no offense to you or your women."

"That makes it better, but one day we will have to fight."

"I look forward to it my Sadeqi!"

We shake hands and he climbs into the backseat of his Rolls Royce. *You know he can hear his voice as well right? I'll explain him to you later, good man to know.* I watch the cars pull away and my family watches me. I walk back toward them, "What a day!"

That afternoon we arrive back at the hotel and John is waiting on us. I park and he comes to me and says, "You guys are leaving in the morning Sir?"

"Yes John, we have to leave tomorrow."

"So you are going to come to the casino this evening?"

My parents park their jeep and my dad sees John and me talking and waves to us. I understand what John is getting at, "Well John, our parents are finished gambling, but I wouldn't mind giving it a one last shot."

"Excellent what time Sir?"

I look at Kaye; "We would like one blackjack table, one craps table and one roulette table to ourselves as soon as possible."

We go to our rooms and cleanup for our showdown with the casino. We walk in the casino and my sister and Mike run up and join us.

"Right this way Sir, I have one of each table waiting for you now."

I say to Kaye, "Baby are you going to be able to handle this? I am about to lose ten million dollars!"

"No way! So how much are you actually going to leave with?"

"I can't tell you that, it would ruin the surprise."

"I don't care. I loved you when you were poor and I will love you if you are rich, so either way I know I will love you!"

"That's my girl I knew I made the right choice with you!"

That is scary, where did we hear that today? That is odd, now you have me quoting old ladies or Angels?

We step into the private game section and my sister says, "Can I play some too?"

I whisper to her, "Remember our objective Sis!"

"John could you give me a hundred thousand from our marker please?"

I lean against the rail of the craps table and he replies, "Yes Sir, no problem. That will make your new balance $122,000."

"Thank you John."

The dealer pushes the ten die at me, "Kaye Honey, pick two dice please." Kaye reaches down and selects two and begins shaking them.

"John can she have a practice roll she has never done this before?"

"Certainly, it is your table Sir."

Kaye tosses the dice, a seven falls, and the dealer says, "Nice roll Ma'am!"

I look at her shocked, "Think you can do that again Babe?"

"I hope so!"

"All on the seven gentlemen! Roll it again Honey!" Kaye tosses the dice and another seven appears. And just like that we now have seven hundred thousand. I hand my sister a tray of a hundred thousand and one to Kaye and one to Mike. "Good luck my people!"

We are served drinks and then we gamble for what seemed like hours. I take a tray over to the roulette table and bet a hundred thousand on black and lose.

I walk back over to the craps table, "I want to bet it all!"

The dealer counts the chips, "One million five hundred thousand."

"I changed my mind! I'll bet one million on the field. Put one hundred and fifty thousand back on the marker please." The rest I put in a chip rack.

The dealer pulls a million to the field and pulls $150,000 back to the house for my marker.

"Ok Kaye, roll a number in the field."

"What field?"

"Baby, right here! 2-3-4-9-10-11 or 12" I point to the numbers and she says, "Oh any of those numbers!"

"Yes please!"

She tosses the dice and a twelve comes up I cheer as our parents walk up.

Her dad says, "What's going on?"

"Your daughter just won me three million dollars!"

They all hug her and I prepare for the next roll, "If you are squeamish you may need to leave she might lose it all for me too!"

I look over at my sister and she is down to about twenty thousand, "Hey Sis, bet it all on the next hand! I just did and I won!"

She bets the whole pile of chips and wins with a blackjack. She runs over and kisses me on the cheek.

I look back at the craps table and say, "All of it on the seven again!"

The family comes over to watch. The dealer says, "Three million on seven." John comes over to the table, "Sorry Sir, we cannot cover that bet. I know I said it was an unlimited table but we must limit your bets to one million per table. I apologize for any inconvenience."

"No John, I apologize I was assuming too much. Ok one million on seven here. Sis, take this one over to blackjack and mom set this on black on the roulette table. Dealers, take two thousand for a tip from each million. Kaye roll the dice" Kaye starts shaking the dice and the dealers all say thank you sir at the same time. Kaye rolls another seven for a win I hug her and mom says, "You won over here too!"

My sister says, "You have seventeen against a ten showing over here."

I walk over to the blackjack table, "Leave it!"

The dealer flips his bottom card and has another ten. "Sorry Bro!"

"It's alright, that's why I hate blackjack!"

"Kaye, so what is our balance on the table now?" She looks as she sips her drink and the dealer whispers an amount to her, "$10,350,000 Sweetie! Can we go home now?"

I look at John, "How about ten million on black at roulette?"

He looks over at the table and nods in agreement. My family goes crazy, "What are you doing?"

Kaye smiles at the chaos that I created. We place the bet on the black and my dad just watches as if he knows what is going to happen as well. The croupier rolls the ball around the wheel and we wait for it to bounce and fall on a number and color. The ball stops on green zero and I yell, "No!" for a more dramatic affect. John tries not to appear happy, but I can see in his mind, he is very happy.

I look at the 350,000 in chips and try to decide what to do. Should I keep it and have over half a million or lose it and not worry about these guys hunting us down? *LOSE IT!*

"John I would like to bet this 350,000 on blackjack."

Now my dad is getting upset, "Come on kid, know when to quit!"

John smiles as I place the bet. As the cards are dealt I see my hand of 13 against an Ace. "Oh come on! Not my lucky number against an Ace! You are killing me!"

I look around the room in disgust, I look at the dealer, "Hit me lightly please."

"Would you like insurance Sir?"

"No"

He places my next card and it is a seven, "Yes, 20. What you got under there, big boy?"

The dealer flips his hole card and there is the suicide king staring at me, as I yell, "No! Damn, king of hearts for a stupid Blackjack! Told you I hate Blackjack, and that is why."

My family and spectators all sigh and say tough luck. I again look at John and can see he is relieved and now my family leaving with close to three hundred thousand does not seem as bad.

I walk over to Kaye and she hugs me and says, "It's alright Baby you can get it back some day."

She almost laughs as she pretends to cry.

"You got anymore sevens in you babe?"

"Nope all done!"

John comes up, "What would you like to do Sir?"

"Get my ten million back please!"

My father puts his hand on my shoulder and says to John, "What do we have left on our marker, anything?"

"Yes Sir you have $272,000 on that marker."

"John, what I'd like to do is close that marker. How do we do that?"

My sister loses the rest of her money and yells, "Crap!"

John looks at her and then my father, "There are several different ways we can handle it."

"Would it be possible to receive a check for $150,000 and $120,000 cash?"

"What about the two thousand Sir?"

"John, you guys have been so good to us. I would like for you to have it, the casino or hotel. So when we come back you will treat us the same way."

"Sir, you will always have a free room here and we will eagerly await your return to us. There will be no charges for your stay this time as well."

The two men shake hands and John says, "You will be able to pick up your cash and check whenever you want, tonight or in the morning."

"Thank you John, see you next trip, I hope."

We walk out of the casino and I say to my dad as he has his arm around my neck and Kaye has her arm around my waist, "Nice job people we pulled it off."

Kaye says to me, "Hey, thanks for warning me what you were going to do or I would have been freaking out over losing that much money."

"Kaye Honey, you need to find a middle ground because you did not act upset enough. Nice job Dad! I couldn't have done better myself!"

"Thank you Son, see I have skills and I didn't have to lose ten million to walk out with my two hundred thousand."

"Right, I took that bullet for you!"

He laughs as we walk out the door and our family follows.

Kaye smiles, "I'll work on my drama to get it just right."

Dad looks over at her, "You're doing fine, Girl!"

We walk to the pool area and sit at our patio chairs in front of our rooms.

"What a way to end the year? Son what would you have done if you won that money?"

I look around and notice all the ears ready for the information.

"I would have put it in the bank and canceled your insurance, bought some airplanes to do my training and make some money, invested some of it, and given some to a couple of needy churches and other charities that need it. Like that one up in Washington, DC."

My mom says, "Which one in Washington?"

"I think it is called the US Government, they always need money for some reason. Something about taking care of poor people like us, since we are broke again."

They laugh and enjoy my poke at the mighty government they fall under and complain about. Funny to me the first to complain about something are usually the last to make an effort to change things.

We dress for dinner and I talk Kaye into letting me watch her dress for dinner. I want to see the process and ritual she goes through to make herself presentable to the masses. She comes in my room and lays her gown on the bed and as she is dropping the robe she is wearing she ask, "Are you sure you can handle this?"

"No, but it is a demon I want to face once and for all!"

The robe hits the floor and her nakedness slaps my face as she steps in my shower. I am sitting there watching her and am amazed by her beauty. She washes her long blond hair seductively. I have already dressed for dinner or I would probably jump in the shower with her after that maneuver she just made. I sit on the toilet watching her and she finally looks at me as I gaze pleasantly at her beauty, "How long do we have to wait before we can?"

I come back to reality, "Um I can't tell you! We might have already and you just don't remember."

"If that is the case then come show me how we did it."

"Kaye, shut up and color!"

She laughs at me as she rinses the soap off her body. She steps out of the shower and I hand her a towel. "Hey give me a kiss!"

"Sorry Kaye not right now, I could not resist that temptation right now."

She dries herself, "Then why are you torturing yourself?"

"Something I need to do! This makes me not wonder and only think of you tonight."

"Thanks!"

"I mean I will still think of you, but not be obsessed with what is under that dress all night. The other night when you wore it all I could think about was getting it off of you. Now it should not bother me as bad, I hope!" She wraps a towel around her wet blond hair, slaps on makeup, then grabs her gown, and slips it on.

"Hey girl, no panties or bra?"

"Nope, can't. You will see the lines and straps."

I slap my forehead and say, "Well this didn't work, because now I want to tear that dress off again!"

She removes the towel from her head and blow-dries her hair for what seemed only to be a minute, flips her hair and taps my face, "Oh poor baby! You look good in that tux by the way!"

She laughs and leaves the room. *She loves knowing she has some power over you, which is why she normally is so insecure around you. She will get better I promise!* Why is she insecure? *She feels she loves you more than you love her.*

"Girl, are you finished?"

"Yes why?"

"You realize you just got ready in fifteen minutes? If we get married, are you still going to be able to pull that off?"

"As long as you help with the kids I will be able to!"

"Ha, very funny. Kids, can we just get the grown kind not the babies?"

"No, I want a little you or me running around terrorizing my mom and dad!"

There is a knock at the door, Mike opens it and lets the parents in. "You kids look nice!"

I say, "Kaye I need you in the bedroom for a moment."

I grab her mother's arm as I enter and drag her with me. With our back to Kaye, I show her mom a necklace I bought for Kaye. Her mom smiles and says, "Very nice!"

We turn to Kaye and show her the necklace that is diamond and pearls. Not a choker, but should hang just above her breast tastefully. "Oh that is beautiful! For me?"

I place it around her neck and say, "Happy New Year Babe!"

She tears up and hugs her mom and then me.

We head down to the hotel ballroom and we are escorted in and given our first round of drinks. We sit and talk about the accomplishments of the year and the things we hope to accomplish in the future. Kaye leans over and says, "Tell me about our future?"

I look at her and her beautiful dress, "I can't hear you. Your dress is too loud!"

She smiles, "Either you tell me or I will take it off right here and tell everyone you dared me to!" *She is serious tell her this.*

I look deep in her eyes, "Every road has decisions we have to make. If we make a wrong turn, our roads may go in opposite directions . . . Let's play a game, you tell me places you would like to go during your life. I can only see places I go and I will know if you are there with me. That will give you an idea and that is all I am allowed to let you know."

She looks at me in wonder and says, "Paris?"

"Yes!"

"London?"

"Yes!"

"All of Europe?"

"All the good places, and some not on a tourists map!"

She looks at me wishing she knew more, "Mexico and Hawaii?"

"Yes and Yes!"

She smiles and says, "Sounds good! How many children will we have?"

"How many do you want?"

"As many as we can afford!"

"We are not going to have that many! You would never be on your feet."

She smiles, "Then how about five or six?"

"That sounds like a plan my girl!"

The party starts becoming more and more crowded. A group of high rollers just arrived and we can tell these boys are used to partying and have it down to a science. One of them walks over to us and says, "Hear you guys are the new hot stuff on the block!"

My father and I say nothing and watch the man, as he is obviously drunk. "What you boys too good to talk to me?"

His friends start to gather around him. My father says, "Oh I'm sorry, I thought you were just making a general statement. I heard you address no one."

The man looks my father up and down and says, "Well then let me introduce myself. I am Jimmy Taylor. I have won enough off this casino to own the place, but I like to let them think they still own it. Now back to my original statement. I hear you boys are the new hot stuff around here!"

My dad smiles at the man, "Nice to meet you Mr. Taylor we have really enjoyed your casino. We had the opportunity to win a couple of million but we lost it as quick as we won it. If that qualifies us as hot stuff then yes, to answer your question or statement. I'm still not sure which it was, but we consider ourselves lucky tourist that had a fun week in the Bahamas."

The man studies my father as he was speaking and now says, "So you boys aren't pros? You are just down here having fun and had some luck in the process?"

My dad looks at me and then back at the man, "That is correct Sir. I am a business man and my kids are still in school."

He looks around at our group and says, "Tourist? Guess I was misinformed! From what I hear you should be pros and if you do go pro give me a call. We could own this island!"

He hands my father his business card and shakes his hand. "Good luck to you and your family!"

He waves and walks away.

"Dad let me see that business card," my dad hands it to me. I look at the card and notice the girls with the man. He is somebody important I can feel it.

Kaye leans over, "What's up?"

"Nothing, there is something about that guy that is odd." I look at the card and my conscience explains the type of stuff the man is into and predicts I will see him again.

"Let's go to that party at the Xanadu."

I stand up and the rest of my group stands to join me.

My dad says, "How are we getting there?"

"I have a limo waiting on us Dad!"

We walk out the front door and John follows us, "Leaving so soon gentlemen and lovely ladies?"

My dad turns around and says, "We promised some friends at the Xanadu we would make an appearance there. We will return. You want to come with us?"

"Thank you Sir, but I cannot leave here. We will see you later then?"

"Most definitely we will return. Bye John."

We all squeeze into the limo and the car pulls away from the building. As Kaye sits on my lap, I whisper to her, "Sitting on my lap is not the best idea with that dress on and no panties!"

She turns to me, "In a couple of years you will be begging for me to do this! I love my necklace by the way, thank you very much."

"You are welcome I got it for losing that money . . . the ten million."

We arrive at our destination and walk toward the elevator. As we reach the top floor we see the volleyball girls, I notice the Prince sitting in the corner talking to people about his age. We talk to Trish, Lindsey, and the rest of their friends. They admire each other's attire, as girls seem to like to do. We dance and have a good time and the New Year is only minutes away.

The Prince approaches me and says, "You have many women friends!"

"This is my custom, they are my friends."

He looks around at the girls, "They are very lovely. May I have one or two for the evening?"

"Turkihe it doesn't work that way here. Let me help you in our way of doing it."

I raise my hands to get their attention, "Excuse me ladies! This is Prince Turkihe from Saudi Arabia. He is a friend of mine and would like to know if any of you or all of you would care to dance with him and usher in the New Year with him?" A couple of the girls walk over and shake his hand and begin talking to him and as he backs up to the dance floor, I give him a wink and he nods to me. Kaye takes my hand and leads me to the dance floor. As we begin slow dancing, she whispers in my ear, "You are a good man and I am glad you are mine! I want to spend the rest of our lives making you happy."

I look her in the eyes, "That sounds nice and I think we are off to a great start."

I kiss her and as our chest squeeze together, I can feel her heart beating faster and harder like a frightened puppy. We stop kissing and just hold each other; she begins to breathe and relax and melts like butter in my arms. Hope I never lose that power over her. *As long as you continue to love her like you do and are always honest with her, she will always love and respect you.*

". . . 5, 4, 3, 2, 1 Happy New Year!" The crowd shouts and everyone begins hugging and kissing each other. Kaye and I kiss and she says, "Here is to a great life my friend!"

She kisses me again. We look up and see the girls from Florida rush towards us giggling and kissing everyone in their path. When they reach us, they place their arms out to us, we hug and kiss them, and I felt violated by a few of them. Some kissed me passionately and some kissed me as if it was the first time they ever kissed anyone. One of the girls put her tongue in my mouth and it felt like a windup toy went off in my mouth. One girl's tongue felt like she was looking for something in my mouth. My favorite was Lindsey, she was talking dirty as she kissed me and was inviting me to her room.

The girls were very smart with their tactics. They got Kaye far enough away from me but not far enough for her to worry. They blocked her vision and some even tried to French kiss her. They finally leave us and I say to Kaye, "Honey, I think I just got raped . . . Hold me!"

Kaye laughs and hugs me, "Great! Now you are going to be a lesbian! I think I can make that work to my advantage though!"

She laughs and I look at the floor sadly, "Sure, pick on the victim! I was sexually assaulted and you are making fun of me?"

She laughs and plays with my hair, "It will be ok Baby!"

The next morning we are awoken for breakfast by the phone ringing. "Five minutes, patio my Baby!" I sit up and look at Kaye sleeping. I watch her for a moment and then caress her breast to see if I could get away with it. I am going to miss waking up with her when we go home. *Yeah, poor thing, in two years she will be there all the time.*

She rolls over, "I am not hungry, and I want to sleep, rub my breast some more that felt good."

"Good luck with that dream! You know our moms. Plus we have to leave in an hour girl, so get your pretty butt up!"

I walk out of the bedroom and Mike and my sister are there drinking coffee. Their suitcases are beside them ready to go.

"You guys going somewhere?"

"Ha-ha very funny! We leave in one hour!"

"Sis, we have our own plane rented, I don't think it will matter if we are late."

She smiles, "Yes, I guess you are right!"

I walk out the door and jump in the pool one last time. As I swim around my father walks to the side and says, "Need you to come to my room please!"

I step out of the pool and follow my father. Walking past the food table, I grab a slice of bacon and my mother tosses me a towel. I dry off and enter the room and my father has the money sitting on the bed. I see the check for one hundred and fifty thousand and the cash sitting next to it. "Your mother and I counted it and it is all there."

"Good, so what's the problem?"

"I can put the check in my wallet, but the cash is not going to fit."

"Put it in your carry-on bag."

"I saw a briefcase in the lobby I was thinking about buying."

I think for a moment, "That is so the movies Dad! If a customs agent happens to see us at the general aviation terminal and they see you with a briefcase. Don't you think they would want to check it more than a carry-on bag?"

"Good point and if it was in your bag it would be even less suspect, right?"

"Yes Dad I believe it would."

He smiles and says, "Go get me your bag and we will put it in there."

"Yes Sir."

Walking past the table again, I reach down and grab more bacon.

I go in my room and Kaye is up and moving making sure she has everything. "What's wrong girl, you look like you have lost something important?"

"Have you seen my necklace I can't find it?"

"The last time I saw it was last night when that girl was taking it off your neck."

"WHAT!?"

Everyone rushes in the room, "What's wrong Honey?"

"You said some girl took it off my neck last night?"

"Yes one of those Florida girls. I thought you were giving it to her."

"Why would I do that?"

"She needed the money and I thought you were being nice and helping her out."

Kaye screams and says, "I loved that necklace! It was a gift from you and I would not just give that away!"

"Actually it was a gift from the hotel. They gave it to me, I passed it on to you, and I thought that was the spirit you were giving to that girl."

Kaye looks in shock and says, "Maybe I was drunk, but I don't remember this happening."

We walk out to the breakfast table on the patio, "The girl was talking about her parents getting thrown out of their house."

"I remember that part."

I make a plate of food for Kaye and say, "Well you were being very compassionate towards her, and at the countdown she was removing it from your neck. I was about to say something and then you hugged her. So I thought you had given it to her. I was so proud of you and thought it was the most selfless act I had actually witnessed."

Kaye smiles, "She stole my necklace, and you thought I was giving it to her. That is strange?"

Kaye's mom says, "Honey, I was there and thought the exact same thing. You were doing a good deed Sweetie!"

Kaye looks sad and pats my hand, "I thought that was a gift from you."

I hug Kaye, "I'm sorry if I misinformed you. I wanted to take credit for it, but that girl needed it more than you did. It was a gift from the hotel and I wanted you to look and feel nice last night, but I planned to give it to her anyway. Roxanne told me the story yesterday. I will buy you another if it means that much to you."

She says, "No, no . . . you're right. Where would I wear a diamond necklace anyway?"

I laugh and say, "Yeah you could never wear that dress to our school anyway. Next time you need that dress I will make sure you have as good or a better necklace."

She hugs me and says, "Thank you! Some things you do are going to take some getting used to."

"Got to keep it interesting girl."

We arrive at the airport and they put our bags on the plane. I see the pilots and shake their hands, "Happy New Year! You ready to go back Sir?"

"No, I don't want to go back to the cold weather. I want to stay here where it is warm."

"Hey it was snowing when we were leaving this morning."

"Great! Where is your copilot? Same guy?"

"Yes Sir, he is doing the preflight on the plane."

"Let's go find him; he is going to like me."

I pull out a wad of cash, "He is going to love this! Remember that five bucks he gave me?"

I smile at the pilot, "He won a couple of times."

We walk into the cockpit of the airplane and he says, "Welcome aboard Sir, what's with the cash?"

"I did like you said number twelve on roulette. I saved half and bet the rest the next day and so on. The last day you lost, sorry."

He takes the cash, "Thank you Sir!"

He hugs me and says, "How did you do?"

I smile as Kaye walks in behind me and say, "I won a little, and some lesbian raped me."

Kaye slaps my butt as the pilots laugh at me. "Honey it is snowing at home!"

The pilots continue to laugh at me.

I look at the copilot, "So is that worth you giving up the right seat for a while on the way home Buddy?"

"Sir I have no objection if the captain doesn't!"

The captain looks at me and says, "I will let you sit up here for takeoff and one hour of flight if you can answer a question."

"I will try my best Sir."

"What is the difference between rotate and flare?"

I look at the floor and then the pilot, "They both have to do with raising the nose of the airplane. Rotation is for takeoff and flare is for landing."

He smiles at me and hands me the flight manual, "Very nice! Look through this and get familiar with the takeoff speeds, procedures and emergency procedures."

I take the book, walk to Kaye, sit on her seat with her, and flip through the book. Kaye looks over my shoulder and says, "What are you doing, Lesbian? Are you going to fly us home?"

"Yes, I am Darling!"

"Really? That is cool for you!"

I look at her, "You ok with that?"

"Sure, the pilot won't let anything happen right?"

"That is correct, no worries."

I continue flipping page after page memorizing every speed, setting, and procedure.

I walk to the cockpit, "I'm ready Sir."

He looks at me in shock, "Really then you can answer any question I ask?"

"I hope so."

"Then what runway should we depart on?"

"What is it with you guys and your trick questions? That's not in the book. But looking at that windsock out there the wind is coming from the north so our best option would be runway six."

The two pilots look at me in shock and the captain says, "What is our takeoff speed?"

"What is our weight? I saw a lot of variations depending on our weight?"

"We are right at twenty thousand."

"At that weight we should rotate at 108 KIAS and takeoff with 8 degree of flaps and takeoff at 120 KIAS."

"That is very good, one last question and you can fly with me. What is maneuvering speed and what is ours at our current weight and why is it important?"

"That is the speed you need to fly at in turbulent air, our speed at that weight should be 225 KIAS. We slow it down to keep the wings from breaking off or making my girlfriend sick."

Kaye smacks me on the back, "How did you know I was here?"

"Honey I bought you that perfume, remember?"

"Have a seat and let's get this party out of here."

I sit in the copilot seat, don the radio headset, and flip the mike switch, "If everyone could take their seats please. We will begin our taxi here shortly, thank you."

My family looks to the cockpit in question and do as they have been instructed. I read the steps in the checklist to the captain and he performs the step or says check. We start the engines and then get our clearance for departure. As we start to taxi the pilot explains to me about the operation of the rudders of the airplane, tells me the direction and yellow line to follow, and says, "You have the airplane." I step on the rudder controls and guide the aircraft to runway 6. The pilot helps me with the throttle and says, "Our taxi speed should be that of a brisk walk." I nod in agreement and continue to steer us down the taxiway as we roll he explains how to takeoff and things I should pay attention to. We reach the end of the runway, and the tower clears us for takeoff. The pilot says to me, "Take her on the runway we will stop for a final check and then we go." He presses the mike button, "Roger tower clear to go for 38 Alpha Juliet." He points to the number painted on the runway, "Stop just before the numbers." He flips the radio switch to cabin and says, "Ladies and gentlemen and Kaye prepare for departure." We hear Kaye from the back, "Hey!"

He explains how torque is going to make the nose of the aircraft go to the left and how to correct for it and how the wind will affect us. "Concentrate on getting us airborne when I say rotate I will help as needed. Throttle full forward and let's go." I push the throttle levers forward and feel the thrust of the aircraft. I keep the airplane rolling straight down the runway and apply slight backpressure on the yoke, the nose wheel starts to rise, and I hold it at that point and no more. He says rotate and I apply more pressure and we become airborne. I feel him push the yoke a bit to bring the nose of the airplane down. "Gear up." I put the handle up and feel the wheels retract. *You did it tough guy, you got this bird in the air and now you are flying!* I feel like a puppet, the captain pulls my strings and I do his bidding. I continue flying and making the corrections requested by the pilot and turns to new headings.

We get to our cruise altitude and the captain says, "You did very well, but how do you feel?"

"A bit overwhelmed, that is a lot to process in a short period of time."

"Yeah, but you get use to it, it becomes second nature. Remember you just started in a jet and most people start in a smaller aircraft with less going on and less to do."

I scan the horizon for traffic and the captain says, "Any plans to be a pilot?"

"Yes Sir, but not for hire. I will fly my own aircraft and that's about it."

"That sounds nice what do you plan to have?"

"I'm not real sure, but something that I can fly this crowd around in." He looks at them and says, "Nice group, all family?"

"No Sir."

I point everybody out, "Kaye is my girlfriend and that is her family and my sister's boyfriend. These here belong to me."

He chuckles at me, "Well you definitely seem like a pilot. Whatever you do, good luck to you and if you decide to fly come see me. I'd hire you soon as you got rated."

"Thank you Sir! I will start lessons in a couple of weeks."

He hands me his business card, "Call me, and I will get you going I have my own little Cessna and I'll be glad to teach you."

I look at his card and see CFII Jerry Lowery. "I'll call you next week and we can set up a schedule."

"Sounds good Buddy."

We are almost home and I get up and go to the back of the plane. I sit down with my sleeping Kaye and she just snuggles into me as if I was there all the time.

"Did you have fun Babe?"

"Yes, but it is a lot of work!"

"You still want to do it?"

"I sure do, Jerry is going to teach me."

"Our pilot?"

"Yeah, he is an instructor and has his own plane."

She puts her head on my shoulder, "Sounds good, take a nap with me."

Chapter 19

The phone rings and my sister answers it, "Tommy it's for you!"

I come to the phone, "Hello!"

I hear my friend Chris on the other end, "Hey, yeah we just got in around lunch time. How have you been?"

I listen to his Christmas and New Year's stories, "That sounds great what you doing today and tonight?" I listen to him say nothing and then say, "I thought we could get caught up and help me move at the same time."

He checks with his mom, "Great, thanks I'll see you in a bit and I'll get to see your new car."

I yell through the house, "Chris is coming to help!"

My dad yells, "Great the more the merrier!"

My mom tells us stuff to take and stuff to leave for a yard sale or goodwill. Not much is going since mom has bought new furniture. So mostly just clothes and personal stuff is all we have to move. We drive up to the new house just as the pizza delivery guy shows up. I pay him for the six pizzas and give him a nice tip for our future pizza deliveries. Chris sees the house for the first time and can't believe it, and hugs my mom, "Which room is mine Mom?" She laughs at him and continues unloading boxes. He looks at the pool and Jacuzzi, "No way! The storage business must be very good this place is nice." I show him around and he is very happy for us.

Kaye finds us in the gym above the garage and says to Chris, "Did he tell you he is gay now?"

Chris looks at Kaye, "I knew that before he left. He did not need to go to the Bahamas to prove that."

"No, it happened while we were there!"

"Girl, how bad are you in bed that you made him gay on his first try? Come here Buddy give me a hug!" We all start laughing at Chris being stupid. Kaye says, "No New Year's eve we were at this party and he was attacked by these six lesbians. So now he is a lesbian."

"Why was I not at this party I am already a lesbian trapped in a man's body." He looks at me and then starts laughing louder, "Kaye you wish he was a lesbian, you freak!"

We all laugh and make our own stupid comments.

"So you guys had fun in the Bahamas? Are you still virgins?"

We look at each other and then at Chris, "You know friends don't tell that kind of stuff!"

"Good! You still are. I just didn't want to be hanging out with a couple of sluts, especially gay ones!"

We all start laughing again and my mom comes up the steps, "Sounds like you are having fun!"

I look at her, "Yes Ma'am we are. Do you need some help?"

"No, and it was a lot easier to move when we had new stuff delivered and old stuff not brought here."

Mom looks around, "Do you kids like my gym?"

We all nod in agreement, "But Mom where we gonna keep the beer?"

She snaps to look at the reaction in the room, "In the fridge of course, but you want be having any for a while will you!"

Kaye says, "We need to move to the Bahamas!"

We all chuckle and watch everyone coming up the steps to join us.

Mom says, "I will get the final stuff we need tomorrow and then we are moved in."

Kaye looks over at me and says, "Did you tell Chris how much money you lost in the Bahamas?"

I smile and say, "No, he wouldn't believe it anyway."

My aunt says, "Then tell me I will believe it."

"No you won't Aunt Nette, you will just get mad."

The room looks at me in anticipation and I say, "Ok I'll tell but don't get mad! The first time I lost half a million and the second time ten million."

You could have heard a pin drop in the room, total silence and then an eruption of noise. Are you crazy, what were you thinking? All these questions and Kaye just sits back and laughs as they badger me.

We finish our task and everyone goes home and my sister says, "Can't we stay here tonight?"

My mom and dad look around and I say, "Yeah we could just sleep here in the living room under a blanket and watch TV."

My dad nods and says, "Fine by me, we really have nothing at the old house anyway."

We cuddle up together and talk about our trip and future plans in front of the fireplace.

"Son, my stockbroker called today and was telling me to buy this stock that is supposed to be the next IBM."

"What is the name and what do they do?"

"He said it was something with computers, software, or something. I forget the name, something soft. He said the owner was a man named Gates."

"Microsoft?"

"Yeah that was it! The broker said the stock was at fifty cents and should be big someday."

The voice in my head goes crazy with excitement, "Dad, buy as much as we can afford or as much as allowed! I'm talking, like a million shares. You won't regret it!"

I tell my dad what we should expect from the stock and he smiles and says, "I'll do that first thing in the morning." We talk some more and then all fall asleep. That is what we do the first night in our new big house.

The next morning dad and I go to the bank to deposit the check from the casino. My dad fears the check will be no good or that it will get us in trouble with the IRS. The teller takes the check from dad and looks at it suspiciously. She picks up her phone and calls someone and says, "Just a minute, gentlemen."

Dad looks at me, "This is what I was worried about."

"Don't worry; they are just verifying the funds from that bank. It will be fine, I am sure."

The teller says, "Mr. Adams will be right with you, please have a seat. Next please."

We sit down and Mr. Adams rushes towards us, "Gentlemen, please step in my office."

As we walk in the office, I notice how nice it is in comparison to the rest of the bank. *I wonder if he has any dirty dealings going on. May need to check this guy out.* Mr. Adams sits down and types on his computer. He looks at us and smiles as he waits for information to appear on his screen. He makes an odd face and says, "The activity on your account has changed dramatically."

"My dad smiles and says, "Yes, we have made some changes."

"It appears that for a couple of months you spent no money and had a bit more than a normal income."

We just stare at each other as I think how to handle this.

We smile and I say, "Yes . . . Was that a statement or a question?" My dad is obviously getting nervous and I continue, "This is not our only bank, and we had to change our spending habits to start our new businesses." The man looks satisfied with my answer and smiles as he looks at the check.

"Now you have a very large check from a bank in the Bahamas."

"Yes, my father did well at a casino down there. Would you know the best way to pay the taxes on that? Should we pay it now or set money aside for the end of the year?"

The man looks satisfied with my responses and says, "Pay it now and you avoid any chances of penalties later on. Congratulations on your winnings. How did you win so much?"

My dad smiles at the man, "On a really big slot machine and a roulette table."

We all smile and Mr. Adams pulls out a form to deposit and one for paying the IRS. Mr. Adams seems pleased with our answers as we fill out the forms. He looks at the check again and says, "Seems like a waste. Win all this money and then have to give almost half to the government."

My dad says, "Why? They need their share also. They have mouths to feed just like the rest of us."

The man raises his eyebrows in understanding, "Yeah, I guess so."

We shake hands with the man as we leave and I still feel uncomfortable about him. We leave the office and dad says, "Everything alright here."

"Not sure, something is not right." *He is just unsure about us, it will be fine. Don't worry I'll fix it so he won't bother us anymore.*

I look at the man as we walk out of the door and he is on his phone. Wish I could hear that conversation. *He is warning the IRS about us. Again, don't worry.*

Chapter 20

"Are you ready to get started?" I look at my instructor getting in the plane with me, "Yes Sir, I've been waiting for this for a while!" He smiles and says, "I am going to point at gauges and you tell me what they are and what they do. I know you can fly, but now you have to learn from the ground up. You must know everything about it and how to explain it in detail. You should have no problem from what I've seen from you so far."

"I understand and will try my best, but I want to enjoy it as well, not just lesson after lesson. I want to sightsee and have fun with it."

He smiles at me, "Man after my own heart. Let's get started."

He points to an instrument and I tell him the name and what it is used for. We do this for every instrument and then we inspect that the aircraft is safe for flight. We re-enter the airplane, go through the starting procedures, and then start the plane. I am given another lesson on taxiing as we roll down the taxiway. We roll to a stop at the end of the runway and I do my final preparation check for takeoff. He explains all the stuff that could go wrong and why.

We are cleared for takeoff, and roll into position and he says, "Take us flying Sir!" I press the throttle knob in all the way and the little Cessna comes to life. I watch my speed and rotate at 65 knots. We lift off the ground and it is an amazing feeling. I look out the side window and see the gap between the wheel and the ground widening. I look at our instruments to ensure we are flying what is expected, not climbing to fast or to slow or turning before I should be.

Jerry gives me instructions as he talks to the controllers on the ground. Once we are a safe distance from the airport we begin doing maneuvers so I can see how the plane will react to different movements. *Wonder who showed the Wright brothers this stuff? Isn't it beautiful and peaceful from up here.* "Think we could fly over my house?"

He looks at me, "Sure no problem. Do you think you can find it from up here?"

I look at the ground, recognize a store, and follow the road, "Sure I can, I will just follow this road over to there, and I can almost see it now."

He chuckles, "You're an IFR pilot already!"

I look at him oddly, "No I followed the road not an instrument."

He smiles at me hoping I will realize what I just said. I point at him, "Oh I get it, I Follow Roads instead of Instrument Flight Rules."

He chuckles again as we fly over my house, "Hey you have a pool. Maybe I am not charging you enough?"

"Why? People with pools get charged more?"

"No, but they can normally afford it."

We go back to our flight lesson, I learn the characteristics of the Cessna airplane, and I realize how much I love flying.

He says, "Ok, let's head back to the airport."

I look at him, "You have another student, or another flight?"

"No most people get tired and can retain no more information after an hour. If you want to keep going I will stick it out with you."

"Thanks, now keep teaching."

He continues with what would be our next lesson. Then we do some more sightseeing. We both agree that it is time to return to the airport and work on some landings. The first approach Jerry lands the plane, explains what he is doing, and says, "That is what it should look like, your turn."

We takeoff again and stay in the traffic pattern and as I come in for a landing I try to mimic his actions from earlier. My landing is not as skilled as his is, but we survive. I try again, the next is actually quite nice, and he praises me for my effort. On my last attempt, I bounce to a stop on the runway. Jerry explains what I did differently and how to avoid it happening in the future.

"Jerry let me try one more, I can't finish on a bad landing."

"Go ahead."

I takeoff and I am determined I will make this one, a good one. As I turn on final approach, everything is looking good. I scan over everything in the cockpit just as the wheels are about to touchdown. I adjust the nose up a bit to flare the aircraft, as I was instructed. The sound of the wheels touching ever so softly on the asphalt is all I hear and then Jerry says, "Nicely done my friend. Are you done now or do you still want more?"

I smile and say, "I want more, but I guess I am done. I have to go to the bathroom."

"Very well then we will turn here and park this bad boy."

We park the plane and as the engine is shutting down Jerry says, "Cheated death again!"

I chuckle at his joke and see my sister looking at the airplane.

She walks over, "Did you get lost? I've been waiting for over an hour."

"Sorry Sis, I was having so much fun that I did not want to come down."

"Well, until you get your driving license mister you need to come back when you are supposed to."

"Got it and I will not let it happen again."

Jerry says, "Can I borrow him for ten more minutes?"

"Sure, I'll just sit her bored like I have for the last hour."

"Thanks. He Buddy you wouldn't be interested in buying a plane of your own, would you?"

"Yes I would, that was my original plan until I met you. Why, you don't want me crashing your plane anymore?"

"No, actually my older friend is going to stop flying for medical reasons and wanted to sell me his plane. My credit is maxed out right now with three other planes, and I could use another for my flight school."

I notice my sister on the phone and I yell over to her, "Is that dad by any chance?"

She nods yes and I say, "I need to speak to him."

She holds the phone in the air to me. "Jerry, come over to the car with me."

I walk over to the car, "Sis, I apologize." I take the phone, "Hey dad! Yes, it was great! May I buy an airplane?" I listen and then say, "Not sure, but enough to pay for itself. Can you come out here? Great see you in a few minutes then."

I hand my sister the phone, "He is on the way here if you want to leave you can, I will ride home with him."

"You know we don't buy stuff without me baby Brother."

"Good let's go inside where it is warm and talk with Jerry."

We walk in the building and all grab a cup of coffee. My dad walks in, "One sugar and one cream please, it is cold out there! Your sister was getting worried and called me. Come back on time when people are waiting on you Son!"

"Sorry I . . ."

"It's ok Son we understand. Now let's hear what I came here to hear."

My dad watches Jerry walk in, "Hi Jerry, good to see you again. How did he do?"

"Good Sir, the kid is a natural and I hope all is well with you."

Jerry looks at me and says, "He did very well and catches on really fast."

"So what are you talking about us buying?"

"Like I was telling Tommy, it is a sweet little Cessna 172. My friend wanted me to buy it but I am tapped out on credit right now with three airplanes. If you buy it and let the school use it I will teach Tommy for free."

"What happens to the money the airplane makes?"

"It would go to the flight school."

"Is the school going to make the payments on the bank loan for the plane?"

"Well no . . . what we could do with the money the plane makes is, we make the payment and then the school keeps the rest."

My dad looks at Jerry and is not sure whether to trust him or not, "How much is this plane gonna cost?"

"He would sell it to us for thirteen thousand."

"Let me talk to the kids for a moment."

"Sure thing."

Jerry leaves the room and we start discussing details of the deal. Dad looks at me, "Is this a good deal?"

"It is not what I had hoped. I wanted to rent the plane and make enough to pay for it and my lessons. If I fly for free it balances out though."

"So it cost what for you to get your license?"

"Fifty hours times fifty dollars per hour is $2500. Then I need to build up hours to get my instrument rating and commercial license and multi-engine. We need to find out how much Jerry was planning to cover for my license. Multi-engine is around two hundred per hour."

"Jerry could you join us again, please."

He walks in and we get specific on who pays what and who is responsible for what. At the end of it all I realize my license will cost nothing, I will own an airplane and make or lose no money for three years. We all agree and go to look at the airplane. We walk into the hanger and I see this beautiful sight, an almost brand new looking airplane. My dad says, "This looks nice. Why is it being sold?"

"My friend is old and can't get a medical anymore. To keep it close to home so he asked me to buy it, but I am involved in too many ventures at the moment."

"What do you think Son, will this work for you?"

I look at it and see no flaws anywhere, "Yes Sir, it is great!"

My dad is talking to Jerry and the old man that owns the plane and Roxanne comes over to me, "You sure this is a good investment?"

"It is perfect and it won't lose any value, actually I bet when and if we sell it, we make a profit."

She smiles at me, "Sounds good baby Brother."

"Roxanne, Tommy, could you come with us?"

We get over to my dad and Jerry and dad says, "Jerry wants to know if we would care to go into business with him?"

I look at my sister and then dad. I listen to my conscience and say, "If we can look at the company books and everything looks ok, I say yes!"

Roxanne and dad agree. My dad writes the older man a check for the plane and they do the paperwork to transfer the certificates and registrations. My sister and I look at the books and she whispers, "Everything on the up and up?"

"Yes, but if I forget in ten years we need to sell and we will have done very well."

She nods and says as dad walks in, "I agree with my brother dad, we should invest in this business."

Jerry explains the business plan and our share of the profit and the way we should expect things to happen. We leave owning half a charter service and half a flight school. As we walk to the vehicles my dad says, "Son ride with me and explain what just happened and what I should and should not expect." Roxanne yells, "Call me so I can hear too!"

We get in the truck and my dad's phone rings, "Hello? No Sweetie you haven't missed a thing."

I explain to both of them how our company is now multileveled to best suit our needs. I explain the benefits and pitfalls to them and tell them our new monthly income will now surpass one hundred thousand per month. That makes them both happy and I continue saying after taxes each year we still bring in one million. I explain the next area we enter is buying property and this makes my dad very happy. I tell him the area he needs to buy his property for his wildlife reserve or killing field.

My father has a dream to own a property that he stocks with wild game and hunts as he sees fit. He would have his very own utopia of wildlife. He stocks the land merely for viewing, like a safari, or for hunting when it becomes over populated. He needs a lake for fishing and fishing tournaments. He needs over a thousand acres for the wildlife to roam, eat, live, and die. He would fence the area for unauthorized hunting and so the deer would not leave the area as easy. He would have fields for the animals to eat and meadows for them to relax and woods for them to hide. For himself and fellow hunters he would have log cabins to rent for a week of hunting, a butcher shop, and taxidermist on the grounds. He would like this to be right on the bay, so some ocean fishing would be accessible as well. He would line the bay beach area with little bungalows for tourist as well as hunters. He would start an oyster bed so you could have fresh oysters every day. If he can obtain the spot he has in mind, he will call it the Sandbar and Powder horn Ranch.

We pull into our driveway and my sister pulls in behind us. I grab the map from my dad's truck and we walk straight to the dining room table in the house.

"Rosa, we are home and in the dining room!"

Mom yells back, "Dinner in thirty minutes and Kaye is on the couch!"

Kaye yells, "Not anymore, I'm in the dining room now!"

Kaye kisses me as I layout the map on the table, "How was it? I was starting to get worried. It was taking longer than I thought?"

"It was great! Now we own half the company and we'll explain more over dinner."

I point to the map, "Dad this is the land you showed me a couple of weeks ago that you want."

Roxanne comes back in the room, hands me some paper, and hugs Kaye. I explain the state owns most of it and would be willing to sell with what we have in mind for it, and would give a tax break for improving the area.

"The only problem is this one family here. They don't want to move and we could tax them out or buy a property at this lake here and swap them."

My dad says, "We explain how this refuge will surround them and they will be watched and their fields won't be safe from the deer. We tell them they will be fined for shooting our deer. They will probably jump at the chance for the other land; it is closer to the one town and better for them."

Dad looks and points at the map, "So I buy this place tomorrow no matter what?"

"Yes Sir, approach these people after you buy this one. Tell them nothing except you are interested in buying their land first. We will deal with it after that."

Mom walks in the room, "Dinners ready! Get that stuff off my table and come grab a plate!"

We do as mom says and then return to the dining room, "Mom I really like your new house."

Mom smiles at me and says, "Me too, and I like that it is paid for."

Chapter 21

The first day back to school after the Christmas break; as I walk in the school something feels weird. People stare, but not in the normal adoring way. I see Kaye, "What is going on here girl?"

"I think they heard about you losing 10 million over the break."

"What!? Need I remind you this is a Christian School and I could get kicked out for something like that, plus I don't need a reputation as a gambler?"

"It wasn't me Honey! Think about it I was drunk most of the time there."

Chris walks up and says, "Hey buddy, can I borrow some money? Oh wait I forgot you lost it all!"

Chris and a couple of our friends start laughing. "Chris! Don't forget that was just a joke, and never really happened."

"Sure whatever you say!"

I grab Chris by the arm and pull him away from the crowd, "I thought you were my friend?"

"I am. What is the problem?"

"Hello! Look around, they could kick me out of here for something like that."

"I thought that is what you wanted?"

"Not anymore, things have changed and I need to be here. So it was a joke and nothing else, got it!"

"Yeah sorry Buddy, I wasn't thinking like that." *You call this guy your friend? Sounds like a jealous kid trying to destroy you. I'll check him out for you.*

The bell rings and we head to homeroom, on the way I explain the same thing to Kaye and that it did not happen. She agreed and we sit down in homeroom. The door opens and the principal and both my basketball and football coach are with him. The group of men looks at me and asks me to go with them to the school office. They walk solemnly without a word. We enter the office and they begin their inquisition, "Have a good Christmas break?"

"Yes Sir, very nice thank you. How about you guys? Good time?" They all reply with yeah it was good.

"The reason we brought you here is to ask you a question."

Please don't make me lie to them!

"There is a rumor going around that you went to the Bahamas and that you were gambling and drinking over the break."

"Yes Sir, I heard that rumor this morning as well."

They look at each other and the coach says, "Any truth to it?"

"Yes Sir, my family and the Lewis' went after Christmas for New Years. It was fun."

"So the rumor is true? You were gambling and drinking as well." *Don't forget womanizing also!* "Gentlemen I am fifteen and not old enough to commit those sins. I went snorkeling, parasailing, jet skiing and met some nice people, but that is about it."

"So the rumor is half true? You and your family went to the Bahamas and you did not gamble?"

"That sounds better. You can call my parents if you like or ask Kaye."

I look at the questioning men and say, "I think I know what happened. Chris was helping us move and we were joking and I said I lost ten million gambling, but I never thought he would take us seriously or go around saying such nonsense in public."

The three men talk and decide my collective fate. They look back at me and the principal says, "We would like you to speak Wednesday in Chapel about the ills of gambling and the wickedness the tongue can spread when the mind is misled."

I look at them and say, "Interesting topic I should be able to work with that. The only reference I know to gambling is the casting of lots at Jesus' feet. I am pretty sure it is not one of the commandments. I may need some help with that topic if you guys don't mind? I'll be ready though."

"Good we look forward to it."

The bell rings and they say, "Head on to class and stay out of trouble you are one of our good ones!"

As I enter the hallway, I see Chappy and he says, "How was the Bahamas? I hear you lost your shirt down there."

We walk away from the office and I say, "Now you know that's not true. Why would you repeat that crap?"

"Yeah, but it is funny!"

I point to the office, "Wish the faculty felt the same way!"

He laughs and walks away and I join Kaye walking towards me, "What did they say?"

"I get to speak in Chapel Wednesday about big tongues and gambling."

"Sorry Honey! At least you get to do something you are good at to prove your innocence."

"But then I am a hypocrite for denouncing gambling. I think I can put a twist on it though and make gambling legal here!"

"You are a bad boy!"

"Hey, you know as well as I do, the power of suggestion is a powerful tool if used at the right time. Timing is the key."

"Explain men of power to me?"

"They take the power, how else did they get it! Unless you are an American, and then you take it buy making people think they gave you the power."

"You are scary sometimes!"

"I know, but answer this. How did the person in charge of countries become in charge, back in the old days?" The bell rings and class begins.

Driving to school Wednesday morning I watch my sister speed through traffic. Wonder if she can sense how nervous I am with her driving and putting on makeup at the same time. *She is doing fine just relax.*

My sister pats my knee, "Are you nervous Bro?" *Guess she can.*

"If I was not prepared I would be, but I am going to own this service today."

"No wonder all the girls in school are after you. You are so confident. How many girls have asked you out?"

I smile and say, "I lost count, one girl asked me right in front of Kaye the other day. I thought Kaye was going to lose it." We laugh as my sister pulls into the school parking lot.

Walking into the school Chris walks up beside me, "I hear you are starting the basketball game tonight!"

"That's funny I heard the same thing about you. Do you just sit home and make up rumors."

"No, I was talking with Kim and she said the coach mentioned it as a possibility."

"Kim, you mean the girl that does the statistics for our team?"

Chris nods in agreement. I say, "That sounds good to me, but why do you find pleasure in sharing information all the time. You're completely random about who you share information with half the time. Make sure you listen to my sermon today."

Chris looks at me like I just insulted him, "Just thought you would want to know and would be happy about it."

"Thank you for trying to share what you thought would be good news to me, but the reason I have to speak in Chapel today is because you are always sharing information. Can you do me a favor and keep me off the headlines. Only talk about me in emergency situations or tell me stuff that is really important and not just so you can be the first to tell me."

Looking insulted by my comments I continue, "Let's start over. Good to see you this morning! How are you?"

He smiles and hugs me with one arm, "I was fine until one of my friends crapped on me this morning."

We walk into school and what seemed like three minutes later it was time for me to speak in Chapel. Three periods had passed, but my anxiety brought me to this point in time. I could not remember anything I had done for the past two and a half hours. *Why are you so worried I am the one speaking and don't worry I will make you a hero again.* I go on stage and sit down. When they do the announcements, I listen due to our basketball game tonight and the time we need to be on the bus. I also hear the reason I should be starting in the game tonight, "Stephen Williams a senior broke his leg last night, and needs our prayers for a speedy recovery." *Unlucky for him, but yet another chance to shine for us, that will make it our court for the rest of the season.*

My name is announced and I walk to the podium and the crowd mildly applauds. *Looks like we lost some fans over the gambling, I'll win them back for us.* During my speech, I mention the fate of rumors and whom they hurt. I explain why rumors are wrong and why they are also wrong to listen to. I throw in some biblical references for backup. I talk about the fact that gambling is wrong in the eyes of the church and why the church feels the way they do. I explain that gambling is very addictive and can be detrimental to families not just the person gambling. I work in my own agenda that if you do gamble even though it is wrong, you should never exceed your means and know your limits. I explain sin is something that hurts yourself, people around you, and your reputation as a Christian. "Christianity should not be used as a crutch or an easy way out or an excuse for why you act a certain way. It should be the reason you act the way you do! Thank you!" *That should do it!* I walk away from the podium and the crowd goes wild. I walk back to my seat and the Principal closes the service with prayer.

I stand up to walk away, the three men surround me again, and Coach Bolton says, "So are you for or against gambling? By that speech I could not quite tell?"

I look at the three men, "I am not going to say that when I get older I won't gamble. But for right now, I am going to say against gambling, due to the company I keep."

They look at each other and then the Principal says, "So it is safe to say you are on our team and we will hear no such rumors of any gambling activities."

I think for a second and say, "Sir I can't control rumors, but I will make sure no jokes are made to create such rumors. If said rumors surface I can guarantee they will not be valid claims."

He looks at me and the crowd is building off the stage waiting for me to exit, "Good let's keep it clean around here, your public awaits!"

I turn to walk to my friends waiting for me and Coach Bailey stops me, "Nice speech, Son! I am going to need you to start in the game tonight is that good with you?"

"Yes Sir, I am glad to help out anyway I can Coach."

"Great, we'll go over our plays on the bus."

I walk off the stage and the girls all try to touch me, congratulate me, and tell me I did a good job. I see Kaye in the background watching and getting angry. I talk to them and thank them and the teachers motion us out of the Chapel.

I finally get close to Kaye and say, "Hey my girl!"

She stands with her arms crossed and biting her lip.

"Kaye let's go Honey, don't say a word. I know what you are thinking and saying something to her won't make it better." We walk to our locker and Kaye says nothing until her friend Lucy comes up to her.

"Can you believe she said that? 'Are you sure you are going out with Tommy?' I would really like him to go out with me!"

Kaye huffs, "I can't believe the nerve of that girl!"

Lucy says, "Why would she say something like that to you!"

I watch the two girls argue about a senior that wants me, and for Kaye to leave me alone. I almost laugh a couple of times, but I fight the urge knowing how upset Kaye is right now. We walk into our next class and Kaye is still angry and turns to me, "I am going to that game tonight. I don't trust that girl at all."

The teacher begins teaching and I think to myself. I could have my own cult right about now and I would not get out of bed until Sunday to preach. *Yeah you could preach on sins, since you would know them all first hand.* Is that what happens to these cults, they get drunk on power? *You got it Buddy, most people cannot handle the added power, and it knocks them off balance. You know now in life you must have balance.* Yeah I am still waiting to see what mine will be. *You are doing well.*

I sit on the bus and the coach steps on and says, "Mr. Dunn did you sign up for Miss Lewis to travel with us on this trip." I look out the side window and see Kaye standing there, "Yes Sir, if it is not a problem."

"No, just wish you would have told me sooner."

"She wasn't sure if she could go or not. Sorry Coach!"

He lets Kaye on the bus and she sits next to me, "Where is that girl? I will kick her butt if she comes near you!"

"Well I'm not sure where she is right now, but a few minutes ago she was on my lap." Kaye is quiet for a moment and then she punches my arm.

I chuckle and say, "Feel better?"

"I wish that was her face!"

"You need to be good Honey! We talked about this and you know you have nothing to worry about."

I continue reading the playbook the coach handed me.

Lisa walks up to the front of the bus, "Hey Tommy, how are you doing?"

I look up and see Kaye's nostrils flaring, "I am fine Lisa, thanks for asking. How are you?"

"Good! I was told to ask you a question. Do you have a girlfriend, and if you do? How serious is it?" Kaye is about to rip this girl apart with her bare hands, "I do have a girlfriend, she looks out for me and I look out for her and we are very happy together. She is very jealous though so you better beware."

I pat Kaye's hand and I can feel her about to uncoil, as she was about to strike.

"Lisa this is my girlfriend Kaye. Kaye this is Lisa."

They say hello and shake hands, "Sorry Kaye, I did not know, and he is a hot topic right now. If you get tired of him just let us know and we will take care of him for you."

Lisa walks away and Kaye says, "Was that an apology or a way of saying watch it missy or we will take your man away from you?"

"Which ever you want to believe, but you are going to have to learn to deal with this graciously or you won't be able to be around me. Unfortunately, this is just the beginning. I will let them know I am off the market as long as you can control your temper."

"So you are saying girls will always hit on you?"

"Yes! I can live with it and I hope you can."

"You are telling me you would not sleep with her if she asked?"

I look back at her and whisper to Kaye, "She did ask, and I said no. Kaye, if I wouldn't sleep with you after I saw you naked in the shower, what makes you think I'd sleep with her." Kaye smiles as I continue, "I mean look at her, after you get passed the long brown hair, nice smile, pretty eyes, big breasts, that cute mole on her inner thigh, and nice round bottom what have you got anyway?"

Kaye's smile turns into a frown and she starts punching me again. I laugh as the coach asks her, "Please stop beating on my player. Nobody is allowed to do that today." The bus pulls away from the school grounds and the cheerleaders start doing cheers.

We arrive at our rival school and the varsity girls' basketball team steps off the bus first and go directly to the locker room and we head to the snack bar. Kaye and I sit on the bleachers and watch the girl team walk out onto the floor. They shoot the ball to warm up for the game. I look behind me and see Jimmy setting up the video camera.

"Kaye let's go sit with Jimmy."

We sit down next to him, "Hey Jimmy!"

"Hey what's going on?"

"These cameras are getting smaller and smaller aren't they; I bet one day they will be small as your hand."

"Yeah right, that might happen!"

We sit with Jimmy while he videos the game. "Hey Jimmy, how's your dad?"

"He's good; he will be here for our game."

"Good! I still want to talk to him."

"Hey, there he is now walking in the door with your dad."

I look and see the two men entering the gym. They both see us, and walk up the bleachers to join us. We greet each other as I say to Mr. Stephens, "Any interesting cases going on Sir?"

"Yeah remember that bank robbery last week? I'd like to get some leads on that."

I sit closer to him and whisper, "What would you say, if I told you I saw it happen in my head the night it happened?"

He looks at me curiously, "Like a premonition? Or you actually saw it happen?"

"Not sure, but sometimes I get weird feelings or see things I can't explain or care to . . . Can you keep a secret, just between me and you?"

He looks around, "Sure I think so?"

"I don't want to be involved, but I want to help you get these guys."

I look around to make sure no one is eavesdropping on us. "That bank job . . . It was an inside job. Watch the video for the last hour of the day before the robbery. You will see the security guard talking to two guys. Those are your guys. The money is under the house of one of those guys."

He looks at me strangely and I say, "Why did the bank say it was 1.2 million that was stolen? I only saw eight hundred and eighty thousand."

Mr. Stephens looks at me as if he does not believe me, I say, "Question the guard, have the tape going with him talking to his friends and he will breakdown and tell it all, I guarantee it."

The coach calls us and tells us to enter the locker room when the girls come out after halftime. I stand up and hug my dad and Mr. Stephens stops me from leaving, "So what do you want from this, if it is good information?"

"I just would like the chance to help you again in the future, no fame, or money."

He smiles at me, "I'll look at the video and decide what to do from there. Have a good game Buddy, you too Son!"

Jimmy and I walk down the bleachers and walk to the locker room as the girls exit from their halftime break.

The girls come out of the locker room and I grab my sister and say, "Number twenty-two is going to be their shooter this half. Play her tight and watch number three, her passes are sloppy and you should be able to get some steals." Roxanne hugs me, and runs to join her team.

Our coach has more pride than the girl's team coach does. The girls go out and win their game and that is about the end of it. We come out of the locker room like a well-oiled military machine. We use fear as a weapon, much like our football team did. We come out passing the ball like the Harlem Globetrotters. Our coach screams ball control and defense to us all the time; we try to keep him happy. Our coach had a promising career, but lost it all when he blew out his knee on a dunk attempt. He was the person that had the longest rim roll on a basketball rim. The ball was said to have made four complete rolls around the rim before falling in the goal. He can handle a ball so well that when I play against him I feel like a toddler.

The game tips off and we get the ball. The ball is thrown to me. I call play number three and the team spring into action as I bring the ball down court. I see Chappy wide open under the goal and I toss it to him. He throws the ball in for the score. We rush down to get on defense and the opposing team pushes the ball up the court and misses their shot. We get the rebound, bring the ball down, and score again. I start to feel cocky, and I fight the feeling, I know how quick this game can turn on you.

We play like men possessed by the basketball gods. At the halftime break, the coach announces he will be starting other players since we are beating them so decisively. The second half I sit where I normally do on the bench, but this time the people next to me are different. Chappy leans over, "You play baseball as well?"

"No, I am going to start flying lessons seriously, so when I turn sixteen I can get my motorcycle, car and pilot license all in the same day."

"That's impressive, good luck with that."

"Thanks, hey did you ever hear anything from Carolina?"

"Yeah it was the amount of scholarship we thought and the letter said that it could change in training camp this summer for more depending on me. You got me in the door and now I have to do it on my own. Thanks for that by the way!"

"No problem that's what friends do!" *That explains why we have seen no bill from his dad.*

The coach looks down the bench at us, "You two Chatty Cathy's, ready to go back in? They are catching up to us?" I look over at the scoreboard and we are winning 49-46. I stand up and head to the score table to check in and Chappy follows. The buzzer sounds as the ball goes out of bounds. We enter the game and the score is now 49-48 with 2 minutes to go in the game. I walk the ball down court and two guys come to defend me. *Two guys covering you means someone is wide-open hero!* I look down the court and see Chappy, all by himself under the goal. You have to be kidding me, it cannot be this easy. I dribble in between the two guys and throw the ball as hard as I can to Chappy, he catches the ball and puts it in the goal for the score.

When we get on defense, Chappy runs by me and gives me a high five. "Chappy, when you see me go for the steal take off!" He nods as he has seen me do this play with my friends on Sunday afternoons. The guard brings the ball down and I pretend he is not going to be a threat. I lunge towards the guard, the ball bounces behind him, and Chappy takes off towards the ball. He picks it up and goes in for the slam-dunk. I look to the bench and see the coach is breathing easier now. The other team calls a time out, we walk to the bench, and I look at the scoreboard and notice that with 1:01 left to go we are winning 53-48.

"You guys are doing well! Just continue to play good defense and we can leave here winners!" We all do our little cheer and head back to the floor, but now we have all starters back on the floor.

We wait for them to bring the ball down court, when they do it is not long before they score. We bring the ball down and it is no easy task as they are trying to foul us, but we pass the ball too fast for them. As I have the ball thrown to me, I am almost tackled by my defender and a foul is called. I walk to the free throw line and when given the ball I line up my first shot. It bounces around and falls in. I wink at Chappy, hope he understands the next shot will be a miss, and bounce off to him. As I shoot, it is almost as if a light bulb goes on over Chappy's head, as he realizes what I meant. The ball hits the rim and bounces right in his hands. He dribbles the ball and passes it out to me, I see three defensive guys rushing towards me and I shoot the ball. I make the shot and I am fouled again. I go back to the free throw line, shoot, and make the goal. The score is now 57-50 with 20 seconds to go. We run and take our defensive stance, as they run down the guard shoots and misses. Our guys let the ball fall innocently to the ground trying to avoid fouls. The opposing team gets the ball, shoots and makes the goal with 10 seconds remaining in the game. Chappy and I run to the other end of the court as Tony throws me the ball, I catch it, dribble and toss the ball up on the backboard. Chappy catches the ball and dunks it and the time expires. The buzzer sounds and we hug and bounce around the floor after our victory of 59-52.

The coach runs up to me, "Now that is the kind of basketball I like to see."

"Thought you would like that one Coach, we did it for you!"

We begin leaving the floor and my dad comes up to me, "Nice job Son, but a bit too much showboat for my taste."

"I know dad, we did that for the coach not for you. He likes that kind of stuff."

"Ride home with me I need to talk with you."

"Yes Sir! I'll tell the coach."

I run into the locker room, change my clothes, and rush out. I come out of the locker room to my dad telling the coach that me, Kaye and Roxanne will be riding home with him.

Mr. Stephens walks up to me, "Anything else you can think of specifically? I don't want to screw this bust up."

"The bag of money under that house is in a gray bag and the bigger guy has a limp. Check the video of the robbery versus the afternoon before. I think they are wearing the same clothes both days."

"If we break this you want no praise or attention at all?"

"No Sir! I just want to be allowed to help you in the future from behind the scenes." He smiles and shakes my hand.

We walk out of the gym and my dad says, "You sure you want to be a cop."

"I am not going to be a cop. I want them to be our friends as opposed to them wanting to catch us doing something wrong."

"What are we doing wrong?"

"Nothing, but I don't want any dirty cops trying to get us to pay them on the side to protect us. If we have friends on the inside, we can avoid that."

"I don't like it, but I will trust you and your judgment."

We get in the vehicle with Kaye and my sister as dad says, "Good news children, I have obtained a karate instructor. We start Saturday morning. Kaye you will be there also Honey."

She looks at me, and then dad, "Yes Sir, what time?"

"We start at 8 am, so Roxanne and her mom can get to the mall by 10. Our instructor is Mr. Lee."

Kaye and I cuddle and she says, "Yes Sir. Can I sleep over so I can be on time?"

My dad gives a displeased face and she says, "Just kidding." Looking at me she says, "Nice game Honey! So now I have to take karate?"

"You will thank me some day, I promise."

"I bet it won't be Saturday morning though."

"Not this Saturday, but maybe some Saturday."

We chuckle as dad pulls into a fast food area and says, "Burgers or chicken?"

"Yes please!" We all laugh as dad stops the vehicle.

"We bought that land and the family that we were talking about jumped on the chance to move. It was an even swap."

My dad looks at my sister and I, and says, "We entered negotiations over the big part of land with the state."

I look at my sister, "Hey, find out who is in charge of that. Maybe we can make them see things for us." *We just took care of that with the bank. Excellent work my friend. You just enjoy the ride mister.*

Chapter 22

Saturday morning and it is too early for this crap, but I really enjoy our new gym over our garage. I should make this my room; I like the cedar smell and look . . . *Pay attention before I let Kaye kick our butt! You need to learn this we need to be able to protect ourselves. Kaye looks cute in her karate gi though doesn't she?* She is starting to look cuter every day and her personality is amazing. It is going to be hard to leave her alone for much longer. How long do I have to wait? *Until you can afford to support her and your kids, then you can have her.*

Mr. Lee decides to make me Kaye's punching bag. I stand in front of her as she practices her punches. She yells, "Keaa!" and nearly hits my nose. She continues this as Mr. Lee explains the power of control. The girls look at the time and realize they need to clean up before they leave for the mall. They bow and leave our make shift dojo. Kaye says to me, "I am going to use your shower." I nod as she leaves. My father and I are the only students left. My dad has always prided himself on being a fighter, but this is new to him. Mr. Lee teaches us more difficult defensive moves that he felt the girls were not ready to do. We go through the maneuvers and from what Mr. Lee says that we are getting good.

At the end of the lesson Mr. Lee pulls me to the side as my father leaves, "What do you want from this experience?"

I think how to answer him, "I just want to be able to defend myself and be able to stop lying about karate."

"What do you mean lie about karate? From your motions and understanding I would think you already had some training."

"I did when I was ten, but that place only wanted to teach me Kata. I wanted to fight not dance."

"I bet since then you have not been in one fight."

"That is correct. People heard I was taking karate and they left me alone."

"So the dance, as you call it did benefit you?"

"Yes Sir, I guess it did."

"Yes, martial arts can open up a lot of doors for you. It can lead you to an inner beauty or an inner peace beyond understanding." *He has a good conscience as well; admit to nothing, he already knows us.*

Mr. Lee looks me in the eyes and says, "I feel a power within you."

"What are you some kind of Jedi? I feel the same with you!"

Mr. Lee bows to me and I hear in my head. *Can you hear me my young student?* My voice says, *do not answer him!*

I smile and bow to him and wait. *He is going to punch all around you, don't flinch.*

Mr. Lee screams and hurls punches inches from my face and chest and stomach and I stand fast.

He smiles at me, *these you will need to block my student.*

How did this guy get inside my head? I block the flurry of punches with the techniques I had learned today and prior to today.

He stops and bows, "You are good, and why do you need training?"

"A future adversary told me I needed to."

Mr. Lee smiles and says, "He can talk to his conscience as well. He will be dangerous for you. I will train your mind and body."

Mr. Lee bows to me, and then screams and punches my chest with what appears to be a great force, but I feel nothing. He smiles at me and says with his inner voice to me, *I knew you could hear me earlier.* "You speak to your conscience as well Mr. Lee?"

"No, I just listen."

He bows to me and says, "See you next lesson."

He turns and looks at me; *your secret is safe with me.*

I go downstairs into the pool area and see my dad climbing into the hot tub. Mr. Lee talks to him and then leaves through the house. I walk over to my dad and say, "I don't see how you can get in there with it so cold outside?"

"Mind control my Son, mind control. It is about mind over matter, I don't mind and it don't matter." He laughs loudly and continues, "I would like to make this area like a greenhouse during the winter, and take it down for the summers."

"That sounds good to me Pop! Where do you know Mr. Lee from?"

"He used to work for me at my old job. When I quit they fired him and now he is out of work and almost homeless, so I thought he would be great for us right now."

"Hey why don't you hire him to work the Storage at the west end of town?"

"I am way ahead of you this time my Son; I already did when I learned of his predicament."

Mr. Lee walks back out to us with Mr. Stephens and another man.

"Mr. Dunn these gentlemen were knocking on the door as I was walking out."

Dad says, "Thank you Mr. Lee." then says, "Mr. Lee may I speak to you a moment."

My father greets the men and then whispers to Mr. Lee.

Mr. Stephens smiles and says to me, "We just want a few moments of your time."

Mr. Lee still smiling very big says to my father, "I will meet you gentlemen there in 2 hours then."

He leaves and my father says, "How may we help you gentlemen? Please forgive me not getting out of the Jacuzzi, but it is cold out there."

Mr. Stephens says, "We are here because of my big mouth gentlemen and for that I apologize. This is Mr. Smith from the bank and he wants to talk you about something you requested."

Mr. Smith says, "Thank you Mr. Stephens. Gentlemen I represent the bank as a board member, but I am also in charge of a request of yours to purchase five thousand acres of land."

My father does not understand what is going on and expects the worst while I expect this best. Mr. Smith continues, "Mr. Stephens overheard me speaking to a friend and heard us mention your name."

He looks around at all of us, "The short story is we were discussing whether or not to sell the land and Mr. Stephens stood up for you. We have had proposals like this before and they never came through." Looking at the ground and then back at us, "The reason we have come to you today is because Mr. Stephens told us of your help in recovering a large amount of money stolen from the bank. He told us Mr. Dunn that your son's suggestion helped in the capture of the criminals and the recovery of the money."

My dad smiles at me as Mr. Smith continues, "He also said your son wanted no reward or publicity for his acts. We would however, like to give you the option to buy the land that you requested and request if it is possible or feasible for you to purchase the land around it? There would be no taxes for the first three years. That should give you a chance to build it up."

My father looks at me and I hand my father his robe as he steps out of the Jacuzzi, "Son I am not sure what you have done, but this is like a dream come true!"

My dad picks me up and hugs me. He sets me down on the deck, "How much land are we talking about and at what price Mr. Smith?"

The man reaches in his briefcase as we walk in the house and pulls out a map. Mr. Smith says while pointing at the map, "We know you were able to get that family out of there and you requested this land around it, we are willing to sell from the lake to a half a mile out into the bay for a total of seven thousand acres. You would have full rights to the lake and the shoreline on that side would be yours. We would like to sell this to you at half the market value."

My dad does the math in his head, "That's about 2.5 million."

"Yes Sir, we did a calculation of 2.67 million and my bank would be happy to loan you the money at one percent below the current interest rate. After it is all said and done, the total cost would be 2.89 million."

I interrupt, "May we pay that off early and save some money?"

Mr. Smith smiles and says, "Sure you can Son, just like a standard loan."

My dad walks over to me and says quietly, "Boy, you did real well this time and I am very proud of you. Can we pull this off?"

I wink at my dad, "Yes Sir, I have a plan."

My dad spins back to the two men, "Mr. Smith do I have any building restrictions on this land?"

"No Sir, but what did you have in mind?"

"My Son is going to need his own landing strip down there once he gets his pilot's license."

Smiling at my father, "No, that sounds great and once you get your Sandbar up and running I would love to visit it and hunt some white tail deer out there."

"Mr. Smith you have a deal! Where do I need to sign?"

"Just come into the bank Monday and we will have the paperwork ready for you."

The two men shake hands and my dad says, "Thank you Sir!"

"No Sir, thank you and your son."

Mr. Smith walks over to me and shakes my hand, "Son if I can ever do anything for you, please don't hesitate to ask."

"Thank you Sir and you are welcome on that bank thing. It was just a lucky guess, but I am glad it worked out for all of us."

Mr. Smith looks at me oddly, "Hey didn't you preach at my church a couple of weeks ago?"

I smile and say, "Yes Sir that was me."

"Son, now I am even happier about this transaction. Mr. Dunn I will see you Monday morning whenever you would like to arrive."

Mr. Stephens walks over to me, "Sorry about this, but I saw it as an advantage for you, and I hope it is ok?"

I look around, "You need to come up and check out the gym real quick Mr. Stephens."

On the way up the steps I say, "You didn't say anything to anyone else did you?"

"No!"

"Then you did great Sir, thank you. Hey, do you have any leads on that poor girl that got raped the other night?"

"No, do you have any leads?"

"I think so, but I am not sure? The story of these State students keeps running in my head, but I am not sure if it is the same case or not, but there seems to be many similarities. I'll let you decide . . . I don't know how this part of the law works."

I sit on the weight bench and say, "The girl was submissive and then changed her mind in the middle of the act. The boys wouldn't stop and that is when she got upset. Then this third guy found her walking home and was trying to comfort her and then he had his way with her also. So, which guy is she after?"

Mr. Stephens looks at me and says, "The last guy. So that's why she had inconclusive results when they checked the sperm. There had been too many rats in the hole."

I look at him after his odd analogy, "I'm not trying to judge the poor girl, but she put herself in two bad situations."

I tell Mr. Stephens the name of the guy. "Again please leave me out of it. Ask the girl if anyone else might have seen this going on. Something tells me she does not want to get the guy in trouble she just wants him out of her life and off the campus. I am pretty sure she knows the guy and she did not expect him to do that to her."

He looks at me strangely, "I will talk to her today, and then we will talk to this guy. Thanks for your help."

We walk down to the pool area and I shake hands with both the men as they leave. My dad puts his arm around my neck, "Boy I am not sure what you are up to, but I sure like your results."

"Dad you know that land will never pay for itself?"

"Yeah I know, but it will take care of a want I have had for a very long time. Thank you my son! Now how do we pay for it?"

"Don't worry I have a plan, but you have to take us to Disney World this summer as payback for me."

"You got it, let's go to the mall, and tell the girls!"

We look around and my dad for the first time in his life seems genuinely happy with his life. He has the woman he married and loves, his dream house, and dreamland. *Yeah we did well, and it is going to get better.*

Chapter 23

At the mall, I talk with my sister as she plays the baby grand piano to the pleasure of the crowd in her store and people passing by. We talk about what we have accomplished and she is happy and amazed. I look over at the runway in the middle of the store. There are two cute little girls pretending to be models walking up and down the runway showing off their dresses that they want their moms to purchase. "Can I do my gay super model routine?" My sister continues playing the piano and looks around at the crowd she has, "One minute, when I finish this song, get Kaye to start your walking music. Hey, any chance you think Kaye might be the one for you? I really like her." I kiss my sisters cheek, "If things continue going the way they are, I would have to say, yes."

I trot over to Kaye and tell her, what I am about to do and she sets up my music as I tie my shirttail in a knot. My sister finishes her song and the crowd applauds moderately, hey it is a mall. I walk over to the adorable little girls and say in a loud gay voice, "What are you girls doing? That is not the way to work my runway!" The girls laugh at the crazy man, they have obviously heard of my antics before. In my best gay voice and attitude I say, "Come on girls let me show you how to work a runway!" The little girls follow me as they giggle. My dad laughs but says, "I hate it when he does this!" The house lights go dim and the spotlight hits the stage and a montage of runway music begins to play over the store stereo. I go into gay overdrive on the runway, as I throw my hips side to side and prance down the catwalk and stop at the end. The ladies in the store start cheering and a crowd from outside rush in the store. The Gap store empties into our store and I see Debra running to the front of my store to watch me. I put a hand on my cheek and then pretend to use it to spin me around and the crowd goes wild. I can here Kaye cheering from behind the counter where she is working.

As I return to the starting point, I tell the little girls, "Now that is the way you have to work it girl!" The first girl laughs and hugs me and walks the runway to a cheering crowd, she spins and returns way to fast. I try to tell her to slow it down, but it falls on deaf ears. The next girl sees the mistakes of the first and walks the runway like she owns it. She does a curtsey to the cheers, and does a spin and returns, ever so gracefully. I walk out on stage and pretend to hand dry my crying eyes and the crowd loves it. I take the two girls by the hand and saunter down the runway one last time, as a designer would do at the end of his show. I bow as the girls curtsey to the crowd while they still cheer for us. I do the gay clap and nod to the crowd and mouth thank you to the crowd and exit the stage.

The store stays full and the ladies browse and begin buying odd and end type items as they feel they owe the shop something for the show. I talk to the two little girls and tell them, "You girls were wonderful out there! You both look very lovely in those dresses are you going to buy them or steal them like you did my heart?"

They laugh and say, "Mommy is going to buy it. You are funny!"

"Well thank you Ladies for coming to my sisters store."

The girls both hug me, and then run to the dressing rooms.

Kaye is working hard at the counter as is my sister and mother. I walk over and say, "You Ladies need help?"

Mom looks around, "We are ok, just go to the front, and make sure nothing walks out unpaid for."

I head to the front and women say thank you for the show and tell me that was fun for them as I pass by. I stand at the entrance and watch people come and go as a security guard would.

"You snot nose brat!" I look at the man and say, "Yeah . . . yeah I love you too!"

Smiling at me the man says, "You saved my life. Thank you."

I stare at the man with the expression, I know you, but from where, "It was fun, but not that good of a show."

The man sticks his hand out for me to shake and I do. "No, a couple of months ago I asked you for money in front of the mall. You told me to go home and get back to my life. I did . . . and, well, thank you."

The memory comes back to me and I smile and say, "You are welcome. Glad I could be of service. I am Tommy by the way."

"I know, been waiting for the right time to approach you. My name is Jim. Fun show by the way, my daughter loves this store." The man's family approaches and he smiles and says, "Thanks again." I notice one of my little models from the show running up to Jim and hugging him. She waves bye to me as they exit the store. I smile and wave as I hear. *Makes it all worth it doesn't it?* I nod my head and fight back the tears.

Debra comes over to me, "Love your show, when is the next one?"

I smile as I see Kaye watching me, "Whenever some sweet little girl is too scared to walk that runway I show them the way."

"I'm scared, so when are you going to show me the way?"

I look at her, "If I didn't have a girlfriend I would be all over that suggestion."

"So what? I have a boyfriend and I would still do you right now."

I look at her beautiful legs and say, "That is where we are different then. I feel relationships are supposed to mean something and sex is only for people in love."

"Wow, when you come back to reality, come see me and I will rattle your cage good."

"Thank you Debra, I appreciate the offer of you rattling my cage. That sounds like fun."

She walks away and I mumble to myself, "You poor misguided gorgeous slut!"

The store is thinning out except for ladies ordering dresses to be made by my mom. I walk up to Kaye and she says, "Every time you pull that stunt this store makes money!"

I smile, "That's why I do it. Did those little girls' moms buy those dresses?"

My sister nods yes to me, "Thanks Bro! You are the man!"

I smile at her and Kaye says, "What did that slut want?"

I look to the entrance where Debra and I spoke, "The same as always. Me!"

"I am going to kick her butt once I get good at karate."

"Why? You already have the trophy!"

Kaye and Roxanne look at each other like, what is he talking about. I try to say it better, "Why fight for a prize when you have the prize already," pointing at myself. I continue, "That is like wiping your butt before you take a poop! It doesn't make any sense."

They both start laughing and say, "You are so stupid! Good to see your ego is still intact."

I decide to check on my deli and listen to ideas of my sandwich fixers and watch pretty women walk by. I check the money versus supplies and everything is going very well.

I start making myself a sandwich, "Hey Roger you know anybody interested in doing yard work?"

He looks at me and then at my father walking up, "Sure I know a guy. What do you need?"

My dad says, "Son, buy me a unloaded turkey sub. No, change that. Load it up with everything."

I laugh and say, "And then throw it in the dogs bowl boys, he'll eat anything!"

The guys laugh at my father and Roger says, "Six inch or foot?"

"Foot, my boy is buying! I am officially broke I just bought a couple thousand acres near the beach. So you better make me two."

"Wow Boss, what did that land cost?"

"Can't really say just yet boys, I'll find out Monday!"

I look around and the people in and near my deli, all listen like EF Hutton is speaking about what stock to buy. I take my father's arm and whisper, "Dad I know you are excited, but you may want to tone it down a bit."

"Yeah, I guess you are right, sorry."

"Dad how long is it going to take to get to our west end storage?"

My father looks at his watch, "You are right, better make those sandwiches to go boys."

Roger looks up at me as he cuts a sandwich, "Yes Sir! What were you asking about yard work Boss?"

I look at him as he makes the sandwiches, "This area is growing like crazy and all these Yankees are moving down here now. They are not going to be used to cutting their own grass. So I want to start a lawn service and keep the area looking good."

"That sounds good I'll check around for you."

My dad and I take the three sandwiches and head out the door.

We pull up to the gate at the storage area and cars pull into see what is going on. We see Mr. Lee waiting for us and talking to a car full of people. We open the office and walk in; the people follow us in and ask when we are going to open. My dad says, "We are opening today we finally found someone to manage it for us."

Mr. Lee smiles and says, "So how may we help you?" to the people.

They start asking questions and I hand Mr. Lee a price list as he tells them things about the storage that he should not know yet, but answers every question correctly. My dad looks at me, smiles and says to me, "Good choice eh Son? He is good!"

"Dad I thought he was your choice?"

My dad leans over to me, "Yeah, but I wanted you to say it!"

We chuckle as Mr. Lee asks, "Is there a master key so I can show these people some units?"

Dad reaches under the counter and picks up a set of keys, hands them to Mr. Lee.

We watch and eat our sandwiches as Mr. Lee gives a tour of the facility.

"Hey Dad, how does he know so much about this place?"

"He met me here the other day and I showed him around. I didn't think he would want the job, but I'm glad I was wrong."

"So he is willing to live here?"

"Look at his car. I think he is glad to have some where to live."

I look to the parking lot and notice the car is full of clothes and belongings. "So what's his story? Is He a drunk or something?"

"You would think after what he has been through. His wife died a year ago and he was battling with insurance companies over payments. When I quit the company, they let him go six months before his retirement. I feel responsible since I was not there to protect him."

The people return to the office with Mr. Lee, "We would like the big unit for two months."

Mr. Lee asks for a contract from me and I hand it to him. He explains it to the people and asks how they would like to pay. They pullout cash and pay for the month and a security deposit. We mark the unit they request as occupied and give them a key. The people leave and we hand Mr. Lee the sandwich we had bought for him. We talk about what we want and what we expect from him as he eats his sandwich and he thanks us for the opportunity. We sit around for a couple of hours talking and renting out storage units.

Dad looks at me, "What was that talk about a yard crew or whatever?"

"I was thinking of getting a truck and trailer. A couple lawn mowers, leaf blowers and those new weed eaters and have some guys go around and cut peoples yards. Ours would be on the list and let them work out of one of our storage units, like maybe here if Mr. Lee would supervise the operation."

Mr. Lee smiles, "I have just the guys too! When do you want them to start?"

My dad looks at me and then at Mr. Lee, "How many guys do you have and what would they want for pay?"

"I know two guys that do that kind of thing, but are out of work right now, they use to work for our company also. Pay would be negotiable."

My dad nods, "I know the guys you mean. They'd be great."

My dad looks at me, "Guess we need to go and buy a truck and trailer and some equipment."

We drive away and my dad says, "Is there a business you are not going to get into?"

I laugh and say, "I don't think so. I was thinking when the grass starts growing I don't want to cut it. Plus all our properties will need the grass cut and I don't want you to make me do it, so I will own the company that does it. These guys should be able to cut 5 to 10 yards a day at twenty dollars each as a minimum. It will mushroom like crazy and the grass grows back so they will do it week after week. I think we can make a hundred bucks a day profit and I'll be happy."

"Son the storage will make in a month what you hope to make in a year."

"But three things are accomplished; I don't have to cut grass, I have just created jobs for people who need them, and I make some money."

My dad sees a used truck for sale that looks good and pulls into the lot to look at it. Next thing you know, we are in the lawn care business as well.

The spring flies by after our basketball season ends with us losing the State championship. My sister enters her pageant and comes in 1ST runner up. The dress my mom made for her evening gown competition only stayed on the wall for one day in the shop and some lady bought it. The deli is still doing well and I work there sometimes because my father says, "I think you should know how to do an honest day's hard work."

My lawn care company is really taking off and I am about to buy another truck now. I have four guys cutting 100 yards a week, commercial and residential, way over my expectations. I work with those guys from time to time to get a feel for some real hard work. I see how people look down on these type people and decide real quickly, I will not treat them that way, ever! I clear around $1000 a week from that company and save all of it as I think these guys are smart enough to figure out they need to buy it from me someday, so they can keep all the profit for themselves. The workers seem really happy and are making my company grows faster and faster.

Mom's dress shop is doing well and has famous visitors from time to time. We actually had some of my little models get discovered there. Debra got a little upset when her boyfriend was discovered by an agency while playing model with me on the runway one day. Hey, we were just having fun, so it really wasn't my fault, *or was it*.

My deli is doing well also as my friend's hangout there hoping to catch a glimpse of a super model leaving my mom's store. Sometimes when business is slow, I call Chris and give some false hope of a model to get the word out. People just mysteriously appear at the mall and have no real idea as to why they are there. It always makes me laugh.

Chapter 24

Last day of school and last day as a sophomore, soon I will be old enough to drive and then take over the world! *Yeah, soon you will be a flying donkey also, little Hitler!* Hey, you know I am just kidding! *I know, but you still need to keep your ego in check. Too many people have gotten to where you are and lost their mind one way or another.*

Kaye comes walking towards me and sarcastically says, "You're lucky you are in school or I would be kissing you right now!"

"How in any sense would that make me lucky? I like it when you kiss me!"

She kisses me and says, "Ok, you are no longer safe anywhere!"

"What are they gonna do? Kick us out the last day!"

We chuckle and walk the halls of our school and look around one last time before the summer break. We both sign yearbooks of underclassmen on our way out of the school.

My sister is waiting on us and says, "Hurry I am hungry and want to eat before I go to work. We are meeting Chappy and the gang at Pizza Palace."

As we get in the car my sister says, "Thank you."

"For what?"

"For everything it has been a good senior year for me, and getting me my beach house."

"Hey, you deserve that, but you are welcome."

"I would have never thought I would own a house at the beach. So thank you very much!"

"You're welcome. You can pay me back though!"

Roxanne parks the car at the Pizza Palace, "How can I do that?"

"Find us a big enough house that you, Kaye and I can live in at college. We will be there in two years. Until then you can rent out rooms and you can have that money."

She smiles at me, "Deal! I'll get one of those big pretty houses near the planetarium."

We get out of the car and Roxanne says to Kaye, "His planning ahead ever freak you out?"

"Yeah, but I am thrilled I am in his plans!"

"Me too!" The girls giggle as we walk in the pizza place. My sister is graduating tonight and she is a little over excited about everything and I need to help her stay grounded and level headed.

Later that night at the graduation I say to Kaye, "This is boring as most of these ceremonies are."

"Shh . . ." My sister gives the Valor Victorian speech and I enjoy the elegance of her speech. Kaye keeps me awake for the rest of the ceremony by tickling me and promising me things. Things I should not be thinking about here. At the end I hug the seniors that had become my friends: my Sister, Chappy, Leigh, Kim, and Scott. I tell them all good luck and I would see them soon. I got season tickets to the Carolina games so I would see Chappy every weekend and I plan on attending their football camp. Scott will be leaving for the Marines in a couple of weeks and Leigh was off to Bible College to get her MRS. degree in marriage to a preacher man. My sister is handling our family business so I will still see her, so no problem there.

My sister and her friends leave for the beach for their senior party that normally last three days, if they follow the lead of senior classes in the past. My sister uses my beach house instead of hers because she does not want her house trashed and if she does something stupid she will not have to relive the memory every time she walks in the house. Maybe they will burn it down so I can build a nice new house.

"Mommy dearest let's go to the beach!"

"I can only go for one day and then I need to be back. I have to make two wedding gowns before June 10th."

"So what's the problem? Kaye's parents can go with us and take care of us little kids while you can't." She snarls at me, "Boy, I will be glad when you are old enough to drive!"

We laugh and I say, "Dad you can break away for how long?"

"I could go straight to the sandbar from there, so two days. When do we leave for Florida?"

"Next Sunday."

"Yeah, that will work for me. Let's go now."

My mom jumps up and goes to pack, "Good, I wanted to do something at that house anyway, new curtains and comforters."

My dad looks at Kaye and I, "You guys going to pack?"

"Dad you taught me as a child to always be prepared. I keep a bag packed!"

Kaye smiles and says, "I'm with him, he told me to do the same thing. I bought clothes to keep in a suitcase for just such an emergency."

He smiles, "Good kids!"

Kaye and I smile at each other and she says, "You need to buy me a new bathing suit when we get there."

"I need to buy you a surfboard also!" I start tickling her and we wrestle on the living room floor.

Kaye says, "Who are we riding with?"

"Sounds like both my parents are going to have to drive. I vote for the Caddy with my mom. Call your parents and see how they are going."

Kaye makes the call and then puts my mom on the phone with her mom and I ask, "What happened, Girl?"

"My parents need to do the same as yours. So my dad is riding with yours and my mom with your mom. I wish we could drive!"

Dad walks in the living room, "Sorry guys, we have a new plan. You either have two days at the beach and then three at the Sandbar. Or one day at the beach and then back here."

Kaye and I look at each other, "The beach and Sandbar Dad."

Dad looks at Kaye, "Honey, you ever been camping?"

"No Sir."

"You are not too delicate are you Honey?"

Kaye looks at me and says, "I hope not!"

"Son, come help me load up the dirt bikes on the trailer and bring your bag."

Kaye looks at me, "This is going to be fun, right?"

We are in the backseat of my mom's Caddy, "Sure it will be, until we get to the Sandbar. Then it will be hell. My dad loves camping, but only works and sleeps. He does nothing fun. My dad will make slave laborers out of us for those days. It will be like going back in time as we build the pyramids. I can teach you to ride the dirt bike, and we can escape occasionally. But after this we will be having fun at Disney World!"

She smiles and says, "If we survive!"

We get to the beach and unpack and mom opens up the house. I look at the house and it is an older beach house. The house is on stilts and doubles as a carport for our vehicles. There is a deck on both sides of the house, the staircase to the house leads up into the middle of the house. The beach side has a walkway over the sand dune to the beach and other balcony overlooks the street. Kaye and I walk up the stairs that enters the house between the kitchen and dining room area. We inspect the house together and then walk out on the ocean side deck. The sun is about to set behind us; I smile at Kaye as we look at the ocean with the sun on our backs.

I yell in the house, "Mom we are going for a walk."

Kaye's mom walks out on the deck and says, "Don't go too far we eat in an hour."

"Yes Ma'am, back in thirty minutes."

Pat smiles at me as Kaye takes my hand and we start walking, "Why did you do that? She was giving us an hour! She already loves you more than me!"

"Sometimes moms need reassuring they are in charge especially when they are afraid of losing control of their babies. Kaye, we are those babies!"

Kaye laughs and kisses me, "Let's enjoy the time here. The woods are going to be harsh on us!"

"Life is what we make it Kaye. Don't dwell on the bad, just enjoy all the good."

"Hush with the philosophy. Hey, you have any money on you?"

"Always! Why?"

She points to the surf shop and I say, "Girl, you are going to make someone a good wife someday!"

"If you are lucky it may be you!"

"No! I'm not a lucky kind of guy!"

"So what, now you don't want me?"

"No! Now I want you more than ever. I just hope I deserve you. Buy me a surfboard girl."

She laughs as I open the door for her.

We look around the surf shop and she walks over to the surfboards, "I want this one!"

I smile and say, "For me, right?"

"No for me. It is too pretty for you."

"But look Honey, it has a reserved tag on it and . . ."

The salesclerk walks over, "Mr. Dunn good to see you again Sir. The surfboard you ordered is in the back. We forgot to take the tag off this one. Did you want this one Ma'am?"

I look at him in shock as the other clerk brings an identical one out of the back of the shop.

Kaye says, "Yes please!" She licks the board and says, "Mine!"

Then she licks my cheek; "Mine!"

The two clerks laugh at her absurdity. She goes over to the bathing suits and begins searching for a suit. She looks at her new surfboard and tries to match the colors for the combo. I walk over to the surfboard and rub it like a cherished artifact, or like a spirit I am trying to become one with. A six-foot Natural Arts classic design with dual fins and it's all mine, and now I actually have two.

Kaye yells to me, "Honey, come help me try on this suit."

The salesclerks' chuckle as Kaye drags me to the dressing room. She drops her clothes and puts on the bathing suit, "What do you think?"

I stare at her, "I think you are beautiful."

She kisses me, "What about the bathing suit!"

"What bathing suit?"

She laughs and I say, "It looks great! Just put your clothes on over it and let's steal it!"

She hands me the hanger and tags, "Go pay, we need to get going."

"You know Kaye; it amazes me how comfortable you are about being naked around me."

She puts her clothes over the bathing suit and says, "I'm hoping you will rape me eventually!"

"My Dear, when the time is right I will, don't you worry!"

I kiss her and she says, "Then I'll keep tempting you until then."

"Once we do. Are you going to still want me or are you going to throw me to the wayside?"

"I will never throw you away, I am going to keep you, and you will be stuck with me forever!"

I leave the dressing room and she follows me out slapping my butt, "Mine!"

A salesclerk says, "Is that your girlfriend Buddy?"

I look back at her still shopping, "Yeah why? Is she stealing again?" They laugh at us and I say, "More like wife sometimes."

"You're a lucky man. She is cute and surfs, that is an awesome combo, Dude!"

I look at her walking towards us, "Cute enough to give her that bathing suit for free?"

"Sorry Dude! She would have to be my girlfriend for that to happen." I laugh and hand him the hanger and tag for the suit. "Guess we are paying then."

He enters the surfboards and bathing suit in the cash register and I give him the cash. I look at my watch, "Let's go babe we are running out of time."

I put a board under each arm, we walk out, and the clerk chases us out, "How far do you need to go?" I point at the house about a football field length away, "Come on I'll give you a ride."

I set the boards in the back of the truck that he just sat down in and we crawl in with him.

"Thanks for the ride!"

We jump out and I could swear I see him wink at Kaye. I put the boards in the shed next to the steps and I look at Kaye as the guy drives away.

"Kaye, do I need to say anything?"

"No, I can see in your eyes you are jealous and that is enough. I did nothing wrong."

I kiss her, "Yes you did! You are just too cute and adorable!"

She chuckles, "How do those shoes feel?"

I look at my feet, "What do you mean?"

"I have to stand in those shoes all the time and now they are on your feet."

I look at the ground understanding her metaphor and she continues, "I didn't even look at that guy and if he ever tries to talk to me I would ignore him."

"Thank you Honey, but we may be able to use this to our advantage. If we see him again I will let you know how to act or react around him. I trust you like you trust me, and I am not upset with you at all. But it bugs me that people will try anything for their own self-satisfaction and not care who they hurt."

Kaye hugs me, "Let's go eat I smell your mom's shrimp cooking."

We eat dinner on the deck and enjoy the sea breeze and I explain to the family why the wind blows toward the beach in the daytime and towards the sea at night. Kaye's dad says, "Those flying lesson going to make you a pilot or weatherman?"

We all chuckle at his humor, "Both I hope, and then I should be able to get a job somewhere."

We all laugh and my dad says, "What do you plan to do for a job Son?"

I look at the parents waiting intently for an answer, "That depends on a couple of variables."

Our parent's smile at each other and my mom ask, "So I can retire in five years?"

"Mom you could retire now if you want."

She smiles, "But I am finally enjoying work, so I will keep working."

Mom looks at my dad and says, "Honey, let's take a walk while the kids clean up this mess."

Kaye's parents smile, "May we join you?"

"Sure!" The parents look very happy as they walk towards the beach.

Then looking in Kaye's eyes I say, "Kaye if we get married would you sign a prenuptial agreement?" *The ultimate test, you are bad Mister.*

She looks at me, "For what I will never leave you."

"That clause will be in there. What I and my dad are looking for is in worst case scenario, that you can't touch the family fortune."

"I would never leave you, so it won't matter."

"Hear me out Babe . . . I never want our relationship to be about money. When and if we get married I will give you an account with one million in it for emergencies only. We will have a joint account that we use for living. Each child we have will be given a million dollar account at birth. When they turn eighteen, it will be worth over two million. So, worst case scenario is if we split up, there is no messy court case. You would be given a house and we split that one account and you would keep whatever car you have and that original million dollar account and whatever interest it has accumulated."

"You have thought this out haven't you?"

"Prepare for the worst and hope for the best is my motto!"

"I would sign that and never take anything from you but what you want me to have. I love you!"

"I love you Girl!"

"So is our future going to end in divorce?"

"I really don't think so! I think your answer just insured us a long and happy life together. I had no idea how much you loved me until just now."

She looks at the dishes and says, "Let's get this mess cleaned up and go for a walk."

The next morning I hear the waves crashing on the beach as the sun peeps over the horizon. "Kaye Honey, wake up!"

"What's wrong?"

"Nothing, it is time to surf! Let's go! We have to hit the Dawn Patrol!" Looking at the clock I say, "It is surf thirty."

"I want to sleep! What is dawn patrol?"

"It is when you surf the good waves at high tide at sunrise. Come on Babe wake up!"

I pull the covers off of her. She looks cute lying there in her white cotton panties and my white tee shirt. If I were a bad man, I would just crawl back in bed with her and take advantage of her.

She sits up, "I'm up Baby!"

She walks in the bathroom, washes her face, and brushes her teeth. I walk in and she is putting on her bathing suit, and I brush my teeth. I smack her butt as I walk out and I say, "Mine!"

She laughs and says, "Bout time you figured that out! Come back here! You need to kiss me if I am going out there with you."

I kiss her and say, "That sounds like an even trade to me."

We sneak out of the house and grab the twin surfboards. I hand Kaye a wet suit, "What is this for?"

"The water might be to cool for you this early in the morning and that will keep you warm."

She slides it on, "This feels nice!"

I look at her, "And it looks even better!"

I kiss her as we head towards the surf.

Once on the beach I make her a little mound of sand and I balance her board on it. I give her a quick lesson explaining how to balance herself and how to stand up. She listens like someone eager to learn. "When you feel the board being pulled by the wave that is when you stand up." I tell her about the water currents, and how to duck dive under the waves. She lies on her board and practices standing up. On the first try, she gets to her knees and stops. The next try she makes it to her feet and tries to get a feel for the board and a good stance.

"You ready to try Babe?"

"Sure let's give it a shot."

We paddle out and she has limited problems for a first timer. I let her stay in front of me so I can watch her and help her if I need to. We get in position and she takes the first big wave, and gets pounded by it. I fear the worst. I catch the next wave and see her paddling back out to sea. I ride the wave and then paddle back out. After I get beyond the wave I see her paddling toward the next big wave and she crest the wave as it passes her and I have to duck under it to keep from being crushed by it. I ride a wave and then catch up to her. Kaye lies on her surfboard obviously tired, "I think I passed all the big waves. Did I go too far?"

"No Girl you did perfect, now you wait for the next set."

"Come here you."

I paddle closer to her and she kisses me, "You have a clue yet how I feel about you?"

"I have no doubt at this point, thanks for everything. Isn't that an awesome sunrise when it comes out of the water like that?"

She looks at the sun, "Still not as awesome as you. Thanks for making me do this. Now you catch a wave to show me how and then come back here and I'll try."

I look out at the wave swelling up, "Ok here I go."

I begin paddling and watching the wave. I feel the pull from the wave and stand up. I look back at Kaye and she is sitting on her board and clapping. I exit the backside of the wave and paddle back to her.

"Very nice you show off!"

I smile as she laughs, "If you fall try to do it to the ocean side of your board so the board does not hit that pretty head."

"So if I fall wrong the board could crack my skull?"

I nod in agreement and say, "Then you are fish food!"

She laughs and starts paddling with the wave and she misses as it rolls by. She sets up for the next one as I give her more pointers. The next one she catches but does not stand up. She belly rides to the beach and seems to be happy with her accomplishment, so I clap for her. I ride the next wave and then paddle back out with her. I look to the beach and see someone on our deck. "Someone is awake."

Kaye looks, "One of our moms. I am going again."

"Try to stand up this time!"

She paddles and drops in on the wave and stands for a moment and falls off. I paddle for the next wave to make sure she is ok and I see her and she is paddling out and looks fine. I exit the wave again and paddle to her, "You ok Girl?"

"Fine, I think I am getting the hang of it. If I ride one more let's go get something to eat. I am starving!"

"You got it Babe!"

I get to a good waiting point and she begins paddling and catches the wave and stands up. I see Kaye riding the wave right at me. She yells, "Get out of the way!" She turns and barely misses me as I watch in amazement. She teeters a bit but rides for a long time and jumps off the board at the beach. She looks at me, bows as I clap above my head to her. *Told you so! She is awesome!* She's mine! Thank you! *No problem!* She smiles and waves me in. So I catch the next wave and ride it to the shore and jump off just like she did. I run to her and hug her. "You did awesome Girl!"

"That was fun! We can do it after we eat right?"

I look at the waves, "I hope so? The waves tend to get smaller in about an hour."

She looks at the house and then the ocean, "We had better surf for about thirty more minutes then." *Told you she was the one!*

We grab our boards and head back out to the surf. We play in the waves and Kaye is actually quite good. More surfers show up and some migrate to our area just because they see a girl, and an opportunity to impress her. Our mom's wave at us, and Kaye says, "We need to head in Babe!"

I look around at the staring guys, "Yeah, it is getting crowded anyway."

As Kaye and I paddle in a guy rides the same wave and gets as close to Kaye as he can. She gets nervous and falls off her board. I look at Kaye as she pops out of the water and I see the anger on her face as he just smiles. She is about to say something as I stop her.

"You ok, Girl?"

The guy laughs, "Get your little girl off my waves!"

"Your waves! You look like you can't afford a car, so I know you can't afford a wave Buddy!"

"You think you own this beach?"

"This part I sure do!"

"You tourists don't have a clue do you?"

"Sounds like you are the one asking the question Einstein!"

The guy says, "Don't make me leave this surf and kick your butt!"

"What would it take to get you out of the water then tough guy? Say the word or I could just come back in there and drown your stupid ass."

"Just try it!"

"You come near me or my girl again and I will make you regret it!"

I walk towards the house and I hear, "You gonna talk that shit with all my boys here!"

I look out at the water and say, "Yeah, and you're going to need more boys, if you want it to be fair! Hell, my girlfriend could beat you, and your boys!"

He comes out of the water and approaches me, "That's about enough out of you boy, and after I am done with you I am going to have my way with your slut!"

"Then shut your mouth and let's dance Punk!"

He punches at me and I duck out of the way. The rest of the guys rush over as they see us getting physical. He swings again and misses.

"One more swing and I have to hurt you Buddy, you better be glad my girl is not fighting you. She would have already kicked your butt."

He swings at my stomach and still only hits air. I grab his hippy hair and swing him around and kick the back of his legs making him drop to his knees. Holding him by his long hair and aiming him at Kaye I say, "Apologize to the lady!"

Wincing in pain as I hold his hair and squeeze the hand that he used to throw three punches at me he screams, "Kiss my ass!"

"Maybe later, but we need to deal with this right now!"

I release his hair and punch him in the back of the head. One of his braver buddy's approaches me and I kick him in the chest and he falls to the ground. Our parents see what is happening and they rush towards us. I wrap my arm around his neck.

"Last chance, Punk!"

Our dad's stop right in front of me and I say, "Hey Buddy, tell this man how you said you were going to beat me up so you could rape his daughter!"

Kaye's dad walks up, "Is that true Boy?"

The guy says nothing, but stares at Mr. Lewis. Then he says, "I said no such thing!"

I release him and say, "Then why am I hugging you here on the beach?"

"Cause you're gay!"

His friends and I laugh, "I didn't think it was possible! But you are as dumb as you look!"

He stares at me and I say, "Get out of here before I get mad and do something I will regret!"

"Just fight me man to man!"

"Fine, go get me another man; I don't want you crying to the police or anyone when this is over. Also, now I have witnesses that I heard me ask you to leave my property and you refused."

My dad says, "Boy, if you are smart you and your friends will leave now!"

"Dad, he has already proven he is not smart!"

His buddy tosses him a knife and now I get excited, "Thank you! Now I can kill you in self-defense!"

I walk over to the guy and he swings the blade at me. I dodge the swing and say, "You couldn't hit me with your fist, what makes you think you can cut me?"

He swings again and Kaye punches one of the guys approaching her and he drops to the ground crying. I start laughing and I say, "Told you! She has no mercy!"

The guy swings again and I punch him in the chest and he drops the knife and falls to the ground. My father stands on the knife so no one else can pick it up. I punch the guy in the face again and again. It was suddenly not fun and made me sad. I felt like I was beating on a retarded kid. I stop hitting him and hold him up by his hair, "Apologize to her! And you better be nice to her!"

"Let go of him Son!" I turn around and a cop is standing on the beach behind me. I release the guy and he falls to the sand and I say, "Thank God! Maybe you can talk some sense into these clowns!"

I walk over to my dad and the cop says, "What is the problem here?"

My dad says, "Assault, trespassing, attempted murder, and attempted rape!"

My dad points to the knife in the sand, "Here is the knife he tried to use."

The cop picks up the knife, "Anybody hurt?"

No one says a word and he says, "I think it was just a bunch of kids horsing around and it got out of hand."

My dad looks at the boy and then the officer, "He's your boy isn't he?"

The officer looks at him, "No! My brother."

"Well Sir, if that is your attitude, then let the boys finish horsing around. You can give that little Punk back his knife. So it will be a fair fight and if he dies, he dies."

"That sounds like a threat Sir!"

"No it is a promise! Get those punks out of here."

My dad steps over to Kaye and gives her a hug. The officer yells at the boys, "Get your sorry butts out of here!"

The officer approaches my dad and my dad says, "We will be at the station later to fill out a report! Now get off my property Officer!"

We walk up the stairs to the house and watch the boys and the officer leave.

Dad sits down to the table with us, "You know we are going to have problems with this town from now on. You know that right?"

"Yes Sir! These boys are out of control and the only answer is not one I want."

"You are right Son, so we sell the property and leave these rednecks alone so we don't have to kill them."

"They will come after us, they are not going to let go of this unless they think they have won."

"So what do you suggest?"

"Let me take care of it. Mom you take everything out of the house that you want to keep. Dad we will go down and fill out a report. First we call Mr. Stephens back home, maybe he can call and talk sense into these cops before it gets out of hand."

Dad picks up the phone and calls Mr. Stephens. A few minutes later I get on the phone and explain it to him. He says he will call them. We hang up and there is a knock at the door. Mom opens the door and it is the sheriff. She invites him in and says, "Thank God you are here."

"Oh, I was told we probably would not be welcome here."

My dad says, "If you think a knife wielding teen is horse play like your officer did, then yes, you would not be welcomed here."

"Now Sir, you know as well as I do, boys will be boys and there are two sides to every story. I am here to hear your side of the story."

My dad huffs and says, "Like it will matter!"

I shake hands with the sheriff and a chill comes over me. *Wow this guy is evil. No wonder his two boys are bad.* I say, "Actually Sir, there are three sides to every story, your side, my side and the truth."

I walk over to my dad and say, "Mom would you get the sheriff some coffee please."

I whisper to my dad, "This guy is bad news. If you are going to be angry, leave now. But no matter what is said you say nothing else!"

I look in my father's eyes and he realizes how serious I am. I walk over to the sheriff and sit down and explain the story as calmly as I can. I explain how they were bullying us to the part where the knife was pulled and I started beating the boy badly and then the officer showing up. The sheriff smiles and says, "I am sorry this happened, but you beat those poor boys pretty bad. I will talk with the boys and assure you this will not happen again."

"Thank you Sheriff, that's all I wanted."

The sheriff apologizes to me and leaves the house. My father comes over to me as we watch the sheriff leave and dad asks, "Is it over Son?"

"Sorry Pop, this town is one sick circus and we just met the ring leader. We have insurance right?"

"Yeah, we are fully covered."

The rest of the day we tan on the beach and play in the water. Kaye, our two dads and I toss football and we end up forgetting the incident as our moms prepare to leave. "Dad, when mom leaves follow her out of town and stop at a store and get some gas or something. Don't speed or even blink wrong, they are watching us." When our moms leave he does as planned and has no problems.

Kaye and I sit on the beach that evening watching as the waves get closer and closer to us. "Tommy, I am glad you made me take that karate with you now."

"Is today Saturday?"

She kisses me, and I say, "See I told you I would lookout for my girl."

The sunsets behind us, as we look at the ocean and I say, "Kaye Honey, go get me a beer please. No matter what you see or hear walk normal speed, grab the beer and then come straight back here. If by some chance I am not here, wait here for me." I kiss her and she leaves as a guy approaches.

"You the guy that beat my cousin's butt this morning?"

"Maybe, did he deserve it?"

"Most likely, he is a little smart ass! Still he is family and we don't stand for that around here. So now I have to beat your ass."

I look up at him, "Come on, this ain't worth dying over!"

"I am not going to kill you, just make you wish you were dead. Stand up!"

"This is the only warning I am giving you Sir! Leave now and I will pretend this never happened."

He starts laughing, "Warning noted, now stand up and do your worst, Buddy!"

"I just can't believe you were stupid enough to come out here by yourself. Two questions, can you swim and do you know Jesus?"

"Yeah, I can swim and I know Jesus!"

"Good! Last chance to walk away before my girl gets back."

"Is she going to bring me a beer? So I can drink it when I am done with the two of you!"

I smile and stand up, "That's it! Go to Jesus to save you! I tried you dumb redneck!"

I kick him in the throat with the heel of my foot and he drops to his knees gasping for breath. I grab him by his hair and pull him into the ocean.

As we enter the water I say, "Now it is Jesus' decision whether you live or die!"

I swim out in the water with the man in tow by his long hair in my hand. I pass the point of the breaking waves and stop. I look at the man, as he appears lifeless. I remove his shirt and pants and put them on as he floats in the water. I grab his hair again and swim towards the deeper water and towards the direction of the beach the man had approached me from. I look at him and hold him above the water and give him mouth to mouth.

As he spits and gargles I say, "What did Jesus tell you? And what the hell have you been drinking?"

The man stares at me blankly as I spit and wash my mouth out as I say, "Oh, sounds like Jesus doesn't know you! You want to live or die Buddy?" He tries to fight as I continue pulling him to the deep water, "Last chance, is this over or do we continue hoping Jesus will save you?" He looks at me out of the corner of his eye as he still struggles, "You kiss my ass!"

"I just did that! That is why you can breathe again. So, I take it you and your family will never stop! Am I right?"

He flips over and tries to grab me and says, "I am going to drown you now, and it will be over you Punk." The man grabs me and holds me under the water, but instead of resisting, I take him with me deeper and deeper into the dark water. I swim backwards like a porpoise would into the blackness of the sea and hope the bottom does not strike me too hard as I pull the man down with me. The man tries to release me and swim to the surface, but I hold his hands and continue downward. I feel him go limp as I feel something hard and jagged bump against my back. I put my hand out and feel a reef below me and to the side of me. I tug on the man and he feels stuck and lifeless. I pull at him and I cannot pull him free. Almost out of breath I release him to return to the surface. As I float to the top it seems a lifetime is passing. I release my last bit of air and hope I can continue floating to the top. I swim hard trying to pull myself upward and I finally surface gasping for air. I look around the moonlit water to see if the man floated up with me. I regain my composure and continue scanning the area for a body. I take a deep breath of air and go under in an attempt to find the man that was obviously drunk.

As I swim downward, so many feelings flow through me: anger, sadness, pity, and joy. Joy, that I can defend my family and myself. I reach the bottom and I feel around in the darkness and only feel sand. Where is the reef I felt down here earlier? Then I hear as I begin to float upward, *forget it, he is gone and we just did a lot of people a big favor. You tried to help him and let him live, but he gave you know choice. Let's head back. You need to do one more thing to end this. You will never hear a thank you for this, but you will see this little beach town grow when the tyranny ends here.* I float to the surface and swim to the beach, and my conscience continues as I listen to the plan. *Unfortunately this is war and we must protect our family.*

I walk onto the beach and look out at the water to see if he is floating yet, and I see nothing. I take off his shirt and pants and throw them up on the beach, above the point where the high tide should come. I feel my back to see if I bled when I hit the reef. I feel no open wound and I do not have that feel of air hitting an open wound. The extra clothes must have protected me.

I walk towards Kaye sitting on the beach sipping a beer. I sit beside her and she looks relieved. *Don't tell her about what happened. She couldn't handle it yet.*

"Went on a midnight swim without me?"

I sip my beer and say, "Yeah, I was afraid you might try to rape me by giving me that, let's go skinny dipping routine."

She laughs and says, "Our dads are watching us. I think today shook them up!"

I look up at the house and say, "Can't imagine why?"

She laughs and puts her arm around my neck. "Kaye, rub the middle of my back. I felt something bump me in the water." She lifts my wet shirt, inspects, and rubs my back, "Nothing here!"

"Good."

I look to the water to see if I see anything floating yet. *Well if he didn't know Jesus, he has at least met him by now.* That's for sure.

"Hey Girl, let's swim!"

We run to the water and she gets scared, "There might be something in the water that will get me."

"No, I am still right here."

I pick her up and walk in the water and say, "It's the same stuff that would get you in the daytime."

"But during the day I have a better chance to see it and avoid it."

"Good point!"

I begin to shake, "Kaye something is chewing on my leg!"

Kaye screams and I fall in the water and drop her. We both go under and she stands up and runs to the shore and says, "See I told you it was dangerous!"

I laugh as she runs back to me in the water and tackles me. We play and splash for a bit and then walk back to our beers sitting in the sand. I look at the ocean one last time as we walk to the house and I still see nothing floating on the water.

The next morning I get up and look out at the ocean and the beach and see no body or anyone on the deserted shore. "Kaye Honey, you gonna try surfing this morning?"

"If you are, then I am!"

"Then let's go!"

We hop out of bed, wash up again, walk out, and grab our surfboards. I hear the screen door shut again and I spin to see my dad standing there, "I'll have you some food ready in about thirty minutes. Is that long enough?"

"Yes Sir, that is perfect!"

Watching us he says, "That sure is a beautiful sunrise, have fun you two!"

Kaye's dad walks out holding two cups of coffee and hands one to my father. They scan the beach as a centurion on patrol would. This is fine by me; my conscience said we were at war.

Kaye and I paddle out, just beyond the breaking waves and we sit on our boards and talk for a moment. Then she tries to catch a wave with no luck. I paddle and drop in on a beautiful wave. The wave pushes me towards the beach as I gracefully glide on the wave. As I paddle back out, I notice the boys from the day before entering the beach. I notice our fathers going on high alert. Kaye catches a wave and rides about halfway and slips off her board as she tries to adjust her footing. We paddle out together and the boys pick a spot about a hundred feet from us. As we wait for a wave, the boy I beat up the day before yells, "Sorry about yesterday!" I hold my fist up to heaven and he does the same, and then we both catch waves. We keep our distance and everything is smooth. My dad hollers for us to come eat, and Kaye and I catch waves to the beach.

We walk to the house and Kaye says, "That was better!"

"Yeah Honey, you did very well!"

"No, I mean that guy being nice and acting like he had some sense."

"Yeah, I just wish he meant it."

"What do you mean?"

"Hopefully I am wrong, but I am betting he will be dead tomorrow. Tell our dads to keep an eye on me, I will be right back."

Kaye and our dads watch as I talk to the guys and then I jog back to the house. As I get closer my dad says, "What was that about?"

"I was asking them to find Jesus and change their life styles."

"And what was their response?"

"They laughed and had rude comments to say, so I told them I would pray for them and hoped God would have mercy on them."

"Well, at least you tried and sometimes that is all we can do."

As we eat breakfast on the deck, we see cops go down the beach and find clothes on the beach. We watch them come towards us as they go house to house asking questions. When they get to us they ask us each if we saw the man. When they get to me I say, "I saw a man last night come on the beach take off his clothes and he went swimming." They ask me the time and I tell them as close as I could. I tell them, "My girlfriend and I were sitting on the beach, but she went in the house for a soda. I didn't want her seeing some naked man swimming." I point to the area I last saw him and they call for a dive team.

They thank me for my help and leave.

An hour later they were pulling the guy out of the water. "Dad, I think we should go ahead and go, right after the cops come back by and make sure they see us packing up." He nods in agreement. Thirty minutes later the Sheriff pulls in our driveway. "Thanks for your help Son." I smile at the man and look at the ground as I say, "Sorry I didn't call you last night, but I didn't think he was doing anything but swimming."

The Sheriff shakes my hand and it does not feel like it did the day before. I can see his future getting clearer and nicer. Yesterday it felt muddy and dirty, but now it looks like it is clearing. The Sheriff says, "His blood alcohol level was pretty high. While he was swimming it appears his hair got tangled on the reef and he drowned."

"That is a shame Sir. Was he a local boy or a visitor?" Kaye walks over and takes my arm and caresses it. "He was my cousin."

I open my mouth wide, "I am really sorry to hear that. It is even worse when it is family. I know if it was someone I cared about I would be crushed." He sees my hidden meaning in my statement and I fear I have said too much.

He looks at me sternly, "That son of a bitch deserved it! He caused more trouble around here than he was worth."

My father walks over to us as the sheriff says, "So, he was with no one or said nothing to you?"

"Sir, I don't think he even knew I existed. I saw him stripping and I sent Kaye in for a drink so she would not notice him and he went swimming. When she came back I kind of forgot about him, if you know what I mean." The sheriff looks at me in wonder. *Don't worry; he can't do the trick like your mom and dad.* "So, you guys leaving?"

"Yes Sir, my dad is building a hunting resort and we are going to mark off the land."

He looks at our group, "That sounds nice. You guys bought this house?"

My dad almost speaks but I say, "It is my sisters actually. Would you help keep an eye on it for us?"

I wink at him and put my hand out to shake. He shakes my hand and notices the hundred-dollar bill. "I can't accept this Son."

Refusing to let up I say, "Why not? I am a citizen paying you a bonus for an extra effort that I am requesting you to keep an eye on my sister's house."

He looks at the money, "Since you put it that way I will tell my guys to keep an eye on it for you like we watch all the houses here."

"Thank you Sir, and tell your son I am sorry about yesterday and there are no hard feelings."

He smiles at me and says, "I will do that Son, and you folks have a nice day!" We watch the sheriff get in his car and drive away.

My dad pats my head, "Is it over now?" I look at my father and give him a yeah-right look.

We finish loading the vehicle and I look at the house, then I set the trap. We all get in my dad's suburban truck, as he drives away; I notice all the stuff in the back. He has chain saws, food, generators, building tools, TV's, camping gear, a box of something and several weapons. "Dad, you never took this much stuff when you use to take us camping."

"I couldn't afford it back then, and I need your girlfriend to enjoy her first camping trip. I would hate to scare her from camping ever again."

Kaye smiles and I say, "Oh, we are going camping at the mall?" The two dads laugh as Kaye starts hitting and wrestling me.

Dad looks at me in the rearview mirror, "It's time for the radio to go back to country music."

Kaye and I frown at each other, "Where is the gun? So I can put myself out of my misery first."

Kaye laughs and my dad says, "Right behind your seat, but don't get my truck dirty please."

He changes the radio station and says, "We missed the last ferry so we need to drive the long way."

"Isn't it the same amount of time?"

"Yeah, but on the ferry I save gas."

I hear my conscience and then say, "Dad something else we need to buy is some stainless steel and aluminum so we can build some huge gas tanks."

Dad looks in the rearview mirror, "Why? Is there going to be another fuel shortage?"

I look at everyone in the car and say, "Yes and no. The fuel people want you to think so and then they will jack up the prices. We buy a bunch now and save the money later."

"When we get home I'll get some place we can build a gas station and convenient store and put a huge tank behind it."

"We need a tank out here as well dad so we can stock pile it."

Kaye's dad speaks up, "Can I buy in with you guys on the gas station?"

My dad looks at me in the mirror, I nod yes, and my dad says, "You going to let your daughter marry my son?"

Bob looks in the backseat at Kaye and I smiling, "I thought they were already married!"

We all laugh and my dad says, "Of course we will let you own half."

The two men shake hands and that is when we became a real family tied together with gas.

Chapter 25

"Wake up you two, we're here."

I open my eyes and look around, "We are where? I see nothing but trees and bushes!"

"Let's set up camp so we have some where to sleep in a couple of hours."

I look around and say, "Now I know how the pilgrims felt. We are here, but there is nothing here."

I step out of the truck and Kaye follows, "Look Tommy a deer!"

The deer hears her and runs away. Kaye smiles and says, "That is the first real wild animal I have ever seen. Are there wild animals out here like bears, snakes, or lions?"

"Kaye, we are not in Africa."

My dad says, "I have seen a lynx out here and three black bears."

"Great Dad, now you have scared her!"

Kaye smiles, "No, I think it is cool!"

I look at her in surprise, "You think it is cool! Really?"

She smiles, "I am going to use your theory about a better outlook."

I kiss her cheek, and whisper, "I have never wanted you more than I do right now."

Kaye kisses me, and my dad walks over. "Break it up you two, we have work to do."

My dad gives us the lay of the land and where we are to use the bathroom and where to put our tents. I look in the woods a bit and see a huge pile of lumber, "What is that for Dad?"

"We are going to build a ten foot stand for my satellite receiver, a shelter for the generator, and a log cabin."

"We are going to do all that today?"

Dad laughs, "That would be nice, but I seriously doubt that."

We set up the tents and gather firewood for the fire. My dad hands Kaye two cans of bug bomb and sends her up wind of our campsite. He shows her how to use them and she walks into the breeze. She looks back at us, "Is this far enough?" My dad yells yes to her and we see a big cloud coming towards us, "Cover up boys!" and it slowly fades as it reaches us then another cloud begins coming near us but passes more to the side of us. Dad yells at Kaye, "Perfect Honey, now come back."

Dad looks at me, "You and Kaye build the shelter for the generator, and we will start the tower."

"Yes Sir! What specs do you want me to use for the design?"

"Do what you think best to block the noise away from camp."

We help our dads as requested by helping set up the camp and then I build a three sided, four foot by four foot box around the generator. Then Kaye and I start helping on some of the permanent buildings. I see Kaye growing weary but not wanting to complain.

"Dad, we are going to take the bikes out and do some reconnaissance work and survey the land. Maybe find the lake for a swim."

He smiles at our accomplishments around camp and says, "Be safe. Take a pistol in case you need it."

We unload the motorcycles and I show her, the gear set up and how to balance the bike. I am lucky she learned to drive a car with a clutch so she picks it up pretty quick. We ride around the campsite and then out to the road. I point at a trail, "You ok to do this little path?"

Kaye looks at it and nods yes. "Let's find the lake!"

I drive down the path and she follows me and I look back periodically to make sure she is still there and ok. It is flat forestland so there are not a lot of terrain problems. We find the lake and stop the bikes. I look over the lake and realize how big it really is. Kaye pulls up beside me and shuts off her engine. "Is this whole lake ours?"

"No, we only have a quarter of it, about five miles of the shoreline. Wow it is a big lake!"

"You have any idea how big it is?"

"Straight across from here is close to ten miles and from east to west is 15 miles."

She looks at me in disbelief, "You are just making that up! You have no idea!"

I look at her sternly, "I measured it on my flight chart, and it was mentioned in our land papers."

She smiles and unbuttons her shorts, "Yeah sure, smart guy! Let's go skinny dipping."

I take off my shirt and pull down my shorts and I jump in the water. I swim out and look around in the water as it is very clean, no one can get to this lake. No roads are within five miles and there is no access for the public, so it is unknown to most people. Kaye finally is undressed and jumps in the water and swims to me, and she holds onto me as I tread water for both of us. "Can you touch the bottom?"

I grab her butt, "Sure can. Why?"

She smiles and says, "I meant the lake bottom."

I feel around with my foot and I peer into the water. "No, it is about fifteen feet deep here."

"You get that from a chart also?"

I begin to get tired of treading water for both of us, "No, that is a guess. Honey, could you ride on my back, this is way too tempting of a situation and I am very weak in that department right now."

She makes a face and slips around to my back, "Are you sure it is not me. If I were someone else would you?"

"I would not be naked out here with anyone else. If I have sex now I will lose my gift and I am not ready for that to happen."

"I didn't know that! I will not try anymore then until you tell me we can."

I swim around with her on my back and she says, "I just thought of something. This is the first time I've seen you naked . . ."

She stops talking and I say, "And . . ."

"I like it very much, but I will still leave you alone until you say we can."

Smiling at her over my shoulder I say, "Thank you Girl!"

She rubs my chest as I swim towards the shore. "So what rules do we have about sex?"

"I will guide us Kaye, once we do make that move, you are free to make all the moves and suggestions on me that you want. From that point on we will be tied to each other forever."

She smiles, "Deal!"

I stand on the muddy floor of the lake, "Gross! Stay on my back until we get on shore. This mud has a nasty and slimy feeling." I reach the shore and she jumps off my back and looks at me naked.

I smile, as she is obviously impressed and I say, "How do those shoes feel?"

She looks down at her feet, "I am not wearing . . ."

She points, laughs, and thinks for a moment, ". . . I am use to these shoes."

She hugs me as I look over the lake and I say, "Right now we are like Adam and Eve. There is no one around for miles and we are naked in the wilderness."

She looks around and says, "Then where is the tree of life?"

I look in her eyes, "Do you really not know?"

She looks around, and then looks back at me, "No! Why, is there one here somewhere?"

I put my hand on her crotch and say, "It is right here."

She stares at me intently and does not try to remove my hand nor does she try to be seductive.

"The Bible is using the tree as a metaphor! Why do you think people say their family tree? The fruit was not an apple, it was sex."

She looks at me in awe as I remove my hand and she says, "So Eve had sex with a snake first?"

"Kaye, are you sure you are ready for this information?"

"Sure tell me your theory Honey, I will listen. So far it makes sense, but this next part is bound to be gross."

I look at her, "Ok sit down, and I'll try to explain the best I can."

She picks up her clothes and watches me as I begin, "The Bible says that Lucifer entered a serpent not a snake and tempted Eve."

Kaye gets dressed and sits in the grass, "What is the difference?"

"It was lost in translation, but the serpent was actually a dinosaur."

"What? Are you crazy?"

"Yeah, but that is a different subject. I can prove the dinosaur thing though."

"How?"

I smile at her and say, "A couple verses later it talks about the punishment of man for their sin. It talks about them realizing they were naked symbolizing they lost their innocence, and then talks about the pain of childbirth for Eve. Why would that be necessary for any other reason?"

"That makes sense, but what about the dinosaur?"

"A few more verses later it says the serpent was cursed and made to crawl on its belly, thus the extinction of the dinosaurs. They could not eat and the snakes we have now are all that survived."

She shakes her head and says, "That makes as much sense as the way it is written in the Bible. You should go to Bible College Honey!"

"No way!"

"Why?"

"I would not get those hard heads to listen. They still think creation happened in seven days. They would have me crucified as a heretic. Look what they did to Christ!"

"So how long was it for creation then?"

"Think about ancient times. Those people did not care about time like we do today. Time was new to them and they did not ever expect it to end like we believe today. They thought Noah was nine hundred years old. That should be the first clue about their timetable and these were a much simpler people back then. Plus, don't even get me started on Noah."

"What's wrong with Noah?"

"Nothing, I just get frustrated by people getting the number of animals wrong."

"Two of each is what it says."

"No, and that is what I am talking about."

"Yes it was! That is what it says in the Bible!"

"If you believe that then you need to read your bible again. It says seven of each and two of each unclean animal."

"What is the difference?"

"Clean was what they could eat and unclean was what they could not eat."

I look at Kaye and she looks like it is the first time she has heard this stuff. "I thought we went to the same school?"

"They didn't tell us this stuff!"

"I know, but some things we should be able to figure out for ourselves."

I go back to talking about time. "You know they used the lunar calendar when they did start keeping track, and it is shorter than the calendar we use today."

She looks at me and says, "So how long did creation take?"

"We won't be sure until we get to heaven, but I think the scientists are more right than the church interpretation of the Bible. I believe the part about; God said it and it happened. But the timeline is different than we know time today. Later in the Bible, I forget where, it says; 'one day to God is like a thousand years to man'."

She looks confused and I say, "Man didn't show up until the sixth day, so how would he know except what he is told, and what he can understand. Women . . . it gives no time that woman was created just how. So, does time really matter? We could do this type stuff all day."

Taking a breath I say, "Speaking of time! If you want to see something cool, next time you see my dad and he has no watch on, ask him what time it is and watch what he does. He claims we have some Indian blood in us, and that he can tell time by the sun. The scary thing is, he is usually right within a few minutes."

She smiles, "Can you do that too?"

"Yes, but I was bragging on my dad right now."

She looks at her watch and covers it up, "So, what time is it nature boy?"

I look at the sun, "Ten after five. But my dad puts on a show when he does it."

Her mouth drops and says, "How do you do that?"

"Ask my dad to do it; with my dad he has fun explaining it."

I look at the lake and throw a rock in the water, "You know the greatest irony of the Bible?" She says nothing as I continue, "It's not about who is wrong or right about creation, or any other story in the Bible. It is there so we will continue to talk about God. Some people just need to argue to have a conversation about meaningful stuff. And God just wants us all to be good children and love each other and remember him and praise him."

"Speaking of controversial topics. Tell me about you and the number 13?"

I already told you. Didn't I?"

"No, is this something I need to worry about?"

I smile at the beautiful young girl, "Many reasons . . . you realize I was born on the 213th day of the year? That is one reason. The big reason is numerology."

"What? Why?"

"Well, remember Bible class where we discovered meanings for different numbers?"

"Yeah, but isn't 13 bad?"

"Not for me. Remember man was created on the sixth day and God rested on the seventh day?"

Kaye says, "Yes, I recall that. So, man represents 6 and God is 7 and the two together equals . . ."

"You got it, plus Jesus was the thirteenth disciple."

"What? Jesus was not a . . ."

"Yeah we could argue that all day. To me, it is respect to my religion."

She smiles and lays her head on my lap, "You are amazing! Yeah the Bible College would have you locked up as a lunatic or heretic." I say nothing and she says, "You are like a mud puddle. Nice and calm on the surface, but if you take a close look you see all the stuff floating around. You can never see the bottom because you are so deep."

I rub her head, "Nice analogy! So now I'm mud to you!"

We wrestle on the grass and start kissing.

In the distance, I hear a horn blowing Morse code. Kaye does not hear it at first and she says, "What is it?" As I look like a dog hearing a whistle call. "Hush my dad is sending some message by Morse code." I listen and I understand,—.—. C—.—K,. I—. N The noise stops and I hear the horn again, CK IN.

"My dad is worried about us and wants us to check in with them. Let's go."

I start Kaye's dirt bike and she jumps on. I walk to mine and crank it as she starts rolling by. I follow behind her down the small trail. We go down the little trail and I squeeze my clutch and rev the engine, so hopefully dad will hear we are on the way. We get to the road and Kaye stops as a semi log truck rolls by. After it passes we then cross the road to the dirt road headed to our campsite. We pull in I notice the satellite dish is up and they have the TV going. Kaye and I turn off the engines of the bikes and Kaye says, "Looks like you boys are roughing it out here!"

We all chuckle and my dad says, "Where you guys been? We were starting to worry you might be hurt." Kaye hugs my dad, "Sorry Dad! We found your lake and went swimming and then while we were drying in the grass Tommy was telling me his philosophy of creation and the original sin."

Kaye looks startled as my dad and her say at the same time, "Sex."

Kaye points at us and says, "I never understood that before!"

She hits me and says, "You were right and I will never doubt you again! All the signs point to it."

The two dads look at each other in question and Bob says, "So you guys were talking about sex? You two are still good kids, right?"

Kaye hugs her dad, "I can honestly say Dad, and we were both tempted, but we did not give into temptation. We are both still virgins and will be for some time. Tommy told me that we should not rush things, because sex is what caused the trouble in Eden. We decided we are not going to risk it until we are in a place in our lives where we can support ourselves and not embarrass you guys."

Bob says, "I guess there goes our dinner conversation."

He hugs me and puts me in a headlock.

Kaye looks around, "Where did you say we need to go potty?"

My dad reaches in his bag and pulls out a roll of toilet paper and a plastic baggie. Handing it to her he says, "Just in case. Turn the bag inside out and use it as a glove to pick it up."

"Gross! Thank God, I am not doing that! I just have to pee."

My dad points the direction and Kaye walks to the side of camp dad pointed to. We look at the TV so she is not worried about us listening or watching her. The sun starts going down as we start the campfire and watch Wheel of Fortune on TV. I try not to cheat and listen to my conscience that knows the answer as soon as they say the category and I look at the puzzle. Hey, we could make money on game shows! *No, then we would be considered a freak. Scratch that idea.* We eat our dinner and Kaye and I both enjoy the beef stew. We talk around the campfire with our dads about our future plans and it starts getting late.

My dad says, "Let's clean up the camp and go to bed. I want to build two sheds tomorrow and cut down some trees for a path to the lake."

I look at Kaye, "Told you we would be slave labor out here."

We put the food in the suburban and dad puts the sacrificial leftovers a safe distance from camp downwind, but away from our toilet area.

Bob hugs Kaye as he says, "You are sleeping in here with me tonight." They get in the tent and they zip it up. We then do our best imitation of the Walton's TV show back in the seventies. At the end of the show all eleven people say goodnight to each other all through the house one at a time; goodnight Mary Ellen, goodnight John Boy, goodnight grandma. Then my dad yells, "Goodnight!" and we all laugh and shut up. I start to say one more goodnight and my dad punches me, "Shh!" I listen as my dad only acts this way when something out of the normal is going on.

"Bob are you still awake?"

"Yeah, what was that noise?"

The two men are quiet as they both stick their heads out the two tents to look around. My dad brings his head back in the tent, "Great!" I look at my father's face and know it is not good. My dad thinks how to handle the situation and he gives me the hand signal he made up for me as a child for bear. I move slowly and quietly to the front of the tent and see the bear going towards Bob and Kaye's tent. The bear begins clawing at the tent lightly and softly growling. I run out of the tent and smack the bear on the butt, and run back into our tent. The bear stands up on its hind legs and spins around, "That's what I was afraid of Dad!"

"Have you lost your damn mind Son?"

I smile at him, "Dad if we can handle those stupid cops we can handle a stupid bear."

My dad says to me in shock, "My bears aren't stupid. So what were you afraid of?"

I point at the bear as he goes back to all fours, "Male bear!"

My dad thinks for a moment and I see it hit him as I say, "Kaye, by any chance did you start your female cycle today?"

"Yes why?"

"There is a big guy outside your tent interested in meeting you!"

I begin chuckling softly and I look at my dad, "Dad, do you have a steak in that cooler?"

"Four, but he is after tail, not food!"

"Well, he is looking for love in all the wrong places then. The scent may throw him off long enough to get Kaye in the truck."

I walk out to the cooler, grab the first steak, and wave it at the bear. He rises up again and I notice he is still young, only about six feet tall on his hind legs. I toss the steak at him and it falls to the ground in front of him. He drops down to all fours again, picks it up, and starts eating it. My dad tosses me another one and I walk away from the camp holding the steak where the bear can see it, as I try to lead the bear away from the tents. The bear finishes the steak and is now interested in the one I am holding.

"Kaye when I say now you and your dad need to walk calmly to the truck and get in."

The bear approaches me as I back pedal away from camp. When he gets close I toss the steak to him and he stops and picks it up and starts eating. "Now!"

My dad tosses me another steak and I catch it as Kaye and her father get in the truck. I now dangle the next steak and continue leaving the campsite area. The bear walks towards me again and I let him take it from my hand, and he sits down to eat it. I walk past him and pat him on the back as I pass, the bear does nothing but continue eating and I walk back to camp.

I look around and now my dad is in the truck also. I walk to the truck, open the door, and jump in, "What are we going to do now?"

Kaye says, "Where is the bear?"

I point as he walks away from our camp, "He is going back home he is a big softy. He is only about two years old!"

Kaye hugs me, "Thank you!"

"Hey, I told you I would protect you and I mean it!"

Her dad pats me on the shoulder, "You're either brave or very stupid Buddy!"

I smile at him, "There is a fine line between those two and I like to dance on the line so no one really knows the truth, but I think I lean more towards the latter." I look at my dad and I see the pride in his eyes on how I handled the situation.

I look at our group and say, "Suggestion, we are not sure what else may be out there tonight, we go to that house down the road that we bought Dad. We can stay there and come back in the morning." There is no objection and I jump out of the truck and grab the sleeping bags. When I get back in the truck my dad starts the truck and says, "I'm just glad we didn't have to kill one of my bears." As he puts the vehicle in drive I notice the rifle across his lap.

We drive down the road to the abandon house and I say, "Dad, since you have bears you need to set up an area for them so they don't come visiting in the middle of the night."

Kaye and her dad chuckle as my dad says, "I won't cage my bears."

"Not a cage, but an area more attractive than where the people are. Or you could put a fence around the camp so they won't wonder in the camp area." He pulls into the driveway of the house we bought on our land, "I like that second choice better, a fence around the camp."

Kaye says, "Me too!"

I look around the truck, "Fine, we cage the people then." We laugh and step out of the truck.

We walk into the old farmhouse with no power and it is dirty from being closed up for weeks. We look around the best we can in the dark using flashlights. Kaye screams as we see a rat scurry across the floor and I say, "We have no AC in here and I have never been in here before. I would feel safer at the campsite." Kaye holds my arm, "I agree!" My dad and Bob look around not sure what to do and Bob says, "We could just leave Kaye here and we could go back."

"Dad, that is not funny!"

We laugh at the two of them playing.

"How about this, Kaye can sleep in the truck and we can return to the tents?"

We all look around at each other and Kaye says, "Why don't we go home! Or Tommy and Kaye sleep in the truck?"

The dads look at each other and they say in unison, "Tommy and Kaye sleep in the truck." We climb back in the suburban and drive back to camp. Kaye and I crawl in the back and slip into our sleeping bags. We talk for a minute and I almost fall asleep when Kaye puts her hand on my chest and says, "Thanks."

I lean over and kiss her, "Goodnight Girl!"

"One last question, how did you do that with the bear?"

"Do what?"

"Don't make me beg or ask stupid questions. I do what you want for you. Something I want you to do for me is explain things without me having to ask. Not always right away, but first chance you get."

"I will do that. Ok, I saw the bear going to your tent. I knew there was no food in there and I remembered your potty break earlier and the bear came from that direction. When I was sure it was a male bear I knew what he was sniffing around for, like a dog."

"So how did you know the steaks would work?"

"I didn't, I was hoping they would and I got lucky."

"So you were never scared?"

"I was shaking like a leaf! I was scared out of my mind!"

"Stop being silly! You're so brave?"

"No, but the fear of something happening to you was greater than my fear of the bear. My conscience told me what to do and it worked out just like I was told it would."

She kisses me, "Well, I hope you want to keep me around, because now it is going to be very hard to get rid of me." She snuggles into me and gives a big sigh as she drifts off to sleep.

The next morning my father wakes us up by shaking the truck. I look out and see the sunlight bouncing across the water of the bay. Kaye sits up and says, "Where do we wash up?"

I point at my dad, "Ask the great white hunter."

We step out of the truck and my dad starts telling us what to expect from our day, "Kaye we've setup a temporary toilet for you over there and your dad will be back in a moment with fresh water for washing up. Eat breakfast and throw trash here so our friend Harry da Bear does not return. We are building a temporary cabin first thing. I have tied ribbons on trees to be cut down. So let's get started."

We hear the dirt bike approaching and see Bob riding with two big jugs of lake water. He stops next to me and says, "Good morning sleepy heads!" I take a water jug from him and he shuts off the engine, "Swimming in that lake felt nice this morning." We both smile at him and Kaye hugs her daddy.

We do the work my dad requested and at lunch I lean against my dad, "You know Roxanne's beach house is gone don't you?"

"I was afraid it might be."

"Plug in your phone and see if you can get a signal. I think they are trying to contact us."

My father takes his phone out of the truck and shimmies up the satellite tower he had built the day before. He plugs in his phone, using a wiring disaster waiting to happen that he created. He sits for a moment and I grab his and my food and join him. I sit next to him on his new tower and look across the bay. "You can see pretty well from up here." We watch a shrimp boat pass and we can just barely see the islands off the coast in the distance as the phone rings.

"Hello!" My dad listens and then says, "Ok, we will head back down there, we can be there in about two or three hours." My dad hangs up the phone, he looks at me, and his eyes tear up.

"Come on Dad, it is just a house. We can rebuild it."

Kaye and her dad walk over to the tower as dad says, "Those boys that you had problems with yesterday . . ."

"Yeah I know Dad, they burnt the house down. I told you that was going to happen."

"They died in the fire."

I look at him in shock, "Are you serious?"

He nods his head in agreement and says, "I guess we never know how long we have, do we?" *I do! I knew it was time for those evil punks to exit this planet.*

We pack up, make the camp area safe, and then drive back to the beach. Kaye looks sad and I caress her hand as she says, "This has been an eventful week."

"I know girl, but we have to have weeks like this to appreciate the calm ones that we normally never notice."

"What do you mean?"

"What did you do last week? Did you have car trouble? Homework problems? Boyfriend problems?"

"Nothing like that, just a normal week."

"Well I guess it balanced out with this week then."

"That's for sure!"

"God can rest then the world is back in balance. Just think how many people he has to do that for before your next selfish wish like world peace!"

She hits me, "You are not funny!"

"Think about it? And yes I am!" I cuddle into her and she rubs my head.

We pull up to the rubble that was my sister's beach house. My dad looks at it and is disgusted and the sheriff pulls in behind our vehicle. I look over at him and I see his eyes are swollen from crying over the loss of his son. He comes near me, I put my hand out to him, he shakes it, and I say, "I am sorry for your loss Sir."

"Son, I am sorry for yours as well."

While holding his hand his spirit is clear and clean and the darkness around him is gone. He walks over to my dad, "Sir, I really need to apologize for what happened here. Those boys broke in and they burnt the place down with themselves inside. We have no clue what happened, but as much as it pains me to say. It seems they unfortunately got what they deserved, a cruel twist of fate. I loved my boy, but if he was up to no good like that . . ."

The sheriff starts crying and my dad hugs him, "I understand Sheriff. I am Sorry for your loss."

The sheriff calms down and says, "The town is going to help you rebuild this place for free. Just see our builder with whatever plans you want. We will have a crew come in tomorrow and get this debris out of here. Do you think anything valuable may have survived?"

"We only bought this place a couple of weeks ago and had no chance to put anything in it, but some curtains and comforters. That type stuff so nothing of any real personal value."

I hug Kaye, "Sorry to be so stressful for you! You sure you can handle being with me? I can't promise you much different. It will always be a challenge in my life with my gift."

She kisses my cheek, "I am your problem from now on and you are mine. I will get us through this. I am your rock and you are mine. I am your girl!" I kiss her and thank God for her.

The clerks from the surf shop walk up, "Heard what happened Bud! Sorry about your troubles! Did you get those boards out?" Kaye puts me between the guys and her like a shield. I am about to say, yes they are in the truck when the guy continues; "I'll make you two more surfboards just like them at no charge. I'll make your girls two inches longer to help with her style of riding. Yours, I am going to chop two inches so you can grind the wave easier."

"But . . ."

"No buts . . ." Then he says, "They will be finished in about two weeks. Just come by and pick them up. Hey girl, next suit you want from my shop. Steal it, because your money is no good next trip."

He shakes my hand and waves bye to Kaye, and the two guys walk away.

My dad walks up and says, "What did your surf buddy want?"

"Condolences and thanks for relieving him of stress and tyranny. I guess those guys that died were real bad news around here."

The sheriff's other son the deputy pulls up as we sift through the rubble looking for anything of value before the cleanup crew arrives. He walks straight to me and I expect the worst from him. An accusation that I did this somehow is what I expect to hear. "Mr. Dunn I am sorry my brother did this to your house."

He hands me a hundred dollar bill and he says, "My dad said you gave us this to watch your house and we let you down so we don't deserve it." I try not to take the money but he forces it into my hand, "I would not feel right keeping it. I told my brother and his punk friends to stay away, but when dad's cousin died he blew a gasket." He looks at the ocean, "I am sorry this whole ordeal happened, and I wish I had handled the beach situation differently." *Yeah me too and this would have never happened!*

"Thank you Officer. I am sorry for the loss of your brother and cousin as well." We shake hands and he walks away.

I see my sister's Mustang coming down the road with a convoy of her friends. I look at Kaye, "This should be interesting." My sister parks across the road and she is crying, "What did you do to my house?" My dad runs over to her, calms her down, and explains the loss of the boys and she becomes silent. She walks over to me, "What did you do?"

"Sis, let's go for a walk!" Chappy and the gang look around in shock.

I am about to explain the entire incident to Kaye and her. "Are you both sure you can handle this? It will not be a good story!" They both agree, not sure of what I was about to say. We walk towards the beach and I begin telling them the part about the guy on the beach and Kaye's mouth drops open. When I explain how I set up the house to explode if it was broken into they both stopped walking. I told them how once one door was opened they had five minutes to leave; if that door was not touched again the house would blow up. "I guess they were still inside when it went up."

My sister says, "You killed all those guys?"

"No, I gave these guys choices and they chose poorly."

I look at the ocean, "I tried and tried to let them live, but they were hell bent on winning against me. They cared about nothing but winning and it cost them their lives."

The two girls look at me as my sister asks, "Why should I believe you?"

I think for a moment, "What would it take for you to believe me?"

"These voices you say you hear? Are you going to blame it for everyone you kill?"

I look at her sternly and I point at her and say through my voice. *That kind of talk is not going to be tolerated!* She was staring at me and heard my voice but saw no movement of my lips.

"Kaye, did you hear him say that?"

"No, but he does that to me all the time isn't it cool?"

My sister is overwhelmed with fear and begins to run away. *STOP!* My sister stops and Kaye and I walk to her as she sits on the beach crying.

Kaye hugs her, I say, "Maybe I should not have told you the whole truth, but I was hoping you two could be my confidants. I need to have people I can trust around me. Kaye has agreed and I hope you will also Sis. My conscience says that most people who have this gift go crazy if they have no one they can download with."

"What do you mean, by download?"

"If I don't tell things to someone my brain gets full and I go crazy. Ever seen a movie with a crazy house in it where a guy is going around mumbling things uncontrollably?"

Kaye says, "Yeah, I saw one like that."

"That could be me! If I am not careful."

Roxanne says, "So are you going to be going around doing vigilante justice the rest of your life?"

"No, I have to maintain balance in my life though."

"What do you mean?"

"An easy way to explain it is by a blind person. The rest of their senses are heightened since they have the loss of their sight. My gift works the same way, but I have to control it. If I get greedy and buy myself a bunch of stuff, challenges will come at me, left and right. Not immediately, but eventually I am faced with hard decisions."

"We all are. What makes you different?"

"My conscience helps me decide on stuff that normal people don't see. Things that normal people ignore, like if I come to an intersection, if I choose the wrong way things go wrong for me and others around me. Like when I take a test I can see the answers on the page and none of the wrong ones, but I learn from it as well."

My sister looks at me and says, "So why did you lose that money in the Bahamas?"

"For a bunch of reasons!"

"Give me some; we could have used that money."

"For what? Who do you think owns the casinos? I just showed them I could leave with a lot more than I did. Those guys will want their money back, and in a couple of months, I will go to the Bahamas and lose their money back to them. It was merely a loan until we have our own money coming in. Plus, we already have more than we should. Do you realize out of this catastrophe we will make forty thousand dollars and get a free house in the process and this town will love us forever? You can't buy love, but you can earn it through actions. When is the money enough?"

"Why will this town love us?"

"Those boys obviously were bad news and terrorized this town. They had a choice to leave us alone, but they came to the house to trash it. It backfired on them, and if it had not. The feud would have continued and never ended."

My sister says, "So I feel better about this deal here. Tell me about the money in the Bahamas in my head, and I will believe you and never question your methods again."

Kaye says, "Yeah me too!"

I look at the two of them sitting on the beach. *Can you both hear me; this is a first time try for me?* They both nod yes and I explain to them why I lost so much and how a fifteen-year-old kid should not be in a casino anyway. The casino would have researched losing that much money.

With me losing ten million, it made it easier for them to lose $300,000. In addition, by losing that much money, it kept my gift in balance. I give them a play by play as they sit on the beach with their eyes shut.

My sister says, "So this balance you speak of is when you do something for someone you get something in return and vice versa?"

"Yes, in a sense that is correct."

"You are full of crap my Brother! We all have that."

"That is correct some just use it more than others."

"I still don't believe you! Tell me something I will be shocked about?"

"Out loud?"

"Yes!"

"You lost your virginity this week."

I walk away and she stands in shock and stares at me as I return to the house remains. My sister catches up to me, "Ok, I believe you, this is just overwhelming!"

"For you? Try being in my shoes pal!"

"Don't say anything to mom and dad!"

"Why would I do that? That has nothing to do with me, just be careful."

"Hey, if I were pregnant would you know?"

"Yes I would and . . ." I put my hand on her stomach ". . . you are not."

She hugs me and says, "What do we do here?"

"I am going to talk to you in your head so no one hears us."

She nods and I say, *that lady over there is the insurance adjuster. This town wants this to go away fast. Take the money she offers. The town is rebuilding your house as soon as you tell them what you want at no cost to you.*

My father joins us as we talk to the lady. She offers us ten percent more than we paid for the house to cover any items we had in the house. My sister agrees and she tells us the check will be mailed to us. My sister looks up and down the beach at the different houses. The sheriff comes over, apologizes for the house, and asks if she wants the house rebuilt the same way. She points at a house down the road that should be equal in value. They shake hands and my sister winks at me.

Kaye looks down the road and then at my sister, "Balance! I get it now."

Chapter 26

Disney World, from fifth grade until now I dreamed of coming here, now we are here, and I feel out of place. I need more roller coasters and fewer theme rides. The world becomes a lot smaller when you are stuck on 'It's a Small World' ride for thirty minutes. I like staying at the Grand Floridian though it is really nice.

I look around the parks and look at the work force they use to run the place. I look at the grounds and I am amazed by the cleanliness of the place. I take mental notes of the park so if I ever want my own amusement park I will have an idea of what to do.

Kaye watches me and says, "You are here to have fun, right?"

"Yes and no. I am going to build a park someday and I have to be as good as or better than this place to draw a good crowd."

She looks around, "You better come up with some cartoons and movies then."

"I will be going for more of a roller coaster theme than cartoon characters. I just want mine to look as nice as this place."

I see an official looking man with a walkie-talkie radio on Main Street USA as they are setting up the parade for that day. Kaye and I walk up to the man and I say, "Excuse me Sir, may I ask you a few questions?"

"Sure how may I help you?"

"We were admiring your park here and were wondering, how many people would you say come in here a day?"

"Thanks for enjoying the park. I would say a slow day would be 40,000 and a high traffic day would be around 80,000 to 100,000 people per day average."

Kaye's mouth drops and she says, "And you make $30 per person?"

"No way, that would be great. With all the different discounts, we average around 10-15 dollars per person. We make our money with the food and souvenirs sales."

I look at him and say, "Out of all the cost for food and employees. What would you say a good guess would be for profit per day?"

He looks at us wondering what we are asking these type questions for, "I would say a safe guess would be somewhere around fifty to a hundred thousand. Why do you ask?"

Kaye looks at me and I am about to tell the truth when she says, "School research paper. We start our economics class this year and we wanted some good info so we know what we are talking about. We are also doing research on owning franchises."

The man smiles, "Sure I understand."

I look at Kaye and say through my voice as she smiles, *Very good Honey.*

He begins telling us cost of everything from lawn care to concessions to actors in costumes. He tells us the cost and liabilities of roller coasters and other rides, insurance is a killer. We thank the man for his time and he leaves just as our parents walk up.

"What are you two up to?"

"Dad I was thinking about opening an amusement park, but now I think we should start an insurance company instead. That is where the real money is." My dad laughs and I say, "No Dad, I am serious."

We watch the parade and I crunch numbers in my head. I tap my dad on the arm, "How much is your car insurance?"

He looks to the sky and then down at me, "Your mom and I is about one hundred a month. Your sister by herself is a hundred a month since she is a new driver still."

"What about health insurance?"

"We have none right now since we both stopped working, but the company paid the majority and I think we paid like $12/month."

"What about life insurance?"

"Around $14/month per person for a hundred thousand dollar policy, but that price will go up as we get older."

"I wonder what our startup cost would need to be."

My dad looks at the parade, "A couple of million at least."

"We will have that next week!"

My dad looks at me, "I thought we were going to pay off my land with that money and stock pile the rest?"

"We are, but dad we have to spend money to make money you know that. Even if we stay small and have a hundred customers, we can make $25,000 per month and until we have a big payout we bank money. As the money grows we pull our personal money out, plus we are self-insured. So no premiums for us to pay then I could open my theme park and have no expense there. This place spends a thousand a day in insurance."

"That's it! Three hundred thousand a year is all they pay?"

We smile at each other and dad says, "Get me a cost verses income ratio and I will tell you what I think." I look at him and whisper in his ear, "Dad you can pretend you are in charge and I will never disrespect you, but I make the decisions and your job is to enjoy the benefits. You will either allow me to keep you involved or I will wait until I am old enough to do it on my own."

My dad raises his eyebrow at me and says, "You are still my son and I will be in charge of you no matter what."

I smile and say, "Yeah I hear Hitler had a father also, but no one ever mentions him do they? Let me do the thinking and you are the pretty face up front. I will give you the requested chart showing you how much money we will make, but you have to trust my decisions as you have the past year."

My dad looks at my mom and then the parade, "You have done well Son, and I will trust you. If you turn into Hitler I will take you out though."

I laugh and say, "I would hope you would, Sir!"

My dad looks at me in the eye, "That would be terrible to have to kill your own son! I now feel sorry for Abraham in the Bible."

"But he got lucky Dad, at the last moment God saw his faith and said he did not have to."

"Hope I am not faced with that!"

"Me too Dad, me too!"

Back at the hotel, I walk out to the pool area with Kaye and find our family lying out tanning by the pool, "Hey Mom, I asked the concierge to get us a limo so we could go to the convenient store."

She stands up and says, "That is funny, a limo to the convenient store. You want to go through the trailer park and McDonald's on the way? Anybody need anything from the store?" They all come up with odd and end items such as chips, lip balm, and suntan lotion and so on. My sister puts on a shirt and shorts and says, "Can I go?" I wave my hand in a come on gesture and we head to the lobby.

The limo pulls up and we step in. My sister asks how the lottery will work and what to expect. Being from a state with no lottery, we really have no clue. We walk in the store and start grabbing junk food and the supplies our family had requested. My mom asks the clerk about the lottery and the way it works, I listen to their conversation.

Mom looks at me and I whisper in her ear. Mom then tells the clerk, "Let me have three quick picks and two tickets to pick my own, please."

The woman does as requested and says, "That will be five dollars and just give me those cards when you pick them so I can enter them in the computer."

I give my mom a five and she pays. We walk over to the counter for marking down the numbers and I say, "3-13-26-31-69 and 7." She colors the boxes, then just picks numbers on the other ticket, and takes it to the clerk. The lady enters the numbers in the computer and gives us our tickets, "Good luck, the drawing is tonight, it is up to 18 million now."

"Thank you!"

We pay for the rest of our stuff and we buy fifteen lottery scratch cards for fun. We get in the limo and head back to the resort, I tear the tickets and hand them out and say, winner, loser, loser, big winner, loser. My sister holds up one of the tickets to me, "Winner, but how much?"

I look at the back of the ticket, "Five dollars."

I continue handing out the tickets and I say, "Kaye, hand that one to the driver."

She does and he says, "Thank you!"

My sister scratches her ticket and says, "You were right five bucks!"

The driver stops at a traffic light and he scratches his ticket and says, "Thank you Sir! Twenty-five dollars!"

I smile at him and hand the rest to my mother. Mom looks through the tickets, "Which one was the big winner?"

I point at Kaye, "I gave it to my girl."

Kaye scratches and yells, "Five hundred dollars!"

My mom holds up her purse, "But I have the real big one!"

"Yes you do Mommy Dearest!" She hits me as Kaye attacks me with kisses.

We pull up to the hotel and the door attendant opens the door for us, mom says, "We need to go get cleaned up, we have dinner reservations at Cinderella's Castle in an hour."

Kaye smacks my butt, kisses my ear, and says softly, "Do we have time for a quick shower?"

"Since we are still virgins and have to stay that way for a while yes we do!"

Kaye and I head to the room as mom goes to the pool to make sure the rest of our group is getting ready. "What do you want Girl?"

She looks around as we enter our room, "Big fake breasts!"

I smile, "When you get older maybe, but not now. You are perfect for your age."

Kaye strips and turns on the shower, "Come on we need to hurry."

I walk in the bathroom and she is in the shower all lathered up. I step in and she rubs her soapy naked body all over me and dumps shampoo in my hair I begin rubbing it in my hair. I massage her back and she says, "Rinse and get out and get dressed." I stand under the shower and the soap is washed away. I step out and begin drying off as she rinses off.

I hold up a towel as she says, "Hand me a . . . Oh thank you." I finish drying off and walk into the bedroom of our suite, "Kaye what do you think I should wear?" She comes out of the bathroom with a towel on her head but the rest of her is naked, "I think you should wear . . ." She jumps on me and we fall on the bed, ". . . me!"

"You are a bad girl Ms. Lewis!"

We kiss and she jumps up. She opens a drawer, pulls out a pair of khaki shorts and a blue polo, and throws them at me. I get dressed and there is a knock at the door. "Housekeeping!"

I open the door and it is my sister, "Yes, my darling Sister."

"You guys ready for an enchanted evening at Cindis' house?"

"I am and Kaye needs five minutes."

"Can Mike and I hang out here until you are ready?"

"Kaye baby, are you decent?"

I hear nothing and say to my sister, "Sure come on in."

We sit down and watch TV and Kaye comes out, "I'm ready."

Roxanne says, "Oh cute. Twins!" I look and Kaye is wearing the same as me in a girl's style.

I smile, "Guess everyone will know who I belong to. Let's go!"

I take Kaye's hand as we walk down the hallway and she asks, "Is it ok we are dressed alike?"

"I am fine with it. I bet we hear about it all night, and we will both get tired of hearing it."

We get to our parents room as they are walking out. We walk out to the little bus that will take us over to the Magic Kingdom. We arrive and rush to the castle for our reservations. When we show up we discover our reservations only allowed us to wait in line for a table. We take pictures with Cinderella in the mock ballroom while we wait, it may make for an interesting conversation piece one day, especially the look on Cinderella's face. Kaye looks at the picture and then at me, "I can't believe you did that!"

I laugh, "She seemed to like it."

My sister leans into look at the picture and says, "What did you do to get Cinderella to make that face?"

"Think about it!"

We sit down to dinner and have a wonderful dinner much better than I would have expected from a cartoon castle. At the end of the meal, a host of Disney characters surrounds me and sings to me, as Happy Birthday plays on the PA system. My family looks at the situation in shock and Kaye laughs at them having fun with me. I try to say it is not my birthday, but they do not seem to care. They take me up on the little stage and make me be the little teapot from the song as they sing the song. Then they pretend to turn me into a piñata. The restaurant laughs as the characters have their fun with me as they sing and dance around me. Daisy Duck grabs my butt as the person inside the costume laughs. They escort me back to my table and Cinderella is sitting in my chair. She stands and offers me her hand and I take it and kiss her gloved hand. She comes close and says, "When you are about to leave I request your presence in the Ballroom downstairs."

Playing my part in her joke I say, "Of course your highness!" as I bow to her.

She walks away and my dad looks at the picture, "You grabbed her butt! Didn't you?"

I look at Kaye and say, "We both did."

Kaye laughs and says, "I only put my hand there I did not squeeze."

The family laughs at the situation and mom says, "What did she say as she left? That she is going to kick your butt as you leave the castle."

I smile in a concerned smile, "Just to see her in the ballroom."

I stand up as we are leaving and two guards approach me, hand me a tuxedo jacket with tails, and ask me to put it on as they escort me to the ballroom. I do as instructed and follow the men out. Some old women say, "Good luck Honey!" As I walk past their table. I walk down the stairs and Cinderella is sitting on her throne taking pictures with more guests. The guards escort me to the throne and says, "Your Prince my Lady." She holds her hand out to me, I take it in mine, and she says, "Do you waltz?"

"I have no idea? I have never tried!" *Good, now you lie to the girl that you grabbed on the butt.*

She smiles and says, "Good luck and don't step on my feet." *Don't worry Buddy I got you, just smile and have fun.*

The music starts and I hold her in the proper way and I see the shock in her eyes. At the right moment, I direct her and lead the dance. As we slowly spin, turn, and do the waltz she smiles and I hear claps and sighs as we glide around the ballroom floor. I see Kaye's face, she is impressed, and wishing it was her I was pushing around the floor. A couple of the cartoon characters try to join us with small children, but are only doing it to be funny, at least they stay out of the way.

At the end of the dance I bow to her as she curtseys and then we bow and curtsey to the crowd that is applauding wildly. She smiles at me and gives me a hug and says, "Well this backfired tremendously! Mister you can grab my butt anytime you want."

"I can do that now if you like?"

She backs away from me, and smiles as she says "Enjoy your day in my kingdom Sir!"

She walks toward her throne, but holds my hand so I must escort her. She releases my hand as she sits on her throne. I bow to her and back away reverently. I walk past the camera area, remove the jacket, and hand it to the girl taking pictures and she says, "Lovely job out there, Sir!"

"Thank you, I enjoyed it." I walk towards my family and they hug me and tell me that I did very well.

We walk out of the castle and decide what to do. Kaye and I say, "Space Mountain!" Mike and Roxanne agree with us, our parents decide to go and wait in a spot to watch the fireworks and for Tinker Bell to fly out of the castle, like the end of Disney movies.

The camera girl runs out of the castle and says, "Sir! Excuse me! Princess Cinderella wanted you to have this picture." I take the picture and the girl runs back inside the castle. I look at it and Kaye looks at it and grabs it, "I'll kick her Princess butt!" My family comes over and looks to see what is going on. The picture is of Cinderella and me dancing from just moments earlier. "She signs the front Cinderella, but on the back puts her real name, phone number, and address! And a joke about her glass slipper. Kaye says sarcastically, "I'm surprised Shelly didn't put her bra size on here!" Kaye's mom tries to calm her down and I say, "Thirty-four C's. She told me while we were dancing." Kaye drops the picture and turns to raid the castle. I stop her, "Honey I was just kidding!"

She stops and looks at me, "These shoes are hurting my feet!"

"I know and I am sorry I put you in those shoes. I'm sorry you are upset, but it was all in fun. She is not that pretty close up." *You are the worst liar in the world, that girl was beautiful!* I know, but what am I supposed to say here. *I got this one for you Buddy.* My mom picks up the picture and puts it in her purse. My conscience talks to Kaye and calms her down.

My sister says, "Come on let's hit the roller coaster before it closes!"

The parents go shopping on Main Street and we head to Space Mountain to stand in line to ride the roller coaster.

Kaye takes my hand and says as we walk, "You better be glad I like you or I would kick your butt and burn down her castle."

"Sure wish it was that day!"

Kaye looks at me in confusion, "What are you talking about?"

I look at her as we enter the line for the roller coaster, "You know that day when we look back on this day and laugh about it."

She smiles and hugs me, "You're right, I don't have anything to worry about do I?"

I squeeze her, "Not unless that is something you like doing!"

As we stand in line, I notice two guys staring at Kaye as we go through the serpentine line. I want to say something to them, but I just watch since they obviously know we are together. I almost bring it to Kaye's attention, but I see her smile one time at their attention to her and I decide it is best not to say anything.

We ride the roller coaster, then join the family for the fireworks display, and talk about this being the last day of being poor and wondering how different life will be. Kaye's family and Mike just think we are joking around, but the next morning they find out different.

The morning paper arrives as Kaye and I walk out the door. I pick it up as we walk to breakfast. Passing my sisters door I knock and keep walking. The headline reads we have a winner in the lottery. The article says where the ticket was purchased and they are waiting for the arrival of the winner. Kaye and I smile at each other as my sister pops her head out of the door and says, "We'll be down in five minutes." I hold up the paper and yell, "They have a winner!"

We keep walking and we hear her door shut. When we get down to the lobby we see the Disney characters signing kids autographs. We see Pooh, Mickey, Chip and Dale, and Pinocchio and I say, "He looks like a real boy."

The actor looks at me as I pass and says, "You too!"

I smile and keep walking and Kaye says, "Wonder if he has heard that one before?"

We laugh and enter the dining room and see our parents and they are reading the morning paper as well.

I kiss my parents and say, "Hey Mom, you see that headline? That was the same store we bought our tickets at."

She says, "Really? Maybe I should check our numbers to see if we won?"

She gives a little giggle and smiles at me.

Roxanne and Mike join us and my sister has her paper in her hand, "Did we win?"

People look around at her and she sees them and sits down with us. The Disney characters enter the dining room as we eat. Kaye leans over and says, "Your girl Cindi, or should I say Shelly is here. How would you like me to act?"

I look up and see the girl playing Cinderella the night before coming towards me. "Act anyway but jealous." Kaye smiles and says, "I will be your sister and you put the moves on her if you want and I will do nothing."

I look at Kaye in shock as Cinderella says, "Good morning kind Sir. Are you enjoying your meal?"

I look up at her and say, "Yes my Lady, very much so. Thank you for asking."

She walks on and greets other people eating, but every time I can see her she is staring at me, and Kaye notices as well. As we leave the restaurant the actress is by the door and puts her hand out to me, and I reluctantly take it and kiss her hand.

"My Lady, allow me to introduce you to my Lady Faire Kaye."

She looks at Kaye and then me, "It is a pleasure to meet you. Your Prince here, is quite the dancer."

Kaye looks at me and says, "Yes he is, he is quite impressive in many aspects."

She smiles at Cinderella and now I feel very awkward as I say, "It has been a pleasure, have a lovely day."

I bow to her and she says, "A moment of your time in private please."

Kaye says, "I'll wait for you in the room, Honey."

I nod to her and she walks away with the family.

The actress leads me down a hallway, "I would like to apologize for last night. I was intending to embarrass you and it backfired and I was really impressed with you. If you ever find yourself alone and somewhere near here, call me and I will come to you or anywhere you want." She smiles and continues, "I don't normally do this, but there is just something about you that . . ."

"Shelly, I need to apologize to you for my actions as well. I was messing with you to get a funny picture. I enjoyed your joke you played on me. You are very lovely and if I find myself single, I would definitely like to contact you."

She looks down the hallway, sees no one, leans in, and kisses me passionately. She pulls away slowly and touches my cheek, "Until then my Prince." She walks away and I stand in awe of the situation. *Think I should turn down the charm a bit.* Just a bit or my bed is going to get full quick. Shelly reaches the end of the hallway and turns to wave. I smile and wave and she disappears.

I walk back to the room and mom has her door propped open, so I walk into their suite. Mom sees me and says, "When do we need to do this?"

Dad looks at me excitedly as I say, "We go and visit Universal Studios this morning and on our way back this afternoon we stop in the store and turn in the winning ticket."

"Why not do it first, so we don't have to feel nervous about holding on to it all day and worry about losing it."

"If we turn it in first, who knows how long it will take. Then the media will swarm us and then the beggars show up wanting a handout."

My dad looks at me, "Good point, but you hold the ticket. I don't want to worry about it."

My dad hands me the ticket and my mom calls the concierge for a limo.

As we ride to Universal Studios theme park, we pass the convenient store we purchased the tickets from, and the media is waiting for the winner to arrive. I chuckle and point, "They are going to have a long day." The family looks and laugh and Kaye's mom says, "Do you really have the winning ticket?" The driver peeps at us in the rearview mirror and I say, "I'm not sure, but wouldn't that be cool if we did? Guess we had better check our tickets." Kaye leans over and whispers to her mother, and she gives an understanding look. The limo driver tells us how to get in touch with him so we can get back to our hotel.

We enjoy our day at the park riding the Jaws ride; King Kong and we even helped ET get home. That evening we leave the park and ask the limo driver if we had the winning ticket to the lottery, where would we need to take it to claim it. He tells us that the store that sold it gets a kick back and the store that receives it gets a kick back.

"Hey Mom, let's take it somewhere else to turn it in and help out two stores."

The limo driver says, "You have it!"

My mom says, "Yes we do."

He pulls into a convenient store with a police car there and no one else. We walk in the store and the clerk says, "You are the winner!" to my mom.

Everybody is excited, the clerk calls the officials, and they tell us what we need to do. What a day, but now we are in the public eye more than ever. The next day we pack up to leave and we set all the bags in my parent's room. Kaye and I go sit by the pool and she asks, "Now that you are some rich guy are you going to dump me for some rich hot sex kitten?"

Trying to mess with her mind I say, "Woo, that sounds like a good idea!"

She sits there looking sad at me and I say, "Remember our talks?"

She nods in agreement as I continue, "I have been preparing you for this. I don't want some rich high and mighty girl bleeding me dry of money. I want the lovely girl I created to continue loving me like she did before I was rich. Not to take advantage of me, but enjoy our new found wealth and to love me as much as I love her."

"So I can say we are rich?"

"Not yet, by the time we graduate from college we will have our own money and you want have to say a word. People will just know."

She smiles and says, "Then you are stuck with me?"

"I hope so as long as we both play by the rules."

We ride the limo out to Executive Airport and our jet is waiting on us and so is a news crew. Jerry helps grab the luggage and says, "Congratulations Buddy!"

I shake his hand, "Thank you Sir!"

We load up as my mom answers questions by the press about the ticket.

My mom says, "My family just guessed all our lucky numbers and we got lucky!"

The reporter asks, "What do you plan to do with the money?"

"Spend it!"

"Any charities you plan to help out?"

"Yes!"

The reporter wants more, "Do you care to share which ones?"

"No, but it is a long list. I will say this though . . . all the people that helped us when we were broke. They are on the top of the list. The people that refused to help us, I hope they show up, so I can laugh in their face." That was the scoop the reporter wanted and my mom walks away to get on the plane. I smile at the cameras and wave as I walk to the plane.

Chapter 27

I hang up the phone at the dress shop and Kaye asks, "Who was that?"

"Debra's ex-boyfriend, that guy that helped me with a model show one time and wanted to be a model. He is now living in New York and struggling, but making it as a model."

"You still hear from him?"

"Funny story, he still sends me thank you notes every time he gets a different modeling job."

Kaye goes on with her work and I start to think about when I discovered him. The first note from him was a couple of months ago when he moved to New York. I can't believe he left Debra for New York, *yeah I can.*

It is a slow Saturday at the mall, and only a week before Kaye and my birthday. I'm sitting with Kaye and mom when Debra walks in our shop.

"Hope you are happy Mister?"

I look up at her tall slender frame, "Not too bad, just a little happy though . . ."

She looks at Kaye and says, "Your boyfriend stole my boyfriend, so now I have to steal yours!"

Kaye looks at me in shock, "I told you to stop doing that gay runway show! First, the lesbians attack you and now you are stealing girl's boyfriends. I told you it would make you gay if you kiss lesbians."

My mom chuckles at us but sees Debra is really upset. "My boyfriend ran off to New York to be a model. So now you are my boyfriend, you need to pick me up tonight at eight." She turns to walk away and I put my hand on Kaye's arm, as she is about to strike like a rattlesnake.

"Where are we going, because I have tickets to the opera at eight?"

Chris walks in, as she says, "No, we are going to the movies and then back to my place for some exercise."

"Sorry Debra, but this is an engagement I can't break. Mozart has his show planned just for me."

She looks at me in disgust, "Debra, this is my friend Chris. He just broke up with his girlfriend and is still getting over her, but maybe he could take you out tonight."

She looks at him and says, "Yeah, he is cute! Pick me up at eight?"

He looks at her, "Here, or somewhere else?"

"At the Gap next door."

He takes her hand and kisses it, "See you at eight."

She smiles and walks out of the store.

Chris shakes my hand and says, "Who's the psycho?"

"Remember super stud from the show we did a couple weeks ago?"

"Yeah, the pretty Boy."

I nod yes and say, "He went to New York and left her waiting in the wings."

"That the girl been trying to bed you down, even though she knows you and Kaye are a couple?"

My mom looks over at us, "Guys Kaye and I are right here!"

We both look at my mom and Kaye and we say, "Sorry Mom!"

I wink at Kaye and she continues folding shirts and smiling at me.

I look at Chris, "You are welcome, but when you are getting busy with this girl you have to do me a favor."

"What's that Buddy?"

"If you get her to the point where she is screaming and really enjoying it you have to yell my name."

He starts laughing, "You are insane! But she will already be doing that though! I always scream your name when I get excited. I will do it, Oh Tommy!"

We laugh as mom says, "Boys we are still right here! Don't make me kick you out of here!"

Kaye laughing at our nonsense says, "No, I want to keep them where I can see and hear them."

My mom walks to the front of the store and begins playing the piano.

I walk over to Kaye and kiss her, "I love you Girl!"

"I know, but why do you always call Chris' name when you get excited."

She starts laughing loud and Chris and I chuckle and Chris says, "No way! You two been getting busy?"

Kaye still laughing says, "No, but when we do he better be yelling my name!"

Chris tries to change the subject by saying, "So you guys heading to the beach after your birthday Tommy?"

"Depends on if we both get our licenses or not. Kaye takes her test on Wednesday. Her dad, Kaye, and I are going to get her car that evening.

Thursday the party is at my house from ten to ten. Friday I take my test for car and motorcycle in the morning and that afternoon for my pilot's license. If I pass them all we will leave that evening."

I look at them and say, "Kaye will probably drive my Corvette and I will ride my bike."

"Can I ride with Kaye then?"

"What is wrong with your car?"

"You are taking a Ninja and your girl is driving your Corvette down, I don't want to drive my Junker down there. I might class up the joint too much."

"Good point! Kaye can drive her car then and you can drive my Corvette!"

We all look at each other and I say, "That's the plan then."

Chris smiles, "If me and psycho work out, can I bring her?"

Kaye and I look at each other and Kaye says, "You keep her out of our bed and we don't care. Keep your freak on a leash!"

Kaye gets her license with no problem as me and her dad watch and wait. After she does we drive straight to the car lot where Kaye has a brand new blue Mustang convertible picked out. Her dad pays for it with the money he won in the Bahamas for her. She hugs her dad and kisses me as the paperwork is done. Kaye and I get in her new car and her dad waves bye as we drive off the lot. "Thanks for making this happen, Honey!"

"You are welcome Girl! Told you, play by my rules and I will take care of you forever."

As she drives through downtown she says, "You nervous about your birthday?"

She stops for a red light and presses the button to put the top down, "Yeah I actually am. I'll be fine though."

We drive around and she visits all her friends and gives some rides in her new car. Riding around with four cute girls in a convertible, don't try and tell me there is no God. He is definitely my friend at this point! I review my pilot's handbook as we ride around and guys try to hit on Kaye and the girls. I try to pretend not to be concerned, but it does bug me. "Kaye these shoes do hurt."

She smiles at me and says, "I know Honey, I know."

The next day at our co-birthday party our friends enjoy my family pool, Jacuzzi and gym. Chris asks, "When are you getting your car Tommy?"

"After I pass my test tomorrow. My dad is making me do my test in one of my lawn trucks since I need the trailer to pull my motorcycle out there. If all goes well I will drive straight to the airport from there."

"Good luck Buddy!"

"Thanks Chris."

"Hey, why don't we fly to the beach?"

"Two reasons. Kaye has never driven to the beach and that would give us no car for the whole week."

"Good point."

"Future plan is to get a hangar down there and we can keep a car in there so we can just fly in and have a car waiting on us."

"Good plan. Hey Debra is going to be coming."

"Good work my friend! So what did she say when you screamed my name?"

"She started looking around for you!" We both start laughing and he continues, "She got excited thinking you were going to join us."

"No way!"

"Yeah, she is a freak man. Thanks for the hook up! She still wants to steal your virginity; I will try to keep her on a leash though at the beach."

Kaye walks over and kisses me and tries to push me in the pool. I use my balance and I dance on the edge to keep from falling in. I laugh at her and she tackles me and we both go in and all of our friends jump in at the same time. My mom comes out on the back deck and yells, "You kids ok?"

"Mom help! They are gang raping me!"

Chris yells, "Me too Mom!"

"You boys wish! No sex in my pool!"

Kaye hugs and kisses me, "Thanks for a great birthday, Honey!"

"You are welcome girl. Did you like my present?"

She looks around, "Haven't seen it! Where is it?"

"On the kitchen counter." Kaye jumps out of the pool and rushes to the counter.

Chris swims over, "I can say one thing for that girl of yours. She sure has a cute butt!"

"Chris, don't make me drown you here in front of God and everybody."

"Yeah like that could happen!"

"How long can you hold your breath Buddy?"

Chris says, "Almost two minutes!"

"See you then!" I grab my friend and hold him under the water. He squirms about trying to get free but is having no luck against my karate move. I hold him under as he slows his fight trying to conserve his breath. The people still in the pool watch and fear Chris is about to drown.

"Does anybody know CPR! I think we are about to lose him?"

I look around and no one says a word, "No? Better let him up then." I pull him up and he gasp for air.

"Don't push me Chris! You are my best friend and I love you like a brother, but I think you know what line not to cross again."

He nods in agreement and I hug him, "You ok?"

He is still breathing hard as I say, "Your turn to try and kill me! I am only up to a minute underwater so keep that in mind." Chris attacks me and holds me under the water.

Kaye comes out, "Where is he?"

Chris smiles and looks down at the water, "I am drowning him do you mind?"

"At this point no I don't. He gave me ten dollars and a key for my birthday."

Chris still holding me under says, "A key to what?"

"That's what I want to know. So don't let him die until I find out."

She watches, as I lay lifeless under the water. "It's been a minute, when is he coming up?"

"He is starting to fight back now."

I spin and twist as Chris increases the pressure on me. I twist around Chris' legs and pull him under and I stand up. I take a big gasp of air and Chris pulls me under.

My mom walks on the patio again and looks at us wrestling in the pool, "Kaye, tell them I said no sex in my pool!"

Kaye and friends laugh as I come out of the water holding Chris over my head on my outstretched arms. I throw him in the water and Kaye says, "What does this key go to?"

As I start to answer her, Chris attacks me again. This time Chris gets the advantage and comes out of the water with me on his shoulders, I reach down, and pinch is nipple. He drops me as we all start laughing.

I stand up and say, "You want your nipple back Buddy?"

Everyone laughs and is disgusted by the gesture and he says, "No you can keep it, spoils of war.

Chris and I hug and call a truce.

Kaye holds up the key and the ten bucks. I look at her and smile, "It's a treasure hunt." Everyone gathers around.

"The money was impersonal, but has a clue for you, and the key goes to my heart and that is personal." All the girls give a big sigh as Kaye kisses me. "That is sweet Kaye you have a good man!"

My mom laughs, "Stop messing with the girl and give her the real present."

Everyone gets quiet and looks at my mom and then me. Kaye looks at me confused and then at my mom. My mom says, "I am supposed to give you clues to find your present. Your first clue is on the money. He is turning you into a pirate and this is your birthday treasure hunt."

Kaye smiles big and thinks as she stares at the money.

Mom continues, "The gift is something you lost precious in the Bahamas, but you have to find it. It is somewhere here on the property, good luck!"

Kaye jumps in the pool, "My necklace?"

I smile and kiss her and whisper, "Could be your virginity?"

"Nope I still have that."

I laugh, "At least the box it came in."

Kaye jumps out of the pool and begins looking around for a box that the key will work in. Her friend swims up to me, "Is the box in her car?"

"Lucy, she has to use the clues to find it and I am not a clue."

Lucy yells, "Kaye what is the first clue?"

Kaye looks around, "I have no idea?"

I yell, "Does the card or the money tell you anything?" Kaye grabs the card and reads it and looks at the ten. She runs up to the gym and finds another clue. She thinks for a moment and then takes off to her car. Lucy says, "Look at her go. That must be some expensive necklace?"

"It has a better story than how much it cost though."

"How much did it cost?"

"About ten."

"Ten dollars? That story has definitely got to be a good one."

I lean over to Lucy and whisper the amount to her. Her mouth falls wide open and she stares at me. She finally calms down and says, "The story can't be better than that amount!"

"After she finds it we will tell the story and you can be the judge."

Kaye runs back out to us at the pool with a bunch of clues in her hand and looks up at my bedroom window. She walks over to the pool house and pulls out yet another key and she recognizes it as my bedside table key.

"Uh oh boys and girls, I think she has it!"

Kaye heads up stairs to my room and she finds the heart shaped box. She comes downstairs and back to us at the pool.

"Honey this key doesn't work!"

"Of course not! I told you, that was the key to my heart! Not your heart shaped box. The key you want is right here."

I hold out my hand and give her the key, "Happy Sweet Sixteen Honey!" I kiss her, she opens the box, and her friends see the diamond and pearl necklace and the girls are in awe.

"Kaye is that the necklace you told us about from New Year's Eve?"

She nods in agreement and starts to tear up.

She kisses me repeatedly and says, "Ok tell the story from the beginning, because there are gaps I don't know about."

Our friends sit around us at the pool and Jacuzzi as I begin.

"It started in the hotel jewelry store. The casino manager saw me looking at it in the store. I told him Kaye liked it and my mom had told me if I won enough to get it for her. That was the day I lost ten million." They all interrupt, so it was true you loser! This type of comment came from them all.

"That almost got me kicked out of school! Remember as far as the school is concerned this whole story never happened, please guys!" They agree and I continue with the story.

"The hotel manager was so happy he did not lose ten million to me that he gave me this ten thousand dollar necklace to give Kaye. I was happy, but wanted the necklace to be from me and not the casino. I gave Kaye the necklace and she wore it New Year's Eve until almost midnight. This girl from Florida had . . ."

"That lesbian, slut, thief!" Our friends laugh at Kaye's outburst. I look at her, she apologizes, and I continue. "Please excuse my girlfriend's Tourette Syndrome."

We all chuckle and I continue, "The girl had been complaining for two days about her parents going broke and she was gambling trying to help them out. She was doing worse by her family and was about to end it all. Kaye was talking to her for a few moments, and at the end they hugged and Kaye's necklace was gone. At first, I thought she was being kind and did it on purpose. The next morning Kaye was freaking out because she could not find her necklace. Then I realized what had really happened. I went to the girl and bought the necklace from her and now I had actually bought it for Kaye and I could actually give it to her as a gift." They all say aw, and what a nice story and her friends all hug me.

Chris says, "Why didn't you turn her into the cops for stealing it?"

"How would that help her family? My sister got a letter from her the other day and her family is doing great, and her mom and dad are both working again."

Kaye says, "Tell them how much you had to pay for it?"

"Why? You don't even know that?"

"Fine, I will tell them then. These girls were a bunch of lesbians and he had to sleep with each one of them, all six to get the necklace back."

They all start laughing and I say, "I wish, then I could have, and saved a bunch of money!" Everyone starts laughing and my mom yells, "Food is ready kids!"

I put Kaye's necklace on her and say, "I am putting the key to my heart here on the clasp so you know where it is."

After I get it on her she turns and says, "I love you and I will be whatever you want me to be, because I love you that much. You are fun and full of thrills. I will never doubt you or not trust you ever again. Plus I have the key to your heart and I am going to keep it forever!" She kisses me and we walk in the house. *Told you she was the one!*

Mom looks at the necklace and Kaye in a bathing suit, "Kaye Honey, you are a bit over dressed for a barbeque."

Mom hugs her, "I am glad to see you got your necklace back though."

"Thanks Mom!"

We eat our steaks and baked potatoes and corn on the cob that mom had cooked on the grill. We talk with our friends and tell them the true story about the Bahamas and if it ever comes up in school we will deny it ever happened.

Lucy says to me, "You were right the story was worth more than the necklace."

She hugs Kaye and me, "You two are so good for each other."

Chapter 28

The next morning I load my motorcycle on the trailer and my mom and dad both come out of the house. Dad says, "What do you want to drive to the airport your bike or your car."

"The bike, but I will have my books with me. I had better take the car."

My dad smiles, "We need to go by the storage area west."

We pull into our storage yard and there is Mr. Lee rubbing a yellow Corvette with a cloth. I look at it and kiss my mom's cheek and then my dad. I trot over to the car and I hug it as Mr. Lee yells, "Get off my car Punk!" He laughs and tosses me the keys.

I jump in the car and he says, "You are not going to do your driving test in this are you?"

"Not sure, why?"

"The person doing your test might be jealous and fail you for the smallest mistake."

"Good point!"

"But if your examiner is some fine woman, you may want to use this car."

"Another good point, Sir!"

I smile at him and I see his face and realize I am about to be attacked.

Mr. Lee throws a flurry of punches and kicks at me; I block and duck the punches and kicks, but do not attack back. I only defend myself.

Mr. Lee stops and smiles, "Either way good luck and when you are done today come by here and let me kick your butt!"

"Thank you Sir!" We bow to each other and he walks to the office.

My mom walks toward me, "I will ride with you, but you leave that roof on."

"Yes Ma'am."

My dad turns the truck and trailer around and pulls onto the road and we follow him.

Mom smiles and looks around, "This car drives ok, but it is too low for my taste."

We hit a bump in the road and she says, "Ok I don't like this car."

"But it likes you Mom!" She smiles at me and says nothing else as I program my favorite stations on the radio.

We pull into the DMV parking lot and no other cars are there. We park and my dad says, "Go take the written test and I will unload your bike for you."

"Thanks Pop!"

"Good luck Son!"

My mother and I walk in and she knows everybody. I forgot she dealt with these people when she worked for the state. She hands me the two tests I need and I sit down and take them. Mom and her friends catch up, and they tell my mom how good she looks. She tells them about her store in the mall and they say they have heard of it and will stop in. They look at me and mom says, "Hopefully sometime when he is putting on a runway show." They all laugh as I have reached some legendary status now for my gay stunt.

I hand them my test, and the girl grades the test and says, "Perfect score on both!" I look in the parking lot at my dad riding my bike through the cones on the course. She says, "Let's check your eyes," as my dad does a wheelie on my bike past the front window, waving at me. I look at the window, "Did you see that?"

"See what?"

"Maybe we should check your eyes."

"Baby I know my eyes are bad, that's why I wear glasses."

I do the eye exam and she determines my eyesight is 20/17. "Is that good? I thought good is 20/20."

"Yeah average, but 20/17 is better. Go do your driving portion and come back to me."

"Yes Ma'am!"

I walk to the front and a cute blond examiner comes over to me, "You ready, Sir?"

"Do you think we should date first?"

The other two ladies laugh but the old guy is not amused. "We are going to do the driving portion of your exam. Where is your vehicle Sir?" She walks out to the parking lot.

My father smiles at me, "What are you doing first?"

I point to the Corvette and he nods in agreement. I open the door for the examiner and she thanks me as she steps in the car. I walk around the car and get in.

She says, "We will go around the block and then come back here and have you parallel park."

"Yes Ma'am."

I adjust my mirrors and she says, "It is nice of your dad to let you use his car for your test."

She is fishing be careful Buddy. My dad is a Ford man and won't even get in this car," I pullout of the parking space, "and before you suggest it is my mom's car, you should know since dad bought her the Caddy she has driven nothing else."

I turn the corner and watch for traffic, "This is my birthday/4.0 GPA present. The bike I had to buy myself."

She smiles, "So you have a job or something?"

"Sort of I own Tommy's deli and Tommy's Lawn Care."

"That deli in the mall?"

I nod in agreement and she says, "I love your subs!"

I smile and say, "Thank you, and next time you are in there, tell the guys you passed me on my exam and they will give you a free sub."

I stop the car and she says, "If you pass that is!"

"What? You want me to do it again?"

She looks around and notices we are parked in the parallel parking space as she had requested. She is embarrassed and says, "Nicely Dunn!" We both laugh at the joke she made with my name. *You could have that poor girl right now if you wanted her. She is a gold digger though.*

We step out of the car and the old guy walks out and speaks with her quietly and then comes to me.

"You ready for your motorcycle portion Son?"

"Yes Sir!"

He explains the course to me, and what he expects. I walk over to the bike and my dad says, "I don't see how you ride these bikes?"

"I know it is not your Harley, Dad. When I turn thirty I will give the rocket to my son and get a chopper to ride with you."

He smiles, "Sounds like a plan."

I get on the bike and my father and the old guy watch and make comments about my style to each other. I do the course as explained and the man turns and walks in the building.

I stop beside my father, "Did I fail or something?"

"Don't think you can fail Son! These are your mom's friends and you would have to do something pretty stupid to fail."

"Does she have any friends with the Federal Aviation Administration?"

"Nope, sorry. They're a different branch of vehicle, but you should be good there as well."

I walk into DMV and they all say, "Congratulations. Be safe out there." They take my picture and hand me my license.

"Thank you ladies and gentleman, have a great day!"

My mom sits talking to this one lady and I walk over and kiss her cheek, "Bye mom I am off to the airport."

The lady says, "What are you going there for? You work out there?"

My examiner says, "No he owns Tommy's deli and Tommy's Lawn care."

The girl was checking to see if I was lying, and to see what my mom would say.

My mom smiles, "That's right, but now he is going to get his pilot license."

Their eyes get big, "Driving and motorcycles aren't enough huh?"

"I would have had my pilot license months ago but like you guys they wanted me to be sixteen."

"Good luck Buddy!"

"Thank you Ma'am! Good bye and Tina don't forget to come get that sub."

She smiles and waves bye to me as I walk out the door.

In the parking lot, my dad already has my bike back on the trailer and he is sitting in the truck. He holds his thumb up and I nod in agreement.

He smiles, "Two down and one to go. What time do you have to be there?"

"After lunch, at twelve thirty, let's go grab some shrimp."

"Get your mom in the car and I'll meet you there. I'll get our regular table."

Dad drives away as I take the top off the car and set it in the trunk.

Mom runs out of the building, "He left me?"

"We are meeting him at Bob's. When are you ever going to learn when it is time to go?"

"I am still trying to keep you boys on my time!"

"Good luck with that Mom."

She hits my head and says, "Drive boy!"

"Yes Sir Master!"

I drive out of the parking lot nice and slow and when I get out of earshot of the DMV I stop the car. "Mom put on your seatbelt next year it will be a law."

She snaps the belt on and says, "That's a good boy!" *You're clear, go ahead!*

"Not really Mom, just want you strapped in for when I do this, my celebration drive!"

I stomp the gas pedal and a cloud of smoke comes from the tires as I propel us down the street. My mom says, "Is that something new? Get your license and lose it the same day?"

I stick both arms out the top of the car and then drive with my knee and yell. My mom is getting nervous and I slam on the breaks and drive normal.

"Are you done being crazy?"

I point to the police car up ahead that just pulled on to the road. "You got lucky Buddy! What if he had been behind us?"

I look at my mom, "No luck involved my conscience warns me when there is a chance I could get in trouble."

Mom looks at me, "So I don't need to worry about you at all? You have it all covered?"

"You can worry if you want to, but there is not much point in it."

"Good, I resign as worrier then just pretend you need me every once and a while."

She kisses my cheek as I park the car next to my dad and I say, "Yes Ma'am!"

After lunch I drive to the airport and Jerry is waiting on me, "How did it go this morning? I assume good since you drove up here."

"It went fine Sir! Is the examiner here yet?"

"Yeah she just went in a moment ago. Go wow her and let's be done with it."

I walk in the building and introduce myself to her. I give her my driver's license as an ID and my logbook with endorsements and she starts asking me questions immediately.

"You just get this license? It is still warm."

I smile at her and say, "Yes Ma'am"

The oral exam last about twenty minutes and then she asks me to plan a trip to the beach for us. As I do the weight and balance I get nervous knowing I need to know her weight for the computation. I ask her as delicately as possible, "What weight should I use for you Ma'am?" She is impressed with the way I handle a delicate situation, as most women do not like disclosing their weight. "I am 115." I do the weight and balance for my airplane, then take the map and plot our course. She is impressed and says, "Let's go flying Buddy."

We walk out to the plane, I do my preflight, and she continues asking me questions about airspace and pattern entries and weather. I handle each question with ease. *She is looking to trip you up not fail you. Next hard question get it half wrong so she will stop badgering you.* She asks me about the coefficient of lift versus drag and I tell her the answer backwards, which is a common mistake. She smiles and says no and explains it to me. *Nice job she was afraid we thought we were perfect and now she is ok!* "Thank you Ma'am I got it backwards." She smiles and we get in the airplane. I do the flight test and have no problems other than one landing was not as pretty as I wanted and I offered to try it again and she said it would not be necessary. I get my license and am legal to fly for fun, but not pay. My next step is to be allowed to fly in the clouds and bad weather.

I tell Jerry about the test and he laughs when I mention the weight and balance question. He says, "At that point your test was over! You were golden after that. You would have had to crash the plane to fail! Good job my friend. You are getting closer to being able to actually help me run this place. Don't worry, it won't be long."

I spend the rest of the day with the family and talking about the 213th day of the year and how it was a very good day for me. We celebrate at my favorite Japanese restaurant. When we walk in my favorite cook sees me and gives a big, woo-woo, "Mr. Big Spender is back guys!"

I smile at him and yell, "This time it is really my Birthday!"

"Like I care, you eat all my food. I gonna burn yours so you no come back."

"How would that be different from how you usually cook it?"

The restaurant laughs hysterically as the man gives me a one arm hug.

Kaye gives a nervous smile and says, "I guess you know this guy?"

Sha-nay-nay looks at her disgusted, "This not the girl you have last week. She much prettier."

Taking Kaye by the arm as she chuckles he leads us to our table and fixes us a fabulous meal.

Life doesn't stop, we can only slow it down sometimes, but it just keeps going and going. So let's enjoy it. Now that I am fully grown in my mind, my body, and age need to catch up. Though I feel like an adult, I am trapped in what most people consider a kids body. In some cultures I am considered a man; here I am still a kid. I am learning balance for my abilities, love, and life. My conscience has helped me discover a life I never thought possible and taught me that life is what we make of it. I plan to make it a good one . . .

ThEnd is near but not here . . .

Made in the USA
Lexington, KY
06 September 2014